EVALUATION
AND
QUALITY IMPROVEMENT
IN THE
HUMAN SERVICES

Peter A. Gabor
The University of Calgary

Richard M. Grinnell, Jr.
The University of Calgary

Allyn and Bacon
Boston • London • Toronto • Sydney • Tokyo • Singapore

Senior Editor: Karen Hanson
Vice-President, Publisher: Susan Badger
Editorial Assistant: Laura L. Ellingson
Editorial-Production Administrator: Annette Joseph
Production Coordinator: Holly Crawford
Editorial-Production Service: Walsh Associates
Composition Buyer: Linda Cox
Manufacturing Buyer: Louise Richardson
Cover Administrator: Linda K. Dickinson
Cover Designer: Suzanne Harbison

Copyright © 1994 by Allyn and Bacon
A Division of Paramount Publishing
160 Gould Street
Needham Heights, Massachusetts 02194

 This book is printed on
recycled, acid-free paper.

Library of Congress Cataloging-in-Publication Data

Gabor, Peter
    Evaluation and quality improvement in the human services / Peter Gabor, Richard M. Grinnell, Jr.
        p.   cm.
    Includes bibiliographical references and index.
    ISBN 0-205-15427-1
    1. Human services--Evaluation.   2. Human services--Evaluation--
Case studies.   I. Grinnell, Richard M.   II. Title.
HV40.G33   1994
361'.0068'4--dc20   93-43841
                                                                                         CIP

Printed in the United States of America

10 9 8 7 6 5 4 3 2 1   99 98 97 96 95 94

BRIEF CONTENTS

CONTENTS

PREFACE

This book presents a unique approach to describing the interrelated roles of *evaluation* and *quality improvement* in the human services. More specifically, we maintain that their mutual purpose is to assist organizations to strive for excellence and accountability; that is, organizations must deliver what they promise. To this end, we believe that any type of an evaluation should be directly linked to the quality improvement process that the organization utilizes.

Audience

This book is intended for a variety of beginning human service students and practitioners: social workers, welfare workers, community workers, recreational workers, early childhood workers, case aides, child and youth care workers, juvenile justice workers, family support workers, therapists, counselors, nurses, and educators. It is designed to be used as a main text in introductory evaluation courses, case management courses, or in applied research courses. It is also suitable as a supplementary text in practice methods and administration courses that place an emphasis on accountability.

In a nutshell, our goal is to provide human service students with a sound conceptual understanding of how the concepts of evaluation and quality improvement can be used in the delivery of services. In addition, this book will provide students with the beginning knowledge and skills they will need to demonstrate their accountability. Our approach is realistic, practical, applied, and most importantly, "user-friendly."

Pressures for Excellence and Accountability

Pressures for accountability in the human services have never been greater. Organizations and practitioners of all types are increasingly required to document the impacts of their services not only at the program level, but at the case level as well. Continually, they are challenged to improve the quality of their services, and they are required to do this with scarce resources. Few human service organizations can afford to maintain an internal evaluation department or hire external outside evaluators.

Thus, this book provides a straightforward view of evaluation in the context of the quality improvement process, while taking into account: (1) the current pressures for accountability in the human services, (2) the current available evaluation technologies and quality improvement approaches, and (3) the present evaluation needs of students, as well as their needs in the first few years of their human services careers.

Rationale and Approach

Over the years, little has changed in the way in which most textbooks present evaluation. A majority of texts focus on *program-level* evaluation and describe project type, one-shot approaches, implemented by specialized evaluation departments or external consultants. A few recent books present *case-level* evaluation, but place most emphasis on inferentially powerful, but difficult to implement, experimental and multiple baseline designs.

As human service educators and evaluators, we are convinced that neither of these two distinct approaches adequately reflects the realities in the field or the needs of human service students and *beginning* practitioners. This book describes how data obtained through case-level evaluation can be aggregated to provide timely and relevant program-level evaluation information. Such information, in turn, is the basis for a quality improvement process within the entire organization.

In short, we have blended the two distinct evaluation approaches to demonstrate how they complement one another in contemporary human service practice. The integration of case-level and program-level approaches is one of the unique features of this book; we are convinced that this integration will play an increasingly prominent role in the future of human service evaluation.

Much of the approach we describe builds on monitoring client progress. These data can then be used by human service workers to make well-founded decisions about their interventions. This form of monitoring provides the opportunity for practitioners to be accountable. It is also the form of evaluation that most human service workers will likely have the opportunity to implement in their day-to-day practice activities. While we cover, briefly, traditional program-level evaluation material, our emphasis is on program-level monitoring approaches. Systems of program-level monitoring can be designed to make use of data collected for case-level monitoring purposes and can be integrated as an ongoing part of service delivery.

Since the approach described relies on data that can be collected by practitioners in the course of their practice, it can be implemented with minimal disruption and at a fraction of the cost of traditional program evaluation approaches. Thus, it is highly suited to the circumstances of present-day practice settings.

We have omitted more advanced methodological and statistical material such as a discussion of celeration lines, autocorrelation, effect sizes, and two standard deviation bands for case-level evaluation, as well as advanced statistical techniques for program-level evaluation.

Some readers with a strict methodological orientation may find some of the described approaches simplistic, particularly the material on the aggregation of case-level data. We firmly believe, however, that our approach can be implemented more easily by beginning practitioners than more complicated and technically demanding approaches. Moreover, the aggregation of case-level data can provide valuable feedback about services and programs and be the basis of an effective quality improvement process. It is preferable to have such data, even if it is not methodologically airtight, than to have no aggregated data at all.

Format

We have written this book in a crisp style using direct language. The book is easy to teach *from* and *with*. Figures and tables have been used extensively throughout the book to provide visual representation of the concepts presented.

We have deliberately made an attempt to explain single ideas in several different ways through repetition, not only within the chapters, but among the chapters as well. Instructors who have taught evaluation and quality improvement to human service students are fully aware of the need to reemphasize fundamental evaluation concepts such as agencies, programs, program and practice goals, program and practice objectives, activities, and measurement. Likewise, to encourage students to become accountable, we have presented the evaluation process simply and clearly.

Key Terms and Glossary
A list of key terms is provided at the end of the chapter where each term is first used. These should be useful in drawing students' attention to key concepts prior to reading the chapter, and to help them test their understanding after completing the chapter. Key terms have also been collected and presented in a cumulative glossary at the end of the book.

Study Questions
The study questions at the end of each chapter provide a focus for students' thinking, as well as for group discussion. Some of the study questions also provide an opportunity, via the case studies (Part VI), for students to see how the methods described in the book have been utilized in the human services.

Content and Organization

The book is divided into six parts. Parts I to III are designed to help students obtain a sound conceptual knowledge of evaluation and quality improvement. Parts IV and V are concerned with the practical applications of the foundation information gleaned from the first three parts. Part VI presents three case studies that clearly illustrate how the contents of the first five parts can be used in the quality improvement process.

The sequencing of chapters reflects our experiences in teaching evaluation courses. We recognize that others may prefer to order the contents differently. As much as possible, we have written each chapter so that it will stand alone, thereby enabling instructors to alter the sequence suggested in this book.

In general, our problem was not so much what to include as what to leave out. This book is an introduction to evaluation and quality improvement, intended to provide students with a sound conceptual understanding of the process as well as some basic practical skills. Those students who desire to undertake more advanced studies in evaluation will have obtained a sound foundation upon which to build.

Part I: Introduction to Evaluation and Quality Improvement

Part I provides basic background knowledge about evaluation and sets the context for the evaluation and quality improvement process. Chapter 1 provides a brief historical overview of evaluation and considers how evaluation has traditionally been used in the human services. The chapter also discusses more contemporary uses of evaluation. The next two chapters provide an overview of the major types of evaluations (Chapter 2) and describe the two most frequently used approaches to quality improvement (Chapter 3). Attention is paid to the use of evaluations in the quality improvement process. Together, these three chapters lay a foundation that is vital to understanding the philosophy of this book.

Part II: Working toward Quality Improvement

The quality improvement process is an integral link between the organization of human services and the services they provide. In this sense, the quality improvement process can connect organizational goals to service activities at the client level. The three chapters in Part II describe such an integrated model. Chapter 4 focuses on the organization of human services, describing how the goal of an agency must be reflected by the goals of the programs offered within the agency. Ultimately, program objectives are translated into client-centered practice objectives (Chapter 5). It is these practice objectives that provide a focus for services at the client level and make it possible to establish measurable indicators of client change.

The final chapter in Part II, Chapter 6, is concerned with measurement. This chapter provides basic information on how the achievement of program and practice objectives can be measured.

Part III: Evaluation Designs for Quality Improvement

The quality improvement process uses various research designs. Part III describes the most frequently used design options available. Practitioners desiring to evaluate changes in their clients' progress will rely on one of several case-level evaluation methodologies (Chapter 7). In case-level evaluation, the focus of interest is clearly on the single case. However, at other times it is appropriate to evaluate entire programs or specific components of programs. In such situations, the progress of a group of cases is of interest and evaluators will choose one of several program-level evaluation designs (Chapter 8). Closely associated with group-level evaluation is the selection of a sample, which determines the extent to which results may be generalized. Commonly used approaches to sampling are described in Chapter 9.

Part IV: Decision Making

Part IV focuses specifically on one approach to quality improvement, monitoring. Monitoring is highlighted because for the human service practitioner it is the most practical approach to quality improvement that can be readily implemented as an integral part of service provision. Chapter 10 describes both case-level and program-level monitoring designs, providing several examples of how they may be implemented. A key feature of this chapter is a discussion of how, using the same data, case-level designs can be built into group-level designs. This discussion is followed in Chapter 11 by a description of the data that are yielded by case-level and group-level designs and consideration of how such data can be analyzed and interpreted. The chapter concludes with a detailed consideration of the use of such data for quality improvement purposes at both the case and the program levels.

Part V: Implementation

There are a number of important considerations in implementing evaluations. A commitment to quality improvement requires that evaluation activities become an integral part of service provision. To achieve this, a system that can collect the appropriate data and organize it into meaningful information must be established (Chapter 12). Establishing a continuous, internal evaluation system requires the involvement of motivated, knowledgeable staff members. Thus, a key consideration in implementing a quality improvement system is fostering an environment that commits an organization to excellence in service and encourages and supports evaluation activities (Chapter 13).

Underlying all implementation decisions is a requirement that the quality improvement process be designed in a manner that meets ethical standards in order to safeguard participants, and others affected by the results of evaluations, from harm. Although Chapter 14 is of fundamental importance, it has been placed near the end of the book because a sound understanding of the quality improvement process will help to clarify the ethical dilemmas and issues that often arise.

An applied summary is presented in Chapter 15 to complete Part V. This chapter provides a concrete real-life application of all the material presented in the previous fourteen chapters.

Part VI: Case Studies

One of the unique features of this book is the presentation of three case studies. These case studies demonstrate how relatively simple evaluation designs can be implemented in the day-to-day delivery of human services. These studies also illustrate how monitoring can yield a continuing flow of information upon which decisions can be based to improve client outcomes, leading to an improvement in the quality of services.

The studies also illustrate how the contents of this book can be used in a variety of practice settings with a variety of clients. For example, Case Study A demonstrates the use of monitoring approaches in a residential care facility for children, Case Study B focuses on the elderly in their own homes, and Case Study C evaluates the effectiveness of outreach counseling and a support group program for battered women.

A Look toward the Future

The field of evaluation and quality improvement in human service practice is continuing to grow and develop. We hope that this book contributes to that growth. If, at some time, we prepare a second edition, readers' comments will be most appreciated. If you find any of the book's content particularly stimulating and useful, or boring and useless, or have suggestions for the improvement of this book, we would like to hear from you.

If this book helps human service students to obtain basic evaluation knowledge and skills and prepares them in more advanced evaluation and practice courses, our efforts will have been more than justified. If it also assists them to incorporate evaluation and quality improvement techniques in their professional practice, our task will be fully rewarded.

P. A. G.
R. M. G., Jr.

ACKNOWLEDGMENTS

Both authors have been teaching case-level and program-level evaluation to human service students for over two decades. We thank the countless number of students whom we have had the privilege of teaching (and learning from) as they have directly contributed to the conceptual development of this book.

Special thanks also go to Dick Edwards, University of North Carolina at Chapel Hill; Maria Roberts-DeGennaro, San Diego State University; and John Stretch, St. Louis University; who reviewed the manuscript in its entirety. Within the limits of time frames and resources, we have tried to follow the suggestions offered by these three colleagues. However, they should not be held responsible for our sins of omission or commission.

We would like to thank our dean, Ray J. Thomlison, Faculty of Social Work at The University of Calgary. Without Ray's support and encouragement, this book would have never seen the light of day. Our thanks to Ray for providing us with an academic atmosphere in which to work and for establishing one of the finest social work faculties that we have seen.

We would like to extend our sincere appreciation to Yvonne Unrau and Gwen Lyon for the study questions contained at the end of each chapter. Yvonne also wrote the key terms at the end of each chapter, Chapter 15, and the glossary. Our thanks go to Margaret Williams and Terry Teskey for copyediting the initial drafts of the manuscript, and to Kathy Whittier for copyediting the final draft.

INTRODUCTION TO EVALUATION AND QUALITY IMPROVEMENT

Chapter 1

Introduction

Chapter 2

Types of Evaluations

Chapter 3

Approaches to Quality Improvement

Part I provides basic background knowledge about how evaluations are used in the quality improvement process within human service organizations. The first chapter in this section provides a brief historical overview of evaluation and discusses how evaluation is one of the core ingredients of accountable and quality practice. Chapter 2 provides an overview of the five major types of evaluations that can be used in the quality improvement process; Chapter 3 presents two complementary approaches that utilize evaluations to improve the delivery of human services.

1

INTRODUCTION

Myths about Evaluation and Quality Improvement
    Philosophical Bias
        Perceptions of the Nature of Science
        Perceptions of the Nature of Art
    Fear

The Need for Evaluation to Improve the Quality of Services
    Increase Our Knowledge Base
    Guide Decision Making
        Policymakers
        Executive Directors
        Practitioners
        Funders
        General Public
        Clients
    Demonstrate Accountability
    Assure that Client Objectives Are Being Achieved

Evaluation as Feedback

Internal and External Evaluations

Summary

Key Terms

Study Questions

THE HUMAN SERVICES have never been under greater pressure. Public confidence is eroding, funding is diminishing, and calls for accountability abound; the very rationale for human services is being called into question. The human services have entered a new, unfamiliar world where only the best organizations, those that can demonstrate that they provide excellent services, will survive.

Quality improvement is the process through which human service practitioners and organizations reach for excellence. Quality improvement is a philosophy; it is a commitment to continually look for and seek ways to make human services more responsive, efficient, and effective. Quality improvement means continually monitoring practitioner and organizational performance and making adjustments, as warranted, to improve that performance. Evaluations provide the means to this end. Quality improvement is a process through which excellence is sought and all types of evaluations provide the tools for the quality improvement process. In short, the goal of quality improvement is to deliver excellent services.

Human services can be viewed at two levels: the case level and the program level. It is at the case level that services are actually provided to individuals, couples, families, groups, organizations, or communities. Program level services are simply aggregations of services provided at the case level. Corresponding to these two levels are two levels of evaluation: case level and program level. Case level evaluations monitor the progress of clients while program level evaluations monitor the progress of groups of clients and organizational performance.

There are sound reasons why human service practitioners and organizations should embrace the techniques of evaluation and commit themselves to the quality improvement process. In today's current environment it is a matter of survival. Moreover, it is ethically and professionally the right thing to do, Nevertheless some human service students, practitioners, and administrators resist performing or participating in evaluations that can enhance the quality of the services they deliver.

Why is there such resistance when, presumably, most would agree that the pursuit of quality improvement is a highly desirable aspiration? As discussed above, evaluation offers the basic tools for the quality improvement process and the resistance is essentially founded upon two interrelated myths: that scientific methods cannot properly and usefully be applied to the art of human service practice, and that evaluation, by its very nature, is to be feared. Each of these myths will now be briefly explored.

Myths about Evaluation and Quality Improvement

The two myths that sometimes undercut the concept of evaluation as it is used in developing quality human service programs spring from two very different sources: philosophy and fear.

Philosophical Bias

Resistance to the general notion of evaluation is sometimes based on a philosophical bias (Bryk, 1983). Our society tends to distinguish between the arts and the sciences.

Far from being an objective feature of the world, however, this dichotomy is a social construction peculiar to industrial society. It leads to the unspoken assumption that a person may be an artist *or* a scientist but not both, and certainly not both at the same time.

Artists, the myth has it, are sensitive and intuitive people who are hopeless at mathematics and largely incapable of logical thought. Scientists, on the other hand, are cold and insensitive creatures whose ultimate aim, some believe, is to reduce humanity to an equation (Carter, 1983).

Obviously, both of these statements are absurd, but a few practitioners may, at some deep level, continue to subscribe to them. They may believe that human service workers are artists who are warm, empathic, intuitive, and caring. Indeed, from such a perspective, the thought of evaluating a work of art does seem almost blasphemous. For example, they may argue that the artwork on the front cover of this book cannot be evaluated.

Other human service workers, more subtly influenced by the myth, argue that evaluations carried out using valid and reliable scientific methods do not produce results that are relevant in human terms. It is true that the results of some evaluations that are done to improve the quality of services to clients are not directly relevant to individual practitioners and their clients. That may be because those evaluations were never intended to be relevant to those two groups of people in the first place. Perhaps the purpose of such an evaluation was only to gather data required by a program's funder or only to increase the knowledge base in a specific theoretical area.

Or perhaps the data were not interpreted and presented in a way that was helpful to the line-level practitioners who are employed by the program. Nevertheless, the relevance argument goes beyond saying that an evaluation produces irrelevant data which spawns inconsequential information to line-level workers. It makes a stronger claim: that scientific methods *cannot* produce relevant evaluation information, because human problems have nothing to do with numbers and objective data. In other words, science has nothing to do with human service practice.

The above paragraph used the words *data* and *information*. The two words are often used interchangeably. In this book, the term *data* signifies isolated facts, in numerical or descriptive form, that are gathered in the course of an evaluation: for example, the number and demographic characteristics of people in a specific lower socioeconomic community or the number of clients referred by a particular source.

Information is the interpretation given to the data when they have all been collected, collated, and analyzed. For example, *data* about client referrals and their referral sources gathered from a program's intake unit may indicate that the program accepts 90 percent of those who were referred by other human service programs but only 5 percent of people who are self-referred. One of the many pieces of *information* (or conclusions or findings) generated by these data may be that the program is somehow discriminating between clients who were referred by other human service programs and those who were self-referred.

The simple reporting of data can also be a form of information. However, the distinction we would like to make between data and information is simple—data are obtained to provide information to help guide various decision-making processes in an effort to produce more effective and efficient services to clients.

The idea that science has no place in the human services springs from society's perceptions of the nature of science and the nature of art. Since one of the basic assumptions of this book is that science *does* belong in the human services, it is necessary to explore these perceptions briefly.

Perceptions of the Nature of Science

It can be argued that the human soul is captured most accurately not in painting or in literature, but in advertisements. Marketers of cars are very conscious that they are selling not transportation, but power, prestige, and social status; their ads reflect this knowledge. In the same way, the role of science is reflected in ads that begin, "Scientists say . . ." or "Scientists have determined . . ." Science has the status of a minor deity. It does not just represent power and authority; it *is* power and authority. It is worshipped by many—not, notably, by scientists—and denigrated with equal fervor by those who see in it the source of every human ill.

Faith in science can of course have unfortunate effects on the quality improvement process within the human services. For example, it may lead one to assume that computers reveal truth and that conclusions (backed by scientific methods) have an unchallengeable validity. Computers often do reveal truth, but they can also spew nonsense at an alarming rate. Conclusions arrived at by scientific methods are often valid and reliable, but if the initial problem conceptualization is fuzzy, biased, or faulty, the conclusions are suspect (Bisno & Borowski, 1985). The point here is that science is not infallible; it is only one way of attaining knowledge. It is a tool, or sometimes a weapon, that human service workers can use to increase the effectiveness of the services they deliver (Borowski, 1988; Grinnell, Williams, & Tutty, 1995).

The denigration of science can have equally unfortunate results. If science is perceived as the incarnation of all that is materialistic, in possible opposition to common human service values, then either scientific methods will not be applied or their results will not be believed and hence not incorporated into day-to-day practice activities. In other words, practitioners will have deprived themselves and their clients of an important source of knowledge (Davis & Humphreys, 1985; Siegel, 1988; Siegel & Reamer, 1988). A great deal will be said in this book about what science can do for human service professionals. An attempt will also be made to show what it cannot do, because science, like all tools, has its limitations.

Perceptions of the Nature of Art

Art, in our society, has a lesser status than science but it, too, has its shrines. Those who produce art are thought to dwell on an elevated spiritual plane that is inaccessible to lesser souls. The forces of artistic creation—intuition and inspiration—are held to be somehow "higher" than the mundane, plodding reasoning of the scientific method as presented in some academic texts. Such forces are also thought to be delicate, to be readily destroyed or polluted by the opposing forces of reason, and to yield conclusions that may not (or cannot) be challenged.

Art is worshipped by many who are not artists and defamed by others who consider it to be pretentious, frivolous, or divorced from the "real world." Again, both the worship and the denigration can lead to unfortunate results. For example, intuition is a valuable asset for human service workers. It should not be dismissed as unscientific or silly, but neither should it be regarded as a superior form of "knowing" that can never lead one astray (Grinnell & Siegel, 1988; Grinnell, Rothery, & Thomlison, 1993).

The theme of this book is that the art of caring and the use of concrete and established evaluative techniques in the quality improvement process can and should coexist. Human service workers can, in the best sense and at the same time, be both artists and scientists. Science and art are interdependent and interlocked. They are both essential to contemporary human service practice.

Fear

The second myth that may fuel resistance to the quality improvement process via evaluations is that an evaluation is a horrific event whose consequences are only to be feared. Human service workers, for instance, may be afraid of an evaluation because it is they who may be evaluated; it is their programs that are being judged. They may be afraid for their jobs, their reputations, and their clients, or they may be afraid that their programs will be curtailed, abandoned, or modified in some unacceptable way. They may also be afraid that the data an evaluation obtains about them and their clients will be misused. They may believe that they no longer control these data and that the client confidentiality they have so carefully preserved may be breached.

In fact, these fears have some basis. Programs *are* sometimes curtailed or modified as a result of an evaluation. In our view, however, it is rare for a human service program to be abandoned because of a negative evaluation. They are usually shut down because they are not doing what the funders intended, or they are not keeping up with the current needs of the community and continue to deliver an antiquated service which the funding sources no longer wish to support. They can also be shut down because of the current political climate.

On the other side of the coin, a positive evaluation may mean that a human service program will be expanded or similar programs put into place. And those who do evaluations are seldom guilty of revealing data about a client or using data about a staff member to retard career advancement. Since the actual outcome of an evaluation is so far removed from the mythical one, it cannot be just the results and consequences of an evaluation that generate fear: It is the idea of being judged (Edelstein & Berber, 1987).

It is helpful to illustrate the nature of this fear using the analogy of the academic examination. Colleges and universities offering human service programs are obliged to evaluate their students so that they do not release unqualified practitioners upon an unsuspecting public. Sometimes, this is accomplished through a single examination set at the end of a course. More often, however, students are evaluated in an ongoing way, through regular assignments and frequent small quizzes. There may or may not be a final examination, but if there is one, it is worth less and feared less.

Most students prefer the second, ongoing course of evaluation. A single examination on which the final course grade depends is a traumatic event; a midterm, worth 40 percent, is less dreadful; and a weekly, ten-minute quiz marked by a fellow student may hardly raise the pulse rate. So it is with the evaluation of anything, from human service programs to the practitioners within them.

An evaluation of a human service program conducted once every five years by an outside evaluator is traumatic. On the other hand, an ongoing evaluation conducted by the practitioners themselves as a normal part of day-to-day program operations becomes a routine part of service delivery. The point is that "evaluation phobia" stems from a false view of what an evaluation necessarily involves.

Of course, one of the disadvantages of an ongoing evaluation of a human service program is that the workers have to carry it out. Some may fear it because they do not know how to do it: They may never have been taught the quality improvement process during their studies, and they may fear both the unknown and the specter of the "scientific." One of the purposes of this book is to alleviate the fear and misunderstanding that presently shroud the quality improvement process, and to show that some evaluations can be conducted in ways that are beneficial and lead to the improvement of services.

The Need for Evaluation to Improve the Quality of Services

We have now discussed two major reasons why human service workers may resist the concept of evaluation. The next question is, Why should evaluations *not* be resisted? Why are they needed? What are they *for*? We have noted that the fundamental reasons for conducting evaluations is to improve the quality of services. More specifically, evaluations (1) increase our knowledge base, (2) help guide decision making, (3) help demonstrate accountability, and (4) help assure that our clients are getting what they need.

Increase Our Knowledge Base

One of the basic prerequisites of helping people to help themselves is knowing what to do. Knowing how to help involves practitioners possessing both practice skills and relevant knowledge. For example, child sexual abuse has come to prominence as a social problem only during the past few decades, and many questions still remain to be answered. Is sexual abuse of children usually due to the individual pathology of the perpetrator, to a dysfunction in the family system, or to a combination of the two? If individual pathology is the underlying issue, can the perpetrator be treated in a community-based program or would institutionalization be more effective? If familial dysfunction is the issue, should clients go immediately into family services or should some other form of help be offered? In order to answer these and other questions, we need to acquire general knowledge from a variety of sources in an effort to increase our knowledge base in the area of sexual abuse.

One of the most fruitful sources of this knowledge is from the practitioners who are active in the field. What do they look for? What do they do? Which of their interventions are most effective? For example, it may have been found from experience that family services offered immediately is effective only when the abuse by the perpetrator was affection-based, intended as a way of showing love (Mutschler, 1979). When the abuse is aggression-based, designed to fulfill the power needs of the perpetrator, individual services may be more beneficial. If similar data are gathered from a number of evaluation studies, theories may be formulated about the different kinds of treatment interventions most likely to be effective with different types of perpetrators who abuse children.

Once formulated, a theory has to be tested (Smith, 1985, 1988). This, too, can be achieved by means of the evaluations using simple evaluation designs. However, it should be noted that in the human services, very few evaluations test theories because the controlled conditions required for theory-testing are more readily obtained in an artificial setting (Rothery, 1993b).

Another purpose for evaluations is the development of human service program models (Hudson & Grinnell, 1989). A program model is a diagram of the way in which the program itself is run and is intended to illuminate such questions as: What resources does the program need? What objectives does the program hope to achieve? What activities do the line-level workers undertake in order to achieve the program's objectives? (Program objectives, practice objectives, and activities will be discussed fully in Chapter 4.)

Since most human service programs are complex, with a number of interlinking parts, a program model can be developed only through careful study of a program's operations; once developed, of course, it has to be tested to ensure its accuracy. Evaluations can thus be used to increase knowledge both about social problems and about the ways in which human service programs address these problems.

The data gathered to increase general knowledge are often presented in the form of means, percentages, statistical tests, and probability levels. The conclusions drawn from the data usually apply to groups of clients rather than to individual clients, and thus will probably not be helpful to a particular practitioner or client in the short term (Hudson, 1982). However, many practitioners and their future clients will benefit in the long term, when observations have been synthesized into theories, those theories have been tested, and effective treatment interventions have been derived.

Knowledge-based evaluations then, can be used in the quality improvement process in four ways:

1. To gather data from human service professionals in order to develop theories about social problems
2. To test developed theories in actual practice conditions
3. To develop treatment interventions on the basis of actual program operations
4. To test treatment interventions in actual practice settings

Guide Decision Making

A second reason for doing evaluations to improve the quality of services is to gather data in an effort to provide information that will help decision makers at all levels (Hudson & Thyer, 1987). The people who make decisions from evaluation studies are called *stakeholders*. Many kinds of decisions have to be made in human service programs, from administrative decisions about funding to practitioners' decisions about the best way to serve a particular client (e.g., individual, couple, family, group, community, organization).

Six stakeholder groups benefit from evaluations: (1) state and federal policymakers, (2) executive directors of the programs, (3) practitioners who work within the programs, (4) funders of the programs, (5) the general public, and (6) the clients served by the programs.

Policymakers

To policymakers in governmental or other administrative bodies, any particular human service program is only one among many (Kidder & Judd, 1986). Policymakers are concerned with broad issues: How effective and efficient are programs serving women who have been battered, youth who are unemployed, or children who have been sexually abused? If one type of program is more effective than another but also costs more, does the additional service to clients justify the increased cost? Should certain types of programs be continued, expanded, cut, abandoned, or modified? How should money be allocated among competing similar programs? In sum, policymakers want comparative data about the effectiveness and efficiency of different human service programs serving similar clients.

Executive Directors

An executive director is mostly concerned with his or her own program (Barlow, Hayes, & Nelson, 1984). They want to know how well the program operates as a whole, in addition to how well its component parts operate. Is the assessment process at intake successful in selecting only those referred persons who are likely to benefit from the program's services? Does treatment planning consider the client's particular demographic characteristics? Does the termination process provide adequate consultation with other involved professionals? The director may also want to know which interventions are effective and which are less so, which are economical, which must be retained, and which could be modified or dropped (Baugher, 1981).

Practitioners

Practitioners who deal directly with clients are most often interested in practical, day-to-day issues: Is it wise to include adolescent male sexual abuse survivors in the same group with adolescent female survivors, or should the males be referred to another service if separate groups cannot be run? What mix of role playing, educational films, discussion, and other activities best facilitates client learning? Will parent education strengthen families? Is nutrition counseling for parents an effective way to improve school performance of children from impoverished homes?

Of greatest importance to most practitioners is the question: Is my particular treatment intervention with this particular client working? (Thyer, 1993). A periodic evaluation of an entire human service program (or part of the program) cannot answer questions about individual clients. However, case-level evaluations can be carried out by workers as a way of determining the degree to which their clients are reaching their practice objectives.

Funders

The public and private funding organizations who provide money to run human service programs want to know that their money is being spent wisely (Booth & Higgins, 1984). If funds have been allocated to combat family violence, is family violence declining? And, if so, by how much? Is there any way in which the money could be put to better use? Often, the funder will insist that some kind of an evaluation of the program it is funding must take place. Executive directors are thus made *accountable* for the funds they receive. They must demonstrate that their programs are achieving the best possible results for the least possible cost.

General Public

Increasingly, taxpayers are demanding that state and federal government departments in turn be accountable to them (Blazek, 1981). Lay groups concerned with the care of the elderly, support for families, or drug rehabilitation or child abuse are demanding to know what is being done about these problems: How much money is being spent and where is it being spent? Are taxpayers' dollars effectively serving *current* social needs? In the same way, charitable organizations are accountable to donors, school boards are accountable to parents, and so forth. These bodies require evidence that they are making wise use of the money entrusted to them. An appropriate evaluation can provide such data.

An evaluation can also be used as an element in a public relations campaign. Programs want to look good in the eyes of the general public or other parties (Carter, 1983). Data showing that a program is helping to resolve a social problem may, for example, silence opposing interest groups and encourage potential funders to give money. On occasion, an evaluation can help highlight a program's strengths in an effort to improve its public image. In other cases, however, executive directors may merely wish to generate support for what they believe to be a good and beneficial program.

Clients

Only recently have the people who use human service programs begun to ask whether the program's services meet their needs. Does the program's intent (goal) reflect the needs of the people it serves? Are ethnic and religious issues being sensitively considered? Do clients *want* what program administrators and funding sources think they want? In short, is the human service program really in tune with what the clients really need?

A factor relevant to serving client needs is whether the program is administered, to some degree, by the clients' social group. If a community is predominantly

African American or Asian or Mormon, is the program operated, to some extent, by people from these respective groups? If it is not, how much input does the community have in setting the program's objectives and suggesting appropriate intervention strategies for achieving them? An evaluation study might look not only at how well the program's objectives are being achieved, but also at whether they are really appropriate to the clients being served (Nowakowski, 1987).

Demonstrate Accountability

A third use of evaluations in the quality improvement process is to demonstrate accountability (Deschler, 1984). As mentioned, executive directors are accountable to their funders for the way in which money is spent, and the funders are similarly accountable to the public. Usually, accountability will involve deciding whether money should be devoted to this or that activity and then *justifying* the decision by producing data to support it.

Demonstrating accountability, or providing justification of a program, is a legitimate purpose of an evaluation insofar as it involves a genuine attempt to identify a program's strengths and weaknesses. Sometimes, however, an evaluation of a demonstration project may be undertaken solely because the terms of the grant demand it. For example, a majority of state and federally funded human service projects are forced to have periodic evaluations or their funds will be taken away. In such cases, a program's staff, who are busy delivering services to clients, may inappropriately view the required evaluation as simply a data-gathering ritual that is necessary for continued funding.

From a monitoring perspective, Rossi and Freeman (1989) suggest that accountability in the human services can take four forms:

1. Coverage Accountability: *Are the persons served those who are designated as targets? Are there beneficiaries who should not be served?*
2. Service Delivery Accountability: *Are proper amounts of services being delivered?*
3. Fiscal Accountability: *Are funds being used properly? Are expenditures properly documented? Are funds used within the limits set by the budget?*
4. Legal Accountability: *Is the program observing relevant laws, including those concerning affirmative action, occupational safety and health, and privacy of individual records? (p. 144)*

Assure that Client Objectives Are Being Achieved

The last purpose of evaluations in the quality improvement process is to determine if clients are getting what they need from a human service program. Responsible practitioners are interested in knowing to what degree each of their individual client's practice objectives and those of their caseloads as a whole are being achieved; that is, they are interested in evaluating their practice effectiveness (Bloom, Fischer, & Orme, 1994; Corcoran & Fischer, 1994; Thyer, 1993).

Clients want to know if the services they are receiving are worth their time, effort, and sometimes money. Usually, these data are required while treatment is still in progress, as it is scarcely useful to conclude that services were ineffective after the client has left the program (Love, 1991). A measure of effectiveness is needed while there may still be time to try a different intervention.

On a general level, the various human service professions have the responsibility to improve their programs continually. For example, the ethical obligation to evaluate is addressed in the *Specialty Guidelines for the Delivery of Services by Counseling Psychologists* (APA, 1981) which states:

> *Evaluation of the counseling psychological service delivery system is conducted internally, and when possible, under independent auspices as well. This evaluation includes an assessment of* effectiveness *(to determine what the service unit accomplished),* efficiency *(to determine the total costs of providing services),* availability *(to determine appropriate levels and distribution of services and personnel),* accessibility *(to ensure that the services are barrier free to users), and* adequacy *(to determine whether the services meet the identified needs for such services).*

Evaluation as Feedback

It is our belief that all evaluative efforts conducted in the human services provide feedback loops that improve the delivery of services. Feedback provides data about the extent to which a program's goal is achieved or approximated. Based on these data, services may be adjusted or changed to improve goal achievement. Figure 1.1 illustrates how evaluations provide a common feedback loop to improve the quality of services in human service organizations.

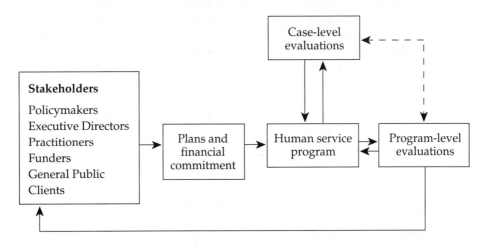

FIGURE 1.1   The Use of Evaluations in the Quality Improvement Process

Internal and External Evaluations

As the APA guidelines suggest, an evaluation may be *internally driven*, that is, initiated and conducted by staff members who work *within* a program. In other cases, the evaluation may be *externally driven*, initiated by someone *outside* the program to be evaluated, often a funding source or sponsor.

The main motive behind internal evaluations is to improve the quality of services to clients. A distinct advantage of internal evaluations is that the evaluation questions framed are likely to be highly relevant to staff members' interests. This is hardly surprising; staff members are responsible for conducting the evaluation and, with their first-hand knowledge of the program, they are in a position to ensure that the evaluation addresses relevant issues. Thus, feedback from an evaluation feeds the quality improvement process. Moreover, a practitioner (or organization) that evaluates his or her practice is in a position to demonstrate accountability to the program's stakeholders.

A drawback to internal evaluations is that they may be viewed as lacking the credibility that comes with an independent outside evaluation. Sometimes funding bodies are therefore not content with data from internal evaluations and request an external evaluation. Because they are carried out independently of the program to be evaluated, external evaluations are often perceived to be more credible. However, because they are commissioned by people outside the human service program, they tend to reflect their interests and may not address questions that are most relevant to program staff. Outside evaluations often impose an onerous data collection burden on program staff as well and tend to be disruptive to normal program operations.

When an externally driven evaluation is to occur, organizations that conduct internal evaluations are in an advantageous position. A prior internal evaluation may identify some things that need to be improved before the outside evaluator appears. It may also identify a program's strengths, which can be displayed. As well, staff members are likely to be conversant with evaluation matters, allowing them to engage in knowledgeable discussions with outside evaluators and thus help ensure that the evaluation process will deal fairly with the program's interests.

Human service workers who are interested in improving the quality of the services they offer via evaluations are well on their way to becoming self-evaluating professionals, or members of a self-evaluating organization. In other words, they are taking responsibility for providing the best possible service to clients through systematic examinations of their strengths and weaknesses via the quality improvement process.

Summary

This chapter introduced the concept of quality improvement and explained how evaluation provides tools for the quality improvement process. The chapter examined two myths that surround the concept of evaluation: philosophical bias and fear. The chapter also presented a brief introduction to why the human service field needs evaluations: to increase our knowledge base; to guide decision making for policymakers, executive directors, practitioners, funders, the general public, and clients; to demonstrate accountability; and to assure that clients' practice objectives are being met. External and internal evaluations were introduced with the notion that internally driven evaluations are usually concerned with the improvement of services and external evaluations are usually required by funding sources who want to know about effectiveness and/or efficiency issues.

With this chapter as a background, the next chapter presents five complementary types of evaluations and will show how each one can provide data to fill the four evaluative needs as outlined in this chapter.

Key Terms

Accountability: A system of responsibility in which program administrators account for all program activities by answering to the demands of a program's stakeholders and by justifying the program's expenditures to the satisfaction of its stakeholders.

Clients: People who use human services—individuals, couples, families, groups, organizations, and communities.

Data: Isolated facts, presented in numerical or descriptive form, on which client or program decisions are based. Not to be confused with information.

Evaluation: A form of appraisal using valid and reliable research methods. There are numerous types of evaluations geared to produce data which in turn produce information that helps in the decision-making process. Data from evaluations are used in the quality improvement process.

External Evaluation: An evaluation that is conducted by someone who does not have any connection with the program; usually an evaluation that is requested by the agency's funding sources. This type of evaluation complements an internal evaluation.

Information: The interpretation given to data that have been collected, collated, and analyzed. Information is used to help in the decision-making process. Not to be confused with data.

Internal Evaluation: An evaluation that is conducted by someone who works within a program; usually an evaluation for the purpose of promoting better client services. This type of evaluation complements an external evaluation.

Quality Improvement Process: An ethical commitment to continually look for and seek ways to make services more responsive, efficient, and effective. It is a process that uses the data from all types of evaluations to improve the quality of human services.

Stakeholder: A person or group of people having a direct or indirect interest in the results of an evaluation.

Study Questions

1. To what degree is the educational program in which you are studying committed to the quality improvement process? What actions give evidence of this commitment? How are evaluation activities a part of this process? Discuss in detail.

2. Examine some research studies in your field. What definition of evaluation is implied or provided in these studies? Select those articles in which the prime objective of an evaluation is to improve the quality of services. In what way is the notion of quality

improvement presented in these articles? Select those articles in which there is some other reason for conducting the evaluation. Identify that reason and comment on its appropriateness.

3. What are the major differences between data and information? How might data and information be used differently in the human services? Can you think of instances where data might be presented or stored without generating corresponding information? If so, what are they?

4. Explain how quality improvement can be used to guide decision making at different levels within a program (e.g., at the administrative level, at the line-level, and at the funding level). How would data collected from administrators, practitioners, and funders differ? Give an example of how one set of data could be used to make different decisions at the various levels.

5. In your opinion, should data collected from clients be made available to them? Why or why not? Discuss in detail.

6. List and discuss in detail the two myths about the concept of evaluation. Do you see yourself believing one (or both) of the myths? Why? Why not? Do you see any of your classmates believing any of the myths? If so, do you feel they will make good human service practitioners? Why or why not?

7. List and discuss in detail the six groups of people that guide decision making in the human services (stakeholders). How can the quality improvement process help each one of these groups of people to make better decisions? Do you see any commonalities between or among the members of the list? Among the six groups of people who make decisions, what group do you feel should have the most say in the decision-making process? What group of people do you feel should have the least say in the decision-making process? Justify your answer.

8. List and discuss in detail the four reasons why evaluation is needed in the human ser-

vices. Present one common social problem (e.g., AIDS, child abuse, family violence, homelessness) that runs throughout your discussion. Upon which one of the four reasons do you feel the quality improvement process should focus the most attention? Why? Justify your answer.

9. Society has drawn an artificial distinction between the arts and sciences. Divide the class into two groups. Using a debate format, ask the two groups to present the pros and cons of the artistic versus the scientific role in human service work. Using the points raised in the debate, and the contents of this chapter, discuss how the two views might be integrated.

10. In a small group, discuss how the group could go about evaluating the artwork on the front cover of this book. Is it evaluable? Why or why not? Justify your answer. Discuss your group's evaluative technique with another group who has the same assignment. What are the differences and similarities between the conclusions reached by the two groups? Discuss in detail.

11. List and discuss the advantages and disadvantages of doing an internal and an external evaluation. Compare and contrast the strengths and weaknesses of the two. Go to the library and find an article that presents the results of an internally driven evaluation. Find another article that presents the results of an externally driven evaluation. Compare the two. What were their similarities? What were their differences? Discuss in detail.

12. Using the APA guidelines for the place of evaluation in the delivery of psychological services, what additional aspects do you feel could be added to make the guidelines even more comprehensive than the five listed? Justify your response.

13. What are some of the recent historical developments in the human services field that have increased the need for and importance of case- and program-level evaluation?

14. You are a practitioner at your local branch of

Helping Families, Inc. Your supervisor informs you that your program will soon be subjected to a governmental evaluation. Your supervisor seems suspicious of and resistant to the evaluation. What may account for this attitude?

15. As a recent graduate of a human service program you find yourself at a local fundraiser debating the merits of how evaluations can be used in the quality improvement process. How would you argue this point?.

16. While recording data for your program's database, your coworker complains, arguing that gathering data has little to do with the decision-making process. How would you respond?

17. You have decided to incorporate the quality improvement process within your practice. What would this mean to you, your clients, your agency, your funders, and to the general public?

18. Read Case Study B. How could the findings from this study address the four evaluative needs in reference to respite care? Discuss each one in detail and relate your answers directly to the topic of respite care in reducing caregiver burden.

2

TYPES OF EVALUATIONS

Evaluations that Can Improve the Quality of Services
    Needs Assessment
    Evaluability Assessment
    Outcome Assessment
    Efficiency Assessment
    Process Analysis

Scope of Evaluations
    Boundary
    Size
    Duration
    Complexity
    Clarity and Time Span of Program Objectives
    Innovativeness

Summary

Key Terms

Study Questions

As we have seen in the previous chapter, people interested in evaluations fall into several groups and have very different but interrelated concerns. Policymakers want to know which programs are the most effective and efficient; funders want to know that they are getting value for money; program administrators want to know how well their programs are achieving their objectives and which intervention strategies are most or least successful; practitioners want guidance with day-to-day practice concerns; and clients want to be sure that a program's objectives are truly reflective of their needs.

Obviously, no single evaluation can satisfy all of these concerns and thus must involve selecting a precise focus (Smith, 1990). What information, via data, is expected? Who requires the information? Why is it needed?

Depending on the answers to the questions above, and depending on the specific questions an evaluation is expected to address, each evaluation will take a specific focus. Some of the many different possible questions that an evaluation can answer are listed below:

- To what extent are clients actually able to access services?
- Does the program meet accreditation standards?
- Is there a need for the program?
- Are program goals and objectives clearly defined?
- Are program processes and outcomes measurable?
- What is the relationship between program components?
- What is the process through which clients progress through the program?
- How satisfied are clients?
- To what extent are client changes attained?
- Does the program cause client changes?
- What is the relationship between program costs and program benefits?

The above is but a small sampling of possible evaluation questions. Whatever the specific focus may be, most evaluations can be conveniently grouped into the five types presented in the following section. No matter what type of evaluation is conducted in a human service organization, its main agenda should be to gather relevant and meaningful data in an effort to improve the quality of service delivery.

Evaluations that Can Improve the Quality of Services

Whatever the focus may be, all evaluations should provide feedback, in the manner described in Chapter 1, for the purpose of improving the quality of human services. This section will present five major types of evaluations relevant to the quality improvement process within the human services: (1) needs assessment, (2) evaluability assessment, (3) outcome assessment, (4) efficiency assessment, and (5) process analysis.

Needs Assessment

Needs assessments usually take place to assess the feasibility of (or need for) a given human service. A needs assessment is intended to verify that a social problem exists within a specific client population to an extent that warrants the implementation of a program.

According to Posavac and Carey (1992), a needs assessment must produce fairly precise estimates of the demographic characteristics of individuals exhibiting the problem under study. A needs assessment seeks to answer such questions as:

- What is the socioeconomic profile of the community?
- What are the particular needs of this community with respect to the type of program being considered (e.g., family support, mental health, employment, education, crime prevention)?
- What kinds of service would be attractive to this particular community?

It must be strongly emphasized that needs, in this context, refers not to the needs of a potential program, but to the needs of the people who will be served within the community (Guba & Lincoln, 1981). Programs should collect data to ascertain the *real* needs of the people they hope to serve and then tailor the structure of their service delivery to meet these needs.

It is often thought that needs assessments should only be conducted *before* a program is conceptualized, funded, staffed, and implemented. Indeed, there is no substitute for a thorough needs assessment at that stage as it helps to ensure that the program is initially responsive to real and important client needs. However, needs assessments also have a role to play *after* a service has been established. Client circumstances and needs change over time as do programs; periodic needs assessments can help to ensure that a service remains responsive and relevant.

For example, although a program may have been carefully designed initially to meet well identified community needs, there may be some doubt that the program is currently addressing the community's *present* needs. The composition of the community may have changed since the program was first established, so that now a high proportion of referrals are African-American children where initially the majority were Caucasian (Ciarlo, 1981). The purpose of the evaluation may be to determine the degree to which the program is responsive to the special needs of African-American children and their families and the concerns of the African-American community. A needs assessment conducted within the community could compare the *current* perceived community needs with the program's *original* intent.

Experienced program directors and funders know that the demographic characteristics of communities tend to change over time (Ihilevich & Gleser, 1982). Perhaps there is now a higher proportion of senior citizens, or perhaps the closure of a large manufacturing plant has created high unemployment and an increase in the problems associated with job loss. The community's human service delivery network may also have changed. Perhaps a program for teens who are pregnant has closed or a meals-on-wheels service has recently been instituted for seniors who are

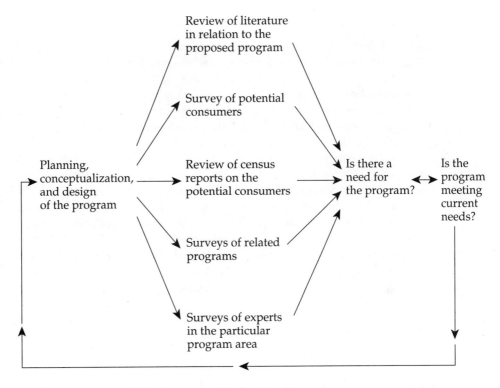

FIGURE 2.1   Needs Assessment Evaluation Process

disabled. Perceptive program directors try to keep abreast of changes by joining interagency committees, consulting with local advisory boards and funding sources, establishing contact with community organizations, and taking similar actions.

Despite all such preemptive measures, however, there is occasionally some doubt that a human service program is meeting the *current* needs of its clientele. On these occasions, a formal needs assessment may be appropriate to ascertain the community's current needs (if any) in human services. Figure 2.1 diagrams the generic process for most needs assessments.

It is possible to avoid periodic and disruptive evaluative efforts if a program's responsiveness to community needs is continually monitored. Indications that a target population is changing can be seen in changing referral patterns, novel problem situations presented by clients, and unusual requests from other human service programs. If a program has a monitoring system for collecting and analyzing such data routinely, any lack of responsiveness can be easily discovered and dealt with immediately. In short, needs assessments provide one type of data for the quality improvement process.

Evaluability Assessment

Evaluability assessments determine whether a program can in fact be evaluated (Rutman, 1980). The main task of an evaluability assessment is to determine whether a program's objectives are conceptualized and operationalized in a way that would permit a meaningful evaluation. This is not, however, simply a matter relating to evaluation. Often, an evaluability assessment indicates areas of the program's organizational structure that interfere not only with the program evaluation effort itself but also with the delivery of its services.

Many human service programs cannot in fact be evaluated as they are currently organized. The written objectives of such programs either do not exhibit common sense, or they cannot be evaluated—by evaluators or funding sources—in their current form. These programs are not necessarily ineffective or inefficient; they just have a great degree of difficulty proving otherwise, as we will see in Chapter 4.

Since it is the program's objectives that are always evaluated, it only follows that if these objectives are not clearly defined, it is impossible to determine whether or not they are being achieved (Hudson & Grinnell, 1989). In such situations, evaluators need to work closely with the program's staff to clarify the objectives so that the program can be properly evaluated. Clearly written objectives not only make evaluation possible but also help to clarify and focus staff efforts, usually resulting in a higher quality of services. Chapter 4 explains in detail how to establish meaningful objectives that are consistent with the program's intent.

Outcome Assessment

Client outcome assessment is an evaluation that determines to what degree the program is meeting its overall objectives (Weiss, 1972). In the human services, this usually means the degree to which interventions are effective. For example, a program in which a high proportion of clients achieve their individual practice objectives (sometimes referred to as treatment objectives, or client objectives) can be considered a successful program. If the majority of clients terminate unilaterally without reaching their practice objectives, the program can be considered less than successful.

An outcome evaluation indicates *whether* the program is working, but it says nothing about *how* it is working (or failing to work). Nor is there any mention of efficiency; that is, the time and dollar cost of client success. After all, if a program achieves what it is supposed to achieve by the attainment of its program objectives, why does it matter how it achieves it? If the program is to be replicated or improved, it does matter and efficiency assessments and process analyses (discussed in the next sections) can answer such questions.

Questions related to outcome generally fall into three categories. First, the evaluator wants to know to what degree the program is achieving its objectives: For example, does participation in a vocational training program improve job skills, and by how much? Second, the evaluator wants to know whether people who have been through the program have better job skills than similar people who have not been through the program. Third, there is the question of causality. Is there any evidence that the services provided by the program caused the improved job skills?

A related question, to do with how long changes last, may also be asked. Many clients terminated from human service programs return to their previous social environment that was at least partially responsible for their problems in the first place. Often, client gains are not maintained, and equally often, programs have no follow-up procedures to find out if they in fact have been maintained.

As will be discussed in Chapter 11, questions about how well the program achieves its objectives can be answered by aggregating, or bringing together, the data practitioners collect about their individual clients. Questions about how well client success is maintained can be answered in a similar way if the program collects follow-up data. However, comparisons between those who have and those who have not been through the program as well as questions about causality require additional data, collected via descriptive and explanatory designs involving two or more groups of clients.

Efficiency Assessment

A fourth type of evaluation is concerned with efficiency: How many hours of service are required, on the average, before clients reach their practice objectives? What do these hours cost in clinical and administrative time, facilities, equipment, and other resources? Is there any way in which cost could be reduced without loss of effectiveness? Is a particular program process—intake, say—conducted in the shortest possible time, at minimum cost?

If an outcome evaluation has shown the program to be effective in achieving its objectives, the issue becomes: Does the program achieve its success at a reasonable cost? Can dollar values be assigned to the outcomes it achieves? Does the program cost less or more than other programs obtaining similar results?

Efficiency assessments are particularly difficult to carry out in the human services because so many client outcomes cannot be realistically (socially and professionally) measured in terms of dollars (Silkman, 1986). For example, the benefits of a job-training program that removes clients from welfare rolls can be more easily quantified in terms of efficiency (cost savings) than a program that is designed to reduce feelings of hopelessness in terminal cancer patients. Nevertheless, there is only so much money available for human service programs, and decisions about which ones to fund, no matter how difficult, have to be made. We do not always need to put a price on program results in order to use costs in decision making, but it is necessary to be able to describe in detail what results have been achieved via the expenditure of what resources.

Note that the four evaluation categories presented so far are linked in an ordered sequence: Without a determination of need, programs to meet the need cannot be planned; without implementation of the planned program, there can be no meaningful outcome; and without a valued outcome, there is no point in asking about efficiency.

Process Analysis

A fifth evaluation category is process analysis, the monitoring and measurement of interventions—the assumed cause of client success or failure. As mentioned previously, an evaluation of efficiency determines the ratio of effectiveness or outcome to cost, but says nothing about *why* the program is or is not efficient, either overall or in certain areas. To answer that question, we need to consider program *process*: the entire sequence of activities that a program undertakes to achieve its objectives, including all the decisions made, who made them, and on what criteria they were based.

An evaluation of process might include the sequence of events throughout the entire program (see Figures 2.2 and 2.3) or it might focus on a particular program part; for example, intervention or follow-up. A careful examination of *how* something is done may indicate *why* it is more or less effective or efficient.

- To put the point another way: When a program is planned, the planning process should include a definition of the population the program will serve, a specification of the needs it will meet, and a description of the specific interventions it will undertake to meet those needs in that population. If the needs are not being met or the population is not being served, the activities possibly are not being carried out as planned. A process evaluation can ascertain whether this is so.

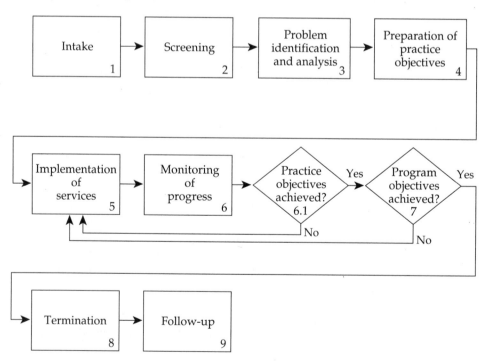

FIGURE 2.2   Flowchart of Client Progress

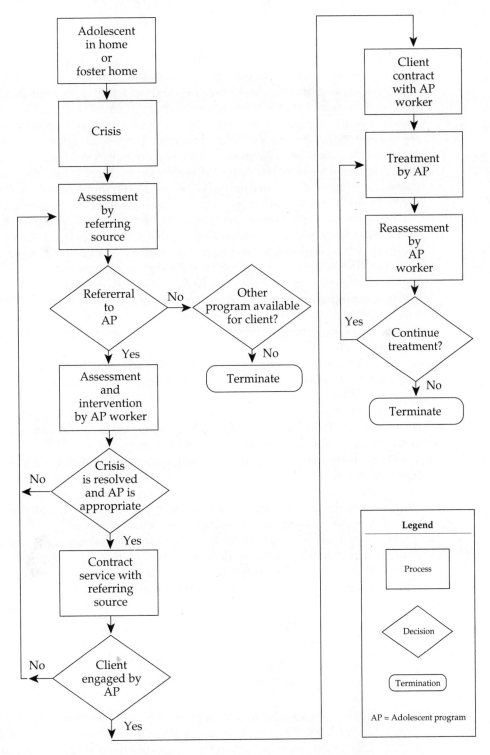

FIGURE 2.3 Client Path Flow of a Crisis Program for Adolescents

Sometimes a needs evaluation will have determined that the program is serving a sufficient number of the people it is meant to serve (Posavac & Carey, 1992). If not, a process evaluation will determine this, and will also determine exactly what interventions (services) are being undertaken by workers with their clients. What procedures are in place for assessment? Are staff members who do assessments thoroughly trained for the job? What modes of services are offered? What criteria are used to decide when a client should move from individual to family services, or into group services, or be terminated or referred elsewhere? What follow-up procedures are in place? How much and what type of staff training is available? How are records kept? What do staff do as compared with what they are supposed to do?

In order for a process analysis to occur, however, the program has to be specifically delineated in a written form so that a client's path through the entire program is clear. In short, a client path flow must be established depicting the key activities, decision points, and client flow through the program in a graphic format. Figure 2.2 presents a generic diagram, in chronological order, showing how a client enters and progresses through a typical counseling program (Kettner, Moroney, & Martin, 1990). Figure 2.3 illustrates an actual example of a client path flow for a crisis program for adolescents utilizing the general format of Figure 2.2 (Hornick & Burrows, 1988).

The data necessary for a process evaluation will generally be available in the program, but rarely in usable form. Clients' demographic and assessment data may be on file but will probably not be summarized. Services provided to individuals are typically recorded by practitioners in handwritten notes deposited in files (Weinbach, 1988). Training courses taken by staff may be included in staff files or general training files or may not be recorded at all.

Where no systematic management data system (presented in Chapter 12) is in place, gathering, summarizing, and analyzing data is extremely time-consuming and expensive. Thus, it is rarely done until a stakeholder outside the program insists on it. Again, the use of routine monitoring procedures will avoid the need for intrusive evaluations initiated by outside stakeholders.

We have assumed that both process and outcome analyses are necessary components of any comprehensive evaluation. If, however, we are concerned only with client outcomes in a program, the need to monitor the program's implementation might be questioned. The answer is simple: An outcome analysis investigates any changes that are believed to be brought about by the program's services. We cannot be certain, however, what these services were unless we study the program's operations.

Scope of Evaluations

The word *program* can refer to a variety of very different things. It may refer to something small, specific, and short term, such as a film developed for use during a training session on AIDS. It may refer to a nationwide effort to combat family violence, and include all the diverse endeavors in that field, with different practice objectives and their corresponding intervention strategies. Or it may refer to a specific treatment intervention undertaken with a particular client.

Obviously, different types of programs will need to be evaluated using different techniques. Thus, the evaluator will have to know, from the beginning, the characteristics of the human service program. The scope of any evaluation that is used in the quality improvement process must be sensitive to the following six program characteristics.

Boundary

The program may extend across a nation, region, state, city, parish, county, community, or it may be more limited, for example, to an individual human service program or school.

Size

The program may serve individual clients, such as single individuals seeking individual services, or many clients, such as people infected with the HIV virus.

Duration

The program may be designed to last for half an hour—a training film, for example. It may be an orientation course on child safety lasting for two days, a group therapy cycle lasting for ten weeks, or a pilot project designed to help the homeless lasting for six months. Or, as in the case of a child protection agency, it may be intended to continue indefinitely.

Complexity

Some agencies offer integrated programs, combining, for instance, child protection services, individual services, family services, and educational services under one common umbrella. Such a program is obviously more complex than one with a simpler singular focus, for example, providing nutrition counseling to adolescents who are pregnant (Price & Politser, 1980).

Clarity and Time Span of Program Objectives

Some programs have simple objectives that can readily be evaluated: for example, to increase the number of adolescents who are unemployed who find full-time jobs within two months after completing a six-week training course (the service). Other programs have objectives that will not become evident for some time: for example, to increase the utilization by high-risk families of a family resource center.

As will be discussed in detail in Chapter 4, a program cannot be evaluated unless its intended results (referred to as a *goal*) are reduced to measurable indicators (referred to as *objectives*). It is important that the program under study have specific objectives (derived from the program's goal) whose degree of achievement can be measured. (The difference between goals and objectives will be discussed in detail in Chapter 4.)

Innovativeness

Some human service programs follow long-established treatment interventions, such as individual treatment; others are experimenting with new ones designed for use with current social problems, such as AIDS.

Summary

This chapter has discussed five different, complementary types of evaluations that can be used in the human services: needs assessment, evaluability assessment, outcome assessment, efficiency assessment, and process analysis. The next chapter extends the discussion of evaluation by detailing how these types of evaluations can be used in the project approach and monitoring approach to quality improvement.

Key Terms

Efficiency Assessment: An evaluation to determine the ratio of effectiveness or outcome to cost. Does not contain data that may explain why the program is or is not efficient.

Evaluability Assessment: An appraisal of a program's components and operations intended to determine whether a program can, in fact, be evaluated for outcome, efficiency, or process. Mainly used to construct meaningful and measurable program objectives which are derived from the program's goal.

Needs Assessment: An evaluation that aims to assess the need for a human service by verifying that a social problem exists within a specific client population to an extent that warrants services.

Outcome Assessment: An evaluation that determines how effectively a program is meeting its stated written program objectives.

Process Analysis: An evaluation in which the entire range and sequence of program activities, including decision making, are appraised.

Program Goal: A statement defining the intent of a program which cannot be directly evaluated. It can, however, be evaluated indirectly by the program's objectives which are derived from the goal. Not to be confused with program objectives.

Program Monitoring: A program activity comprised of the ongoing collection, analysis, reporting, and use of collected program data.

Program Objectives: A set of measurable statements that can be evaluated, derived from a program's goal. Not to be confused with program goal.

Study Questions

1. Evaluation can be used to expand our knowledge base by systematically providing feedback. Identify three types of evaluations that your instructor could use to appraise your learning and performance in this course. Which one would be the best? Why?

Justify your answer. Which one would be the least useful? Why?

2. How do needs assessments and evaluability assessments differ in purpose? How do the results of each affect client service delivery? Explain in detail. Provide a human service example throughout your discussion.

3. Discuss how the scope of an evaluation would be different for a one-time, three-hour workshop on anger management and for an eight-week therapeutic anger management group. Consider aspects of boundary, size, duration, complexity, timespan, and innovation.

4. List and discuss the five different types of evaluations using one common human service example throughout your discussion. What are their commonalities? What are their differences? Which one of the five do you believe is most needed in the human services? Justify your answer. Which one do you feel is least useful to human service workers? Justify your answer using a human service example.

5. In groups of four, agree on a practice problem for a specific client group. Briefly discuss which one of the five types of evaluations could best be used to solve the problem. Discuss the factors that influenced your choice. Present your findings to the class. Discuss how the remaining four types could be used in the same general problem area.

6. What other elements (if any) would you put in Figure 2.2? Why, or why not? From your past experience, trace one of your past clients through the model as presented in Figure 2.2. Did your client go through the entire process? Why, or why not? Explain in detail. Do you think that Figure 2.3 used all of the elements of a client path flow? Explain fully.

7. You work in an agency that enjoys a twenty-year history of serving the community. In recent years, the community has experienced an influx of immigrants from other coun-

tries. Because of this change in local population, your agency intends to evaluate its services. What would be the purpose of the evaluation?

8. Your agency's funder requires data on whether services at your agency have been effective. On which part of your program should the focus be in the evaluation? What questions need to be answered before conclusions can be drawn about service effectiveness?

9. When are efficiency assessments important in the quality improvement process? Why are they particularly difficult to accomplish in the human services?

10. How would the scope of an evaluation of a long-term, nationwide project differ from that of a specific, short-term project? Consider aspects of boundary, size, duration, consistency, timespan, and innovation as you respond.

11. Read Case Study A. Discuss how this program could implement each one of the five types of evaluations to improve its services to children. Be very specific in your response. What would be the scope of the evaluations given the information contained in the case study?

12. Read Case Study B. Discuss how this program could implement each one of the five types of evaluations to improve its services in reference to the use of respite care in reducing caregiver burden. Be very specific in your response. What would be the scope of the evaluations given the information contained in the case study?

13. Read Case Study C. Discuss how this program could implement each one of the five types of evaluations to improve its services in reference to outreach counseling and support groups for battered women. Be very specific in your response. What would be the scope of the evaluations given the information contained in the case study?

3

APPROACHES TO
QUALITY IMPROVEMENT

The Project Approach to Quality Improvement

The Monitoring Approach to Quality Improvement

Advantages of Self-Assessment
       Increased Understanding of the Program
       Relevant Feedback
       Timely Feedback
       Self-Protection
       Practitioner and Client Satisfaction

Types of Evaluations and Approaches to Quality Improvement

Summary

Key Terms

Study Questions

AS WE HAVE SEEN in the previous chapter, many types of evaluations can be done to improve the quality of human services. Each type can be classified under the project approach or the monitoring approach to quality improvement. Sometimes a particular type of evaluation can be classified under both approaches, depending on how often it is done within a human service organization.

An evaluation whose purpose is to assess a completed human service program (or project) has a *project* approach to quality improvement. Complementary to the project approach, an evaluation whose purpose is to provide feedback while a program is still underway has a *monitoring* approach to quality improvement; that is, it is designed to contribute to the ongoing development and improvement of the program as it goes along (Shadish, Cook, & Leviton, 1992). No matter which approach is utilized, its process and logic generally follow the sequence of steps as outlined in Figure 1.1. In addition, the data generated by both approaches must be utilization-focused. That is, the data must be useful to one or more of the program's stakeholders or the evaluation effort is a waste of time and money and is probably unethical! Figure 3.1 presents the generic process that both quality improvement approaches must take in an effort to maximize their utilization potential. Let us now turn our attention to the first approach to quality improvement—the project approach.

The Project Approach to Quality Improvement

As we have seen, evaluations that enhance the quality improvement process in the human services may be carried out daily or they may not be initiated until the program has been in operation for a number of years. A substantial evaluation carried out periodically, at long intervals, illustrates the project approach to quality improvement. This approach tends to give rise to evaluations with the following eight characteristics.

Externally Driven.   The evaluation will almost certainly be externally driven (see Chapter 1), that is, it will be initiated by a stakeholder outside the program who more often than not will decide on the evaluation questions to be answered and the data to be collected.

Resistant Staff.   Program staff may react badly to the idea of an evaluation that is externally driven and may see it as unnecessary, intrusive, irrelevant, and judgmental (Weinbach, 1988).

Intrusiveness.   Evaluation procedures are very likely to be intrusive, no matter how hard the person doing the evaluation works to avoid this. Because the procedures are not a part of a program's normal day-to-day routine but must be introduced as additional tasks to be performed, staff usually have less time to spend on normal, client-related activities. This diversion of attention may be resented when

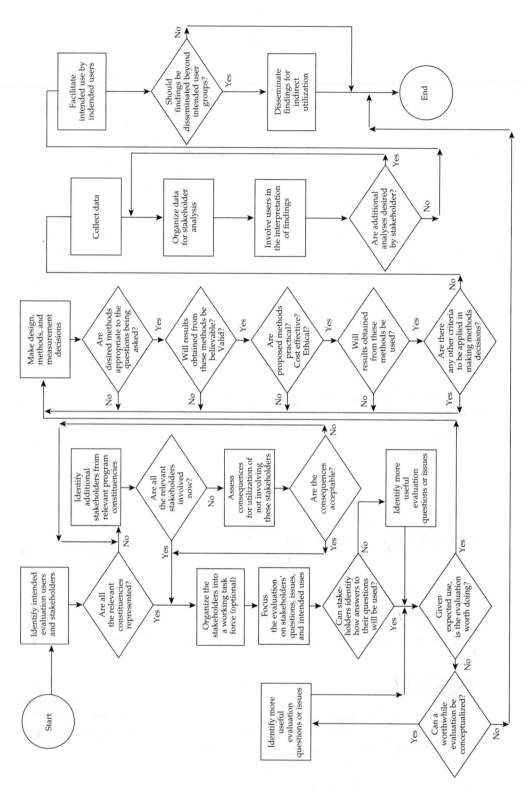

FIGURE 3.1 Utilization-Focused Evaluation Flowchart

workers prefer to spend more time with clients than to participate in an evaluation process that was mandated "from above," or "from outside the program."

Periodic or No Feedback to Staff.   The data obtained from a project approach to quality improvement, even if shared with the practitioners, is usually not directly and immediately relevant to them or to their current clients. This is particularly the case if an evaluation is designed to answer questions posed by administrators or funders, and workers' practice concerns cannot be addressed using the same evaluation methods. If, as sometimes happens, a project approach does yield useful information (via the data collected) for the staff, and changes are made on the basis of this information, the next evaluation may not take place for a long time, perhaps for years. If the evaluator is not on hand to analyze the benefits resulting from the changes, staff members may not be sure that there *were* any benefits (Raymond, 1985).

Resistance to Implementation.   When an evaluation is externally driven, staff may resist implementation of an evaluator's recommendations even if the program's administration insists that changes be made. By the time a project approach is initiated, day-to-day program procedures, both good and bad, may have become set. It is virtually a law of nature that the longer a routine has been in operation, the more difficult it is to change.

Large Recommended Changes.   The changes recommended as a result of a project approach to quality improvement can be enormous. Administrators and evaluators may feel that since an evaluation occurs only once in a number of years, it is a major event which requires drastic findings and recommendations to justify it. When a program is monitored continually, shortcomings can be caught at once and can be corrected with minimal effort. Periodic evaluations, on the other hand, often result in more sweeping recommendations.

Not Practical in Applied Settings.   All evaluations must be based on established scientific principles and methods (Stufflebeam & Shinkfield, 1984). However, the rigorous techniques necessary to obtain cause-and-effect knowledge may not be practical in a normal program setting. Chapter 8 discusses the basic types of evaluation designs that can be used to obtain knowledge at different levels (Grinnell, 1993a). For now, it is enough to point out that evaluation designs used to obtain higher levels of quality improvement recommendations may require that clients be randomly assigned to experimental or control groups without regard for their special needs. Similarly, evaluation designs to measure client change may require that measurement be carried out both before and after the treatment intervention, without regard to clinical time restraints or the client's emotional condition (Gilchrist & Schinke, 1988; Schinke & Gilchrist, 1993).

Usually, rigorous experiments for the purpose of increasing knowledge are carried out in laboratories, not in practice settings (Miller, 1991). However, the same rigorous conditions may be suggested if the purpose is, for example, to evaluate the effectiveness and efficiency of a therapy group. The worker might argue that more time will be spent administering measuring instruments (see Chapter 6) than conducting therapeutic work; the evaluator can easily reply that results will be valid only if experimental conditions are observed (Patton, 1982). The issue here is: Whose interests is the evaluation intended to serve? Who is it *for*: practice or science, the human service worker or the external evaluator?

In a project approach to quality improvement the answer is that it is sometimes for the evaluator, or for the administrative, academic, or funding body that has employed the evaluator. It should be stressed that this is not always the case. Many project approaches use nonintrusive techniques geared to actual practice situations. If, however, the evaluation is only undertaken once in a number of years, intrusion can be considered warranted in order to obtain reliable and valid results.

Difficult to Incorporate in Practice Settings.   A final characteristic of a project approach to quality improvement is that the methods used by the evaluator are difficult for staff to learn and almost impossible for them to incorporate into their normal day-to-day practices. In fact, staff are not expected to learn anything about evaluation procedures as a result of the program being evaluated. Nor is it expected that the evaluation methods employed will be used again before the next major periodic evaluation. The project approach is carried out by the evaluator and, essentially, until the next time, that is that.

The reader may have noticed that all the characteristics we listed for the project approach to quality improvement can be viewed as negative; without a doubt, the project approach is intrusive, traumatic, fails to meet the immediate needs of the workers, and may engender resentment and fear. Nevertheless, this approach must be periodically performed in order to improve the quality of services clients receive. However, this book will not focus on this approach as it is discussed in more advanced evaluation books. We will now turn to a second approach to quality improvement that complements the project approach—the monitoring approach— the focus of this book.

The Monitoring Approach to Quality Improvement

The monitoring approach to quality improvement complements the project approach. It is also based on reliable and valid evaluation methods that can be integrated into a human service program as a part of its normal operating routine. The monitoring approach to quality improvement measures the extent that a human service program is reaching its intended population and the extent to which its services match what were intended to be delivered. In addition, this approach provides immediate and continual feedback on client progress to practitioners. Evaluations resulting from a monitoring approach to quality improvement tend to have the seven characteristics described below.

Internally Driven. Continuous routine use of evaluation methods may have been initially suggested by an administrator or an outside consultant or funder. However, the evaluation methods are put into place and used by practitioners for their own and their clients' benefit without request (or demand) from any outside source. The evaluation may thus be said to be internally driven (see Chapter 1).

Cooperative Staff. When evaluation is a process instead of an event, practitioners generally do not resent it because it is an accepted part of the daily routine of delivering high-quality services to clients.

Nonintrusiveness. By definition, an intrusion is something unrelated to the task at hand that interferes with that task. Evaluation methods that are routinely used to improve services to clients are certainly relevant to the human services. Such methods do not interfere with the task at hand because they are an integral part of that task (Patton, 1986).

Ongoing Continuous Feedback. There are some activities in a human service program that need to be monitored on a continuing basis. For example, client referrals are received daily and must be processed quickly. In order to estimate remaining program space, intake workers need a list of how many clients are presently being served, how many clients will be terminated shortly, and how many clients have recently been accepted into the program. This continually changing list is an example of a simple evaluative tool which provides useful data. The resulting information can be used to compare the actual number of clients in the program with the number the program was originally designed (and usually funded) to serve (Polster & Lynch, 1985).

The list can, in other words, be used to fulfill a basic evaluative purpose: comparison of what is with what should be, of the actual with the ideal. It might be found, in some programs, that the arithmetic of intake is not quite right. For example, suppose that a program has space for 100 clients. At the moment, 70 are being seen on a regular basis. In theory, then, the program can accept 30 more clients. Suppose also that the program has five social workers, each will then theoretically carry a maximum caseload of 20.

In the caseloads of these five workers there ought to be just 30 spaces. But for some reason, there are more than 30. The supervisor, who is trying to assign new clients to workers, discovers that the workers can muster 40 spaces between them. In other words, there are 10 clients on the computer who are theoretically being served, but who are not in any of the five workers' caseloads. What has happened to these 10 clients?

Investigation brings to light the fact that the workers and the intake computer keep their records in different ways. The computer assumes that every client accepted will continue to be served until formally discharged. However, the practitioner who has not seen Ms Kuhlmann for six months, and has failed to locate her after repeated tries, has placed Ms Kuhlmann in the "inactive" file and accepted another client in her place. The result of this disparity in record-keeping is that the program seems to have fewer available spaces and clients who might be served are being turned away.

The problem might be solved simply by discussing inactive files at a staff meeting. What steps will be taken to locate a client who does not appear for therapy? How long should attempts at contact continue before the client is formally discharged? Which other involved professionals need to be informed about the client's nonappearance and the discharge? When and how should they be informed? Is it worth modifying the intake computer's terminal display to include inactive files, with the dates they became inactive and the dates they were reactivated or discharged? Once decisions have been made on these points, a straightforward procedure can be put in place to deal with the ongoing problem of inactive files (Patton, 1990).

Other problems may also come to light. It may be found, for example, that a frequent source of inappropriate referrals is doing so because of inaccurate information about the program's eligibility criteria. Neither the problem nor the solution can be identified unless data are routinely collected about the characteristics of clients referred by various sources. This sort of continuous feedback is obtained through the monitoring approach—problems that would otherwise continue to trouble staff can be immediately identified and solved.

Many programs routinely go through similar processes in order to identify and solve operational problems. They do not dignify them with the term "evaluations," but evaluations, nevertheless, are what they are.

Acceptance of Changes.   Necessary client-centered changes for solving problems are usually agreed upon by line-level practitioners and are usually accepted without difficulty. Resistance usually arises when practitioners are not consulted about the changes or cannot see that they solve any specific problem. This is a fairly common occurrence in the project approach to quality improvement. A monitoring approach, on the other hand, usually allows the workers themselves to identify the problems and suggest tentative solutions.

Minor Recommended Changes.   When changes occur constantly as a result of an ongoing monitoring process, they tend to be small. Of course, continual monitoring can suggest that fundamental changes are needed in the way that the program is conceptualized or structured, but such large changes are rare. Most often, monitoring gives rise to continual minor adjustments instead of the larger, more traumatic changes that may result from the project approach.

Easy to Incorporate in Practice Settings.   The monitoring approach, like the project approach to quality improvement, is based on established research methods. The difference between them can lie in whom the evaluation is intended to serve: the line-level worker or the evaluator. When evaluation is undertaken by the workers themselves for their own and their clients' benefit, there is no doubt about whom the evaluation is intended to serve. Science is merely a tool, used to acquire needed knowledge in a way that is clinically practical. Research methodology provides various established ways to obtain the necessary data, but many of them are too complex and time-consuming to be useful to practitioners who are busy with their caseloads. Later chapters of this text will present evaluation methods that can be used as an integral part of treatment interventions and yet are soundly based on scientific principles.

Advantages of Self-Assessment

Scientific evaluation methods are not the sole preserve of specially trained evaluators. The evaluation methods that will be discussed in the remainder of this book can be easily learned and used by line-level staff as part of routine practice. Becoming a self-evaluating human service professional (or organization) has definite advantages not only for clients, but also for workers. Some of these advantages follow.

Increased Understanding of the Program

A human service program is often a complex entity with a large number of interlinked components. Practitioners are usually concerned mainly with the effectiveness of their treatment interventions. How can the confused sexual identity of an adolescent who has been sexually abused best be addressed? What teaching technique is most effective with children who have learning disabilities? Is an open-door policy appropriate for group homes housing adolescents who are mentally challenged? Answers come slowly through study, intuition, hunches, and past experience, but often the issues are so complex that practitioners cannot be sure if the answers obtained are correct.

Many human service workers stumble on, hoping their interventions are right, using intuition to assess the effectiveness of their particular interventions (or package of interventions) with particular clients. Chapter 7, on case-level evaluation, shows how the use of simple evaluation designs can complement a worker's intuition so that an inspired guess more closely approaches knowledge. However, no amount of knowledge about how well an intervention worked will tell the worker *why* it worked or failed to work. *Why* do apparently similar clients, treated similarly, achieve different results? Is it something about the client? About the worker? About the type of services?

It is always difficult to pinpoint a reason for unsatisfactory achievement of program objectives because there are so many possible overlapping and intertwined reasons. However, some reasons may be identified by a careful look at the program stages leading up to the interventions. For example, one reason for not attaining a client's practice objective may be that the client was unsuited to the program and ought never to have been admitted. Perhaps the program's assessment procedures are inadequate; perhaps unsuitable clients are accepted if the referral comes from a major funding body. In other words, perhaps the lack of client success at the intervention stage derives from problems at intake.

Human service workers who have been involved with a do-it-yourself evaluation may become familiar with the program's intake procedures, both in theory and in reality. They may also become familiar with the planning procedures, termination procedures, follow-up procedures, staff recruitment and training procedures, recording procedures, and so on. The worker will begin to see a link between poor client outcomes at one program stage and inadequacies at another, between a success here and an innovation somewhere else. In sum, practitioners may be able to perform their own tasks more effectively if they understand how the program functions as a living organism. One way to gain this understanding is to participate in a hands-on, do-it-yourself evaluation.

Relevant Feedback

A second advantage of internally driven evaluations is that meaningful and relevant questions can be formulated by the workers within the program (Schuerman, 1983). They can use evaluation procedures to find out what they want to know, not what the administrator, the funder, or a university professor wants to know. If the data to be gathered are perceived as relevant, staff are usually willing to cooperate in the evaluative endeavor. And if the information resulting from that data *is* relevant, it is likely to be used by the practitioners.

Timely Feedback

A third advantage is that the workers can decide when the evaluation is to be carried out. Evaluation procedures can be carried out daily, weekly, monthly, or only once in five years, as will be discussed in the following chapters. The point here is that data are most useful when they help to solve a current problem, less useful when the problem has not yet occurred, and least useful after the event.

Self-Protection

It has been mentioned that most human service programs are evaluated eventually, often by an outside evaluator (Tripodi, 1983). If staff have already familiarized themselves with evaluation procedures and with the program's strengths and weaknesses, they are in a better position to defend the program when an externally driven evaluation occurs. In addition, because improvements have already been made as a result of their self-evaluations, the program will be more defensible. Moreover, the staff will indirectly learn about evaluation designs and methodology by monitoring their practices on a regular basis. Modifications recommended by an outside evaluator are thus likely to be less far-reaching and less traumatic.

An additional consideration is that staff members themselves are likely to be less traumatized by the idea of being evaluated: Evaluation is no longer a new and frightening experience, but simply a part of the routine—a routine that tries to improve the quality of services for clients.

Practitioner and Client Satisfaction

A case-level evaluation can satisfy the worker that an intervention is appropriate and successful, and it can improve a client's morale by demonstrating the progress that has been made toward his or her practice objective. Moreover, data gathered at the case level can always be used at the program level. Improvement of the program as a whole can follow from an improvement in one worker's practice.

Types of Evaluations and Approaches to Quality Improvement

The last chapter presented five types of evaluations that can be used to improve the quality of services within human service organizations. This chapter did not attempt to classify the various types of evaluations into a project approach to quality improvement or into a monitoring approach to quality improvement. Types of evaluations cannot be meaningfully classified by approach. For example, the needs assessment project-type of evaluation can be used in a monitoring fashion if it is undertaken on a regular and systematic basis. The point we want to make is simply that there are advantages and disadvantages to each quality improvement approach and one is not inherently better than the other—they complement one another—each has its place in the evaluative process. That is, they are both used to improve the quality of services delivered by human service professionals.

Summary

This chapter presented the basic ingredients of the project and monitoring approaches to quality improvement. The monitoring approach to quality improvement includes evaluations that aim to provide ongoing feedback so that a program (or project) can be improved while it is still underway. It contributes to the continuous development and improvement of a human service program. On the other hand, the project approach to quality improvement includes evaluations whose purpose is to assess a completed or finished program (or project).

Workers can become, via the monitoring approach to quality improvement, self-evaluating professionals. Program monitoring is a very basic and elementary form of evaluation. However, in order to monitor our practices, we need to know how human services are conceptualized—the topic of the following chapter.

Key Terms

Monitoring Approach to Quality Improvement:
Evaluations that aim to provide ongoing feedback so that a program (or project) can be improved while it is still underway. It contributes to the continuous development and improvement of a human service program. This approach complements the project approach.

Project Approach to Quality Improvement: Evaluations whose purpose is to assess a completed or finished program (or project). This approach complements the monitoring approach.

Study Questions

1. Discuss in detail the advantages of self-assessment in contemporary practice. Provide a human service example in your discussion.

2. Discuss the advantages and disadvantages of the project approach and the monitoring approach to quality improvement in the human services. Compare the two approaches. Do you see any commonalities? Any differences? Discuss the circumstances where one approach would be preferred over the other.

3. This chapter has identified two different complementary approaches to quality improvement. Go to the library and find an article that utilized each approach (one article that used a project approach to quality improvement and one article that used a monitoring approach to quality improvement). Were the contents of the articles consistent with the contents of this chapter? If not, how were they different?

4. In your opinion, how might monitoring approaches be considered more "practitioner-friendly" than project approaches? Compare and contrast the commonalities and differences between the two approaches. Provide a human service example in your discussion.

5. Discuss how a needs assessment evaluation as presented in Chapter 2 could be used as a monitoring approach to quality improvement as well as a project approach.

6. What are some of the advantages for practitioners working in an agency that supports internally driven evaluations?

7. Why are project approaches to quality improvement difficult to incorporate in practice settings? Why are they often impractical in applied settings?

8. Read Case Study C. Discuss how the counseling and support group program could use a monitoring approach to quality improvement and a project approach to quality improvement. Be specific in your response. Discuss in detail the advantages of self-assessment within this program. Do you believe the monitoring approach that the program uses at the case level is effective? If so, why? If not, why not?

Part II

WORKING TOWARD QUALITY IMPROVEMENT

Chapter 4
The Structure of Service Delivery

Chapter 5
Developing Practice Objectives

Chapter 6
Measuring Program and Practice Objectives

Working toward accountability via the quality improvement process is an integral part of how a human service organization delivers its services and becomes accountable to the general public, its funders, and its clients. In this sense, it becomes accountable by linking its organizational goal and mandate to each specific program it offers. In addition, for each one of its programs, it must link the program's goal to specific program objectives, which in turn are linked to client practice objectives. These links form the cornerstone of accountability. Chapter 4 focuses on these links while Chapter 5 shows how a program goal and its associated program objectives can be translated into client-centered practice objectives. It is these practice objectives which provide a focus for services at the client level and make it possible to establish measurable indicators of client change. The final chapter is concerned with the role of measurement in the quality improvement process and discusses the various ways of easily measuring the achievement of program and practice objectives.

4

THE STRUCTURE OF
SERVICE DELIVERY

PART I OF THIS BOOK discussed the concept of evaluations: the types, why they are undertaken, who initiates them, which stakeholders benefit from the results, and how the two complementary approaches to quality improvement differ in their efforts to improve the delivery of human services. During our introduction, brief references were made to *agencies, agency goals, programs, program goals, program objectives, practice objectives,* and *activities.* The specific terminology and the linkages among these terms must be fully understood and appreciated before an evaluation of any kind can take place. This chapter will discuss precisely what these words mean and show the logical relationships among the terms.

Agencies

A *human service agency* is an organization that exists to fulfill a legitimate social purpose—hopefully the purpose was established by some form of a needs assessment as presented in Chapter 1. An agency may, for example, be established to protect children, to provide vocational training for adolescents who are unemployed, or to deliver meals to homebound seniors. It may be public—that is, funded entirely by the state and/or federal government—or private, deriving some funds from governmental sources and some from client fees, charitable bodies, private donations, fund-raising activities, and so forth.

Mission Statements

A human service agency has a *mission statement* that provides a unique written philosophical perspective of what it is all about and makes explicit the reason for its existence. Sometimes mission statements are called *philosophical statements.* They state a common vision for the agency and provide a point of reference for all of its major planning decisions. They not only provide clarity of purpose to staff within the agency, but also help influence stakeholders outside the agency understand its mission.

In general, a mission statement establishes broad parameters within which an agency's goal is developed and refined over time. In addition, it contributes to the development of specific programs that are designed to help achieve its goal. Mission statements are usually given formal approval and sanction, by legislators for public agencies and by executive boards for private agencies.

Mission statements can range from one sentence to many pages in length. They are as varied as the agencies they represent. Five examples of short mission statements are:

1. This agency strives to provide a variety of support services to families and children in need, while in the process maintaining their rights, their safety, and their human dignity . . .

2. This agency strives to promote and protect the mental health of the elderly people residing in California by offering quality and timely programs which will deliver these services . . .

3. The philosophy of this agency views both parents and workers as "partners in care." This approach is consistent whether the family unit is intact or whether the child has been placed out of the home environment . . .

4. The philosophy of this agency believes that treatment services should be short-term, intensive in nature, focus on problems in day-to-day operation of services, utilize beneficial agency and community resources, and be evaluated . . .

5. The philosophy of this agency is to protect and promote the physical and social well-being of Chicago by ensuring the development and delivery of services which protect and promote well-being, while encouraging and supporting individual, family and community independence, self-reliance and responsibility to the greatest degree possible . . .

In short, mission statements guide the conceptualization and operation of the programs within the agency so that the programs will help the agency work toward its goal. The mission statement is important in the development of the agency's goal. However, we feel that some agencies spend too much time developing and redeveloping their mission statements at the expense of refining their goals.

Agency Goals

A human service agency is established in an effort to reduce the gap between the desired state of affairs and what actually exists within a specific target population; it exists to close the disparity between an ideal "goal" and actual "reality." In some instances, however, the goal may be to maintain the status quo in the face of an anticipated decline or deterioration in an existing social situation. For example, a goal may be to avoid further increases in the costs of hospital care.

A *goal* has two purposes which attempt to guide practitioners toward effective and accountable practice. First, guided by the agency's mission statement, the goal acts as a single focal point to guide the entire range of activities within an agency in a specific and common direction. To function effectively as a guidepost, only one goal is specified for an agency.

Second, a goal functions as an umbrella under which all programs, program objectives, practice objectives, and activities within the agency logically fall. A program's goal should be defined at a conceptual level of explication. Having global properties, a goal is not measurable. As such, it is useful to view a goal as a means to an end, rather than an end in itself.

Requirements of Goals

It is essential that a goal reflects the mandate of the agency and is guided by its mission statement. This is achieved by highlighting: (1) the nature of the social problem to be tackled, (2) the client population to be served, (3) the general direction of anticipated client change, and (4) the means for effecting the change. An example of a program goal for a Family Preservation Agency is:

1. The goal of this agency is to preserve family units where children are at risk for out-of-home placements due to problems with physical abuse (current problem and population to be served). The program aims to strengthen interpersonal functioning of family members (direction of anticipated client change) through intensive home-based services (plans to achieve the desired state).

At first glance the above goal can be depicted to have more utility at the program level of operation than at the case level of operation. However, goals that are vague and not used for guidance can quickly lead to unacceptable behaviors of the line-level workers (case-level operations). For example, suppose the agency neglected to use the above goal as a navigational tool. How would practitioners determine the suitability of clients referred? What source would they use to limit the extent to helping clients? How would innovative interventions be assessed for fit within the agency? Every individual worker could offer an answer to each of these important questions. However, an agency must have a common frame of reference to determine whether or not *all* services delivered are effective and efficient.

For the agency mentioned above, losing sight of its goal could cause an overwhelming diversification of its services. Without the focus of "preserving family units" and "strengthening interpersonal functioning of family members," practitioner efforts could inappropriately be diverted to community education, to self-help groups, and to other services that did not reflect the agency's goal. A drastic deviation in worker activity would surely undermine the agency's attempts to demonstrate accountability in services aimed specifically at family preservation (its reason for being—its mandate).

A second example of a goal for a community-based human service agency could be written as follows:

2. The goal of this agency is to help children who are socioeconomically disadvantaged in Boston (target population) who are obtaining low grades in grade school (current state of problem area) obtain better grades (future state) in school by providing afterschool programs within their local communities (plans to achieve the desired state).

Let us look at a third example of an agency's goal. A child protection agency's goal could be as follows:

3. The goal of this agency is to provide temporary services (how the desired state is to be achieved) to children who have been physically and emotionally abused in New York who are in need of protection from their parents and others (current problem and target population) in order for them to return to their natural homes (desired state).

As stated previously, all human service agencies exist for a specific social purpose. The purpose may be very broad—to stop family violence in the United States, or to provide quality in-home treatment services to families where a child has been placed out of the home—or relatively narrow—to increase a community's awareness of family violence or to increase the socialization of the elderly in a specific community.

An agency can be a small organization, operating from a single facility, or nationwide, comprising numerous branches at various locations. However small or large, simple or complex, an agency always functions as one entity which is governed by some sort of executive board. This board, via the input of the executive director, formally establishes policies and procedures for all of its programs which are guided by the agency's mission statement and mandate.

To sum up, an agency's goal must include four statements: (1) it must identify a current problem area, (2) it must include a specific target population with the problem, (3) it must include the desired future state for this population, and (4) it must state how it plans to achieve the desired state. Whatever the current problem, the desired future state, or the population to be served, an agency sets up programs to help work toward its intended result—the goal. In the above three examples the goals were preservation of families, obtaining higher grades, and returning home. These examples also illustrate that a goal does not have to follow a specific format; it only has to contain the four elements mentioned above.

Agency Objectives

The objective of all agencies is to establish specific programs that will help the agency work toward its goal; all programs an agency creates must be logically linked to its goal. In short, no agency should have a program where the services it delivers are not directly and obviously connected to its goal. In the second example above, the agency would be providing specific programs that would help the children it was serving to obtain better grades. It would not have programs such as meals-on-wheels programs, recreation programs, or any other programs that would not work toward the intended result of grade improvement for children who were socioeconomically disadvantaged in Boston.

Programs

There are as many ways to define a human service program as there are people willing to define it. Definitions can be complicated and complex and use terms such as *inputs, throughputs, outputs,* and *outcomes,* which only social systems analysts would be interested in. Definitions of agencies can also be very simple (we support this approach). Matters are further muddied by the fact that the term *program* can be used to refer to different levels of service delivery within an agency (see Figures 4.2 and 4.3 for examples). In other words, some types of programs can be seen as subprograms of a larger program such as the public awareness services under the nonresidential program for the women's shelter as presented in Figure 4.3.

Putting such complexities aside, at the most basic level, a program can be defined according to a simple description of the services it offers. When this is done, a simple program organizational chart can also be used that shows the relationship of the programs to the agency.

The second simple method of defining a program is to use a client path flow that shows the way in which clients move into, through, and out of the program (e.g., Figure 2.4). Despite the differences between the descriptive approach and the client path flow approach, the ultimate purpose of both is to define and represent key elements of the program's structure so that it is understandable.

What is the difference between an agency and a program? Like an agency, a program also exists to fulfill some social purpose. However, there is one main difference: A program has a narrower, better-defined purpose than does an agency. For example, the child protection agency above, with the goal of child protection, may have an investigative program: a staff of workers whose primary function is to investigate allegations that specific children are being neglected or abused. This investigative role constitutes an investigation *program* because the overall goal of the agency—to protect children—has been refined, with an investigative program (which has a narrower purpose)—to investigate allegations of child abuse or neglect.

The child protection agency may also have several group homes for children in care—a group home program. It may be involved with treatment foster parents—a treatment foster care program; with public education—an educational program; or with treatment of abusive families—a child abuse treatment program. It may run special classes for child abuse survivors and their parents who have to appear in court—a survivor-witness program. All of these programs have specialized program objectives (to be discussed later), which contribute to the overall intent or goal of the agency—child protection.

Figure 4.1 presents a simple organizational structure of a family service agency. Note how the five programs are rationally derived from the agency's main focus (families and children), only at a more specific level. For example, the agency does not have a program that is geared toward other target groups such as substance abusers, or the homeless.

It can be easily seen from Figure 4.1 that this particular family service agency has five programs dealing with the agency's target population of family and chil-

FIGURE 4.1   Simplified Organizational Chart of a Family Service Agency

dren: a group home program for children, a family counseling program, a child adoption program, a treatment foster care program, and a family support program.

Figure 4.2 provides a more complex example of an agency that also deals with families and children. This agency has only two programs, a behavioral adaptation treatment program and a receiving and assessment family home program. The receiving and assessment family home program is further broken down into two components, a family support component and a receiving and assessment component. The receiving and assessment component is further broken down into family support services, child care services, and family home provider services.

How many programs are shown in Figure 4.2? The answer is two—however, one should note that this agency conceptualized its service delivery much more thoroughly than the agency outlined in Figure 4.1. This agency has conceptualized its receiving and assessment component of its receiving and assessment family home program into three separate services: family support services, child care services, and family home provider services. In short, service delivery is illustrated much more clearly in Figure 4.2 than in Figure 4.1, and the clearer, the better.

Another example of how programs can be organized under an agency is presented in Figure 4.3. This agency, a women's emergency shelter, has a residential program and a nonresidential program. The residential program has crisis counsel-

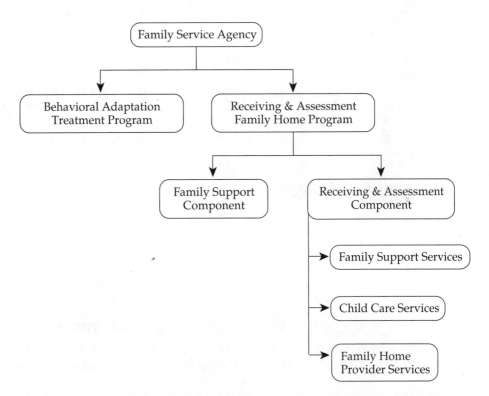

FIGURE 4.2   Organizational Chart of a Family Service Agency (highlighting the Receiving & Assessment Component)

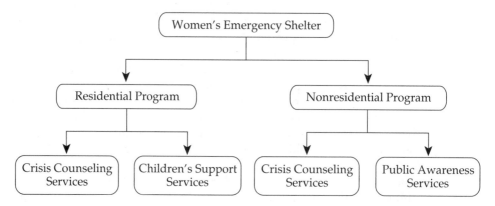

FIGURE 4.3   Organizational Chart of a Women's Emergency Shelter

ing services and children's support services; the nonresidential program has crisis counseling services and public awareness services. This agency distinguishes the services it provides between the women who stay within the shelter (residential program) and those who come and go (nonresidential program).

A final example of how an agency can deliver its services is presented in Figure 4.4. This agency's child welfare program is broken down into three services, and the native child protection services are broken down into four components: an investigation component, a family service child in parental care component, a family service child in temporary alternate care component, and a permanent guardianship component.

It is surprising how many human service agencies establish programs that have nothing to do with their goals whatsoever. Many times, agencies establish programs with a knee-jerk mentality as funds become available for new, but unrelated programs (to the agency's goal, that is), and the agency feels compelled to seek additional revenues.

Classifying Programs

From the previous four figures, it can be seen that how an agency labels its programs and subprograms is arbitrary. For example, the agency in Figure 4.2 labels its subprograms as components and its sub-subprograms as services; the agency in Figure 4.3 labels its subprograms as services—not as components as in Figure 4.2. The main point is that an agency must structure and conceptualize its programs, components, and services logically with reference to its goal, which is guided by its mission statement and mandate.

There is no systematic approach to naming programs in the human services. As can be seen in Figures 4.1 to 4.4, programs can be named according to function (e.g., Adoption Program, Family Support Program); setting (e.g., Group Home Program, Foster Care Program, Residential Program); target population (e.g., Services for the Handicapped Program); and problem (e.g., Child Sexual Abuse Program; Behav-

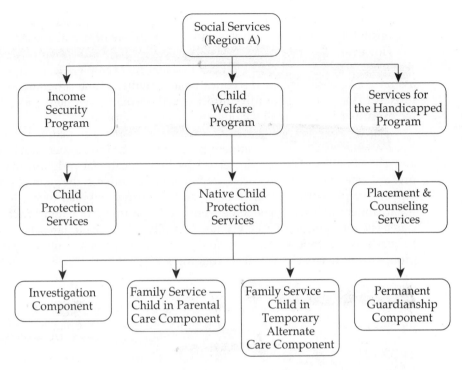

FIGURE 4.4   Organizational Chart of a State's Social Service Delivery System (highlighting the Native Child Protection Services)

ioral Adaptation Treatment Program). Other classifications for program titles include acronyms such as P.E.T. (Parent Effectiveness Training) or catchy titles such as Incredible Edibles (A nutritional program for children). The primary purpose or goal of the program must always be considered, whatever the title. Including the social problem or the main client need in the title simplifies communication of a program's purpose. In this way, the title of the program is linked to the program goal and there is less confusion about what services the program offers.

An elusive program title can easily lead to confusion in understanding the program's purpose. For example, a Group Home Program suggests that the program aims to provide a residence for clients. In fact, all clients residing in the group home do so to fulfill a specific purpose. Depending on the goal of the program, the primary purpose could be to offer shelter and safety to teenage runaways or to enhance functioning of adolescents with developmental disabilities.

Organizational Structure

Another important aspect of human service agencies is structure. An agency can be organized hierarchically, perhaps with a board of directors at the top, followed by an executive director, an assistant executive director, team supervisors, line-level staff, administrative staff, and so forth. Each of these positions carries certain responsibilities to do, for example, with the treatment of sexual abuse survivors.

However, the lines of authority with respect to the educational program within the agency may be somewhat different. Perhaps, for example, a team supervisor has assumed responsibility for the educational activities of the program, and reports directly to the assistant executive director on these matters without going directly to the executive director as all the other team supervisors do.

A final factor in organizational structure is clients. The people served by our hypothetical sexual abuse treatment program will be, say, sexual abuse survivors and their families. The people served by the educational program may include professionals from other agencies, human service students, the general public, and parent groups. As the clients differ, so do the sources that refer them: Referrals for the treatment program may come from the Department of Child Welfare, physicians, lawyers, police officers, friends or family, or other human service agencies. Requests for education more commonly come from various community or student groups or from agencies requiring training.

When an Agency Is a Program

Sometimes an agency may itself have a narrow, well-defined purpose. For example, the sole purpose of a counseling agency may be to serve couples who are sexually dysfunctional. In this case, the agency comprises only one program, and the terms *agency* and *program* refer to the same thing. However, if the clientele happens to include a high proportion of couples who are infertile, it may later be decided that some staff members should specialize in infertility counseling (with a physician as a co-counselor) while other workers continue to deal with all other aspects of sexual dysfunction. There would then be two distinct sets of practitioners, focusing on different goals, and two separate types of clients; that is, there would be two *programs*. Nevertheless, the *agency*, with its board, its executive director, and its administrative policies and procedures would remain.

Program Goals

Probably the most important aspect to remember at this point is that like the agency's goal, a program's goal must also be compatible with the agency's mission statement. They must both flow logically from the mission statement. They are announcements of expected outcomes dealing with the social problem the program is attempting to prevent, eradicate, or ameliorate. Like an agency's goal, a program's goal is not measurable or achievable—it simply provides a programmatic direction. (Kettner, Moroney, & Martin, 1990). Like an agency's goal, a program's goal must also posses four characteristics: (1) it must identify a current problem area, (2) it must include a specific target population containing the problem, (3) it must include the desired future state for this population, and (4) it must state how it plans to achieve the desired state.

Like agencies, program goals reflect the dreams of the people who work within the program. Staff may hope that their program will "enable adolescents with developmental disabilities who live in Boston to lead full and productive lives." More importantly, however, the program goal phrase of "full and productive lives" can mean different things to different staff members. Some workers may believe that a full and productive life cannot be lived without integration into the community. They may therefore want to work toward placing these adolescents in the ordinary school system, enrolling them in community activities, and finally returning them to their parental home, with a view to making them self-sufficient in adult life. Other staff members may believe that a full and productive life for these children means the security of institutional teaching and care and the companionship of similar adolescents. Still others may believe that institutional care with limited outside contact may be the best compromise.

Because these various interpretations of "full and productive life" conflict, the workers may not agree on a more exact program goal. The phrase "a full and productive life" may be the best they can do; it may satisfy all of them precisely because it is a vague phrase, empty of content, and therefore open to various interpretations.

Suppose that the workers finally agree that their program goal of group home X is "to enable adolescents with developmental disabilities to become self-sufficient adults." The question again arises: What is meant by "self-sufficient?" Does it mean that the adolescents must live in the community when they are adults rather than in a supported environment? Or that they may live in a supported environment but must earn enough money from an outside source to pay for room and board? Does a sheltered workshop count as an outside source? Until it is decided exactly what "self-sufficient" means, the workers cannot know whether the adolescents have become self-sufficient adults and, thus, whether the program has met its goal.

Unintended Results

A program's goal may lead to unintended results. For example, a group home for adolescents with developmental disabilities may strive to enable its residents to achieve their full potential in a safe and supportive environment. This is the intended result or goal. Incidentally, however, the group home may produce organized resistance from neighbors—a negative unintended result. This resistance may draw the attention of the media and allow the difficulties in finding a suitable location for such homes to be highlighted in a sympathetic manner: a positive unintended result. Meanwhile, the attitude of the community may affect the adolescents to such an extent that they do not feel safe or supported and do not achieve their potential; that is, the home has not achieved its intended result or goal.

Agency Goals versus Program Goals

Perhaps the group home mentioned above is run by an agency that runs a number of other homes for adolescents with developmental disabilities. It is unlikely that all the children in these homes will be capable of self-sufficiency as adults; some may have reached their full potential when they have learned to feed or bathe themselves. The goal of self-sufficiency will therefore not be appropriate for the agency as a whole, although it might do very well for group home X which serves children who function at a higher level. The agency's goal must be broader, to encompass a wider range of situations, and because it is broader, it will probably be more vague.

To begin, the agency may decide that its goal is "to enable adolescents with developmental disabilities to reach their full potential." Home X, one of the programs within the agency, can then interpret "full potential" to mean self-sufficiency and can formulate a program goal based on this interpretation. Home Y, another program within the agency, serving adolescents who function at a lower level, may decide that it can realistically do no more than provide a caring environment for them and emotional support for their families. It may translate this decision into another program goal: "to enable adolescents with developmental disabilities to experience security and happiness." Home Z, a third program within the agency, may set as its program goal "to enable adolescents with developmental disabilities to acquire the social and vocational skills necessary for satisfying and productive lives." Figure 4.5 illustrates the relationship among the goals of the three group homes to the agency. Note how logical and consistent the goals of the programs are with the agency's goal.

This example clearly illustrates three points about the character of a goal. First, the goal simplifies the reason for the program's existence and provides direction for the workers. The second is that the goals of different but related programs within

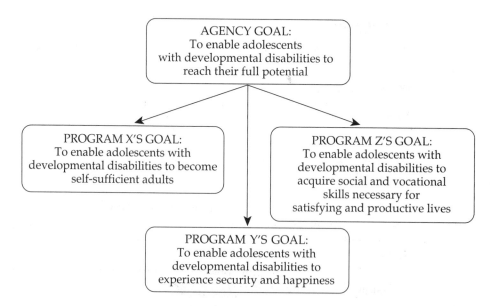

FIGURE 4.5   Organizational Chart of an Agency with Three Programs

the same agency may differ, but they must all be linked to the overall agency goal. They must all reflect both their individual purpose and the purpose of the agency of which they are a part. The third point is goals are not *measurable*. Consider the individual goals of the three group homes in Figure 4.5; none of them are measurable in their present form. Concepts such as happiness, security, self-sufficiency, and full potential mean different things to different people and cannot be measured until they have been more clearly defined. Many human service goals are phrased in this way, putting forth more of a vague intent than a definite, definable, measurable purpose. Nor is this a flaw; it is simply what a goal *is:* a statement of an intended result that must be clarified before it can be measured. Program goals are clarified by the program objectives they formulate.

Program Objectives

Program objectives are logically derived from the program goal. They are nothing more than measurable indicators of the goal; they are more specific outcomes the program wishes to achieve; they are intended results of the goal stated clearly and exactly, making it possible to tell to what degree the goal has been achieved. All program objectives must be client-centered—they must be formulated to help a client in relation to the social problem articulated by the program goal. Since it is the program objectives that are eventually evaluated, they must have four qualities: They must be meaningful, specific, measurable, and directional.

Meaningfulness

A program objective is *meaningful* when it bears a sensible relationship to the longer-term result to be achieved—the program goal. For example, if the program goal is to promote the self-sufficiency of teenage street people, improving the ability to balance a weekly budget is a meaningful program objective; increasing the ability to recite the dates of the reigns of English monarchs is not, because it bears no relation to the program goal of self-sufficiency. The point here—and a point that will be stressed over and over in this text—is that an effective human service organization must demonstrate *linkages* among the agency's goal, the agency's objectives (the programs it creates) the programs' goals, and the programs' objectives.

As mentioned before, the overall agency goal must be linked to the needs of the people the agency intends to serve. If these meaningful linkages do not exist—and, furthermore, cannot be *seen* to exist—the organization should probably be dismantled and its funding diverted to organizations that can demonstrate these linkages.

If at all possible, program objectives should be derived from the existing professional literature and specified on a meaningful and rational basis. Below is an example of how three meaningful program objectives were derived from the program goal.

Program Goal: To preserve family units where children are at risk for out-of-home placements due to problems with physical abuse. The program aims to strengthen interpersonal functioning of family members through intensive home-based services.

Program Objectives: (1) To increase positive social supports for parents, (2) to increase problem-solving skills for family members, and (3) to increase parents' use of non-corporal child management strategies.

In the above example, it should be noted that the program objectives are logically linked, in a meaningful way, to the program goal. We have left out the timeframes for the achievement of each objective so as not to confuse the reader with too much detail at this time. In addition, all program objectives should be formulated, or derived from, the existing professional literature. Or to put it another way, the existing literature should provide enough information to support the creation of a program's objectives. However, it has been our past experience that many human service organizations have program objectives which are not theoretically linked to program goals via the literature (Bouey & Rogers, 1993; Rogers & Bouey, 1993). In addition, many agencies have programs that are not linked to the agency's goal.

Specificity

In addition to having a meaningful program objective logically linked to the program goal, a program objective must also be *specific*. It must have completeness and clarity in its wording. A simple way to write a specific program objective is to use the following model (Royse, 1992):

Model:
To (verb) (specific program objective) (timeframe)
Example:
To increase marital satisfaction of the couple within 180 days.

Three useful verbs for writing client-centered program objectives are: *to increase, to decrease,* and *to maintain.* It must be noted that all three examples of program objectives that were used above in the family preservation example started with the words, *to increase.* These objectives would ideally have specific timeframes contained within them.

Measurability

The third quality required of a program objective is measurability. The purpose of measurement is to define the program objective as accurately, completely, and succinctly as possible. A measurement is usually thought of as a number: an amount of money in dollars, the length of a depression episode, or scores on simple self-report standardized measuring instruments.

The purpose of setting a program objective is to effect client change, which if obtained, will contribute to the obtaining of the program goal. One of the main purposes of making a measurement is to define a perceived client change, in terms of either numbers or clear words. For example, a measurement might show that a woman's assertiveness has increased by five points on a standardized measuring instrument (a program objective), or that a married woman's sexual satisfaction with her husband has increased by 45 points (another program objective). If the hoped-for change cannot be perceived—that is, if it cannot be measured—there is really no point in setting a program objective. Chapter 6 presents a detailed discussion of how program objectives can be measured.

Directionality

The last quality of a program objective is direction. All human service interventions are intended to effect some kind of client change. That is, interventions are undertaken so that clients will come to have more or less of something than they had before; the level of parenting skills, aggression, racist beliefs, or whatever is to be changed, will have gone up or down. The very idea of change involves direction: Without movement in the direction of less or more, better or worse, higher or lower, no change can occur.

To summarize briefly, a program objective is *meaningful* when it bears a discernible relationship to the program goal; is *specific* when its meaning is clearly and completely defined; is *measurable* in that change, when or if it occurs, can be perceived and described; and is *directional* when the direction of the expected change is precisely stated.

Types of Program Objectives

Human service programs often want to change a client's knowledge, feelings, or behavior. "Feelings" here includes attitudes because attitudes are rarely based on knowledge; they more often spring from learned feelings about types of people or things. "Feelings" also encompasses belief systems because a belief, by definition, is not knowledge, but is rather a conviction or feeling that something is true. For example, the mother of a child who has been sexually abused might believe that the child is lying and the abuse did not actually occur.

Not surprisingly, a program objective aimed at changing the client's level of knowledge is known as a *knowledge objective*. Similarly, program objectives concerned with changing feelings are known as *affective objectives*, and program objectives concerned with changing behavior are known as *behavior objectives*.

Knowledge Objectives

Knowledge program objectives are commonly found within educational programs, where their aim is to increase the client's knowledge level in some specific social area. The words "to increase knowledge" are key here: They imply that the recipient of the education will have learned something. The program objective has not been achieved until it can be demonstrated (via measurement) that learning has occurred, and knowledge objectives must be written with this in mind.

For example, "to teach teenage mothers the stages of child development between birth and two years" is not a program objective. As will be discussed below, teaching is an *activity* that may or may not result in client learning. A better program objective would be "to increase the teenage mother's knowledge level about the stages of child development between birth and two years." The hoped-for increase in knowledge level can then be measured by testing her knowledge levels before and after the material is presented to her.

Affective Objectives

Program objectives that relate to feelings focus on changing either feelings about oneself or feelings about another person or thing. For example, a common program objective in the human services is to raise a client's self-esteem; attempts are also often made to decrease feelings of isolation, increase marital or sexual satisfaction, and decrease depression. As well, feelings toward other people or things are important in a variety of situations. To give just one example, many educational programs try to change public attitudes toward minority groups, homosexuality, or sex roles.

Behavioral Objectives

Very often, a program objective is established to change the behavior of a person or group: to reduce drug abuse among adolescents, to increase the use of community resources by seniors, or to reduce the number of fights a married couple has in a month. Sometimes, knowledge or feelings objectives are used as a means to this end. The worker might assume that adolescents who know more about the effects of drugs will abuse them less; that seniors who know more about available community resources will use them more often; or that married couples who have more positive feelings toward each other will fight less frequently. Sometimes these assumptions are valid; quite often they are not. In any case, a responsible practitioner will want to check whether the desired behavior change has actually occurred.

As will be discussed in future chapters, behaviors can be measured through direct observation or through client self-reports. If a program objective is to increase a child's attendance at school, the number of times the child attended school in a month can be easily observed and counted. On the other hand, marital fights and incidents of drug abuse are almost impossible to observe directly, and practitioners may have to rely on clients themselves to report each fight or incident. Such self-reports may of course be fabricated or at least sanitized. Where possible, then, self-reports should be supplemented by other relevant data from involved professionals, court reports, school records, and interviews with relatives.

Maintenance Objectives

Readers should note that the term *program objective* is understood as being client-related. On the other hand, we view a program's maintenance objectives (such as to provide 5,000 hours of counseling, to admit 432 more clients by the end of the year, to enroll 35 adolescents in a certain program by a certain time) as necessary in order for a program to survive, but hardly as criteria by which to evaluate whether it is delivering quality services to its clients.

If a program is to survive, it must set *maintenance objectives*. These objectives are formulated to keep the program viable and involve such objectives as "to increase private donations by 25 percent in 1995," "to recruit 25 volunteers in 1995," "to increase the number of billable hours by 25 percent in 1995," "to have three individuals complete the internship program by July 1, 1995," and "to recruit and utilize four volunteers in covering the telephone lines."

Maintenance objectives may also relate to training staff, recruiting clients, acquiring improved equipment, or restructuring the organization, for example. Thus, program objectives are constructed for the client's benefit, whereas maintenance objectives are constructed for the program's benefit. We should, however, be clear about how these two purposes relate to each other. Maintenance objectives, although necessary to the program's continued existence, are not why the program is being funded. A program is not funded merely to exist and perpetuate itself; it is funded to deliver a human service. Maintenance objectives are to human service programs what food is to human beings: We need to eat, we may even get great pleasure from eating, but in the final analysis we do not live to eat—we eat to live.

Practice Objectives

A *practice objective* refers to the personal objective of an individual client, whether that client is a community, couple, group, individual, or institution. Practice objectives are also known in the professional literature as treatment objectives, individual objectives, therapeutic objectives, client objectives, client goals, and client target problems.

All practice objectives formulated by the practitioner and the client must be logically related to the program's objectives which are linked to the program's goal. In other words, all practice objectives for all clients must be delineated in such a way that they are logically linked to one or more of the program's objectives. If a worker formulates a practice objective with a client that does not logically link to one or more of the program's objectives, the worker may be doing some good for the client but will be harming the program. A program ultimately is evaluated on its program objectives, and workers must fully understand that all of their efforts must be linked to these objectives. After all, why would a program hire a practitioner to do something unrelated to its objectives?

Let us put the concept of a practice objective in concrete terms. Imagine that a resident of group home X is expected to become self-sufficient in order to meet the program's objectives, and to achieve his or her full potential in order to meet the agency's overall goal (see Figure 4.5). But what of this individual's own practice objectives? Is some vocational area of particular interest? What social, personal, practical, and academic skills does he or she need to acquire in order to achieve self-sufficiency? Three plausible practice objectives in this case might be, to increase social contacts outside the home, to increase money management skills, and to increase language skills.

These three interrelated practice objectives demonstrate a definite link with the program's objective, which in turn is linked to the program's goal which in turn in linked to the agency's goal. However, no one can tell, for example, whether the individual has made "more social contacts outside the home" until a "social contact" has been defined more precisely. Does saying hello to a fellow worker count as a social contact? It may if the individual is habitually silent at work. For a different individual, a social contact may involve going on an outing with fellow workers or attending a recreational program at a community center.

Creating Measurable Practice Objectives

As stated previously, all program objectives must be continually measured. However, since we are measuring the program objectives faithfully, do we really need to measure our practice objectives? After all, can it be assumed that if a program's objective is successful, then the practice objectives of the clients must have been successful?

We believe that it is better to have some measurement of a practice objective, no matter how rudimentary, rather than none. If a practice objective is difficult to measure, and no appropriate measurement method seems to be readily available or feasible, it may be easy for the practitioner to decide that this particular practice objective represents an unmeasurable aspiration and give it up. This action, we believe, is unwise. Unlike program objectives that must be measured on a systematic basis, we believe that practice objectives do not have to follow this strict rule.

The function of measuring practice objectives is to provide indicators of change for a particular client on a specified dimension of behaviors, knowledge, or feelings. Measurement strategies for practice objectives can take a wide range of forms. They can be subjective, such as when workers express their professional opinions, or objective, such as when standardized measuring instruments are used. In many cases, measurement strategies for practice objectives rely on the subjective, or descriptive, forms of measurement as practitioners synthesize their practice wisdom with feedback from their clients. Because subjective measurement is usually not made explicit, objective measures should be employed whenever possible.

When objective measurements are used to assess practice objectives, the practitioner typically relies on the context of descriptive data to interpret results. In most cases, the combination of subjective and objective measuring strategies complement one another.

For example, if an adolescent with developmental disabilities adopts the practice objective of increasing his ability to prepare a meal, does this mean merely cooking, or must the meal also be planned, the ingredients purchased, prepared, and cooked, the table set, and the dishes cleared away afterward? If the latter, the practice objective must specify all these things in a way that leaves no room for misunderstanding. "To increase the ability to prepare a meal" is not as good as the practice objective "to increase the ability to plan a meal for two people, purchase, prepare, and cook the ingredients, set the table, and clear the dishes" is. Even now, more precision is needed: "clearing the dishes" does not necessarily include washing them, and the adolescent may be considered to have achieved the objective if the dirty dishes are left in the sink.

With the last paragraph in mind, practitioners must obviously think about how they will know a practice objective has been achieved before they set it. However, this does not mean that desirable practice objectives that are difficult to observe and measure should for that reason be abandoned. The practice objective comes first, the measurement of it comes second. Sometimes workers can get caught up in measuring practice objectives to the extent they have little time for treatment. It must be remembered that effective practice is establishing and doing activities that are specifically geared toward the client's practice objective, which is directly linked to the program's objectives. It indeed would be nice to measure whether we attained all of our practice objectives with all of our clients, but we would spend more time measuring their attainment than in treatment. Much more will be said about the measurement of practice objectives in the following chapter. For now, let us consider another kind of practice objective—the facilitative practice objective.

Facilitative Practice Objectives

To facilitate means to make easier: hence, a facilitative objective is neither important nor desirable in itself but makes achieving a practice objective easier (Nelsen, 1988). For example, consider a boy whose practice objective is to increase his grade in English from a D– to a C+ by the next reporting period. However, he is unlikely to meet this practice objective because he spends every night visiting with friends instead of doing his homework. His parents may set him a facilitative objective: to stay at home, without friends, every school night until the next reporting period.

Staying at home without friends is not a desired end in itself. Further, it is not a true practice objective because it is neither directional nor directly relevant to the practice objective of grade improvement. It may nevertheless be called an objective because it specifies an intended result, but it is only a facilitative objective because its sole purpose is to help the boy achieve his practice objective of higher grades.

Very often, clients have long-term objectives that can be achieved only through a series of intermediate and facilitative activities. Some of these will be related to the program objective and will be desirable ends in themselves. Others will be important only because they make it easier to achieve a practice objective; that is, they will be facilitative practice objectives. In a sense, a facilitative practice objective can be viewed as a practice subobjective. Whatever the terminology used, the ordering of practice objectives and their corresponding facilitative objectives (or subobjectives) must make sense and be linked to the program's objectives. Let us turn now to another kind of objective that helps us to achieve our clients' practice objectives—instrumental objectives.

Instrumental Practice Objectives

More often then not, practice objectives cannot be achieved because practical difficulties lie in their way. This is especially true for community-based human service workers who do a lot of "instrumental" work. Thus, these workers formulate instrumental objectives: objectives that, when accomplished, will remove practical impediments to the attainment of the practice objective (Nelsen, 1988).

For example, a mother of a child who has been sexually abused may be in a treatment program with her daughter. One of the program's objectives is "to eventually reunite the husband and wife." A practice objective may be "to increase her understanding of the role she played in allowing the abuse to occur"—a perfectly reasonable practice objective in light of the program objective. Imagine, however, that she is not increasing her understanding because she rarely attends her therapy sessions and, when she does attend, she seems unable to focus on the matter at hand. Further investigation reveals that she rarely attends because she has difficulty in finding a babysitter for her six-year-old girl, and the agency, where the program is physically located, is a long way from her home. Furthermore, her husband is no longer residing with her, she does not have the benefit of his income, and she has no money to pay the rent. If any progress is to be made in treatment, the practitioner first needs to deal with these issues.

A number of instrumental objectives can be set that deal with obtaining financial assistance, learning how to budget, finding a babysitter, and arranging transportation. These objectives bear no relation to the practice objective, but they are instrumental in allowing the practice objective to be addressed. When the instrumental objectives have been accomplished, a facilitative objective could be set: to attend every therapy session. Achieving this facilitative objective is obviously necessary if the client is to engage in treatment and achieve her practice objective.

Activities

So far, this chapter has focused on the kinds of goals and objectives that human service workers hope to achieve as a result of their work. The questions now arise: What is that work? What do workers *do* in order to help clients achieve their knowledge, feelings, or behavior practice objectives? The answer, of course, is that human service practitioners do many different things. They show films, facilitate discussions, hold treatment sessions, teach classes, and conduct interviews. They attend staff meetings, do paperwork, consult with colleagues, and advocate for clients. Clients also engage in activities: They attend therapy sessions, participate in discussions, complete homework assignments, and do a great deal of intensive, internal work.

The important point about all such activities is that they are undertaken to attain specific practice and facilitative objectives that relate to one or more of the program's objectives. A worker who teaches a class on nutrition hopes that class participants will learn certain specific facts about nutrition. If this learning is to take place, the facts to be learned must be included in the material presented. In other words, the worker's activities must be directly related to the practice and facilitative objectives. In this example, it is assumed that one of the program's objectives has to do with nutrition or the worker would not be teaching the nutritional material in the first place. Or, the nutritional learning may be a facilitative objective where the practice objective is "to increase childcare skills."

This may seem so self-evident as to not be worth mentioning. If no related activities are undertaken to achieve a practice or facilitative objective, it is obviously foolish to expect that the objective will be achieved. Nevertheless, an amazing number of human service programs exist where the activities performed by workers seem to have nothing much to do with their clients' practice objectives, or with the program's objectives, for that matter.

It is critically important that a human service worker who sets a practice objective should also specify what activities will be undertaken to accomplish it and what measures (if any) will determine whether the practice objective is achieved. Over the years we have seen numerous instances where workers say they are trying to raise their clients' self-esteem. When asked what specific activities they are doing to achieve this notable objective, they reply, "nothing specific, just supporting them when they need it." It is rather futile to believe that just supporting a client on a crisis basis will raise his or her self-esteem. Specific treatment interventions must be done to raise the self-esteem of clients—it does not rise automatically just by osmosis.

Below are two practice objectives of a human service program. The goal of this program is to provide services to pregnant teenagers in high school who have elected to keep their babies in an effort to help them to become adequate mothers. Also included are two practice objectives (A and B) and activities that are believed to achieve each of the practice objectives. The measurement of the program objective and the two practice objectives are also listed. Notice the consistency between the concepts of the program's goal, the program objective, the two practice objectives, the various activities, and the two measurements.

Program Objective: To increase the self-sufficiency of pregnant adolescents after they have their babies.

Practice Objective (A): To increase parenting skills.
Activities (A): Teach specific child-rearing skills, role modeling/role playing of effective parenting skills, teach effective child/adult communi-

cation skills, teach and model alternative discipline measures, teach age appropriate response of children, and establish family structure (e.g., meal times, bath times, and bed times).

Measurement of Practice Objective (A): Adult–Adolescent Parenting Inventory.

Practice Objective (B): To increase the number of support systems known to the client.

Activities (B): Review the City's information resource book with the client, provide information sheet on key resources relevant to the client, provide brochures on various agencies, escort client to needed resources (e.g., career resource center, health clinic), and go through specific and appropriate sections of the yellow pages with the client.

Measurement of Practice Objective (B): Measuring instrument specially constructed for the particular city. To show how simple measuring instruments can be, Figure 4.6 presents one that was used with this practice objective. Figure 4.7 presents the correct answers.

Measurement of Program Objective: Self-Sufficiency Inventory.

If a certain set of activities is successful in achieving a practice objective, the worker may want to repeat these activities with another client who has a similar problem. This will not be possible unless the worker has kept a careful record of what he or she did; that is, unless the activities, too, have been clearly defined. The

---

The following is a list of questions regarding resources available in the Calgary area. Please write down as many resources as you know about in responding to each question.

1. Where would you go for help in caring for your children?
2. Where would you go for financial assistance?
3. Where would you go for help with parenting?
4. Where would you go for medical assistance or information?
5. Where would you go for information on improving your education?
6. Who would you call to get help at home?
7. Where would you go for help in finding a job?
8. Where would you go to get help in finding a place to stay?
9. Who would you call if you had an immediate crisis?
10. Where would you go for assistance for food or clothing?
11. Where would you go for legal assistance?
12. Where would you go for counseling?

FIGURE 4.6   Questionnaire on Support Systems in Calgary

1. Social Services
   Community Daycare/Day home

   City of Calgary Social Services
   Children's Cottage

2. Social Services
   local church
   Alberta Consumer Corporate Affairs
   Alberta Student Finance Board

   JIMY Program
   UIC

3. Calgary Health Services
   family doctor
   Parent Support Association
   Calgary Association of Parent

   Parent Aid
   City of Calgary Social Services
   Children's Hospital

4. family doctor
   Hospitals
   Calgary Birth Control Association

   Calgary Health Services
   Birthrite

5. Alberta Vocational Centre
   Viscount Bennet School
   SAIT
   Mount Royal College
   Canada Manpower

   Alberta Social Services
   Women's Career Center
   Louise Dean School
   University of Calgary

6. Homemaker Services (FSB)
   Landlord & Tenant Board
   Calgary Housing Authority

   Relief Society (Mormon Church)
   Alberta Social Services
   City of Calgary Social Services

7. Alberta Social Services
   Canada Manpower
   Career Center
   Volunteer Center

   Hire A Student
   newspapers
   12 Avenue
   job boards

8. Alberta Social Services
   YWCA Single Mother Program
   Renfrew Recovery
   Women's Emergency Shelter
   Park Wood House
   Discovery House
   church

   Avenue 15
   Single Men's Hostel
   JIMY Program
   Alpha House
   Sherrif King
   Macman Youth Services
   Birthrite

9. Emergency Social Services
   Distress Centre
   Sexual Assault Centre
   Suicide Line (CMH)
   Children's Cottage

   Wood's Stabilization Program
   Alberta Children's Hospital
   church
   police/fire

10. Interfaith Food Bank
    Milk Fund
    Salvation Army

    church
    Emergency Social Services
    Alberta Social Services

11. Legal Aid
    Legal Guidance
    University of Calgary Legal Line

    Women's Resource Centre
    Women's Shelter
    Dial-A-Law

12. Family Service Bureau
    church
    Alberta Mental Health
    Pastoral Institute
    Sexual Assault Centre
    Children's Cottage

    Alberta Social Services
    City of Calgary Social Services
    Catholic Family Services
    Parents Anonymous
    Distress Centre

Note: Client may respond to the questionnaire with answers not listed above but which may be entirely appropriate to their own unique situations and thus be evaluated as correct.

FIGURE 4.7 Answers to Questionnaire on Support Systems in Calgary

definition of an activity usually involves a careful description of what precisely was done; when, where, how, and by whom it was done; and in what order it was done.

Such a record will enable practitioners to know more exactly which interventions produced which results. In other words, specifying the activities to be undertaken in order to achieve a certain practice or facilitative objective is another example of establishing *links*. Figure 4.8 presents a graphic example of how practice activities are linked to practice objectives which are linked to program objectives which are linked to the program goal. Figure 4.9 illustrates a brief example of how a program goal has derived three program objectives where each program objective has sample activities used by the practitioners to achieve the program objectives. In addition, instruments which measure the program objectives are included. Note how Figure 4.9 flows from the logic presented in Figure 4.8.

Summary

This chapter discussed what is meant by an agency, a program, a program goal and objective, a practice objective, a measurement, and an activity. Most importantly, it discussed the linkages that must exist among these elements. The next chapter will build upon this one by focusing on how we go about creating and measuring program and practice objectives.

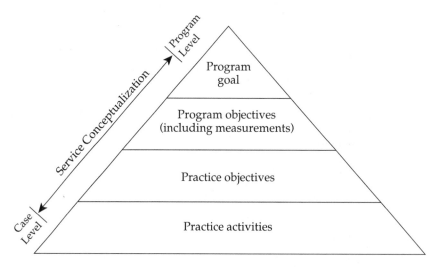

FIGURE 4.8   A Program Logic Model for Conceptualizing Treatment Services

From Yvonne Unrau, A program logic model approach to conceptualizing social service programs. *The Canadian Journal of Program Evaluation, 8.* © 1993. The University of Calgary Press. Used with permission.

Family Preservation Program

Program Goal

To preserve family units where children are at risk for out-of-home placements due to problems with physical abuse. The program aims to strengthen interpersonal functioning of family members through intensive home-based services.

Program Objectives

1. To increase positive social supports for parents.

   Literary Support: A lack of positive social support has been repeatedly linked to higher risk for child abuse. Studies indicate that parents with greater social support and less stress report more pleasure in their parenting roles.

   Sample of Activities: Referral to support groups; evaluate criteria for positive support; introduction to community services; reconnecting clients with friends and family.

   Measuring Instruments: Client log; *Provision of Social Relations* (Turner, Frankel, & Levin, 1987).

2. To increase problem-solving skills for family members.

   Literary Support: Operationally, problem solving is a tool for breaking difficult dilemmas into manageable pieces. Enhancing individual's skills in systematically addressing problems increases the likelihood that they will successfully tackle new problems as they arise. Increasing problem-solving skills for parents and children equips family members to handle current problems, anticipate and prevent future ones, and advance their social functioning.

   Sample of Activities: Teach steps to problem solving; role play problem-solving scenarios; supportive counseling.

   Measuring Instruments: *The Problem-Solving Inventory* (Heppner, 1987).

3. To increase parents' use of noncorporal child management strategies.

   Literary Support: Empirical research suggests that deficiency in parenting skills is associated with higher recurrence of abuse. Furthermore, parents who demonstrate a high need for control and resort to excessive discipline tend to use more abusive discipline strategies.

   Sample of Activities: Teach noncorporal discipline strategies; inform parents about the criminal implications of child abuse; assess parenting strengths; provide reading material about behavior management.

   Measuring Instruments: Self-report log of child management strategies used; checklist of discipline strategies.

FIGURE 4.9 Program-Level Service Conceptualization

From Yvonne Unrau, A program logic model approach to conceptualizing social service programs. *The Canadian Journal of Program Evaluation, 8.* © 1993. The University of Calgary Press. Used with permission.

Key Terms

Activities: What practitioners do with their clients to achieve their practice and facilitative objectives.

Affective Program Objective: An objective that focuses on changing an individual's emotional reaction to him- or herself or to another person or thing.

Agency: A social service organization that exists to fulfill a broad social purpose. It functions as one entity, is governed by a single directing body, and has policies and procedures that are common to all of its parts.

Agency Goal: Broad unmeasurable outcomes the agency wishes to achieve. They are based on values and are guided by the agency's mission statement.

Agency Objective: A program established to help in the achievement of the agency's goal.

Behavioral Program Objective: An objective that aims to change the conduct or actions of clients.

Facilitative Practice Objective: An objective that relates to the overall practice objective (it can be termed a practice subobjective); it also specifies an intended result and makes the achievement of the practice objective easier; constructed for the client's benefit.

Instrumental Practice Objective: An objective that bears no apparent relation to the practice objective, but when accomplished will remove practical impediments to the attainment of the practice objective; constructed for the client's benefit.

Knowledge Program Objective: An objective that aims to change a client's level of information and understanding about a specific social area.

Maintenance Program Objective: An objective formulated in an effort to keep a program financially viable; constructed for the program's benefit.

Mission Statement: A unique written philosophical perspective of what an agency is all about; states a common vision for the organization by providing a point of reference for all major planning decisions.

Practice Objective: A statement of expected change identifying an intended therapeutic result tailored to the unique circumstances and needs of each client; logically linked to a program objective. Practice objectives, like program objectives, can be grouped into affects, knowledge, and behaviors.

Program: An organization that exists to fulfil some social purpose; must be logically linked to the agency's goal.

Program Goal: A statement reflecting the purpose of a program and the individuals it is trying to affect. Because it is articulated at the conceptual level, a program goal is not measurable.

Program Objective: A statement that clearly and exactly specifies the expected change, or intended result, for individuals receiving program services. Qualities of well-chosen objectives are meaningfulness, specificity, measurability, and directionality. Program objectives, like practice objectives can be grouped into affects, knowledge, and behaviors.

Study Questions

1. In your opinion, are the program goal and program objectives (outcome measures) in Case Study C clearly articulated? How could they be improved? What other program objectives (outcome measures) would you see appropriate for Case Study C? Why? Do you feel the program objectives are logically linked to the program's goal? Why, or why not?

2. In your own words, identify additional practice objectives for the outreach program in Case Study C. Compare these with the criteria outlined for objectives in this chapter.

3. The outreach program described in Case Study C was considered an additional service provided by the Austin Center for Battered Woman (ACBW). The core program

was identified as a shelter for battered woman. How would the objectives of the outreach program compare to the shelter program? Would there be any differences? Why or why not?

4. Given the aims and parameters of the program in Case Study C, would the practice objectives more likely reflect aspects of knowledge, behavior, or feelings? What reasons can you offer to support your choice?

5. What instrumental or facilitative practice objectives can you suggest that might have contributed to a higher rate of success with clients in Case Study C?

6. How could data derived from a needs assessment have benefited the program in Case Study C? In your opinion, was a needs assessment necessary? Why or why not?

7. Draw a hypothetical organizational chart to depict a possible structure of the program in Case Study C. Explain how the organizational chart could be helpful in understanding the dynamics of program functioning.

8. In your opinion, does the program in Case Study C contain meaningful links to the agency's goal? If so, what are they?

9. In groups of four, identify the goal and program objectives of your academic human service program. Discuss the dangers your program would face if its goal and program objectives were not clearly articulated.

10. In the same groups of four, discuss the goal and objectives of your class. How do these relate to the goal and program objectives of your academic program?

11. In the same groups of four, have each student develop three practice objectives relating to his or her educational needs within your human service program. Compare practice objectives with one another. Are the practice objectives for each student logically linked to the class's personal objectives derived in Question 10? Why or why not?

12. Chapter 1 discussed the rationale of using evaluative data to increase our profession's knowledge base. With this in mind, how could we increase this knowledge base if workers did not measure program and practice objectives? In your opinion, could the knowledge base of your profession be expanded if practice objectives were not measurable? Why or why not?

13. Chapter 1 presented the various stakeholders who utilize evaluation results. Which group(s) of people do you feel would be the most interested in the outcome of *program* objectives? Why? Explain how each group could benefit from the data. Which group(s) of people do you feel would be the most interested in the outcome of *practice* objectives? Why? Explain how each group could benefit from the data.

14. Discuss how a program objective is really a practice goal. The answer will not be found in this chapter. However, use the logic that this chapter provided in delineating the relationships among an agency, a program, a program goal, and a practice objective.

15. Locate a *goal statement* of a human service agency. Using the contents of this chapter, was the goal statement appropriately written? Why or why not? If it was not written correctly, write it correctly using the criteria as presented in this chapter.

16. Locate a *mission statement* of a human service agency. Using the contents of this chapter, was the mission statement appropriately written? Why or why not? Was it logically linked to the agency's goal? Why or why not? If it was not written correctly, write it correctly using the criteria as presented in this chapter.

17. Locate a *goal statement* of a human service program. Using the contents of this chapter, was the program goal appropriately written? Why or why not? Was the program's goal consistent with the agency's goal? Why or why not? If it was not written correctly, write it correctly using the criteria as presented in this chapter. What other goal could the program have chosen? Why? Justify your answer.

18. Locate a *program objective* of a human service program. Using the contents of this chapter, was the program objective appropriately written? Why or why not? If it was not written correctly, write it correctly using the criteria as presented in this chapter. Was the program's objective consistent with the program's goal? Why or why not? What other program objectives could the program have chosen? Why? Justify your answer.

19. Discuss the differences between facilitative and instrumental practice objectives. Use a common human service example throughout your discussion. Do you feel that there would be certain practical circumstances where they would not be used in an actual practice situation? Why or why not? Provide an example. Do you believe that a facilitative practice objective should be measured? Why or why not? Justify your response in detail.

20. Discuss in detail the main difference between a maintenance objective and a program objective. Provide relevant human service examples of each in your discussion. Under what specific circumstances do you feel a human service program should be evaluated on a maintenance objective? Justify your answer.

21. For the practice objective of "to increase your grade in this class," prepare a list of facilitative objectives and a list of instrumental objectives (no, getting rid of this book and your instructor is not one of them) that you would need to follow to achieve your practice objective of higher grades.

22. What do you feel is the overall goal of your professional human service program? What do you feel are its program objectives? How are the program objectives evaluated? What are its activities?

23. As mentioned in this chapter, all program objectives must be measured. With your present knowledge of evaluation, when do you think these measurements should take place? Justify your answer. How many measurements do you think would be appropri-

ate to ascertain whether a program objective has been achieved or not? Justify your answer.

24. Does the program objective in reference to the pregnant adolescents in high school mentioned in this chapter contain the four necessary ingredients of a goal statement? Why or why not? Discuss in detail.

25. In reference to the above program objective, and keeping the program's goal in mind, rewrite the program objective to make it more meaningful, more specific, more measurable, and more directional?

26. In reference to the above two practice objectives, create a list of facilitative objectives you feel would be needed to increase the chances of achieving each practice objective.

27. Using an agency from your local community as an example, explain what the human service agency is and discuss its purpose.

28. A program can be defined according to a hierarchy of positions of the people who operate the program. Construct a hierarchy of positions of the people who operate your educational program.

29. A program can also be defined in the way in which clients move in and out of a program. Construct a student path flow model depicting how students move into, through, and out of your program.

30. Under what circumstances would a certain set of activities within an agency be considered a program? What if that set of activities were funded independently of the agency?

31. An agency typically has its own board, executive director, and administrative policies and procedures. Under what circumstances would an agency such as this operate two or more separate programs?

32. You are the director of a new women's shelter at your local YWCA. What is the goal of your program? What are some intended and unintended results you could expect from the program?

33. How is the shelter's goal different from the overall goal of the local YWCA? How are they related to each other? How can you ensure that both the goals of the shelter and of the YWCA are being met?

34. Define three program objectives at your shelter. Justify why your three program objectives are linked to the shelter's goal.

35. Define a meaningful practice objective common to the workers who work at the shelter. Remember that program and practice objectives must be client-centered.

36. In developing measurable program and practice objectives for your shelter, you must keep in mind several points about these objectives. What are they? Provide examples of each.

37. Why must you ensure that your program and practice objectives at the shelter are directional? How will you define a practice objective in directional terms?

38. Define one of the client's "knowledge" practice objectives at the shelter. How does this objective differ from an "affective" or "behavior" practice objective?

39. Think about clients at the shelter. What might a typical facilitative objective be for one of these clients? How does this facilitate the achievement of one of the practice objectives?

40. Formulate an instrumental objective for this client in order to help her achieve her practice objectives. Give an example of such an objective.

41. In your initial report to the YWCA, what program maintenance objectives would you include? Why are these important?

5

DEVELOPING PRACTICE OBJECTIVES

Surveying Practice Objectives

Selecting and Prioritizing Practice Objectives

Defining Practice Objectives

Developing Practice Objectives
> *What Is to Be Achieved?*
> *Under What Conditions Is It to Be Achieved?*
> *To What Extent Is It to Be Achieved?*
> *By Whom Is the Objective to Be Achieved?*

Other Issues in Setting Objectives
> *Unintended Consequences*
> *Impediments*
> *Who Should Set Objectives?*

Creating Measurable Practice Objectives
> *Client Logs*

Recording Practice Objectives
> *Presence or Absence Objectives*
> *Magnitude Objectives*
> *Duration Objectives*
> *Frequency Objectives*

Data Collection
> *Who Should Collect the Data?*
> *When Should Data Be Collected?*
> *Where Should Data Be Collected?*

Summary

Key Terms

Study Questions

By far the most important point to be gleaned from the previous chapter is that human service programs are ultimately evaluated on how well they accomplish their program objectives—not on how well human service workers achieve their practice objectives. It is nonetheless true that human service programs are *indirectly* evaluated by how well workers attain their practice objectives. In this sense, the more congruent the practitioners' practice objectives are with the programs' objectives, the higher the chances are that the program will be evaluated as successful.

Human service workers can also measure the attainment of their practice objectives, providing a wealth of data useful in monitoring their clients' progress. They can use these data to determine whether or not their practice objectives are being achieved; if not, they can use different activities in an effort to achieve the practice objectives. In short, why would a worker continue to use the same activities if the practice objective is not changing in the desired direction?

So far, however, almost nothing has been said about how human service workers can formulate practice objectives with their clients, aside from their choosing practice objectives that are congruent and flow logically from the program's objectives. This chapter presents some ways to formulate practice objectives, and provides an introduction to recording them.

Surveying Practice Objectives

It is easy enough to say that a practitioner's efforts should focus upon the problem presented by the client. In many cases, however, neither the worker nor the client is entirely sure where the problem lies. Presenting problems are often phrased in such terms as "My life is a mess," "I'm having trouble with my son," and "I don't know what to do about my life." Human service workers are sometimes no better than the clients they serve when it comes to providing concrete information. Statements such as "We seem to have a problem here," "Our workers need more training," and "It isn't clear what is wrong" are not uncommon expressions within human service offices.

A worker's first task, therefore, is to find out the client's specific problems. Recall that a client can be an individual, couple, family, group, community, or institution. Obviously, the first step is to ask the client to list the situations or people that seem to present the most difficulty. If some definite areas are identified—marital conflict, financial or employment difficulties, a child in trouble with the police—ask for one or two specific examples within these areas. In what way is the child in trouble with the police? Is the employment difficulty to do with finding a job, keeping a job, or problems on the job? At this stage, it is neither necessary nor wise to go into detail; the idea is simply to identify general areas of concern and get an impression of the overall situation. There is often more than one problem; problems can be complex and intertwined and, if there seems to be a single problem, there is an excellent chance that it is not the real problem at all.

If the client cannot identify even general problem areas, give the client a list of commonly experienced problems and ask him or her to check all those that apply. The practitioner can also encourage the client to add problems particular to him- or herself but not included on the list. Figure 5.1 provides excerpts from two different checklists for use with clients at a clinical level and at a community level. The problem selected becomes the client's practice objective, which must be directly linked to the program's objective.

Selecting and Prioritizing Practice Objectives

Once encouraged, the client may identify many potential practice objectives as being problematic. Money may be difficult as well as a child's behavior, the marital relationship, and the job situation; then there may be feelings of anxiety, uncontrolled anger, and alcohol abuse, to name a few. It will not be possible to work on all of these at the same time, although they are all probably interrelated. The client must select one practice objective, or at most two or three, depending on the available time, energy, and other resources (Bloom, Fischer, & Orme, 1994).

Your Name		Today's Date	
Do you want help with:	Yes		No
Managing your money?	————		————
Being less anxious?	————		————
Having more friends?	————		————
Feeling better about yourself?	————		————
Controlling your anger?	————		————

(A)   Excerpt from a Problem Checklist for Clinical Practice

Your Name		Today's Date	
Does your organization need help with:	Yes		No
Increasing participating?	————		————
Getting new members?	————		————
Running meetings?	————		————
Securing funds?	————		————

(B)   Excerpt from a Problem Checklist for Community Work

FIGURE 5.1   Example of Problem Checklists for (A) Clinical Practice and (B) Community Practice

How is a client to go about assigning priority to practice objectives? Obviously, the selected objective should deal with the problem that is causing the client the most concern; however, there are other factors to be taken into account. Perhaps the objective that is most pressing in the client's view is not one that the worker can do anything about. In the case of financial difficulty, for example, steps can be taken to improve money management, but the practitioner will probably not be able to solve the basic problem of insufficient income. It is important to choose the practice objective that has the best prospects for at least a partial solution.

Of course, the objective must also be suited to the resources of the particular worker providing the service. The practitioner may not have the knowledge or experience to address the issues involved; perhaps, for example, the desired change can only be accomplished by a psychiatrist. Or perhaps the worker's agency cannot provide the facilities (as for art therapy or physical activity) necessary to attain the practice objective. In either of these cases, a referral may be appropriate; if not, the practice objective should be put at the bottom of the list of those to be addressed.

Sometimes facilitative and instrumental objectives must be at least partially resolved before practice objectives can be tackled. For example, a client who is abusing alcohol will not be able to accomplish much in the way of managing anger, increasing parenting skills, or improving marital relationships until the abuse has been brought under control. Another important factor is that alcohol abuse has perhaps the greatest chance of producing the most negative consequences if not handled promptly. It should be given priority in the hierarchy of practice objectives, even if the client does not select it as the problem of greatest concern.

Finally, an initial objective should attune the client to the possibilities of success: It should show that some tangible progress can be made and that the maze of problems is resolvable, at least in part. Two factors are involved here. First, when the objective addressed is specific and concrete, the resulting change is more likely to be easily seen. Second, an initial and tangible success may provide the motivation to confront other more difficult problems. Priority should therefore be given to practice objectives that meet these criteria.

To review, priority should be assigned to a practice objective that (1) is of most concern to the client, (2) has the greatest likelihood of being solved, (3) can be addressed by the particular worker using available resources, (4) needs to be resolved before other practice objectives can be tackled, (5) stands the greatest chance of producing the most negative consequences if not handled at once, (6) is specific and concrete, and (7) is likely to produce a tangible desired change.

Defining Practice Objectives

Once the client practice objectives have been delineated, the next task would seem to be to select the first one to be tackled. Before this can be done, however, the problem itself must be clearly defined.

First, the problem must be clarified. It may have been presented in vague terms such as, "I'm having trouble with Elwin," or "I can't seem to control my emotions."

Examples of the problem will help. The "trouble with Elwin" may turn out to be that Elwin skips school, started wetting the bed when he was five years old, is aggressive toward other children, or has been caught by the police for possession of drugs. These problems are much more amenable to action than the hopelessly vague "trouble with Elwin," but further clarification may yet be needed.

Assume that Elwin is aggressive toward other children. Is he aggressive toward his schoolmates, his siblings, other children he plays with at home, children he meets on the street, or all of these? What form does his aggression take? Does he hit other children, scream at them, refuse to share with them, take things away from them? What aggressive behaviors, precisely, does Elwin engage in and toward whom does he direct them?

The practitioner will of course also ask how often the behavior occurs and when it began. Is Elwin aggressive every day, once a week, or was the aggression an isolated incident? Has Elwin always been aggressive or did the aggression begin last month or a year ago?

The client might also be asked if anyone else has observed these behaviors. This question will serve to remove any suspicion that Elwin's aggression exists only in his mother's mind. It will also introduce another source of observation—in terms of when the behavior occurs, how often it occurs, and to what extent it occurs—thus increasing the reliability of the results (Collins & Polster, 1993).

Questions like the above—who has seen the behavior, and what exactly occurs when, where, toward whom, and to what extent—will serve to clarify, first, that there is a problem and, second, what the problem is. However, it is too early to speculate about *why* Elwin is aggressive. Problem definition is a fact-finding mission; the "what" must come before the "why."

At the same time that the worker is pursuing problem definition, he or she must quietly be considering what kinds of practice objectives to set eventually to increase or decrease what particular states. Recall that all human service practice objectives are intended either to increase a desirable state—knowledge, skills, understanding, self-acceptance—or to decrease an undesirable state—hostility, abuse, anxiety, depression. Even objectives that aim to change one state into another—hostility into acceptance or passivity into assertiveness—require that the undesired state be decreased before the desired state can be attained.

In Elwin's case, assuming the practice objective is to decrease his aggressive behaviors, the practitioner has already operationalized "aggressive behaviors" to some extent by asking what the behaviors are; when, where, and how often they occur; and toward whom they are directed. As these initial questions are asked, the worker is also considering what additional facilitative objectives might be used to decrease his aggressive behavior, how the practice objective of "to decrease his aggressive behaviors," might be measured, and what measurement methods might be employed.

The worker is also thinking about how the practice objectives are to be achieved. Such thoughts are at this point very tentative, preliminary thoughts toward what might be done if the objectives are formulated as the practitioner predicts, because setting practice objectives is not a task to be undertaken by the worker alone. The practice objectives are the client's objectives, and their formulation must be a matter of mutual effort and consent.

Developing Practice Objectives

Defining a practice objective is a matter of stating what is to be changed. This provides an indication of the client's current state, or where the client is. Unfortunately, knowing this is not the same thing as knowing where one wants to go. Sometimes, as in Elwin's case, the destination is apparent, but in other cases it may be much less clear.

For example, suppose that a client has presented as a general problem area that she is dissatisfied with her job. Enquiry has elicited that her dissatisfaction has nothing to do with the work itself, nor with the people at work, nor such job-related factors as advancement, pay, benefits, and vacations. Instead, her dissatisfaction springs from the fact that she is spending too much time at work and too little time with her preschool children. Various practice objectives are possible here. Perhaps she should try to find a different, less demanding, full-time job; or maybe she should improve her budgeting skills so that the family can manage if she works only part-time. Perhaps she should make different arrangements for the children's care, so that she feels more comfortable about their welfare. Or maybe the real problem is that she herself feels torn between pursuing a career and being a full-time mother. It may be that what she really wants is to stay home with her children, provided that she can do so without guilt, with her partner's support, and without undue financial stress.

It is apparent that the underlying problem has not yet been really defined. Often, an attempt to formulate a practice objective—to specify where the client and the practitioner want to go—will reveal that the client is not where she thought she was; that the problem so carefully elicited by the worker is not the actual problem after all. If this is the case, additional exploration is needed to redefine the problem before trying, once again, to set the objective.

When the actual problem has been defined, the next task is to establish a related practice objective. If possible, it should be couched in positive terms, that is, in terms of what the client should do or feel rather than in terms of what she should not. For example, if the problem is Antoinette's immaturity, and "immaturity" is operationalized to mean getting out of her seat at school without permission, then one natural practice objective is "to decrease the number of times Antoinette gets out of her seat without permission." But it may just as usefully be written, "to increase the length of time Antoinette stays in her seat during class." Many practice objectives and their corresponding facilitative objectives, that are aimed at decreasing a negative quality, can be reformulated to increase a positive quality while still achieving the desired change.

Finally, as mentioned already, practice objectives must be comprehensive and precise. Each one must stipulate what is to be achieved, under what conditions, to what extent, and by whom.

What Is to Be Achieved?

It is obviously important that the task specified in the practice objective be achievable. For example, if a practice objective for an adolescent with developmental disabilities is that she be able to attend to her own personal hygiene, it would be foolish to choose as a facilitative objective that she should appear every morning bathed and dressed, with her teeth brushed and her hair combed, ready to go to school.

A better facilitative objective would be that she brushes her teeth herself after every meal, without needing to be reminded, in the way that staff have taught her to do. If there is any doubt that the child will be able to remember to brush her teeth, the facilitative objective might say instead that she should brush her teeth herself after being reminded. *It is always better to set practice objectives and their corresponding facilitative objectives too low rather than too high.* Even a small success may motivate clients to continue, whereas a failure can jeopardize the process.

Readers may have noted that the objective of regular tooth-brushing is not a true objective because it is not directional. The direction of the desired change is, however, implicit: We can safely assume that the child has not regularly brushed her teeth herself before. Although the direction of change is permitted to be implicit, then, everything else must be stated. The account of "what is to be achieved" involves a comprehensive specification of exactly and precisely what.

Under What Conditions Is It to Be Achieved?

Itemization of the conditions under which a practice objective is to be achieved should, if at all possible, include details of where, when, and with whom. Continuing with the above example, is the tooth-brushing to be done only after breakfast and dinner, when the child is in the residence, or must it also be done after lunch, when the child is away at school? If the latter, and the facilitative objective is achieved in one location but not in another—if the child remembers at home but forgets at school—an interim facilitative objective could then be set: that the child should brush her teeth at school. Similar interim facilitative objectives may stipulate that the child brushes her teeth at her parents' home over weekends or at the hostel when she is taken on a trip. A number of interim facilitative objectives requiring that an activity be performed in various specific locations should result in the eventual performance of the activity in all desired locations, that is, the achievement of the original practice objective.

When obviously refers to the occasions on which the desired activity or event is supposed to occur: The child must brush her teeth after breakfast and after supper, perhaps also after lunch and after mid-morning, mid-afternoon and bedtime snacks, and possibly every time she eats a candy bar. *When* is not always as simple as it might appear, and much confusion can be avoided if it is spelled out clearly from the beginning.

With whom specifies who will be present when the activity or event occurs. Does "brushing her teeth herself" mean that the child must be all alone in the bathroom, or should a staff member be present to ensure that the tooth-brushing follows the prescribed routine? When practice objectives and their corresponding facilitative objectives involve an interaction between people, however, the question of with whom becomes critical. If Elwin is supposed to share his toys more often with other children, with which others is he supposed to share? His siblings, classmates, friends he invites to his house, the boy next door, or all of these?

To What Extent Is It to Be Achieved?

When a practice objective specifies that something is to be increased or decreased, the obvious question is: By how much? By how much should a mother's knowledge of nutrition increase, before she is considered competent to feed her child adequately? How much improvement is needed before a child is considered to have adequate social skills? How much weight does a woman need to lose before the excess weight is no longer considered to threaten her health? The answers to these questions depend on two factors.

The first factor is the degree, or level, of the problem at the beginning, before any intervention is attempted. A woman who is only slightly overweight will not need to lose much weight in order to remove the hazard to her health.

The second factor is the desired level of performance to be achieved. How much should the woman weigh before the risk is thought to have been removed? The question "By how much?" can then be answered by calculating the difference between the client's initial level and the desired level.

The difficulty here often lies in setting the desired level. In some cases, this is easy: If a practice objective is to prevent a child from wetting his bed at night, the desired level of performance is zero wet nights. However, in the majority of cases the desired level will be less clear. For example, what score on a standardized measuring instrument that measures fear must a phobic client achieve before acrophobia has shrunk to an acceptable level? What is an "acceptable" score on instruments that measure depression or sexual satisfaction?

Further, the level of a problem may be significant to the client even if it is not held to be clinically significant. A woman whose weight does not pose a health hazard may still worry about it to the point that her marriage, social life, and effectiveness at work are jeopardized. The desired level of achievement here will be the level or weight at which the woman feels comfortable. Of course, if the woman fails to feel comfortable at 150 pounds, then 120 pounds, then 90 pounds, the practitioner may safely assume that excessive weight is not the real problem.

A desired level of performance does not necessarily need to be set firmly and finally at the beginning of human service intervention. Imagine that a young woman's practice objective is to increase her social skills with regard to meeting men. An initial facilitative objective could be to say hello to men whom she would like to know in her normal work or school environment. A second, interim facilitative objective could be to hold them in conversation for at least five minutes. A final facilitative objective might be to join them for lunch.

In sum, the extent of the change that needs to be specified in a practice objective is the difference between the initial performance level and the desired level. The desired level may be reached gradually through successive facilitative objectives and may be specified in terms of either clinical significance or the client's subjective satisfaction.

By Whom Is the Objective to Be Achieved?

Some practice and facilitative objectives involve more than one client. For example, a family may (with guidance from the worker) set as their practice objective to clean house together every Saturday morning. They may operationalize "cleaning house" to include vacuuming, dusting, washing floors, and so forth, but fail to specify who should do which of these chores. The probable result is that the family's house-cleaning time will be spent accusing each other of not doing the work. The facilitative objective, naturally enough, will not be achieved, and the related practice objective which is, for example, to improve family relations, will become even more difficult to achieve. It is important that a practice objective specify not only what is to be achieved, to what extent and under what conditions, but also who is to do exactly what.

This same concern over apportionment of responsibility may arise between a worker and a client. It is not uncommon for inexperienced human service workers to assume responsibility themselves for achieving clients' objectives and to set for themselves, perhaps unconsciously, such facilitative objectives as, "I will decrease Ms Wong's depression by providing supportive therapy." Providing supportive therapy is an activity, not an objective. Furthermore, this way of formulating the practice objective indicates that the practitioner is confused about who is to decrease the depression. If the depression is to be decreased at all, it must be decreased by Ms Wong. Put another way, it is Ms Wong who will achieve whatever facilitative objectives are set to lessen her depression. Much confusion may be avoided if the facilitative objective clearly assigns responsibilities for particular tasks.

Other Issues in Setting Objectives

When setting practice objectives, we must also confront the issues of unintended consequences, impediments, and who should set the objectives.

Unintended Consequences

We saw from Chapter 4 that activities designed to achieve a certain program or practice objective may have unintended consequences. For example, an agency's effort to serve more people from a minority group (one of its program objectives) may result in members of the majority group rejecting the agency's services. The actual achievement of a practice objective can also have unintended consequences.

A woman who has become more assertive may be fired by an employer who is affronted by assertive women.

It is a part of the worker's job, then, to help the client anticipate consequences other than those desired. The worker can ask exploratory questions to determine how achieving the practice objective is likely to affect the client's family, friends, co-workers, employment future, and so on.

Impediments

Also, as discussed, practice and facilitative objectives should not be set unless the client is capable of achieving them. However, there may be impediments to achieving the objectives that have nothing to do with the client. For example, a woman whose facilitative objective is to attend therapy sessions as scheduled may not be able to do so because her babysitter is unreliable. Such situations can be avoided if the worker discusses possible impediments with the client as a part of negotiating the objective.

Who Should Set Objectives?

It may be assumed that because it is the client who achieves a practice objective, it should also be the client who sets it. This is often the case, and whenever possible clients should have the primary say in establishing their practice objectives. However, when a client comes up with objectives that are unworkable, impractical, or simply misguided, the practitioner has a responsibility to point out the difficulties and negotiate with the client regarding the formulation of more suitable objectives.

If other objectives cannot be negotiated, the worker may have to refer the client to a colleague or to a different agency, as it is neither advisable nor ethical to put effort into a practice objective that the worker believes is unattainable or wrong for the client.

At the opposite pole from clients who insist on formulating their own practice objectives in their own way, are those who prefer that the worker take sole responsibility for deciding what their objectives should be, and how they should achieve them. Naturally, no ethical practitioner will do this. Negotiation with the client is acceptable and usually necessary; unilateral objective-setting is not. In fact, a large part of the art of the human services lies in helping clients to think through and articulate what it is they really want to achieve.

On occasion, outside sources can bring pressure to bear regarding practice objective formulation. For example, if the client is in a residential home, a hospital, or a prison, the institutional authorities may then have some say in the practice objectives to be achieved: They may require that the client comply more fully with some court order or institutional ruling, and the worker may also be expected to work toward obtaining compliance. In short, the client—or the client and practitioner together—cannot always exercise complete freedom in formulating practice objectives.

In review, the following seven points should be considered when formulating practice objectives consistent with program objectives:

1. The change specified in the practice objective should be one that the client is able to achieve.

2. The change should be perceived as desirable by both the worker and the client.

3. There should be no impediments to achieving the change, and possible unintended consequences should have been thoroughly considered.

4. Wherever possible, the change should be stated as a positive achievement rather than what the client should *not* do.

5. The practice objective should specify precisely what change is to occur, to what extent, and under what conditions.

6. It should be completely clear who is going to do what.

7. If at all possible, some means of measuring change should be established that clearly indicates when the practice objective has been attained.

Creating Measurable Practice Objectives

The last point above mentioned that practice objectives, if at all possible, should be measured to determine if they are being achieved. A valid concern can be raised about the time this measurement takes. After all, program objectives are already being measured and to measure practice objectives would require more time on the part of the human service practitioner. One might argue that we would be spending more time measuring than providing treatment. On the other hand, it must be noted that making measurements of the practice objectives actually increases our ability to define a client's problem accurately and thus provide correct interventions.

Suppose that a worker's practice objective is to increase a woman's self-esteem. There are many ways in which self-esteem can be directly observed or indirectly measured. The woman may voice her opinion more frequently to the group, initiate more social contacts with neighbors, or defend her actions to her boss. She may also achieve a better score on a standardized self-esteem measuring instrument, apply for a job, or make positive statements about her appearance or capabilities.

The practitioner must be sure that whatever measurements are chosen really pertain to self-esteem and are not indicative of something else. Perhaps the job application reflects the husband's opinion that his wife should work, or the woman's statement that she feels she is a nice person was made to please the worker. Perhaps the more frequent voicing of opinions is a sign of increased aggression, not increased self-esteem.

Suppose again that a practice objective for an adolescent is to reduce his aggressive behavior toward his brother. This practice objective must be stated more precisely. The adolescent may claim that he has been nicer, the brother may claim that he has not, and the parents may say—quite rightly—that it depends upon what is meant by "nicer." A practice objective is not useful unless it is specific, defining clearly and comprehensively what is supposed to happen before the objective can be achieved. Thus, the process of trying to measure the practice objective actually refined the concept of aggressive behavior.

A reasonable practice objective to reduce aggressive behavior would be that the adolescent hits his brother less frequently, speaks to him without shouting, does not purposely break anything that belongs to his brother, or does not ruin his brother's homework. Whatever objectives are chosen, their meaning must be agreed upon by all involved. "Hitting," for example, may be taken to include everything from a tap on the shoulder to a severe beating, and "shouting" may be interpreted by any vocalization above a whisper.

Once a practice objective has been precisely defined, it can then be measured. For example, the practice objective to reduce an adolescent's hitting behavior may be measured by asking the parent who is home all day to keep a record for a month of how many times each day the adolescent hits his brother. Similar records may be kept by the adolescent and the brother. If all the records are in agreement, changes in the frequency of hitting incidents can be detected. This process of defining a practice objective in such a way that it can be measured is known as *operationalization*.

The child's aggressive behavior could be operationalized further to include four specific facilitative objectives: (1) to reduce his deliberate physical contact with his brother, (2) to reduce his shouting at his brother, (3) to reduce his destruction of his brother's possessions, and (4) to reduce his touching of his brother's homework.

The index of these objectives may be merely the number of times each day the adolescent exhibits these behaviors over a period of a month; that is, the objective specifies that the behavior is to be measured in terms of the number of times it occurs (as opposed to how long or when it occurs). The measurement method specifies the way that each count is to be made: who will do the counting, when, and how the results will be recorded and displayed. The measurement itself is merely the result of making the count, displayed in the specified manner. Again, the essential linkages between program objectives, practice objectives, activities, and measurements of the program and/or practice objective must be apparent. If they are not, the worker is not performing professional human service practice, but is likely wasting the client's and the program's time, money, and effort.

Further links should be apparent when a concept such as aggressive behavior is operationalized to mean certain specific behaviors. The specific behaviors selected are hardly arrived at haphazardly: They are drawn from the problem initially presented by the client. For example, if the adolescent discussed above has never spoiled his brother's homework, specifying that he should not do so in the future is obviously silly. Another behavior should be chosen that has been found to be problematic. In other words, practice objectives, like program objectives, are client-centered. The point can be generalized: All program goals, program objectives, practice objectives, measurements, and the activities human service workers perform to obtain the practice objectives must be linked to the client's presenting problem. One would expect this to be the case, given that human service programs exist in order to change human lives for the better.

Let us take another example of an adolescent whose practice objective is to plan and make appropriate well-balanced meals three times a day. At first glance, the objective may appear measurable. However, how does one measure the degree to which an adolescent succeeded in planning a meal? In order to make a measurement, it is first necessary to decide exactly what is meant by "planning a meal." Suppose it is decided that meal planning involves first selecting an appropriate menu, and second, writing down on a shopping list exactly what must be purchased in order to prepare the chosen meal for two people.

The worker might establish certain criteria to judge how well the planning has been performed. Did the chosen food items blend well with each other? Were they appropriate to the time of day the meal was to be served? Did they fall within an acceptable price range? Were they items that the adolescent would realistically be able to prepare and cook? Did they take into account the personal tastes of the people who were to eat them? Was every item included on the shopping list? Were quantities of items also included and, if so, were the quantities appropriate? Did the adolescent know in what store or stores the purchases might be made, how they were to be paid for, and how they would be transported home?

Success in meal-planning skills might then be measured in different ways. Perhaps the adolescent will score a point for every criterion met and end with a percentage score. More likely, the practitioner will just make a mental note of which criteria were met and which forgotten, so that these can be discussed with the adolescent and performance will improve next time. Most human service workers would do this quite automatically in terms of "Hey, Vincent, you forgot to put milk on the shopping list." The idea that this was a form of measurement might not occur to them and it almost certainly would not occur to Vincent. For example, if there is no expectation that Vincent's meal-planning skills will ever change by a perceivable or measurable amount, the worker's effort would better be expended on something else.

The second point is that before anything can be measured, it has to be completely and clearly defined. For example, meal planning was *operationalized* above by deciding exactly what steps were involved in planning a meal. The third point is that the definition or operationalization of an objective determines what will be measured. If a person's intelligence is to be measured, the first step is to decide what is meant by intelligence: that is, to *operationalize* intelligence. Is intelligence the ability to remember facts, reason logically, think creatively, respond appropriately to a social situation, all of these, or something else? Whatever factors are included in the definition of intelligence, *it is these factors that are being measured.*

If the definition or operationalization is incomplete or faulty, the measurement will also be incomplete or faulty. Physical scientists have a great advantage here, because the concepts used in physical science are relatively simple. The speed of light is the speed of light, and everyone knows what is meant by the term. Potential program and practice objectives used in social science—utilization, assertiveness, enmeshment, life-satisfaction, and so on—are far more complex and harder to define. Nevertheless, they *can* be defined and, once defined, they can be measured.

The fourth point is that measurement need not be intrusive. Most human service workers assess their own and their clients' progress as they go along. They do this quite naturally, considering assessment to be part of the treatment process and, although they may not call it measurement or assessment, measurement nevertheless is what it is. One of the aims of this text is to encourage human service workers to do consciously what they presently do unconsciously, and to point out ways that they can improve upon the measurement processes they currently use.

The fifth point is that practice objectives must have the ability to reflect small changes in the behavior, feelings, or knowledge level that will be eventually measured (if possible, that is). Often, changes which occur in clients are not dramatic or sudden; they are small, barely perceptible changes, occurring over time. A good objective must therefore have the ability to reflect small changes. For example, if a practice objective is to reduce depression, there may have to be a considerable reduction before the client will engage in such behaviors as socializing with friends or participating in community events. To increase one's socializing with friends may therefore not be a good practice objective to measure, because it will not reflect small reductions in the depression level. If part of the presenting problem was that the client "cries all day," a more sensitive practice objective to measure may be to reduce the number of hours per week the client cries.

Client Logs

In order to develop and monitor a helping strategy, a worker needs to collect as much systematic and accurate data as possible about the client's practice objective. One of the best ways to do this is through a client log. These logs are essentially structured journals in which clients record events, feelings, and reactions relevant to their practice objectives. Client logs are not standardized measuring instruments (discussed in Chapter 6), but they are useful for collecting accurate, ongoing data about a practice objective, both when the objective is being initially explored and when it has been more precisely defined.

The purpose of a log is twofold: First, it jogs the client's memory so that full and accurate data are conveyed to the worker; and second, it can reveal unsuspected connections between events so that new hypotheses can be formulated. For example, a mother who is having trouble getting a young child to school may record that she feels intense anxiety about school attendance every morning when she calls the child to breakfast. Without the log, she may not have mentioned this anxiety to the human service worker, and may not even have realized that it regularly occurred with such intensity. The practitioner may hypothesize that the mother is conveying her anxiety to the child, thereby increasing the child's own anxiety as well as the likelihood that the child will not go to school. A new interventive strategy can then be formulated, focusing on changing the mother's behavior rather than the child's.

All client logs are structured to include at least a description of the event of interest; the time, day, and date the event took place; and the client's reaction to the

EXPLORATORY LOG

Client Name: Peter Kotten   **Day and Date:** April 22, 1995

Time	Place	Activity	Who Was There?	What You Wanted	What Happened	Your Reaction
8:00 AM	Home	Eating Breakfast	Wife and I	Eat; feel reasonably pleasant	She kept trying to talk to me	I got irritated and yelled at her
8:45 AM	In car	Driving to work	Just myself	Wanted to get over feeling bad and get to work relaxed	Driver cut in on me	Started honking and yelling at her
10:00 AM	Work	Completing a letter	Secretary and I	Get work done	She was not finished	Gave her a nasty look, but did not say anything

FIGURE 5.2   Partially Completed Exploratory Log

event. In addition, the client may be asked to note who else was there and what took place before and after the event. Figure 5.2 presents an example of a log partially completed by a client who was having difficulty controlling his anger.

Within the structural outlines sketched above, there is room for much individual variation; a client's log may use whatever format best reflects the practice objective. For example, a client who is having trouble developing effective social skills may be asked to record every social event, including what happened during the event, what happened before and after, who was there, the client's own behavior during the event, and his or her emotional reactions to it. At a later date, the client may be asked to add two more categories: an assessment of whether his behavior during the event was appropriate and any alternate behaviors that might have been more effective.

Recording Practice Objectives

Human service workers devote much of their time and activities to facilitating change in their clients' knowledge objectives, feeling objectives, or behavior practice objectives. Thus, they need some means of pinpointing the level of knowledge, feeling, or behavior, to provide a benchmark for and a gauge of future change.

A client's knowledge level can be defined by obtaining two measures. The first of these determines whether the client has any knowledge at all about a certain subject, such as child development or nutrition—whether knowledge is *present* or *absent*. If some knowledge is present, as is usually the case, a second measure determines the extent or *magnitude* of that knowledge. A more complete definition of knowledge might include the length of time the client retains the knowledge, that is, its *duration*.

A particular feeling such as fear can be defined similarly in terms of its presence or absence and, if present, its magnitude and duration. A feeling that comes and goes may also be defined in terms of how often it occurs, or its *frequency*.

Finally, a behavior such as crying can be operationally defined in the same terms: whether it is present or absent, its magnitude, its duration, and its frequency. There are no concepts common to the human services that cannot be defined using these terms.

Presence or Absence Objectives

To make a determination of the presence or absence of a quality is obviously superfluous when that quality is known to be present. For example, all people, at all times, have some intelligence and some self-esteem, and so there is never a need to establish this fact. However, some feelings or behaviors are present on some occasions and not on others: anger, fear, hitting one's brother, and throwing a temper tantrum. Measurement of presence or absence is most useful when the quality being measured is only sometimes present and can be defined with sufficient exactness to differentiate it from other qualities.

For example, if a practice objective is to increase a child's attention span and a related facilitative objective is to increase the amount of time the child spends working continuously at a particular task, a parent or teacher might be asked to observe the child at work for a ten-minute period. This period can be divided into ten one-minute intervals as shown in Figure 5.3.

If the child works continuously for the first minute, the parent or teacher puts a check mark in the first box. If the child works for part but not all of the minute, there will be no check mark, and if the child does not work at all, there is also no check mark. The same procedure will be followed for the second minute, the third minute, and so forth, up to ten minutes. This kind of *interval recording* is common in the human services and requires the ability to determine the presence or absence of the client's practice objective.

Another measurement method that uses presence or absence data is *spot-check recording*. Suppose that the practice objective is to increase the amount of social interaction displayed by a resident in a nursing home. Social interaction can be measured by the length of time the resident spends out of her bedroom, but staff cannot continuously monitor the whereabouts of one resident. Spot checks on the resident in her bedroom, however, may not be too time consuming; staff members could be asked to check on the resident at two-hour intervals between 9:00 AM and 9:00 PM, when most social activity usually takes place, over a period of a month.

The spot-check recording method is useful for measuring any client practice objective that occurs often or is sustained over a long period of time. Figure 5.4 provides an example of a spot-check recording form that could be used by staff members in the above nursing home.

Readers should note that the presence or absence of a quality is measured by directly observing whether or not a certain event occurs. This method of obtaining a measure, via direct observation, is important in the human services and will be discussed in Chapter 6.

Client's Name	Recorder's Name
Practice Objective to Be Observed: *Increase attention span*	General Comments:
Time Period: *10 minutes*	
Duration of Each Interval: *1 minute*	

Interval

1	2	3	4	5	6	7	8	9	10

FIGURE 5.3   Interval Recording Form

Client's Name		Recorder's Name	
Practice Objective to Be Observed: *Increase socialization*		**General Comments:**	
Day & Date	Spot Check Time	Resident Was Alone	Resident Was Not Alone
Monday, Jan. 1, 1995	*9:03 am*	✓	
Monday, Jan. 1, 1995	*10:15 am*	✓	
Monday, Jan. 1, 1995	*1:14 pm*		✓

FIGURE 5.4   Spot-Check Recording Form

Magnitude Objectives

It is always important to know the extent to which some quality is present. Obvious examples are the amount of weight lost in a weight-loss program and the amount of knowledge acquired by a client. However, magnitude is also important in subtler ways; for example, one may want to obtain a measure of the changing magnitude of a child's temper tantrums over a period of time. To do this, it is first necessary to define, or operationalize, what is meant by various magnitudes. Here is one attempt to do so:

1. Low-volume crying or whining
2. High-volume screaming and shouting
3. Hitting, kicking, or throwing inanimate objects
4. Attacking another person, either bodily or by hurling objects

The progress of the tantrum can then be followed by recording the time when it began, presumably at the lowest magnitude; when it climbed to the second level; and so on. Figure 5.5 illustrates a *magnitude recording* for a hypothetical tantrum.

The same measurement method can be used to track the progress of other practice and program objectives, such as reduction of anxiety attacks (a practice objective), or increased agency responsiveness to community complaints (a program objective). In the case of the latter, responsiveness might be defined as having five levels of magnitude:

1. Refusing to receive the complaint
2. Receiving the complaint but not responding
3. Discussing the complaint with community representatives but making no attempt at solution
4. Devising a solution to the complaint
5. Devising, discussing, and implementing a solution

Client's Name		Recorder's Name	
Practice Objective to Be Observed: *Decrease magnitude of tantrums*		**General Comments:**	
Time	Magnitude	Observer	Additional Comments
6:01 pm	1	Father	
6:08 pm	2	Mother	
6:13 pm	3	Mother	
6:25 pm	2	Mother	
7:05 pm	1	Father	
8:10 pm	3	Mother	

FIGURE 5.5   Magnitude Recording Form

Adapted from Richard Polster & Donald Collins, Measuring variables by direct observation. In R. M. Grinnell, Jr. (Ed.), *Social Work Research and Evaluation* (3rd ed.). © 1988. Itasca, IL: F. E. Peacock Publishers. Used with permission.

It is apparent that magnitude can mean very much more than a simple measure of more or less weight, or a lower or higher score on a measuring instrument. Given that the critical aspect of many objectives is the degree to which the problematic feeling or behavior occurs, magnitude can be the single most important measure.

Client's Name		Recorder's Name
Practice Objective to Be Observed: *Reduce the length of crying spells* Time Period for Observation: *5:00 pm – 6:00 pm*		**General Comments:**
Date	Length of Time Problem Occurred (e.g., minutes)	Additional Comments
March 8	5, 20, 3, 1	

FIGURE 5.6   Duration Recording Form

Adapted from Richard Polster & Donald Collins, Measuring variables by direct observation. In R. M. Grinnell, Jr. (Ed.), *Social Work Research and Evaluation* (3rd ed.). © 1988. Itasca, IL: F. E. Peacock Publishers. Used with permission.

Duration Objectives

Sometimes the most important aspect of a client's problem is not its magnitude, but the length of time it continues. A child's crying may fall into this category, as may an argument with a partner, an illness, a financial difficulty, or a feeling of dissatisfaction with a job. A common method for measuring duration, known as *duration recording*, is to record the length of time that a given event continues during a specified period.

Imagine that a child's crying is to be recorded between 5:00 PM and 6:00 PM. It may be found that the child has four crying spells during this hour, with the first lasting 5 minutes, the second 20 minutes, the third 3 minutes, and the fourth 1 minute. Figure 5.6 illustrates a form on which the duration of these crying spells might be recorded. Similar recordings made on succeeding days will give an accurate picture of the problem, so that intervention strategies may be precisely tailored to the pattern of the crying behavior.

Frequency Objectives

Many human service practice and facilitative objectives have to do with increasing or decreasing the frequency of behaviors and feelings. A large number of objectives can be assessed by measuring how often the relevant activities occur: reducing cigarette smoking, increasing positive statements about oneself or others, increasing the initiation of conversations, doing more chores around the house, and reducing fights with schoolmates, among many others. The measurement method used to track this dimension is known as *frequency recording*; it simply involves recording how many times the relevant event occurs during a specified time period. Figure 5.7 illustrates a form on which frequency data can be entered.

Client's Name		Recorder's Name	
Practice Objective to Be Observed:		General Comments:	
Time Period (Hours/Day):			
Date	Frequency	Additional Comments	

FIGURE 5.7 Frequency Recording Form

Adapted from Richard Polster & Donald Collins, Measuring variables by direct observation. In R. M. Grinnell, Jr. (Ed.), *Social Work Research and Evaluation* (3rd ed.). © 1988. Itasca, IL: F. E. Peacock Publishers. Used with permission.

Data Collection

The next important consideration is the methods that should be used for collecting and analyzing the data. The process of beginning data analyses will be discussed in Chapter 11; here we look at data collection, with particular reference to who should collect the data, when, and where.

Who Should Collect the Data?

Questions about what data to collect and what measuring instruments to use are obviously linked to questions about who should collect the data, when, and where. There are three possible agents of collection: the client, a relative or friend living with the client, or an outside person in the client's environment, such as a human service worker, nurse, or teacher (or, of course, some combination of these).

The Client

Data such as private thoughts and emotions are only available to the client, and hence can only be accessed through the client. If these data are needed, it is apparent that the client must collect them. As a bonus, the process of data collection may help to clarify the problem in the client's mind. However, there are a number of disadvantages to this method of data collection, not the least of which is that the client might be unable or unwilling to collect the data. In addition, the client may consciously or unconsciously bias the data, and there is a possibility that the act of recording will itself effect change. In many cases, therefore, the data will have to be collected by someone other than the client.

Relative or Friend Living in the Client's Home

Many problem behaviors occur in the home, in the presence of the client's family, in which case it is sensible to ask a family member to collect data, especially if that person is usually present while the problem is occurring. This method of collection can be particularly relevant when the problem is in the area of interpersonal relationships or centers on a child.

There are four disadvantages to having a relative or friend collect data. First, the relative or friend may "see" what he or she expects to see, subconsciously distorting the data. Second, the relative or friend may not appreciate the importance of collecting data unobtrusively; if the client notices any scrutiny, he or she may alter the behavior. Third, the relative or friend may not be willing or able to record times and events as accurately as is required. Lastly, the relative or friend may distort the data consciously, either as a result of submerged feelings toward the client or to impress the worker.

Despite these serious drawbacks, in some circumstances having the relative or friend collect the data is the only way to obtain the data. If such is the case, all the worker can do is to try to impress upon the relative or friend the importance of unobtrusive observation and accurate, objective recording.

Outside Person in the Client's Environment

If the problem occurs most often outside the home, the practitioner will need to recruit some person from outside the home. There will probably be a large number of people in the client's environment who could be asked to collect data: family members not living in the home, friends, teachers, volunteer workers, school counselors, nurses, occupational and other speciality therapists, and, of course, the client's human service worker. Many of these people will be too busy to collect data; others, though willing, may not be reliable. Sometimes, too, changes in the behavior being observed are so finely grained that they require data collection by a trained observer rather than a relative or friend. The worker's challenge, in all these cases, is to find an observer who is both willing *and* able.

When Should Data Be Collected?

In the context of data collection, *when* refers not only to what time but to how often. In general, data should be collected as often as possible so long as the collection process does not become tiresome, boring, or overwhelming to either the client or the person collecting the data. At the very minimum, data must be collected before beginning the intervention and prior to termination. If no data are collected between these two points, however, the termination data may reveal only the degree to which the practice objectives have not been accomplished—hardly useful information. Repeated measurements are the *only* way in which the worker can really monitor the client's progress.

If a measurement is to be repeated, the practitioner may have to judge how much time should elapse between administrations. The optimum time interval is generally determined by four factors. First is the time a particular client takes to complete it: The more time-consuming the instrument, the less often it is administered. The second factor is the client's willingness or ability to complete the instrument. Annoyance or boredom are good indicators that the instrument should be completed less frequently. If completion of the instrument requires a great deal of the client's energy, this, too, indicates that the instrument should be filled out less often. The third factor is whether the instrument is the only one being used to measure the particular practice objective. If it is, it will need to be completed often; if it is not, the time interval can be more generous. Finally, it is important that a client who is completing an instrument daily, or every few days, should always complete it at the same time of day. This will help ensure that the conditions under which the instrument is completed are standard; and standard conditions will improve reliability.

Where Should Data Be Collected?

The data will often need to be collected where the problem occurs. If the problem occurs most often at home, the data will be collected at home; if it occurs at school, a teacher may be asked to collect the data in the classroom. Whatever option is selected, it is important that the instrument be completed in the same place every time. Again, this helps to ensure standard conditions and increases reliability.

Summary

This chapter discussed the process of identifying clients's problems: how to survey them, how to select and prioritize them, and how to define them. It concluded by considering how to develop practice and facilitative objectives in relation to what one wants to achieve, under what conditions, to what extent, and by whom. It also presented simple methods for recording practice objective data: presence or absence, magnitude, duration, and frequency. These provide an introduction to the more rigorous ways of measuring program objectives and client practice objectives—standardized measuring instruments—the subject of the following chapter.

Key Terms

Client Log: A form whereby clients maintain annotated records of events related to their practice objectives; structured journals in which clients record events, feelings, and reactions relevant to their problem.

Duration Recording: A method of data collection that involves direct observation and documentation of the practice objective by recording the length of time of each occurrence within a specified observation period.

Frequency Recording: A method of data collection involving direct observation and documentation in which each occurrence of the practice objective is recorded during a specified observation period.

Interval Recording: A method of data collection that involves continuous, direct observation and documentation of an individual's behavior during specified observation periods divided into equal time intervals.

Magnitude Recording: A method of data collection that involves direct observation and documentation of the amount, level, or degree of the practice objective during each occurrence.

Spot-Check Recording: A method of data collection that involves direct observation and documentation of the practice objective at specified intervals rather than continuously.

Study Questions

1. Explain in detail why program objectives and practice objectives must be logically linked. What risks do practitioners incur for themselves and their clients when they set practice objectives that are not consistent with the program's objectives?

2. In your own words, list the strategies a worker could use to delineate practice and facilitative objectives with a client. Compare your list with approaches outlined in the chapter.

3. A parent expresses frustration with his child's noncompliance and wants to hit the child. As a practitioner, what questions would you ask this client to define the problem more clearly? What level of clarity is needed before practice and facilitative objectives can be established? Explain in detail. Use a human service example in your explanation.

4. Why should practice and facilitative objectives be developed jointly by the practitioner

and the client? What are the specific responsibilities of each party? What ethical issues arise for human service workers who do not consult their clients when establishing practice objectives?

5. Rephrase the following practice objectives in positive terms: (a) to decrease the number of times that John interrupts his mother when she is talking on the telephone; (b) to reduce the amount of profanity Jane uses in conversation with her teacher; and (c) to cut down on Ms Tasker's spending at the grocery store during each shopping trip. Does rewriting the above practice objectives in positive terms influence the nature of a worker's activities? Explain your answer in detail and provide a human service example throughout your discussion.

6. How might a human service practitioner modify practice objectives to maximize success for a client? What ethical considerations must be taken into account?

7. Give an example of one practice objective that has stated direction and one that has implied direction. How would the nature of the activities differ for each?

8. What is the relationship between defining a practice objective and recording one?

9. What recording approach would you use for the following practice objectives? Explain your choice: (a) for Joe to establish eye contact with another person; (b) to increase the number of times that Jay asks permission to leave the house; and (c) to increase the amount of time Janice spends in job-seeking activities.

10. In groups of five, assign each group member one of the five types of recording strategy outlined in this chapter. Have each group member develop a short data collection form. Share your group's data collection forms with the class, and discuss the similarities and differences among the types. Compare your data collection forms with those presented in the chapter (Figures 5.2–5.5).

11. In groups of five, choose one of the types of recording strategy discussed in the above exercise. Using the criteria presented in the chapter, outline a step-by-step procedure for developing a practice objective with the recording form in mind. Do the steps follow a logical order? Why or why not? Discuss the ethical implications of the practice objective. Present your discussion to the class.

12. As we know from the previous chapter, a program is usually evaluated on the attainment of its program objectives. Thus, human service workers must continually measure program objectives. Knowing that a program's objectives are being measured, why do you feel it would be worthwhile to measure a client's practice objectives, or facilitative objectives for that matter? Make a case that we should measure not only a program's objectives, but also the client's practice objectives along with their facilitative objectives. Now make a case that we should only measure a program's objectives. Which one do you agree with? Why? What would be the disadvantages if we did not measure our practice objectives in relation to knowledge generation as presented in Chapter 1?

13. Let us say you have a client who has a practice objective of "to increase his self-esteem." List the various facilitative objectives that you would formulate with this client and the activities you would engage in under each facilitative objective. Use this chapter as a guide in formulating your facilitative objectives. How would you go about measuring the practice objective? What advantage would there be in measuring the practice objective? If you did measure the practice objective over time, how do you feel the data could help you as a practitioner? Would you measure your facilitative objectives? Why or why not?

14. In your own words, discuss in depth how the process of measuring a practice objective refines the delivery of services to a client. Use a human service example throughout your discussion.

15. In your own words, discuss how the process of measuring practice objectives has been around since the conception of the human services. Discuss how human service workers have always been measuring the success of their practice objectives. How do you feel the process of measurement has changed during the last several years?

16. Considering the contents of the last chapter and this one, discuss in depth the relationship between an agency's goal, a program goal, a program objective, a practice objective, a facilitative objective, an instrumental objective, activities to meet the practice objective, activities to meet the facilitative objective, the measurement of the program objective, and the measurement of the practice objective. Use one common human service example throughout your discussion.

17. Develop a list of written guidelines that would aid the client in Case Study B to accurately use a client log.

18. Why is congruency between the client's practice objectives and the program's objectives important for the program? The client?

19. How does a worker arrive at a practice objective? What kinds of strategies can a practitioner use to determine practice objectives with a client?

20. A client at your agency, Ms Jones, is experiencing financial problems, is overweight, is having problems with her husband, and has difficulty forming friendships. Through what process would you prioritize your practice objectives with her?

21. As one of your practice objectives with Ms Jones, you decide to tackle her weight problem. Why must "weight problem" be clearly defined before you can do this? As you clearly define "weight problem" think about what specific practice objectives might be used to alleviate her weight problem, how these objectives might be measured, and what measurement methods might be employed.

22. In developing practice objectives with Ms Jones, you both come to the conclusion that weight is not the underlying problem in this case. How will you go about defining the "real" problem? Why is Ms Jones' participation in this process so important?

23. Suppose that the practice objective has been identified as low self-esteem. Establish related facilitative practice objectives. Keep in mind that they should be stated in positive terms and be comprehensive and precise.

24. Specify under what conditions the practice objective is to be achieved. If possible, include a specification of where, when, and with whom.

25. Your practice objective with Ms Jones should specify that her self-esteem should be increased. Specify by how much. Upon what two factors does the answer to this question depend? List some successive facilitative objectives to be reached before the desired performance level can be reached.

26. Specify by whom the practice objective with Ms Jones is to be achieved. Why does confusion sometimes revolve around this task?

27. Design some exploratory questions you will ask Ms Jones in order to determine the likely effects of the achievement of the practice objective will have on those around her. Why is it important to do this?

28. Why is it important to discuss possible impediments with Ms Jones as a part of negotiating the practice objective?

29. Under what circumstances would it be the responsibility of the worker to modify the practice objectives set by Ms Jones? What ethical considerations must be taken into account if you do this?

30. Why should human service workers measure practice objectives?

31. Under what circumstances would human service workers measure practice objectives using presence or absence data?

32. What is the difference between interval recording and spot-check recording instances of a practice objective? Which method would be more useful when measuring Ms Jones' practice objective?

33. When is it important to measure the magnitude of a practice objective? If applicable, demonstrate how you would measure the magnitude of Ms Jones' practice objective.

34. When would it be appropriate to measure the duration of a practice objective? If applicable, how would you measure the duration of Ms Jones' practice objective?

35. Does Ms Jones' practice objective require the increase or decrease of the frequency of certain behaviors or feelings? If so, how? How would you measure the frequency of Ms Jones' practice objective?

36. Under what circumstances would you have a client complete a client log? What is the purpose of such a log? Construct an exploratory "student log" designed to measure your level of stress.

37. Under what circumstances would it be necessary for someone in the client's environment to be responsible for data collection? What are some disadvantages to having a relative or friend collect the data?

38. Read Case Study B. What was the program's goal? What were the program's objectives? What were some of the practice objectives? What were some of the activities that were used to obtain the practice objectives? How were practice objectives recorded? What other recording methods could have been utilized? Why? What additional data would these recording methods provide? *When* were the data collected? Do you think the time the data were collected was appropriate? Why or why not? *Who* collected the data? Do you feel that the person who collected the data was the appropriate one to collect them? Why or why not? *Where* were the data collected? Do you feel where the data were collected was appropriate? Why or why not? What additional program and practice objectives could the program have utilized? Why?

6

MEASURING PROGRAM AND PRACTICE OBJECTIVES

A CONCEPT SUCH AS depression can be defined in words, and, if the words are sufficiently well chosen, the reader will have a clear idea of what depression is. When we apply the definition to a particular client, however, words may be not enough to guide us. The client may seem depressed according to the definition, but many questions may still remain. Is the client more or less depressed than the average person? If more depressed, how much more? Is the depression growing or declining? For how long has the client been depressed? Is the depression continuous or episodic? If episodic, what length of time usually elapses between depressive episodes? Is this length of time increasing or diminishing? How many episodes occur in a week? To what degree is the client depressed? Answers to questions such as these enable a professional human service worker to obtain greater insight into the client's depression—essential for a treatment intervention.

Why Measurement Is Necessary

An evaluation is an appraisal: an estimate of how effectively and efficiently program and practice objectives are being met in a practitioner's individual practice or in a human service program. In other words, an evaluation can compare the change that has actually taken place against the predicted, desired change. Thus, an evaluation requires knowledge of both the initial condition and the present condition of the objective undergoing the proposed change. Therefore, it is necessary to have two *measurements,* one at the beginning of the change process and one at the end. In addition, it is always useful to take measurements of the objectives during the change process as well. Measurement, then, is not only necessary in the quality improvement process—it is the conceptual foundation, without which the evaluative structure cannot exist.

A definition, no matter how complete, is only useful if it means the same thing in the hands of different people. For example, we could define a distance in terms of the number of days a person takes to walk it, or the number of strides needed to cross it, or the number of felled oak trees that would span it end to end. But since people, strides, and oak trees vary, none of these definitions is very exact. To be useful to a modern traveler, a distance must be given in miles or some other precisely defined unit.

Similarly, shared understanding and precision are very important in the human services. A worker who is assessing a woman's level of functioning needs to know that the results of the assessment are not being affected by her feelings toward the woman, her knowledge of the woman's situation, or any other biasing factor; that any other worker who assessed the same woman under the same conditions would come up with the same result. Further, the practitioner needs to know that the results of the assessment will be understood by other professionals; that the results are rendered in words or symbols that are not open to misinterpretation. If the assessment is to provide the basis for decisions about the woman's future, via the treatment intervention chosen, objectivity and precision on the part of the human service professional are even more important.

Objectivity

Some practitioners believe that they are entirely objective; that they will not judge clients by skin color, ethnic origin, religious persuasion, sexual orientation, social class, income level, marital status, education, age, gender, verbal skill, or personal attractiveness. They may believe they are not influenced by other people's opinions about a client—statements that the client has severe emotional problems or a borderline personality will be disregarded until evidence is gathered. No judgments will be made on the basis of the worker's personal likes and dislikes, and stereotyping will be avoided at all costs.

Human service professionals who sincerely believe that their judgment will never be influenced by any of the above factors are deluding themselves. Everyone is prejudiced to some degree in some area or another; everyone has likes and dislikes, moral positions, and personal standards; everyone is capable of irrational feelings of aversion, sympathy, or outrage. Workers who deny this run the risk of showing bias without realizing it, and a worker's unconscious bias can have devastating effects on the life of a client.

A client may unwittingly fuel the bias by sensing what the practitioner expects and answering questions in a way that supports the worker's preconceptions. In extreme cases, clients can even become what they are expected to become, fulfilling the biased prophecy. The art of good judgment, then, lies in accepting the possibility of personal bias and trying to minimize its effects. What is needed is an unprejudiced method of assessment and an unbiased standard against which the client's knowledge, feelings, or behaviors can be gauged. In other words, we require a measurement method from which an impartial measure can be derived.

Precision

The other ingredient of the quality improvement process is precision, whose opposite is vagueness. A vague statement is one that uses general or indefinite terms; in other words, it leaves so many details to be filled in that it means different things to different people. There are four major sources of vagueness in the human services.

The first source of vagueness is terms such as *often, frequently, many, some, usually,* and *rarely* which attempt to assign degrees to a client's feelings or behaviors without specifying a precise unit of measurement. A statement such as "John misses many appointments with his worker" is fuzzy; it tells us only that John's reliability *may* leave much to be desired. The statement "John missed 2 out of 10 appointments with his worker" is far more precise and does not impute evil tendencies to John.

The second source of vagueness is statements that, although they are intended to say something about a particular client, might apply to anyone; for example, "John often feels insecure, having experienced some rejection by his peers." Who has not experienced peer rejection? Nevertheless, the statement will be interpreted as identifying a quality specific to John. The human services abound with statements like this, which are as damaging to the client as they are meaningless.

A third source of vagueness is professional jargon, the meaning of which will rarely be clear to a client. Often professionals themselves do not agree on the meaning of such phrases as "expectations-role definition" or "reality pressures." In the worst case, they do not even know what they mean by their own jargon; they use it merely to sound impressive. Jargon is useful when it conveys precise statements to colleagues; when misused, it can confuse workers and alienate clients.

The last source of vagueness is tautology: a meaningless repetition disguised as a definition. For example: a delinquent is a person who engages in delinquent behaviors; "John is agoraphobic because he is afraid of open spaces," "Betty is ambivalent because she cannot make up her mind," "Marie hits her brother because she is aggressive," "John rocks back and forth because he is autistic." Obviously, tautological statements tell us nothing and are to be avoided.

In summary, we need to attain objectivity and precision and avoid bias and vagueness. Both objectivity and precision are vital in the quality improvement process and are readily attainable through measurement.

Measurement and Data

The word *measurement* is often used in two different senses. In the first sense, a measurement is the result of a measuring process: the number of times Bobby hits his brother in a day (a possible *frequency* practice objective); the length of time for which Jenny cries (a possible *duration* practice objective); the intensity of Ms Smith's depression (a possible *magnitude* practice objective). In the second sense, measurement refers to the measuring process itself; that is, it encompasses the event or attribute being measured, the person who does the measuring, the method employed, the measuring instrument used, and often also the result. Throughout this book, *measurement* will be taken to refer to the entire process, excluding only the results. The results of any measurement process will be referred to as *data*. In other words, measurement is undertaken in order to obtain data—objective and precise data, that is.

In any profession, from the human services to plumbing, an instrument is a tool designed to help the user perform a task. A tool need not be a physical object; it can just as easily be a perception, an idea, a new synthesis of known facts, or a new analysis of a known whole. In Chapter 1 the scientific method was described as a useful tool with which to pursue the art of the human services. However, in the human services, a tool used to obtain data—a *measuring instrument*—is a physical object. It is a piece of paper, or a form, on which the client's feelings, perceptions, or behaviors can be recorded in various ways.

In the preceding chapter we considered five simple recording methods, using simple forms, that are helpful to keep track of practice objectives: presence or absence objectives (Figures 5.3 and 5.4), magnitude objectives (Figure 5.5), duration objectives (Figure 5.6), and frequency objectives (Figure 5.7). These are technically not measuring instruments, only vehicles to record data. The observer recording the data is actually the measuring instrument—the one really doing the measuring—and the forms are only a place for the written data (Collins & Polster, 1993). In addition to these recording forms, there is a more accurate method to measure a program or practice objective. This method has more objectivity and precision (as discussed above); standardized measuring instruments replace the recording forms (Bostwick & Kyte, 1985a, 1985b, 1988, 1993).

Standardized Measures

A *standardized measuring instrument* is one that has been constructed by researchers to measure a particular knowledge level, attitude or feeling, or behavior of clients (Jordan, Franklin, & Corcoran, 1993). It is a paper-and-pencil instrument and may take the form of a questionnaire, checklist, inventory, or rating scale. Two factors differentiate a standardized instrument from any other instrument, such as the basic recording forms previously discussed: the effort made to attain uniformity in the instrument's application, scoring, and interpretation; and the amount of work that has been devoted to ensuring that the instrument is valid and reliable (Hudson & Thyer, 1987; Hudson, 1993).

Every instrument, whether standardized or not, is designed to measure some specific quality; if it is valid, it will measure only that quality. The information sheet that usually accompanies a standardized instrument will state the instrument's purpose: to measure anxiety about academic achievement, say, or to measure three aspects of assertiveness (Corcoran, 1988). In addition, the sheet will usually describe how the questions (items) on the instrument relate to that purpose and will say something about the clinical implications of the quality being measured (e.g., Hudson, 1982).

The information sheet may also indicate what the instrument does not measure. A description of an instrument to measure aggression, for example, may specifically state that it does not measure hostility. This statement of purpose and the accompanying description improve chances that the instrument will be used as it was intended, to measure what it was designed to measure. In other words, it is more likely that the application of the instrument will be uniform.

The information sheet may also discuss the research studies done to ensure the instrument's validity, often including the instrument's ability to discriminate between clinical and non-clinical populations. It may mention instruments or criteria with which the instrument was compared, so that users will better understand what validity means in this particular instance. Information about reliability will usually be given via descriptions of the research studies undertaken to ensure reliability, and their results. Again, this information will help the worker who uses the instrument to know what kind of reliability can be expected.

Information will also be given about the characteristics of people on whom the instrument was tested. For example, an instrument to measure loneliness may be accompanied by the information that it was tested on a sample of 399 undergraduate students (171 males, 228 females) from three university campuses. An instrument to measure self-esteem may have been tested on a sample of 240 eighth graders, 110 African American, and 130 Caucasian. In each case, scores will be given for the tested group and subgroups, so that the user can see what the norms are for people with particular demographic characteristics. A *norm* is an established score for a particular group against which the score of a client can be measured (Jordan, Franklin, & Corcoran, 1993).

Let us say, for example, that the mean score of African-American eighth graders on the self-esteem instrument was 40, with a small range in scores about the mean given in terms of a standard deviation. In comparison, the mean score for Caucasian eighth graders was 60. A practitioner who read this information on the sheet accompanying the instrument would know that an African-American client's score should be compared with the African-American average score of 40, and a Caucasian client's score should be compared with the Caucasian average of 60. Without this information, the worker might think that an African-American client who scored 42 was suffering from low self-esteem; although, in such a case 42 is really close to the average self-esteem score for African-American eighth graders.

The concept of norms has an important place in the human services, particularly in the administering of measuring instruments. What is normal for an African-American child from a poor, urban neighborhood is not necessarily normal for a Caucasian child from a prosperous rural neighborhood; what is normal for one ethnic group may not be normal for another; what is normal for an adolescent female may not be normal for an adolescent male. It is very important that a client's score be compared with the average score of people with similar demographic characteristics. If this information is not available, as it sometimes is not, the human service worker should bear in mind that an "unusual" score may not be at all unusual; it may be normal for the type of client being measured. Conversely, a normal-looking score may turn out to be unusual when the demographic characteristics of the client are taken into account.

The documentation sheet should also explain how to score the instrument and how to interpret the score. Scoring may be simple or relatively complex; it may involve summing specific items, reversing entered scores, or following a preset template. Often, it may also be accomplished on a computer. Some instruments may yield one global score while others may provide several scores, each representing a dimension such as self-esteem or assertiveness. Interpretation of the scores also varies depending on the instrument. When interpreting scores, it is particularly important to be aware that some scores represent the magnitude of problems, while others indicate the magnitude of positive attributes such as skills or knowledge. *Depending on what is measured, increasing scores may indicate improvement or deterioration; the same is true for decreasing scores.*

A standardized measuring instrument, then, should be accompanied by at least six kinds of information: (1) the purpose of the instrument, (2) a description of the instrument, (3) the instrument's validity, (4) the instrument's reliability, (5) norms, and (6) scoring and interpretation procedures. The amount and quality of informa-

tion provided may be taken as an indicator of whether an instrument is standardized or not and, if it is, to what degree.

Rating Scales

Rating scales use judgments by self or others to assign an individual (or program) a
single score in relation to the program or practice objective being measured. What
the various types of rating scales have in common is that they all rate clients on
various traits or characteristics by locating them at some point on a continuum or in
an ordered set of response categories, where numerical values are assigned to each
category. Rating scales may be completed by the person being evaluated (self-
rating) or by some significant other, such as a parent, supervisor, spouse, or practitioner. Sometimes a client and a significant other are asked to complete the same
rating scale in order to provide the worker with two different views.

There are two types of rating scales that are useful for evaluative purposes:
graphic rating scales and self-anchored rating scales.

Graphic Rating Scales

Graphic rating scales are structured with a program or practice objective described
on a continuum from one extreme to the other, such as "low to high" or "most to
least." The points of the continuum are ordered in equal intervals and are assigned
numbers. Some or most points have descriptions to help people locate their positions on the scale. Below is one such scale, a "feeling thermometer" that asks
children to rate their level of anxiety from "very anxious" to "very calm" (Kidder &
Judd, 1986). The practice objective in this situation might be "to decrease a child's
anxiety at home."

Check below how anxious you are.

100	____	Very anxious
90	____	
80	____	
70	____	
60	____	
50	____	Neither anxious nor calm
40	____	
30	____	
20	____	
10	____	
0	____	Very calm

A second example of a graphic rating scale asks clients to rate their individual
counseling sessions on a scale ranging from "not productive" to "very productive."
The objective could be to increase a worker's understanding of how her clients view
her effectiveness.

Please circle the number that comes closest to describing your feelings about the session you just completed.

1	2	3	4	5
Not productive		Moderately productive		Very productive

The major advantage of graphic rating scales is that they are easy to use, though one must take care to develop appropriate descriptive statements. For example, end statements so extreme that it is unlikely anyone would choose them, such as "extremely hot" or "extremely cold," should not be used.

Note that the first graphic rating scale above provides data about a client, whereas the second scale provides data about a service.

Self-Anchored Rating Scales

Self-anchored rating scales are similar to graphic rating scales in that clients are asked to rate themselves on a continuum, usually a 7- or 9-point scale from low to high. They differ in that *clients* define the specific referents, or *anchors*, for three points on the continuum on a self-anchored scale. An anchor point is the point on a scale where a concrete descriptor is given to define the condition represented by that point. This type of scale is often used to measure such attributes as intensity of feeling or pain. A self-anchored scale is an excellent source of data, because it is essentially developed by the person most familiar with the subtleties of the problem—the client.

For example, a client who has difficulty being honest in group sessions could complete the following question (the three anchor points are put in by the client), which is intended to measure his own perceptions of his honesty. In the example below, the client writes in the three anchor points (i.e., can never be honest, can sometimes be honest, and can always be completely honest). A practice objective could be to increase his honesty within the group.

Indicate the extent to which you feel you can be honest in the group.

1	2	3	4	5	6	7	8	9
Can never be honest				Can sometimes be honest			Can always be completely honest	

Suppose that a client is feeling trapped in her marriage and in her role as a homemaker. She might develop a 9-point scale such as the one shown below, ranging from "I feel completely trapped," through "I feel I have some options," to "I do not feel trapped at all." If she is not able to analyze her feelings well enough to identify three distinct emotional levels between 5 and 9 or 1 and 5, she may prefer to use a 5-point scale instead. She should certainly be told that the intervals are equal; the distance between 8 and 9 is the same as the distance between 7 and 8, and so forth.

1	2	3	4	5	6	7	8	9
Do not feel trapped at all				Feel I have some options			Feel completely trapped	

If the problem is not the extent to which the woman feels trapped but the intensity of the trapped feelings, she might consider what sort of emotions she experiences when she feels most and least trapped. If being most trapped involves desperate or suicidal feelings, these feelings will define the high end of the scale.

From this example, we can deduce the two major advantages of self-anchored scales. First, they are specific to the client in a way that a scale developed by someone else cannot be. They measure emotions known only to the client, and may therefore yield the most complete and accurate portrayal of the situation. Second, they can measure the intensity of a feeling or attitude. Clients who suffer from feelings of anxiety or guilt or from physical ailments such as migraine headaches are often primarily concerned with intensity, and they may be more willing to fill out an instrument that reflects this concern.

There are also disadvantages to an instrument that is completed by the client. One major drawback is that clients may consciously or unconsciously distort their responses so as to appear more worthy or more deserving in the eyes of the worker. Analyzing an emotion thoroughly enough to rate it on a scale may result in changes to the emotion. This problem is known as "reactivity."

Self-anchored scales, then, are of particular value when the quality being measured is an emotion or thought pattern known only to the client, or when intensity is the primary concern. These scales can be used alone or in conjunction with other types of measuring instruments. They can also be used to supply data peripheral to the central problem: For example, a client whose practice objective is weight loss might use a self-anchored scale to measure changes in self-esteem associated with the weight loss.

Summated Scales

Where rating scales obtain data from one question about the program or practice objective, summated scales present multiple questions to which the client is asked to respond. Thus, summated scales combine responses to all of the questions on an instrument to form a single, overall score for the objective being measured. The responses are then totaled to obtain a composite score indicating the individual's position on the objective of interest.

Summated scales are widely used to assess individual or family problems, for needs assessment, and for other types of case level and program level evaluation efforts. The scale poses a number of questions and asks clients to indicate the degree of their agreement or disagreement with each. Response categories may include such statements as "strongly agree," "agree," "neutral," "disagree," and "strongly disagree." It is our opinion that summated scales provide more objectivity and precision in the concept that they are measuring than the two types of rating scales mentioned above.

Goal Attainment Scaling (GAS)

As seen in Chapter 4, human service workers ultimately try to achieve a program objective(s) with their clients. They do this by creating practice objectives which, if resolved, will accomplish the program objective. The underlying program objective is not the direct focus of a worker's attention. Instead, they create and focus their attention on the practice objectives which are directly linked to the program's objectives. A useful medical analogy is to think of a disease as a program objective and the symptoms of the disease as practice objectives.

Creating Practice Objectives from Program Objectives

By way of example, suppose that a residential home for children who are delinquent accepts a boy, Ron, who is experiencing trouble at school as well as with the police. Ron's teacher reports that he is two grade levels behind on every subject, he has violent temper outbursts in the classroom, and acts as a negative leader to other students. The worker sets three practice objectives for Ron: first, that he should perform academically at his own grade level; second, that he should express anger in appropriate ways; third, that he should display positive leadership behaviors. In using the medical analogy above, delinquency is the disease and Ron's poor grades, inappropriate anger expression, and few leadership skills are symptoms of the disease—the practice objectives. It should be noted that Ron could have displayed other ways in which delinquent behavior could be exhibited (e.g., skipping school, criminal behavior, joining a street gang).

Weighting Practice Objectives

Each of the three practice objectives for Ron presented in Figure 6.1 is assigned a weight between 1 and 10 based on the worker's perception of its clinical importance. The first practice objective receives a weighting of 7, the second of 3, and the third of 9. These practice objectives, with their weights, are shown at the top of Ron's goal attainment scale in Figure 6.1 (Atler & Evens, 1990).

Next, each practice objective is operationalized; that is, a precise meaning is assigned to such phrases as "displays positive leadership" and "expresses anger in appropriate ways" so that the objective is measurable. Each objective is then rated on a 5-point scale ranging from –2 to +2 (see left-hand column of Figure 6.1) where:

–2	=	Much less than expected level of outcome
–1	=	Somewhat less than expected level of outcome
0	=	Expected level of outcome
+1	=	Somewhat more than expected level of outcome
+2	=	Much more than expected level of outcome

As can be seen from Figure 6.1, each point on the scale is anchored; that is, each of the five possible outcomes is operationalized in fairly precise terms. For example, the first practice objective, "Much more than expected level of outcome," is defined

Levels of Predicted Attainment	Scale #1 Ron achieves appropriate grade Weight = 7	Scale #2 Ron expresses anger appropriately level Weight = 3	Scale #3 Ron displays positive leadership Weight = 9
Much less than expected level of outcome (–2)	*Falls behind current level*	*Acts out in more destructive ways*	*Uses others all the time to achieve negative goals*
Somewhat less than expected level of outcome (–1)	*Stays at current level*	*Stays the same*	*Sometimes uses others to achieve negative goals*
Expected level of outcome (0)	*Gains three months*	*Shows some signs expressing anger in acceptable ways*	*Sometimes functions as a positive leader*
Somewhat more than expected level of outcome (+1)	*Gains six months*	*Rarely has tantrums*	*Has become a strong but inconsistent leader*
Much more than expected level of outcome (+2)	*Gains a year*	*Always expresses anger in acceptable ways*	*Never functions as a negative leader*

FIGURE 6.1   Ron's Goal Attainment Scale

as an increase from Ron's present grade level of two years behind to a level of only one year behind, that is, a gain of one year. Similarly, the second practice objective, "Somewhat more than expected level of outcome," is defined in terms of a decrease in number of tantrums, and specifically, their becoming "rare."

The Generation of Data

Once the scale has been established, a baseline score is obtained. As we will see in the following chapter, a baseline measure is a measure of the client's state before any intervention. Without this measure, it is impossible to know whether change has occurred, and so a baseline measurement is always critically important to any series of repeated measurements.

Ron's baseline score is determined by rating him on the scale very soon after he enters the home, when nothing in his behavior will have yet changed. The worker assigns him a score of –1 on the first practice objective, –1 on the second, and –2 on the third. Because the objectives are weighted, the goal attainment score is determined by multiplying each rating by the assigned weight and summing the results. Ron's baseline goal attainment score would then be calculated as follows:

First Practice Objective
   Weight =   7
   Rating = –1
   Score   =   7 × –1 = **–7**

Second Practice Objective
   Weight =   3
   Rating = –1
   Score   =   3 × –1 = **–3**

Third Practice Objective
   Weight =   9
   Rating = –2
   Score   =   9 × –2 = **–18**

Total Goal Attainment Score = (–7) + (–3) + (–18) = **–28**

As the ratings reflect the opinion of the rater, it is always preferable to have two or more people simultaneously rate the client. Let us say that Ron's teacher gives him the same rating as his worker on the first two practice objectives, but on the third she gives him a –1 instead of a –2. Ron's score on the third practice objective is then 9 × –1 = –9 according to his teacher, bringing his total score to –19 from the teachers point of view. Ron's baseline goal attainment score is then calculated as the average of the two scores, that is, (–28) + (–19)/2 = –23.5.

If the scores assigned by the two raters differ greatly, this is a sign that the anchor points on the scale have not been defined with sufficient precision. They will then have to be redefined and the ratings redone. The calculation of a baseline score therefore serves two purposes: It provides an initial score against which change can be measured, and it serves as a test of the measuring instrument.

Once a baseline score is established, the intervention is implemented and the client is repeatedly rated at whatever intervals seem appropriate. If the scale becomes outdated in light of the client's achievements, a new scale can be constructed for one or more practice objectives.

Advantages of GAS

The advantages of goal attainment scaling lie in its flexibility and its individualized approach. It can be used to measure process as well as outcome; that is, it can be used to evaluate what takes place during an intervention as well as the intervention results. It is readily adapted to any client in any situation, to any human service worker who wishes to assess the level of his or her own skills, and to any agency or organization undertaking an outcome evaluation.

Further, although the example given above was qualitative in that the anchor points on the scale were defined descriptively, quantitative anchor points such as scores on standardized measuring instruments or frequency counts can also be used. The term *quantitative*, as its name suggests, has to do with quantity or numbers, and so any measure involving a number rather than a description counts as quantitative.

Another advantage of goal attainment scaling is that the data obtained can be aggregated across a number of clients and put to various uses. For example, suppose the practitioners in Ron's home noticed that most of those who obtained a score of 5 or higher on the scales after a three-month stay succeeded in the program, whereas those with lower scores tended to fail. Goal attainment scores after the first three months might then be used to indicate whether a particular child should remain in the program or be referred to a different facility. In addition, aggregation of a number of individual scores will indicate the degree to which the program is successful as a whole.

Features of Good Measuring Instruments

As one might expect, some measuring instruments are better than others. There are five main features that distinguish a good instrument from a poor one: validity, reliability, sensitivity, nonreactivity, and utility.

Validity

A human service worker who cannot find an instrument to measure a particular practice or program objective—to decrease social isolation, for example—may be tempted to use an instrument that measures something closely related, say, loneliness. If instruments and concepts were really as interchangeable as that, no one would ever be quite sure what it was they were measuring. Note how the objective to "decrease social isolation" can be a practice objective as well as a program objective.

It is important to most human service professionals to know that the instrument they choose will measure what they want it to measure and not anything else. An instrument that measures what it is supposed to measure, and measures only that, is called a *valid* instrument (Bostwick & Kyte, 1993).

If a number of questions on a measuring instrument are intended to measure the degree of loneliness, and if the instrument is valid, these questions should adequately reflect the true substance of loneliness. For instance, people who are lonely tend to feel that they have no one to turn to; they feel misunderstood and out of tune with the people around them; they feel withdrawn and are unhappy about being withdrawn; and they feel that their relationships are superficial. Each of these feelings, common to lonely people, contributes to the overall concept of loneliness.

If a measuring instrument is to truly measure loneliness, it must tap each one of these feelings, or at least an adequate sample of them. That is, it must reflect what loneliness really is and enable the client to measure his or her feelings of loneliness against the entire spectrum of loneliness. For example: a person who feels misunderstood is lonely; a person who feels misunderstood and also feels withdrawn is more lonely; a person who feels misunderstood and withdrawn and has no one to talk to is still lonelier. The measure is all a matter of degree.

Note that in order to construct an instrument to measure loneliness, one has first to operationalize the concept of loneliness, that is, to decide what specific feelings comprise that concept. An instrument purporting to measure loneliness will therefore be valid to the extent that its authors have identified all the requisite feelings and have included an adequate sample of them in the instrument. An instrument containing such an adequate sample is said to be *content valid*. Because it is almost impossible to identify all of the feelings that make up a complex concept like loneliness or depression, no instrument will be entirely content valid, only more or less so.

Reliability

We have seen that, in testing for change, at least two and preferably more measurements are required. A human service worker who uses the same instrument more than once with the same client wants to assume that differences in the results (first measurement – second measurement = difference) are due to changes in the client. If this assumption is false—if the differences instead reflect, say, boredom with the questions—the instrument's results will give a false impression of the client's progress. It is therefore important that a measuring instrument gives the same result with the same unchanged client every time it is administered. An instrument that can do this is said to be *reliable*.

Of course, no client remains completely unchanged from one day to the next. The problem level may not have changed—the client may be just as depressed—but she may be more tired or less anxious about taking the test, or more physically uncomfortable because the day is hotter. These random and irrelevant changes will probably affect his or her score to some degree, but if the instrument is reliable, this degree will not be large. In fact, an instrument is said to be reliable to the extent that results are not affected by random changes in the individual.

Sensitivity

Because changes in a client's problem level are often small, it is important that a measuring instrument be able to detect small changes. What is needed, in fact, is an instrument that is stable or reliable enough to ignore irrelevant changes and *sensitive* enough to detect small changes in the level of the real problem.

The key to achieving such subtlety of discrimination is to select an appropriate measurement method. For example, suppose that a practice objective is to reduce the number of nights on which a child wets his bed. The measure selected might be a count of the number of mornings on which the bed is dry. If the bed is wet every morning for a month despite the worker's intervention, we could assume that the intervention is ineffective. But, if before the intervention started the child was wetting his bed five times a night and after intervention only once a night, the intervention has been successful in reducing the wetting episodes. However, this success was overlooked because the measurement method selected was in this context insensitive. It measured whether the problem occurred, which it either does or does not; there are no degrees of change in between.

The same considerations apply when a problem is indicated by more than one behavior. For example, a child may indicate problems with his teacher both by skipping the particular teacher's class and by being rude to the teacher when he or she is in class. If the rudeness occurs more often than the skipping, it is sensible to count incidents of rudeness rather than of skipping, because the high-frequency behavior is more likely to reveal small changes in the child's attitude toward his teacher than the low-frequency behavior.

Nonreactivity

Sometimes the very act of measurement affects the behavior, feeling, or knowledge level objective that is being measured. For example, cigarette smokers who begin to count the number of cigarettes they smoke may smoke fewer cigarettes simply as a result of the counting, without any other intervention being involved. Staff being evaluated may change their routine because they know they are being evaluated. A child who knows his television watching is being monitored by his mother may watch television less to please her or more to spite her, but in either case, the amount of television watching will have changed. It is therefore important that the instrument chosen be nonreactive or not affect the behavior, feeling, or knowledge objective being measured. A synonym for *nonreactive* is unobtrusive. Put another way, a worker's aim is to record a measurement as unobtrusively as possible.

Utility

Utility means usefulness. If a measuring instrument is to be useful, it also has to be practical in a particular situation with a particular client. For example, the best way to demonstrate to the client such changes as improved posture or more frequent eye contact may be by making video recordings of successive interviews. However, if the client refuses to be videotaped, this particular measurement method cannot be used. It may be a perfectly valid and reliable measure, but it lacks utility.

To give another example, a practitioner may discover a perfect instrument for measuring depression: It is valid, reliable, nonreactive, and sensitive to small changes, but it is also five pages long. In addition, it takes a long time to score and the numerical score, once obtained, is difficult to translate into a meaningful assessment of the client's depression. This instrument, though perfect in every other respect, is useless in practice because it takes too long to complete and too long to score and interpret. Instruments that have utility are acceptable to the client; they are easy and quick to administer and score; and they give results that reveal the client's current state.

Naturally, an instrument that is short enough to have utility may be too short to be entirely valid. It may be impossible, for example, to sample loneliness adequately in a 10-item questionnaire. As is often the case, this is a matter for compromise: a situation in which the instrument developer's best judgment is the only real guide.

Locating Standardized Measuring Instruments

Once the need for measurement has been established, the next consideration is locating appropriate standardized measuring instruments from which to choose. The two general sources for locating such instruments are commercial or professional publishers and professional literature (Jordan, Franklin, & Corcoran, 1993).

Publishers

Numerous commercial and professional publishing companies specialize in the production and sale of standardized measuring instruments for use in the human services. A selected list of publishers is presented in Figure 6.2.

The cost of instruments purchased from a publisher varies considerably, depending on the instrument, the number of copies needed, and the publisher. The instruments generally are well developed and their psychometric properties are supported by the results of several research studies. Often they are accompanied by manuals that include the normative data for the instrument. As well, publishers are expected to comply with professional standards such as those established by the American Psychological Association. These standards apply to claims made about the instrument's rationale, development, psychometric properties, administration, and interpretation of results.

Standards for the use of some instruments have been developed to protect the interests of clients. Consequently, purchasers of instruments may be required to have certain qualifications, such as possession of an advanced degree in a relevant field. A few publishers require membership in particular professional organizations. Most publishers will, however, accept an order from a human service student if it is co-signed by a qualified person, such as an instructor, who will supervise the use of the instrument.

Professional Journals and Books

Standardized measuring instruments are most commonly reproduced in human service journals; in fact, most commercially marketed instruments first appear in one of these publications. The instruments usually are supported by evidence of

Academic Therapy Publications, 20 Commercial Boulevard, Novato, CA, 94947; (415) 883-3314.

Behavior Science Press, P.O. Box BV, University, AL, 35486; (205) 759-2089.

Biometrics Research, Research Assessment and Training Unit, New York State Psychiatric Institute, 722 West 168th Street, Room 341, New York, NY, 10032; (212) 960-5534.

Bureau of Educational Measurements, Emporia State University, Emporia, KS, 66801; (316) 343-1200.

Center for Epidemiologic Studies, Department of Health and Human Services, 5600 Fishers Lane, Rockville, MD, 20857; (301) 443-4513.

Consulting Psychologists Press, Inc., 577 College Avenue, P.O. Box 11636, Palo Alto, CA, 94306; (415) 857-1444.

Educational and Industrial Testing Service (EDITS), P.O. Box 7234, San Diego, CA, 92107; (619) 222-1666.

Family Life Publications, Inc., Box 427, Saluda, NC, 28773; (704) 749-4971.

Institute for Personality and Ability Testing, Inc. (IPAT), P.O. Box 188, 1062 Coronado Drive, Champaign, IL, 61820; (213) 652-2922.

Merrill Publishing Company, 1300 Alum Creek Drive, Box 508, Columbus, OH, 43216; (614) 258-8441.

Personnel Research Institute (PRI), Psychological Research Services, Case Western Reserve University, 11220 Bellflower Road, Cleveland, OH, 44106; (216) 368-3546.

Professional Assessment Services Division, National Computer Systems, P.O. Box 1416, Minneapolis, MN, 55440; (800) 328-6759.

Psychological Assessment Resources, Inc., P.O. Box 98, Odessa, FL, 33556; (813) 920-6357.

Psychological Services, Inc., Suite 1200, 3450 Wilshire Boulevard, Los Angeles, CA, 90010; (213) 738-1132.

Research Concepts, A Division of Test Maker, Inc., 1368 East Airport Road, Muskegon, MI, 49444; (616) 739-7401.

Research Press, Box 317760, Champaign, IL, 61820; (217) 352-3273.

Science Research Associates, Inc. (SRA), 155 North Wacker Drive, Chicago, IL, 60606; (800) 621-0664, in Illinois (312) 984-2000.

Scott, Foresman, & Company, Test Division, 1900 East Lake Avenue, Glenview, IL, 60025; (708) 729-3000.

U.S. Department of Defense, Testing Directorate, Headquarters, Military Enlistment Processing Command, Attention: MEPCT, Fort Sheridan, IL, 60037; (708) 926-4111.

University Associates, Inc., Learning Resources Corporation, 8517 Production Avenue, P.O. Box 26240, San Diego, CA, 92126; (714) 578-5900.

WALMYR Publishing Company, P.O. Box 24779, Tempe, AZ, 85285; (602) 897-8168.

Western Psychological Services, 12031 Wilshire Boulevard, Los Angeles, CA, 90025; (213) 478-2061.

FIGURE 6.2　Publishers of Standardized Measuring Instruments

Adapted from Catheleen Jordan, Cynthia Franklin, & Kevin Corcoran, Standardized measuring instruments. In R. M. Grinnell, Jr. (Ed.), *Social Work Research and Evaluation* (4th ed.). Itasca, IL: F. E. Peacock Publishers. © 1993. Used with permission.

Books Reprinting Standardized Measuring Instruments:

J. R. Cautela. (1988). *Behavior Analysis Forms for Clinical Intervention,* (vols. 1 and 2). Champaign, IL: Research Press.

K. J. Corcoran & J. Fischer. (1994). *Measures for Clinical Practice* (2nd ed., 2 vols.). New York: Free Press.

W. W. Hudson. (1982). *The Clinical Measurement Package: A Field Manual.* Newbury Park, CA: Wadsworth.

J. Krysik, I. Hoffart, & R. M. Grinnell, Jr. (1993). *Student Study Guide* to accompany the fourth edition of *Social Work Research and Evaluation.* Itasca, IL: Peacock.

E. J. Mash & L. G. Terdal (Eds.). (1976). *Behavior Therapy Assessment.* New York: Springer.

P. S. Nurius & W. W. Hudson. (1993). *Human Services: Practice, Evaluation, and Computers.* Pacific Grove, CA: Brooks/Cole.

J. P. Robinson & P. R. Shaver. (1973). *Measures of Social Psychological Attitudes* (rev. ed.). Ann Arbor, MI: Institute for Social Research.

Professional Journals Publishing Standardized Instruments:

Applied Behavioral Measurement
Behavior Assessment
Behavioral Therapy
Educational and Psychological Measurement
Evaluation
Family Process
Journal of Behavioral Assessment and Psychopathology
Journal of Clinical Psychology
Journal of Consulting and Clinical Psychology
Journal of Personality Assessment
Research on Social Work Practice
Measurement and Evaluation in Counseling and Development

FIGURE 6.3   Books and Journals Publishing Standardized Measuring Instruments

Adapted from Catheleen Jordan, Cynthia Franklin, & Kevin Corcoran, Standardized measuring instruments. In R. M. Grinnell, Jr. (Ed.), *Social Work Research and Evaluation* (4th ed.). Itasca, IL: F. E. Peacock Publishers. © 1993. Used with permission.

their validity and reliability, although they often require cross-validation and normative data from more representative samples and subsamples.

Locating instruments in journals or books is not easy. Of the two most common methods, computer searches of databanks and manual searches of the literature, the former is faster, unbelievably more thorough, and easier to use. Unfortunately, financial support for the development of comprehensive databanks has been limited and intermittent. Another disadvantage is that many articles on instruments are not referenced with the appropriate indicators for computer retrieval. These limitations are being overcome by the changing technology of computers and information retrieval systems. Several services now allow for a complex breakdown of measurement need; databanks that include references from over 1,300 journals, updated monthly, are now available from a division of Psychological Abstracts Information Services and Bibliographic Retrieval Services.

Nevertheless, most human service professionals will probably rely on manual searches of references such as *Psychological Abstracts*. Although the reference indices will be the same as those in the databanks accessible by computer, the literature search can be supplemented with appropriate seminal (original) reference volumes.

Figure 6.3 provides a selected list of books and journals that publish standardized measuring instruments that are likely to be found in a computerized or manual search of the literature. In using these sources, one is compelled to rely on the knowledge or judgment of the author or editor. These sources do, however, provide a point of departure for locating appropriate measuring instruments.

Evaluating Standardized Measuring Instruments

A literature search should produce several instruments suitable for measuring a particular program or practice objective. The choice of one instrument over others depends on the strength of the quantitative data the instrument provides as well as its practicality in application. These two dimensions can be evaluated by asking a number of questions pertaining to the validity and reliability of the instrument, the population sample to be used, and the practicality of administering the instrument (Figure 6.4). The validity and reliability of both the instrument and the data collected by it are the most crucial concerns in evaluating any instrument. As these factors were discussed in detail above, the following discussion is confined to issues of sampling and practicality.

Representativeness of the Sample

One aspect of evaluating standardized instruments is the extent to which the data collected in setting the norms for the instrument represent the same types of individuals who are being measured. For example, if the instrument being considered was formulated and tested on a sample drawn from a white Anglo-Saxon population, it might give perfectly valid results when administered to white Anglo-Saxons, but not if it is administered to Native Americans, African Americans, or social minorities such as women. In general terms, the samples used in setting the norms for an instrument must reflect a population that is similar to those who will complete that instrument. Demographic characteristics such as age, gender, race, and socioeconomic status must also be considered.

Another consideration is the size of the sample: the larger the sample, the better. A further concern is when the data were collected from the sample. Data based on samples selected a long time ago may not be an adequate basis for accepting the instrument as psychometrically sound for contemporary use.

The Sample from Which Data Were Drawn:

1. Are the samples representative of pertinent populations?
2. Are the sample sizes sufficiently large?
3. Are the samples homogeneous?
4. Are the subsamples pertinent to respondents' demographics?
5. Are the data obtained from the samples up to date?

The Validity of the Instrument:

1. Is the content domain clearly and specifically defined?
2. Was there a logical procedure for including the items?
3. Is the criterion measure relevant to the instrument?
4. Was the criterion measure reliable and valid?
5. Is the theoretical construct clearly and correctly stated?
6. Do the scores converge with other relevant measures?
7. Do the scores discriminate from irrelevant variables?
8. Are there cross-validation studies that conform to the above concerns?

The Reliability of the Instrument:

1. Is there sufficient evidence of internal consistency?
2. Is there equivalence between various forms?
3. Is there stability over a relevant time interval?

The Practicality of Application:

1. Is the instrument an appropriate length?
2. Is the content socially acceptable to respondents?
3. Is the instrument feasible to complete?
4. Is the instrument relatively direct?
5. Does the instrument have utility?
6. Is the instrument relatively nonreactive?
7. Is the instrument sensitive to measuring change?
8. Is the instrument feasible to score?

**FIGURE 6.4   Questions to Be Asked in Evaluating a Standardized Measuring
Instrument**

From Catheleen Jordan, Cynthia Franklin, & Kevin Corcoran, Standardized measuring instruments. In
R. M. Grinnell, Jr. (Ed.), *Social Work Research and Evaluation* (4th ed.). Itasca, IL: F. E. Peacock Publishers.
© 1993. Used with permission.

Practicality of Application

An instrument's practicality of application depends on its ease of implementation
and ease of analysis of the data it generates. The first three practicality questions in
Figure 6.4 concern the likelihood that the client will complete the instrument, for
even the most valid and reliable instrument has no practical utility if it is left
unanswered.

Likelihood of Completion

A longer instrument is usually more reliable than a shorter one, but it is also more time-consuming and so may not be completed by the client. This fact is especially important in case-level designs where multiple measures are needed, to be discussed in the following chapter.

The social acceptability of a measuring instrument turns on the client's, not the worker's, view of the appropriateness of the content. The content's perceived appropriateness as a measure of the program or practice objective of interest—not what the instrument in fact measures but what it *appears* to measure—is referred to as *face validity*. In addition, an instrument that is offensive or insulting to clients will not be completed. Instruments should also be easy for clients to complete, with content and instructions that are neither above nor below their typical level of functioning, and questions that can be easily answered.

Interpretation of Results

The remaining five questions in Figure 6.4 concerning practicality of application focus on the meaning or interpretation of the results provided by the instrument. Interpretation is easiest when the instrument provides direct measurements, has utility, is nonreactive, is sensitive to small changes, and is easy to score.

Program and practice objectives that can be measured directly are often behavioral. Other practice objectives, such as self-esteem or depression, can be measured only indirectly, or through some behavior that is believed to be associated with the objective.

An instrument is considered to have utility if the results provide some practical advantage or useful data. The significance of the results is obviously influenced by whether the instrument is reactive. The instrument has to be sensitive enough to pick up small changes in the program or practice objective being measured.

A final consideration is what is done with the instrument after it has been completed. It may seem self-evident that if an instrument is to provide meaningful data it must be possible to score it. However, the scoring procedures of many instruments are too complicated and time-consuming to be practical in practice situations. Even though they are psychometrically sound, they should be eliminated in favor of others that can more easily be scored.

Summary

This chapter has discussed the concept of measurement: what measurement is, what a measuring instrument is, what will be measured, and by what method it will be measured. Rating scales, including graphic rating scales and self-anchored scales, were discussed along with summated scales and Goal Attainment Scaling. In addition, we considered the features required of a good measuring instrument.

Key Terms

Graphic Rating Scale: A type of measuring instrument that describes an attribute on a continuum from one extreme to the other, with points of the continuum ordered in equal intervals and assigned numbers.

Measure: A label, usually numerical, assigned to an observation that has been subjected to measurement.

Measurement: The process of systematically assigning labels to observations; in statistics, measurement systems are classified according to level of measurement and usually produce data that can be represented in numerical form; the assignment of numerals to objects or events according to specific rules.

Measuring Instruments: Instruments such as questionnaires or rating scales used to obtain a measure for a particular client or client group.

Nonreactivity: An unobtrusive characteristic of a measuring instrument; nonreactive measuring instruments do not affect the behavior being measured.

Norm: In measurement, an average or set group standard of achievement that can be used to interpret individual scores; normative data describing statistical properties of a measuring instrument, such as means and standard deviations.

Rating Scales: A type of measuring instrument in which responses are rated on a continuum or in an ordered set of categories, with numerical values assigned to each point or category.

Reliability: (1) The degree of accuracy, precision, or consistency of results of a measuring instrument, including the ability to reproduce results when a variable is measured more than once or a test is repeatedly filled out by the same individual. (2) The degree to which individual differences on scores or in data are due either to true differences or to errors in measurement.

Response Bias: The tendency for individuals to score items on a measuring instrument in such a manner that one score is reported for the majority of all items.

Self-Anchored Rating Scale: A type of measuring instrument in which respondents rate themselves on a continuum of values, according to their own referents for each point.

Standardized Measurement Instrument: A paper-and-pencil tool, usually constructed by researchers and used by human service professionals, to measure a particular area of knowledge, behavior, or feeling; provides for uniform administration and scoring and generates normative data against which later results can be evaluated.

Summated Scale: A multi-item measuring instrument in which respondents provide a rating for each item. The summation of items provides an overall score.

Utility: A characteristic of a measuring instrument that indicates its degree of usefulness (e.g., how practical is the measuring instrument in a particular situation?).

Validity: The degree to which a measuring instrument accurately measures the variable it claims to measure.

Variable: A characteristic that can take on different values for different individuals; any attribute whose value, or level, can change; any characteristic (of a person, object, or situation) that can change value or kind from observation to observation.

Study Questions

1. How can demographic information used in developing a standardized measurement instrument influence the interpretation of scores obtained by a single client?

2. A human service practitioner who has 10 years of clinical experience with depressed clients develops a 10-item scale to measure depression. What are the issues of validity

and reliability that this person must consider before using the scale as an interpretive guide to clinical decision making?

3. In your opinion, what were the advantages and disadvantages for the client of using measuring instruments in the intervention process for the client in Case Study B?

4. How might other sources of data (e.g., friends, relatives, worker) have been helpful to the intervention process with the client in Case Study B? Do you think other sources of data would have been useful? Why or why not?

5. In your opinion, did the use of measuring instruments restrict or enhance the clinical creativity of the practitioners in Case Study B? Explain your answer.

6. In groups of four, have each member list his or her biases or beliefs about the use of measuring instruments in the human services. As a group, discuss the nature of each individual bias and determine how such biases affect client service delivery.

7. In groups of four, develop a hypothetical practice objective for a client who has difficulty in managing anger. Assign one type of measuring instrument to each member of the group, and have each individual develop a scale to measure the stated practice objective. Discuss the advantages and disadvantages of each type of scale, and select the best one. Present your decision to the class.

8. Your colleagues wonder why measurement of the practice objectives they have established for their clients is necessary. How do you respond?

9. Why are objective methods of assessment so important in the human services? Why are objective definitions of program and practice objectives important in the human services?

10. What are standardized measuring instruments? What types of information should accompany them?

11. You are a worker at a local immigrant society. You submit all Asian-American clients to a standardized instrument measuring self-esteem. They all perform poorly on the instrument. Would you immediately specify increased self-esteem as a practice or program objective with your clients? Why or why not?

12. What do rating scales measure? How?

13. Specify a practice objective that can be described on a continuum from one extreme to another. Develop a graphic rating scale for this objective.

14. Develop a summated rating scale to measure the practice objective you specified in the above question.

15. Suppose you are a member of a self-help group designed to enhance your ability to interact with others and overcome your shyness. Define your practice objective and develop a 9-point self-anchored rating scale to measure this objective. Why would it be important for your group leader to cross-validate the data gathered from your scale with other sources? What are other possible sources of data?

16. Under what circumstances would a worker measure a practice objective with a summated scale? Why? Explain in detail.

17. As a practitioner you will want to choose good measuring instruments when measuring a particular objective. How will you be able to distinguish good instruments from poor ones?

18. When measuring program or practice objectives, why is it important to choose the instrument that will measure the objective and not something or anything else?

19. What is the optimum time interval between repeated measurement of program and practice objectives? How is this determined? Provide an example in your discussion.

Part III

EVALUATION DESIGNS FOR QUALITY IMPROVEMENT

Chapter 7
Using Case-Level Evaluations

Chapter 8
Using Program-Level Evaluations

Chapter 9
Using Sampling Procedures

All types of evaluations are used in the quality improvement process. Part III describes the most frequently used case-level and program-level design options available. Human service professionals desiring to evaluate changes in their clients' progress can rely on one of several case-level evaluation methodologies (Chapter 7). However, at other times, it is appropriate to evaluate entire programs or specific components of programs. In such situations, the progress of a group of cases is of interest and evaluators can choose one of several program-level evaluation designs (Chapter 8). Closely associated with group-level evaluation is the selection of a sample, which determines the extent to which results may be generalized. Commonly used approaches to sampling are described in Chapter 9.

7

USING CASE-LEVEL EVALUATIONS

THE PREVIOUS CHAPTER discussed the measurement process: what and how program and practice objectives can be measured, who should measure them, when and where they can be measured, and what measuring instruments can be used. This chapter considers how the measurement process can help human service professionals to evaluate their practice efforts at the case level with the use of consultations and case conferences, and with the use of case-level evaluation designs. The advantages and limitations of these designs are also discussed.

Informal Case-Level Evaluations

An empirical method of evaluation is one in which the evaluation is based on the analysis of systematically collected valid and reliable data, that is, on the collation and interpretation of data generated by standardized measuring instruments. Correspondingly, nonempirical evaluations are derived from information developed from theories and descriptions considered relevant by the practitioner. Because nonempirical information collection is relatively less formal and rigorous than its empirical data collection counterpart, it is also known as *informal evaluation*. There are two informal methods that human service workers can use to evaluate their cases at the case level: private case consultations and case conferences.

Case Consultations

Many professionals consult informally with others regarding their cases. These requests for advice are usually accompanied by a description of the client's circumstances, the interventions the worker has tried so far, and the present condition of the client as perceived by the practitioner. Sometimes these descriptions are written, but more often than not, communication is verbal. In either case the consultation is informal because no authority structure mandates or controls it. And it is nonempirical because the information exchanged is not derived from data obtained through standardized measurement.

The disadvantages of case consultations lie in their lack of objectivity and precision, or in other words, in their nonempirical nature. Their main advantage is their efficiency, which is a function of their informal nature: Rapid exchange of ideas and information are facilitated by the absence of formal documentation and procedures.

Case Conferences

Case conferences tend to be more formal than private consultations in that the human service worker and other professionals are usually required to attend, and minutes may be taken and disseminated to participants. Nevertheless, the presentation of the case tends to remain nonempirical, a description reflecting the practitioner's point of view. Concurring and opposing viewpoints are generally couched in the same lack of precision. Although much information of value may be exchanged, it is not data derived from standardized measurements and, therefore, its reliability and validity are unknown.

The major advantage of a case conference is that all human service workers involved with a particular client can meet face to face, share their perceptions or concerns, and perhaps leave the conference feeling that they have been heard, something has been resolved, and future problems can be addressed with the help of people who have already shown themselves to be caring and cooperative. As before, the disadvantages are lack of objectivity and lack of precision. While private consultations and case conferences are a very important part of professional human service practice, these two informal evaluation methods should be used in conjunction with formal case-level evaluations.

Formal Case-Level Evaluations

Formal case-level evaluation designs can be used by human service workers in many ways. Unlike case consultations and case conferences mentioned above, they are formal, empirical methods of evaluation, based on the analysis of collected data usually generated by standardized measuring instruments. They are sometimes known as single-system research designs, single-subject research designs, idiographic research designs, $N = 1$ research designs, time-series designs, and subject-replication research designs.

Whatever name is used, case-level evaluation is a study of one entity—*a* single client, *a* single group, *a* single couple, *a* single family, *a* single organization, or *a* single community—involving repeated measurements over time in order to measure change. The results of a number of formal case-level evaluations can be aggregated to assess the effectiveness of a program as a whole. However, case-level designs are, first and foremost, used to measure client practice objectives.

Formal case-level evaluations focus on practitioners' activities and their clients' practice objective outcomes so that cause-effect relationships can be established in some cases. There are a large number of case-level evaluation designs, ranging from the qualitative to the quantitative and from the exploratory to the explanatory, as illustrated in Figure 7.1. We have seen that the term *qualitative* refers to a description in words, which is less precise than a *quantitative* description, or one given in numbers. An *explanatory* study is one in which the worker manipulates certain factors in order to gain a greater degree of control over the treatment process. A *descriptive* study involves less manipulation and hence less control, and an *exploratory* study involves no manipulation and virtually no control. The case consultations and case conferences mentioned earlier in this chapter fall into the qualitative, exploratory category at the far left of the range.

It should be stressed that the characterization in Figure 7.1 is a *continuum;* that is, there is no point at which qualitative becomes quantitative or descriptive becomes explanatory. Various evaluation designs are placed on the continuum ac-

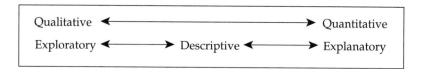

FIGURE 7.1   **Case-Level Evaluation Design Continuum**

cording to the degree to which they manifest descriptive and manipulative qualities. These degrees tend to merge and blend, so that it is often difficult to place a particular design in a particular category.

Formal case-level designs are one of the most promising evaluative tools available to line-level practitioners (Thyer, 1993). A number of features are integral to these designs: (1) baselines, (2) measurable practice objectives, (3) repeated measurements, (4) graphic data displays, and (5) comparisons across phases.

Establishing Baselines

A baseline is essentially a measure of the client's practice objective *before* the professional provides services. By establishing a baseline, the worker attempts to find out how long the problematic event lasts, how often it occurs, at what intensity, or whether it occurs at all in the client's normal life.

For example, suppose that a child throws temper tantrums. Before intervening, the worker will want to know how frequent and intense these tantrums are, when and where they occur, and for how long they last, in addition to trying to gain insight into the events that precipitate or alleviate them. An obvious way to gain such knowledge is to do nothing in the way of intervention while collecting the necessary data. The parents might be asked to keep a client log (such as the one depicted in Figure 5.2) in which they record the day, date, and start and finish time of each episode together with the events that occurred immediately preceding, during, and after it. Alternatively, a standardized measure might be used, over a period of time, to measure the magnitude of the problem. In either case, at the end of the period, the practitioner will have baseline data on the tantrums as well as some data about possible precipitating events. These data provide a standard against which change can be measured, and provide some indication of the most effective interventive method to use.

Measurable Practice Objectives

We have stressed in previous chapters that program and practice objectives must be measurable; they should be defined in a way that allows their degree of achievement to be observed and measured. For example, three distinct practice objectives can be set for the child with the tantrums: to reduce the *frequency* of the episodes, to reduce their *intensity*, and to reduce their *duration*. In each case, it must be clear exactly what is meant by a "temper tantrum." What behaviors, specifically, are observable when a temper tantrum occurs? How can the tantrums be measured when it occurs? The frequency and duration of tantrums can be easily measured using techniques described in Chapter 6; the intensity might be measured using a self-anchored rating scale. The idea that a practice objective must be measurable thus has two conceptual components: The objective must be specifically defined and measurable.

Repeated Measurements

Formal case-level evaluation designs rely on repeated valid and reliable measurements: change is perceived and measured by repeated administrations of the same measuring instrument under the same conditions. Repeated measurements document trends (if any), and how the practice objective is changing over time.

Graphic Data Display

A *data display* is the way in which the collected data are set out on the page; the manner in which they are set out in turn depends on how the original data were grouped or collated. For example: the respective numbers of African-American, Caucasian, or Oriental clients attending a particular program may be presented merely as a list of numerals. For ease of interpretation, these numbers can also be presented in the form of a bar graph or line diagram, or they may be converted into percentages and displayed as a pie chart. Figure 7.2 illustrates these four methods of displaying data. Most people find it easier to see what data mean when they are displayed as a graph or chart rather than as a list. Data collected in formal case-level studies are usually presented graphically, with the level of the practice objective plotted on the vertical line and time plotted on the horizontal line.

Let us take as an example Ms Jarrett, who suffers from depression. The practitioner measures the magnitude of her depression every week for three weeks using a standardized measuring instrument for depression. No intervention is attempted during this time; the object is to obtain a baseline measure of Ms Jarrett's depression. The first time the instrument is administered, Ms Jarrett scores 55; the second time, 52; the third time, 40. The practitioner might plot these scores on a graph as illustrated in Figure 7.3.

The vertical axis of the graph is labelled "Depression Level." What is really being plotted is the magnitude of Ms Jarrett's depression. The horizontal axis of the graph is labelled "Time in Weeks." This indicates that changes in the magnitude of Ms Jarrett's depression are being monitored over a period of time, measured in weeks.

The practice objective, then, is what the practitioner and client are trying to change. Repeated measurement of the objective will show any change that has occurred during the course of the intervention; that is, it will show an *effect*. The

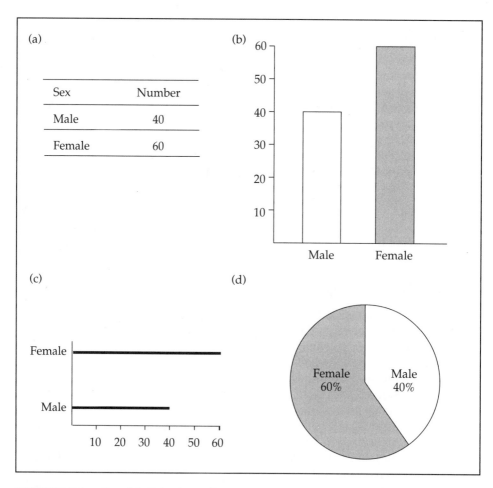

FIGURE 7.2   Graphic Displays of Data: (a) Tabular, (b) Bar Graph, (c) Line Diagram, (d) Pie Chart

length of intervention (activity), undertaken to achieve the effect, is plotted on the horizontal line. For example, a block watch program may be initiated in a community to decrease the number of incidents involving harm or injury to children. This can easily be a practice objective when the community's goal is to "keep children safe." The activities of the block watch program may be measured over time as the number of households participating increases. The months the program is in effect might then be plotted on the horizontal line. The practice objective—the reported number of incidents involving harm or injury to children—will be plotted on the vertical line, as shown in Figure 7.4.

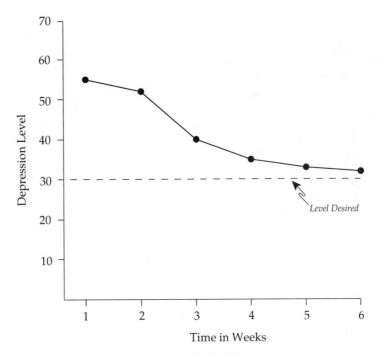

FIGURE 7.3 **Magnitude of Ms Jarrett's Depression Levels over a Six-Week Period**

(Note: high scores = high depression levels)

Comparison across Phases

A *phase* is any distinct part of the contact between a human service worker and a client. For example, the first few weeks of service may be spent collecting baseline data: This is one phase. Then an intervention (services) may be tried: This is the second phase. If the services do not seem to be effective, a different intervention may be tried: This is the third phase.

It is customary to use letters to designate the different phases. The letter *A* represents the baseline phase. Successive interventions are represented by successive letters: *B* for the first, *C* for the second, *D* for the third, and so on. A case-level evaluation design in which a baseline phase is followed by an interventive phase is therefore called an *AB* design. Similarly, an *ABC* design is one in which a baseline phase (*A*) is followed by two different interventive phases (*B* and *C*).

If an intervention is not really different but is merely a slight variation of one tried before, it is represented by the original letter plus a subscript. For example, one way of improving knowledge in a certain area may be to set homework assignments. This may be the first intervention tried, or Phase *B*. If understanding does not improve to the desired degree, the number of homework assignments set may be increased. This second intervention is merely an intensified version of the first and would be designated Phase B_2, with the first intervention now considered B_1. A

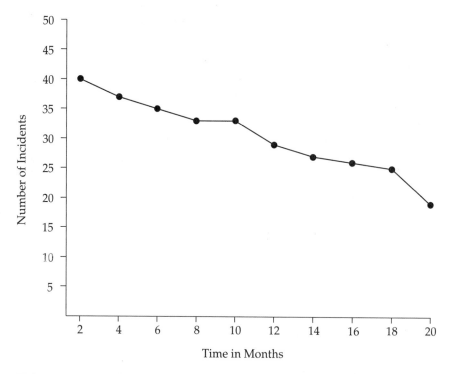

FIGURE 7.4   Incidents Involving Harm to Children over Time

design in which a baseline phase is followed by three versions of the same intervention would thus be written $AB_1B_2B_3$.

Phases are usually represented on a graph by dashed vertical lines and are labelled as shown in Figure 7.5.

Such graphs are useful because they allow changes in the practice objective—in this case, TV watching—to be followed through the various interventive phases. The graph in Figure 7.5 shows that the first intervention was not successful at all (*B*)—the pattern of TV watching scarcely changed; that the second intervention was more effective (*C*); and that the third intervention, a combination of the previous two, was more effective yet (*BC*). Had this graph been presented as three separate graphs—one for each intervention—the complete picture would have been lost. For this reason data for successive interventions are usually presented on the same graph, enabling comparison across phases (Bloom, Fischer, & Orme, 1994).

Formal Evaluation Design Continuum

There are essentially three types of case-level designs: exploratory, descriptive, and explanatory. All three types of designs can be used for purposes of quality improvement as well as for purposes of knowledge building. Exploratory case-level designs

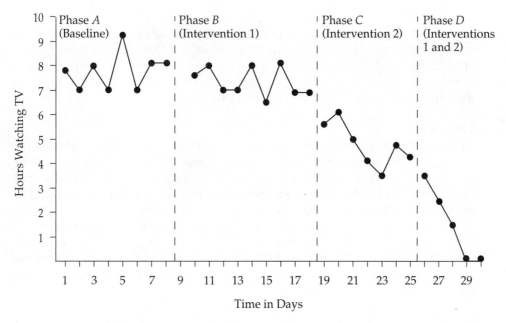

FIGURE 7.5 **Graph Depicting Different Phases of a Human Service Program including Baseline (*A*), Intervention 1 (*B*), Intervention 2 (*C*), and a Combination of Interventions 1 and 2 (*D*)**

are the most commonly used for quality improvement purposes because they involve continuous monitoring of client progress. Nevertheless, the other two types of designs, descriptive and explanatory designs, also produce data that can be valuable for quality improvement purposes. While exploratory designs can contribute to knowledge development, descriptive and explanatory designs are the most useful for this purpose.

Exploratory Designs

The purposes of exploratory designs is to explore, to assess how things are going, and to build a foundation of general ideas and tentative theories that can be confirmed or abandoned later, using more rigorous designs. Exploratory designs will not produce conclusive or statistically definitive results. When an exploratory design is used, it is not possible to *prove* that the intervention caused the outcome; although it may be assumed that if an intervention is followed by a desired client outcome, then the intervention had something to do with the outcome. Exploratory designs measure and monitor the outcome of practice objectives without attempting to prove a causal link between those outcomes and the activities believed to have engendered them.

Although exploratory designs have their limitations from a scientific perspective, they are highly useful for quality improvement purposes. These designs can provide ongoing feedback about client progress, allowing the practitioner to make intervention decisions based on empirical data. This makes it likely that ineffective services will be quickly discontinued or modified and that effective interventions will be maintained—in short, that the most appropriate services will be provided to clients. In addition, these designs are less intrusive, less disruptive, and easier to implement than descriptive and explanatory designs.

B *Designs*

The simplest exploratory design is the *B* design. The *B* design tells us whether the client's practice objective is changing in the desired direction. If the level of the client's practice objective is not changing in the way that it should, we can at least wonder whether other interventions should be tried. The *B* design can monitor the level of the client's practice objective over time (Nelsen, 1988).

Figure 7.6 provides an example of a *B* design that was used by a practitioner to measure the practice objective "to reduce Jeff's clinical stress level over a 10-week period." The design only indicates that Jeff's stress level was decreasing. If the stress levels were not decreasing over time, the worker should at least consider whether other interventions should be attempted.

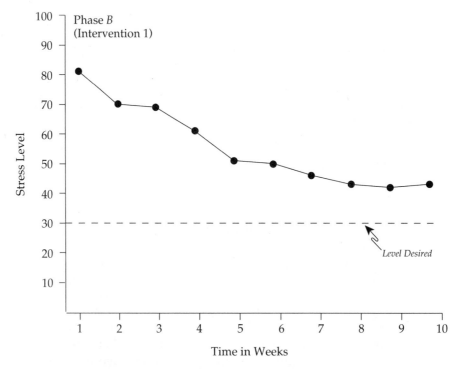

FIGURE 7.6   Jeff's Stress Levels over a 10-Week Period
(Note: high scores = high stress levels)

The *B* design is useful in showing changes in the level of a problem or need. While a *B* design may provide clues about the degree to which a client is achieving his or her practice objectives, no extraneous factors are accounted for, and no suggestion of a causal relationship is possible. Consequently, no conclusions can be easily drawn regarding the relative merits and efficacy of the worker's interventions. The value of the *B* design, therefore, lies in two basic areas. First, it is quick and simple to implement. Second, it allows for the systematic monitoring of changing levels in the achievement of practice objectives.

Descriptive Designs

Descriptive designs are often called quasi-experimental designs. The prefix *quasi-* means "having some resemblance." Thus, a quasi-experiment is one that resembles a true experiment but is lacking some essential ingredient. To understand what the essential ingredient is, it is necessary to say something about the characteristics of a true experiment.

The purpose of a true experiment is to demonstrate with certainty that something causes something else, or, in the cases that concern us, that a certain activity caused an observed change in a client's practice objective. We can demonstrate this causal connection by proving that nothing else could have caused the observed change. For example, suppose that Ms Jarrett is still being treated for depression. Repeated measurement has shown that Ms Jarrett's depression level underwent a marked decrease over a period of one month.

To prove that the interventive strategy alone caused the observed decrease, we must prove that she did not win a lottery during that month, did not have a joyful reunion with her long-lost son, did not find a satisfying job. . . . In short, we have to prove that nothing, aside from the intervention, happened that could have decreased her depression. All of the things that might have happened to Ms Jarrett are called *extraneous variables* because they might also have influenced the attainment of the practice objective; they could have confounded the desired establishment of a cause-effect relationship between the intervention and the client outcome.

Because the number of extraneous variables that may have lightened Ms Jarrett's depression is so enormous, the best way of testing for causality is to have two identical Ms Jarretts, one experiencing only the extraneous variables and the other experiencing both the extraneous variables *and* the intervention. Comparison of the state of mind of the two Ms Jarretts will then reveal how much of the reduced depression was due to the extraneous variables and how much to the intervention. Or, the equivalent of a comparison of two Ms Jarretts can be obtained by comparing groups, as will be discussed in the following chapter. However, in case-level evaluation there is only one Ms Jarrett; some other solution to the difficulty must be found.

The best solution, with only one case (client), is to repeat the experiment: to obtain baseline data, implement an intervention, measure the resulting change, and then bring the client back to the baseline level and do it all again. If the intervention succeeds in bringing about the desired change the second time, it is more probable that the intervention, rather than extraneous variables, was the causal agent.

As should be obvious, there are several problems associated with this procedure. In the first place, it is hardly ethical to return a client deliberately to an original problematic condition; in the second place, it is rarely possible to do so because a useful intervention does not cease to have an effect when it is stopped. For these reasons, it is difficult to implement all the features of a true experiment. Specifically, returning the client to baseline and repeating the treatment are rarely implemented in practice. However, the remaining aspects of these designs, which are more practical to apply, are incorporated in the descriptive designs described in this section.

Three descriptive evaluation designs can be used in formal case-level evaluations: AB designs, $AB_1B_2B_3$ designs, and ABC designs.

AB *Designs*

As indicated earlier, an AB design is one in which a baseline phase (A) is followed by a single interventive phase (B). The assumption underlying this design is that the level of the practice objective in the baseline phase (A) will continue unchanged if the worker does not intervene (B) to change it. On the face of it, this seems like a reasonable assumption but, if the practice objective happens to be Ms Jarrett's depression, innumerable extraneous variables are waiting in the wings. In fact, one can argue that the first contact with the professional is in itself an extraneous variable, and will already have had an effect. Ms Jarrett may feel more hopeful or more understood; her depression may have been lifted to some extent by the very act of leaving the house to attend the interview, by being offered coffee by the secretary, by seeing a new face.

A partial answer to these concerns about measurement impurity can be found in the nature of the baseline itself. A single measure of her depression before the intervention was initiated does not constitute a baseline. After all, a line is defined as the shortest distance between two points—there cannot be a line if there are not at least two points. Preferably, three or more measurements of the original problem level should be made, and in these repeated measures there is some security. The first contact with the practitioner may have lifted Ms Jarrett's depression temporarily, but the effect is unlikely to last for the length of time it takes to establish a baseline. Any effect of extraneous variables is also likely to be temporary. If a stable baseline is established, or a baseline shows the depression to be worsening, it may be assumed that nothing in Ms Jarrett's life aside from the intervention will decrease her level of depression.

Figure 7.7 shows a graph of Ms Jarrett's depression levels, plotted against time, through the baseline phase (A) and the interventive phase (B). Note that higher scores indicate a higher level of depression, so the practice objective in this case is "to decrease Ms Jarrett's depression."

The AB design is a basic component of many more complex designs. It shows only that change has occurred, with a stable or worsening baseline, it supports the assumption that the intervention caused the change. If the intervention includes a number of activities, such as role-plays, films, and discussions, the design will not

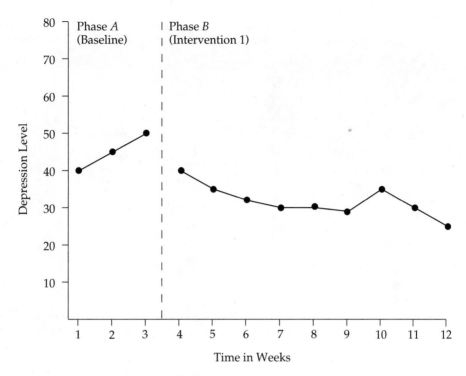

FIGURE 7.7 *AB* **Design: Ms Jarrett's Depression Levels before (Phase *A*) and during (Phase *B*) Treatment**
(Note: high scores = high depression levels)

show which of these activities (or what combination) was most effective in promoting change. Nevertheless, the *AB* design lies within the reach of every human service worker, and it fulfills the major function of a case-level evaluative design: it allows workers to know to what degree their clients are reaching their practice objectives. These data, in turn, help them to decide upon the most appropriate interventions.

$AB_1B_2B_3$ *Designs*

An important extension of the *AB* design is the $AB_1B_2B_3$ design, which consists of a baseline phase (*A*) followed by three variations on one intervention. The $AB_1B_2B_3$ design, also called the changing intensity design, may take either of two forms. One involves increasing the expectations of the client's desired outcome over time, and the other involves changing the intensity of the intervention over time.

For example, suppose that a boy receives a monthly reward of, say, two dollars if he achieves a grade in English that is 5 percent higher than his grade the month before. Here the intervention remains the same—providing the two dollars—but the boy must perform at a higher level every month in order to receive the money. Because the criterion for success has changed, the $AB_1B_2B_3$ design used in this

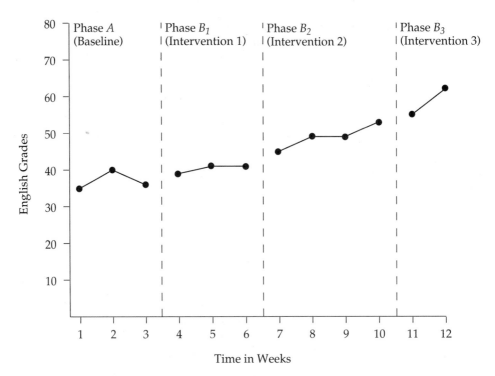

FIGURE 7.8   *AB₁B₂B₃* Design: Boy's English Grades before (Phase *A*) and during Intervention (*B* Phases)

context is called the changing criterion design. Its main advantage is that it allows the client to move in graduated steps toward a final practice objective.

The second form of the changing intensity design involves changing the intensity of the intervention. If a practice objective has failed to reach the desired level, a practitioner may offer more varied or more intense reinforcement, increase the number of tasks per week, or increase the number of weekly sessions. If termination is imminent, the worker may want to reduce the number of contacts or provide more intermittent reinforcement. In either case, the basic intervention remains the same, but its intensity is increased or diminished. Figure 7.8 illustrates this form of changing intensity design.

ABC *Designs*

The *ABC* (and *ABCD, ABCDE,* and so on) designs are extensions of the basic *AB* design and involve a baseline phase (*A*) followed by two, three, or more different interventions (*B* and *C*). Successive interventions are often employed by professionals when data indicate that the first or second interventions are not working satisfactorily and something new needs to be tried.

Another application of the *ABC* designs is the introduction of a maintenance phase, when an intervention has been successful, but the client now needs to be

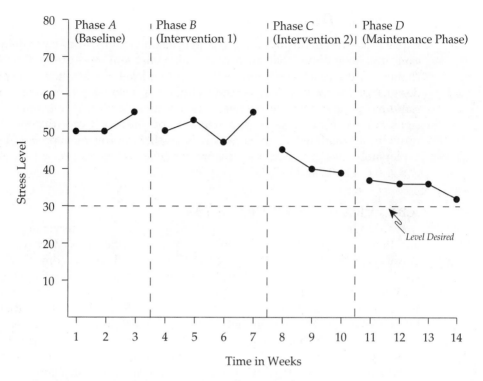

FIGURE 7.9   Mr. Thomlison's Clinical Stress Levels before (Phase *A*), during Two Different Interventions (Phases *B* and *C*), and after Termination (Phase *D*)
(Note: high scores = high stress levels)

taught to use new skills, without the aid of the worker. For example, the worker may have succeeded in reducing stress (practice objective) with the aid of relaxation techniques (activities) applied in weekly sessions, but the client now needs to begin to use these techniques at home. Figure 7.9 shows a client's clinical stress level over time. *A* represents the baseline phase, *B* an unsuccessful interventive phase, *C* a successful interventive phase, and *D* a maintenance phase. Higher scores indicate greater stress, so the desired change is in a downward direction.

The disadvantage of successive intervention designs is that *C* or *D* phases cannot be compared with the baseline phase because an intervening *B* phase has occurred. In addition, the effect of the *C* phase alone cannot readily be distinguished from the combined effects of the *B* phase and the *C* phase, so that the practitioner will not know whether the *C* intervention would have worked without the introduction of *B*. Of course, the more interventions there are, the more confused the picture becomes and the harder it is to ascribe the observed result to any particular interventive strategy.

Explanatory Designs

Explanatory designs are often called experimental designs. They try to demonstrate causality; they show that an activity—the intervention—caused the observed changes in the practice objective—the problem level. As mentioned, explanatory designs are the most rigorous case-level designs. They help to further our understanding of the relationship between interventions and their outcomes; these designs are powerful tools from a scientific perspective. Nevertheless, they also provide information that can be used in the quality improvement process. Five basic explanatory designs used to measure practice objectives are A_1BA_2, $A_1B_1A_2B_2$, $A_1B_1A_2B_2C$, B_1AB_2, and $B_1C_1B_2C_2$.

A_1BA_2, $A_1B_1A_2B_2$, and $A_1B_1A_2B_2C$ Designs

A_1BA_2 designs involve establishing a baseline in Phase A_1, intervening in Phase B, and then removing the intervention, A_2. As a deliberate procedure, this is rarely permissible, but it happens by chance quite often. A client may come for assistance, receive it, and terminate when the problem is apparently resolved. However, when the intervention stops, the problem reappears at its former level; the client returns to the professional, and Phase A_1 is in place again. This second time, though, the worker knows that the B intervention did resolve the problem, if only temporarily. The fact that the problem returned when the intervention was stopped makes it more likely that the intervention caused the resolution of the problem; thus, the worker will be more confident in trying the same intervention again.

When the same intervention is tried again, the A_1BA_2 design becomes an $A_1B_1A_2B_2$ design. If the intervention works for the second time, the practitioner can be still more confident that it was the intervention, and only the intervention, that resolved the problem. However, if the client is not to spend a lifetime on the $A_1B_1A_2B_2A_3B_3 \ldots$ treadmill, obviously something further needs to be done. The worker will probably introduce a C phase in which the intervention is intended to maintain the progress already made. The $A_1B_1A_2B_2$ design now becomes an $A_1B_1A_2B_2C$ design.

There are other circumstances in which a successful intervention may be halted, and so an $A_1B_1A_2B_2$ design (or some variant thereof) may be employed. Perhaps a client has completed a successful B phase with respect to one particular problem when a crisis erupts in another problem area. The worker's efforts are refocused on the crisis; by the time it has been resolved, the success in the B phase has been lost.

In general, it is a common problem in the human services that success, where achieved, is not maintained. One possible reason for this is that termination is initiated prematurely, before the desired change has had a chance to stabilize. It must be stressed that repeated measurements are necessary not just to establish a baseline, but also to establish that a desired outcome has been achieved and maintained. To illustrate, Figure 7.10 shows Mr. Thomlison's clinical stress levels plotted against time through an $A_1B_1A_2B_2$ succession. Note that although the scores in the B_1 phase were decreasing markedly, showing reduced stress, only three measurements were taken, and the intervention was stopped before the measurement

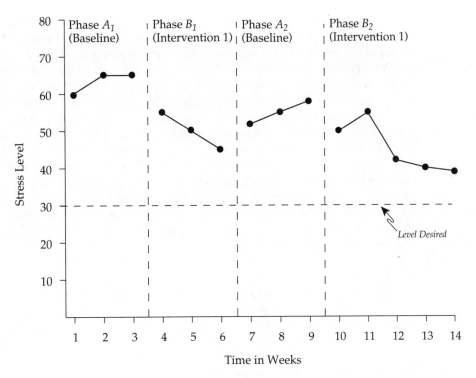

FIGURE 7.10 $A_1B_1A_2B_2$ **Design: Mr. Thomlison's Stress Levels over a 14-Week Period**

(Note: high scores = high stress levels)

pattern was stable. In the B_2 phase, the pattern of decreasing scores was repeated, but further measurements showed an increase in stress before another drop and eventual stabilization.

Note also that the A_2 phase differs somewhat from the first: His stress level is climbing, but less steeply. Very often, the client retains some understanding or skill from the B_1 phase, which continues to alleviate the problem marginally and leads to an improved A_2 phase the second time around. If the A phases are very different, we cannot be certain that the same problem reappeared when the intervention was removed; hence we cannot be confident that the intervention caused the problem to be resolved. Usually, however, the two A phases are sufficiently similar to suggest causality.

B_1AB_2 *Designs*

There are some occasions, especially in crisis work, when taking the time to establish a baseline before intervening would be harmful to the client. On these occasions, a B, or interventive phase, is initiated immediately and terminated when the problem appears to be resolved. As before, the problem may re-emerge without the continued service, and the client may then return to the baseline level. Of course, because the baseline level was never measured, it cannot be known that the client has returned to it. It is also possible that the B intervention continued to have some effect but not enough to prevent the problem from flaring up again.

Practitioners are not entirely defenseless in the face of these different causal possibilities. Initial measurements in the first B phase (B_1) will give some indication of the problem level at the very beginning of intervention, and, if the intervention takes some time to have an effect, these measurements might even constitute a baseline phase. That is, a pseudo-A phase may be established merely because the intervention is not immediately effective. In addition, whether or not the client returns to the same level after the first B intervention (B_1), comparisons between the two B phases and the A phase can still be made. One can at least state that when the intervention was removed, the problem returned, and when the intervention was reinstated, the problem was resolved. This in itself is enough to show causality, although causality is more fully demonstrated if two A phases (A_1 and A_2) can also be compared, as in the $A_1B_1A_2B_2$ design.

$B_1C_1B_2C_2$ Designs

Often a worker may consider two different interventions, but is unsure of which one to try. The $B_1C_1B_2C_2$ design allows both to be introduced sequentially: The B_1 intervention is tried and its effectiveness is assessed. It is then removed and the C_1 intervention is tried in its place; again, measures of effectiveness are made and the C_1 intervention is removed. The original B_1 intervention is then reinstated (B_2), to be followed once more by a C phase (C_2).

This design allows us to compare the effectiveness of two interventions. It is also useful when no baseline data can be obtained, as with the B_1AB_2 design. To see this, suppose that members of the support staff in a hospital are bringing a large number of grievances directly to department heads. The hospital already has a system in place to deal with grievances: Support staff are supposed to take them to their own representatives, who meet with department heads to resolve the issues. This system does not seem to be working well, but the administrator does not want to replace it with an alternative system, which may be even worse, without some preliminary testing.

Using a $B_1C_1B_2C_2$ design, the administrator asks department heads to record for three weeks how many grievances support staff bring to their personal attention. This is the first B phase (B_1) and the "intervention" is the original grievance system. After three months, the administrator discontinues the system in favor of twice monthly meetings in which hospital administrators, department heads, and all support staff meet to discuss issues. This is the first C phase (C_1) and, once again, department heads are asked to note the number of grievances brought by individuals. Three months later, the administrator reinstates the original system, and three months after that, returns to the twice monthly meetings. Figure 7.11 shows that the meetings are more effective than the original system in reducing the number of grievances brought personally to department heads. Because the C intervention (C_1 and C_2) was twice found to be more effective than the B intervention (B_1 and B_2), the

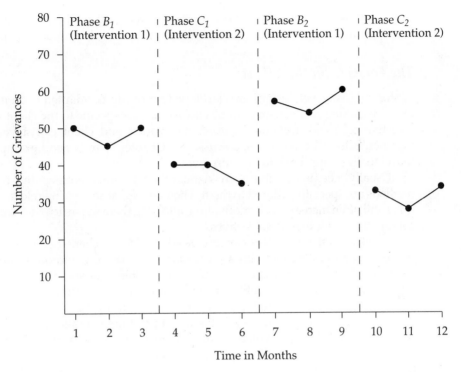

FIGURE 7.11 $B_1C_1B_2C_2$ **Design: Number of Grievances by Intervention over a 12-Month Period**

hospital administrator can be reasonably confident that the meetings really are the better system.

Advantages of Formal Case-Level Evaluations

Formal case-level designs provide the methods by which human service workers can evaluate their success with individual clients. This approach has advantages for the professional, the client, and the human service program.

The Practitioner Is Responsible for Data Collection

Although data may be collected by the client or others in the client's environment, the practitioner has both control over and responsibility for the data. That is, the human service worker decides what data should be collected where, when, under what conditions, and by whom. Given this, it is possible to organize data collection so that if confirmational data are needed (from, say, a teacher or relative), they can be obtained efficiently in time to assist decision making. In addition, workers are free to follow their own theoretical approaches to practice. The data collected will not determine the practice approach utilized but will be determined by it.

The Focus Is on the Client

All formal case-level designs are developed for or can be adapted to an individual case. Measuring instruments can be chosen that are specific to the client's practice objective or, if no instruments exist, the worker and client can develop them together. Self-anchored scales, discussed in Chapter 5, are a good example of this individualized approach to measurement.

Usually, clients are able to recognize that the interventions and measuring methods are specially tailored to them. Their belief that something relevant is being done will often increase their motivation, allowing them to participate more fully in solving their own practice objectives.

Formal case-level designs can also be adapted to the client. For example, it may be necessary to intervene with a particular client at once, without establishing a baseline. However, if the client can provide reliable data about the duration, frequency, or intensity of the problem prior to the interview, a retroactive baseline may be established on the strength of the client's recollection. The design is adaptable in a further sense: It may begin as AB (because a practitioner obviously hopes the first intervention will be effective), but if measurements indicate that it is not effective, it may become ABC or $AB_1C_1B_2C_2$ or $ABCD$, depending on the professional's judgment and the client's response.

Clinical Decisions Are Based on the Data Collected

Formal case-level designs provide continuous data to human service professionals so that they can monitor clients' progress and alter their interventions if that progress is slower than expected. In addition, the collected data can be useful in making decisions to terminate or initiate different treatment interventions.

Problem Analysis Is Facilitated

Case-level designs require that measurable practice objectives be set. Formulating a specific measurable objective compels the worker to think the client's problem through. What is it precisely about Gino's aggression that needs to be measured? Is Gino aggressive in the sense that he is hostile or in the sense that he is overassertive? It is obviously necessary to decide this, as interventions aimed at reducing hostility will differ from those intended to reduce overassertiveness. If Gino is hostile, is he hostile only to certain people in certain situations—for example, his mother or teacher—or is he *generally* hostile? Again, we need to know this in order to plan.

Once the problem is defined, the professional will be able to devise an appropriate intervention. If a similar problem has occurred with another client, the worker may well have formed a hypothesis about the most effective intervention. The intervention can be used again and its effectiveness measured; in other words, the hypothesis can be *tested*. Data serving to strengthen or weaken the hypothesis will enable the worker to reassess his or her own theoretical bases or practice approaches.

The Cost Is Small in Time and Disruptiveness

There is no doubt that making measurements takes more time than not making them. However, this time must be compared to time that is inevitably wasted when the practitioner does not really know how the practice objective is progressing, whether the intervention is working, and whether or not it is time to try something else. Nor should measurement be considered disruptive. A disruption is, by definition, something that disturbs the normal course of events; if measurement is a part of the normal course of events, it is not a disruption, but only a continuous record of progress made.

The Client's Situation Can Be Taken into Account

One of the major advantages of formal case-level designs is that they are infinitely flexible and the client's unique situation can always be taken into account. For example, a rating scale that the practitioner knows will be completed by the client's mother can be designed to fit the mother's capabilities; instruments can be completed at home at times convenient for the client; and designs can always be adapted to fit the client's individual needs.

The Data Collected Is Useful for Program-Level Evaluations

As we know, data collected on individual clients can be aggregated or clustered to provide program evaluation data. For example, a charitable organization that funds a number of agencies might require member agencies to document a minimum level of verified successful case outcomes in order to qualify for funding. The operative word here is *verified*. Individual practitioners would have to provide evidence of successful case outcomes, complete with data clearly displayed on graphs. Formal case-level designs lend themselves to such documentation. An agency staffed with professional human service workers who all use case-levels designs will have less difficulty in demonstrating success and obtaining funding than those agencies that do not use them.

Data collected on clients over time can also be useful in determining eligibility criteria for a human service program as a whole. For example, it may have been found that clients who achieved a certain score on a particular standardized measuring instrument tended to do better in the program than clients who achieved a lower score. A minimum score might then be set as a criterion for admittance.

Limitations of Formal Case-Level Evaluations

There are advantages and disadvantages to most things in life, and case-level evaluation designs are no exception. Two disadvantages are listed below.

Limited Generalizability

As will be discussed in the next chapter, when a study is conducted at the explanatory level with such controls as random sampling and random assignment to groups, the results of the study apply not just to the group being tested but to the entire population from which the sample was drawn. When a case-level study is conducted with an individual client, the results apply only to that client. Thus, they have limited generalizability from one client to the next or from one practice objective to the next. This is a major drawback of case-level evaluation designs.

A number of similar results obtained in similar situations with similar clients make it more likely that the findings are generally applicable; but an individual worker may not have such comparative data available. Workers should therefore resist the temptation to assume that because an intervention worked once it must necessarily work again.

Explanatory Designs Are Difficult to Implement

Only in exceptional circumstances is it ethical to deliberately implement such explanatory designs as the A_1BA_2 and $A_1B_1A_2B_2$ designs, where a successful intervention is removed and the problem allowed to return to the baseline level. Because of ethical difficulties, such designs usually come into being accidentally; consequently, rigor suffers. Very often measurement of the problem level does not continue between the first B phase (B_1) and the second A phase (A_2), as a client who believes that a problem has been solved will not continue to keep records between the apparent solution and the reappearance. There is, therefore, a gap in the data, and it is not possible to say with certainty that the reappearance of the problem had anything to do with the removal of the intervention. Perhaps the problem would have reappeared even if the intervention had been continued. An accidental application of an $A_1B_1A_2B_2$ design thus eliminates one argument for causality: that the problem reappears when the intervention is removed.

Descriptive formal case-level designs are easier to implement than explanatory designs because they require only a baseline phase followed by as many intervention phases as are necessary to solve the client's problem. However, they do not provide causal data, and practitioners who want to know whether a particular intervention solved a particular problem cannot rely on these more practical designs.

Summary

This chapter has discussed various kinds of case-level evaluations which included informal and formal case-level evaluation designs. It highlighted their use by providing brief introductions to exploratory, descriptive, and explanatory case-level designs. The next chapter provides a complementary discussion of evaluation designs that can be used in program-level evaluations.

Key Terms

Baseline Measure: A numerical label assigned to a client's level of performance, knowledge, or affect *prior* to any intervention; the first measure to be made in any series of repeated measurements; designated as the *A* phase in formal case-level designs.

Case Conferences: An informal, or nonempirical, method of case evaluation that requires professionals to meet and exchange descriptive client information for the purposes of making a case decision.

Data Display: The manner in which collected data are set out on a page.

Descriptive Design: A design that approximates a true experiment, but the worker does not have the same degree of control over manipulation of the intervention process; also known as quasi-experimental designs.

Empirical Evaluation: A method of appraisal based on the analysis of data collected by measuring instruments.

Explanatory Design: An attempt to demonstrate with certainty that specific activities caused specific reported changes in practice objectives. The professional manipulates certain factors in the intervention to gain a greater degree of control over the proceedings; also known as experimental designs.

Exploratory Design: A process in which a professional assesses the effects of an intervention process for the purpose of building a foundation of general ideas and tentative theories that can later be examined by more rigorous evaluative methods.

Extraneous Variables: Outside factors that occur at the same time as the intervention and thus may account for some of the measured change in practice objectives.

Formal Case-Level Evaluation: An empirical method of appraisal in which a single client is monitored via repeated measurements over time in order to examine change in a practice objective.

Nonempirical Evaluation: An informal method of appraisal that is not based on empirical data; it depends on theories and descriptions that a professional considers to be relevant to the case.

Phase: Any relatively distinct part of the contact between a professional and a client; *A* represents a baseline phase and *B* an intervention phase.

Private Consultation: An informal method of case evaluation in which a professional exchanges descriptive information about client with another helping human service worker to obtain solid advice.

Qualitative: A description of data that is given in words.

Quantitative: A description of data which is given in numbers.

Repeated Measurements: The administration of one measuring instrument (or set of instruments) a number of times to the same client, under the same conditions, over a period of time.

Study Questions

1. Review the evaluation design used for clients in Case Study C. What features of the study suggest that an empirical method of case evaluation was used? What evidence exists to suggest that informal methods of case evaluation were also used?

2. For each of the six clients in Case Study C, compare the baseline measures for their scores on thoughts, affects, and behaviors. What do the baseline measures tell you about each individual client? What information do the baseline measures provide about the clients as a group?

3. Compare the summated inventory scores for each client in Case Study C. In your opinion, which client made the most change after receiving the intervention? Which client made the least change? What evidence do you have to support your conclusions?

4. The data displays in Case Study C depict summated scores for each individual client during the baseline and the intervention phases. Draft a separate data display to illustrate the results of the clients as a group. Compare your graphic display of data to the ones depicted in the chapter.

5. A simple *AB* design was used to monitor change in program objectives for clients in Case Study C. Explain how the study could have been changed to incorporate an $A_1B_1A_2B_2$ design. What ethical questions would need to be addressed if an $A_1B_1A_2B_2$ design was used with this population?

6. Based on the results of Case Study C, do you think the outreach program should continue? Why or why not? If the outreach services were to continue, what modifications would you make?

7. In your own words, identify the advantages of using case-level evaluation designs in Case Study C. Compare your list of advantages with those described in this chapter.

8. In groups of four, design an explanatory evaluation design for the program in Case Study C. Describe how you would carry out the study. In your description, define the testable assertion, or hypothesis, to be examined by your design. What instruments would you use to collect the data? What sources of data would you use? Present your design to the class.

9. List and discuss the advantages and disadvantages of using informal and formal case-level evaluations. How can they be used together? Explain your rationale in detail. Use a single human service example throughout your discussion.

10. List and discuss the advantages and disadvantages of using only formal case-level evaluation designs to replace case consultations and case conferences. Use a human service example in your discussion.

11. What are some of the disadvantages of using case conferencing to evaluate a client's achievement of his or her practice objective?

12. José, a fellow student in your program, is experiencing problems at school. He is doing poorly in every class, receiving the minimum marks necessary to pass. He is also very shy and has a difficult time forming friendships with classmates. Moreover, he does not attend classes on a regular basis. José asks for your help. Set three practice objectives for José, weighted according to your perception of their importance.

13. Next, operationalize each of your practice objectives with José and scale each objective on a 5-point Goal Attainment Scale ranging from −2 to +2 (Chapter 6).

14. What is a baseline measure? Why is it important in your evaluation of José's problem? Calculate José's baseline goal attainment score.

15. Another student also provides a rating for José. Why is this important and necessary to the evaluative effort?

16. Another classmate wonders why you have used goal attainment scaling in this case. How do you respond? She nevertheless warns against using GAS in isolation in future formal case-level evaluations. Why?

17. José decides that he wants to work on his self-esteem; that is, his practice objective is to increase his self-esteem. Why is it important to establish a baseline for José's practice objective before an intervention takes place?

18. Why are repeated measurements of José's practice objectives necessary to a successful evaluation of his progress?

19. In order to obtain a baseline, you measure José's self-esteem for three weeks. He scores 62, 58 and 63. Graphically display the scores. Remember to plot measures of your practice objective on the vertical axis of the graph and time on the horizontal axis. Why is it important to display your data graphically?

20. You decide to use an intervention strategy to increase José's self-esteem. Repeated measurement may show that his self-esteem problems have declined over the course of a month. Can you prove that your intervention strategy alone caused this increase? Why or why not?

21. You decide to evaluate José's case using an *AB* design. What are the benefits of using such a design? Why is an established baseline of José's level of self-esteem so important? Under what circumstances would you decide to use a successive intervention design with José's case? What are some of the advantages and disadvantages of such a design?

22. How can you increase your confidence in the effects of your intervention strategy? Why is this sometimes not ethical or possible?

23. Under what circumstances would you deliberately not establish a baseline with José? If you fail to establish a baseline, can you still demonstrate that your intervention strategy

caused José's self-esteem to increase? Why or why not?

24. You have just been hired by a human service agency and propose the incorporation of formal and informal case-level evaluations in practice. Summarize the main points of your argument. Be very clear and concise.

25. Read Case Study A. Given the contents of the case study, discuss how informal and formal case-level evaluations could be used in the program, paying particular attention to the program's client population. Discuss how each one of the formal case-level evaluation design categories (exploratory, descriptive, and explanatory) could be used within the program. Now discuss the advantages of using formal case-level designs within the program, paying particular attention to the program's client population and the contextual variables that influence the program's delivery structure. Discuss the limitations of using formal case-level evaluations and present a few solutions that would help overcome these limitations, paying particular attention to the program's client population.

26. Read Case Study B. Given the contents of the cast study, discuss how informal and formal case-level evaluations could be used in the program, paying particular attention to the program's client population. Discuss how each one of the formal case-level evaluation design categories (exploratory, descriptive, and explanatory) could be used within the program. Now discuss the advantages of using formal case-level designs within the program, paying particular attention to the program's client population and the contextual variables that influence the program's delivery structure. Discuss the limitations of using formal case-level evaluations and present a few solutions that would help overcome these limitations, paying particular attention to the program's client population.

8

USING PROGRAM-LEVEL EVALUATIONS

THE LAST CHAPTER discussed simple approaches to case-level evaluations. This chapter is a logical extension of the previous one in that it presents various approaches to program-level evaluations which emphasize the use of groups of clients or cases instead of one client (e.g., one individual, one couple, one family, one group, one community, one organization). As the previous chapter pointed out, case-level evaluations are used mainly to evaluate practice objectives. Program-level evaluations are used to evaluate program objectives. The key difference between case-level and program-level evaluations is the kind of objectives they measure.

The Evaluation Continuum

When the focus and purpose of an evaluation have been determined, the program objectives have been formulated, and instruments have been selected to measure the objectives, it is time to select a program-level evaluation design. Essentially, a design is selected for the specific purpose of an evaluation, or the use to which the results will be put. If the purpose is to make decisions about continuing, abandoning, or replicating the program, the decision makers will need to be very confident about the validity and reliability of the evaluation and a rigorous design may be required.

Like formal case-level designs, there are three levels of program-level evaluation designs: explanatory, descriptive, and exploratory. All three design levels can focus on the evaluation of a program's objectives to some degree; that is, they all can be used to generate useful data that can help human service programs deliver better services to the clients they serve.

Explanatory Designs

Explanatory evaluation designs are sometimes called "ideal" evaluative experimental designs. They involve random assignment of clients (or case files) to groups. It is rarely possible to implement them in agency settings, and less powerful designs, such as descriptive and exploratory designs that are usually less intrusive, will have to be chosen.

Explanatory program-level evaluation designs have the largest number of "design requirements." They are best used in confirmatory or causal evaluation studies where the program objective being evaluated is well developed, theories abound, and testable hypotheses can be formulated on the basis of previous work or existing theory. These designs usually seek to establish causal relationships between the program objectives and the activities the workers perform to achieve them (interventions).

This chapter has been adapted and modified from Richard M. Grinnell, Jr., Group research designs. In R. M. Grinnell, Jr. (Ed.), *Social Work Research and Evaluation* (4th ed.). © 1993 F. E. Peacock Publishers. Used with permission.

Descriptive Designs

Descriptive program-level evaluation designs have the advantage of being practical when conditions prevent implementation of an explanatory evaluation design. They do not control as strictly for the effects of extraneous factors as explanatory designs and are thus less "rigorous." Nevertheless, they are very useful and practical in the evaluation of the human services.

Exploratory Designs

A third type of program-level evaluation design is the exploratory design. These designs only provide an estimate of the relationship between the program objectives and the workers' activities (interventions) with no defense at all against the effects of extraneous factors. However, such a design can be used for a preliminary "non-scientific" look at their relationship to see if it is worthwhile using more rigorous, and also more costly and time-consuming, designs.

Exploratory designs do not produce statistically definitive data or conclusive results; they are not intended to. Their purpose is to build a foundation of general ideas and tentative theories which can be explored later with more precise and hence more complex evaluation designs and their corresponding data-gathering techniques. As is stressed throughout this book, monitoring designs, a form of exploratory designs, are extremely useful in determining if interventive efforts are having an effect on a program's objectives.

Choosing a Design

The two most important considerations in choosing a program-level evaluation design are the purpose of the evaluative effort and how the data obtained will be used. In addition, ethical issues must be taken into account along with political, social, and practical considerations.

Before a discussion of using program-level evaluation designs can occur, it is necessary to distinguish what comprises an "ideal" evaluation, (explanatory design) because any evaluation design finally selected should come as close to an "ideal" evaluation as possible given the social, political, ethical, and practical constraints that surround any evaluative effort. In short, it is useful to understand what an "ideal" evaluation is, so comparisons can be made between the program-level evaluation design selected and the requirements of an "ideal" evaluation. Or, to put it another way, it is always helpful to know how far the evaluation design selected is from an "ideal" evaluation.

Characteristics of "Ideal" Evaluations

An "ideal" evaluation is one in which a study approaches certainty about the relationship between the workers' activities and the program objectives they are trying to achieve. The purpose of doing any "ideal" evaluation is to ascertain whether the conclusions derived from the findings that the workers' activities (their interventions or independent variables) are or are not the only cause of the change they are trying to achieve in the program objectives (dependent variables).

This concept is introduced with the word "ideal" in quotes because an "ideal" evaluation study is rarely achieved in the human services. On a general level, in order to achieve this high degree of certainty and qualify as an "ideal" evaluation, a design must meet the following six conditions:

1. The time order of the intervention (independent variable) must be established
2. The intervention must be manipulated
3. The relationship between the intervention and program objective(s) must be established
4. The design must control for rival hypotheses
5. At least one control group should be used
6. Random sampling and random assignment procedures must be employed in choosing the sample for the study

Time Order of the Intervention

In an "ideal" program-level evaluation, the independent variable must precede the dependent variable. Time order is crucial if the evaluation is to show that one variable causes another, because something that happens later cannot be the cause of something that occurred earlier. Thus X, the independent variable, or intervention, must occur before Y, the dependent variable, or degree of the achievement of the program objective.

Suppose we want to find out if a specific treatment intervention, Intervention X (independent variable), reduces our clients' depression levels (dependent variable) and formulate the following hypothesis:

Intervention X will cause a reduction in our clients' depression levels.

In this hypothesis, the independent variable is the intervention, and the program's objective, or the dependent variable, is the clients' depression levels. The intervention must come *before* a reduction in the clients' depression, because the hypothesis states that the intervention will *cause* a reduction of depression in our clients.

Manipulation of the Intervention

Manipulation of the intervention, or independent variable, means that something must be done with the intervention to at least one group of clients in the evaluation study. In the general form of the hypothesis if X occurs then Y will result, the intervention (X) must be manipulated in order to effect a variation in the program's objective (Y). There are essentially three ways in which human service interventions can be manipulated:

1. X *present versus* X *absent.* If the effectiveness of a specific treatment intervention is being evaluated, an experimental group and a control group could be used. The experimental group would be given the intervention (presence of X) and the control group would not (absence of X).

2. *A small amount of* X *versus a larger amount of* X. If the effect of treatment time (independent variable) on client outcomes (dependent variable) is being evaluated, two experimental groups could be used, one of which would be treated for a shorter period of time (small amount of X) and the other being treated for a longer period of time (larger amount of X).

3. X *versus something else.* If the effectiveness of two different treatment interventions is being evaluated, Intervention X_1 could be used with Experimental Group 1 and Intervention X_2 with Experimental Group 2.

There are certain demographic characteristics, such as the sex or race of clients participating in evaluations, that obviously cannot be manipulated because they are fixed. They do not vary, so they are called constants, not variables (Rothery, 1993b). Other constants, such as socioeconomic status or IQ, may vary for clients over their life spans, but they are fixed quantities at the beginning of the study, probably will not change during the study, and are not subject to alteration by the evaluator.

Any variable that is subject to alteration by the evaluator (treatment time, for example) is an independent variable. At least one independent variable must be manipulated in a "true" evaluation.

Relationships between Interventions and Objectives

The relationship between the intervention and the attainment of the program's objective(s) must be established in order to infer a cause-effect relationship within a "true" evaluation. If the intervention is considered to be the cause in the change of the program objective, there must be some pattern in the relationship between them. An example is the hypothesis: "The more time clients spend in treatment (the intervention or the independent variable), the better the program objective will be (the dependent variable)."

Control of Rival Hypotheses

Rival, or alternative, hypotheses must be identified and eliminated in an "ideal" program-level evaluation. The logic of this requirement is extremely important, because this is what makes cause-effect statements possible in "ideal" evaluations.

The prime question to ask when trying to identify a rival hypothesis is, "What other independent variables might affect the dependent variable?" (What else might affect the client's outcome besides treatment time?) With the risk of sounding redundant, "What else besides X might affect Y?" Perhaps the client's motivation for treatment, in addition to the time spent in treatment, might affect the client's outcome. If so, motivation for treatment is another independent variable; it could be used to form the rival hypothesis, "The higher the client's motivation for treatment, the better his or her progress."

Perhaps the practitioner's attitude toward the client might have an effect on the client's outcome, or the client might win the state lottery and ascend abruptly from depression to ecstasy. These and other potential independent variables could be used to form rival hypotheses. They must all be considered and eliminated, before it can be said with reasonable certainty that a client's outcome resulted from the length of treatment time and not from any other independent variables contained within the rival hypotheses.

Control over rival hypotheses refers to efforts on the evaluator's part to identify and, if at all possible, to eliminate the independent variables in these hypotheses. Three of the ways most frequently used to deal with rival hypotheses are (1) to keep the variables in them constant, (2) to use correlated variation, or (3) to use analysis of covariance. This text will not discuss how to control for rival hypotheses as this discussion can be found elsewhere (e.g., Weinbach & Grinnell, 1995; Grinnell, 1993a).

Use of a Control Group

An "ideal" program-level evaluation should use at least one control group in addition to the experimental group. This is one of the principal differences between an "ideal" evaluation and formal case-level designs discussed in the previous chapter. Instead of controlling for rival hypotheses and achieving internal validity by comparing baseline and intervention phases as in case-level designs, program-level evaluation designs can accomplish the same purposes by comparing outcomes between two or more equivalent groups. The experimental group may receive an intervention that is withheld from the control group, or an equivalent group may receive a different intervention (Reid & Smith, 1989).

A human service worker who initiates a treatment intervention is often interested in knowing what would have happened if the intervention had not been used or if some different intervention had been substituted. Would Ms Gomez have recovered from alcoholism anyway without the worker's efforts? Would she have recovered faster or more completely had family counseling (Intervention A) been used instead of a support group (Intervention B)?

The answer to these questions will never be known if only Ms Gomez is studied, because there is only one of her and it is not possible, at the same time, to treat her, not treat her, and treat her in different ways. But if more than one group of alcoholics is studied, we have a better idea of the outcome of the treatment, because groups can be made equivalent in respect to important variables. Random assignment procedures (see next section) may be used to assure that the groups are not only equal but are representative of all others with similar problems of alcoholism.

In a typical program-level evaluation design with a control group, two equivalent groups, 1 and 2, can be formed, and both are administered the same pretest to ensure that they are the same in all important respects. Then an intervention is initiated with Group 1 but not with Group 2. The group treated, Group 1 or the experimental group, receives the independent variable (the intervention). The group not treated, Group 2 or the control group, does not receive it. At the conclusion of the treatment, both groups are given a posttest (the same measure as the pretest). Some kind of standardized measuring instrument can be used for the pretest and posttest.

Like formal case-level designs, program-level evaluation designs can also be written in symbols. With the notation scheme used later in this chapter, this design is written as follows:

$$\begin{array}{llcccc} \text{Experimental Group:} & R & O_1 & X & O_2 \\ \text{Control Group:} & R & O_1 & & O_2 \end{array}$$

where:

R = Random assignment to one of two groups
O_1 = First measurement of the program objective, the dependent variable
X = Intervention (program or activity), the independent variable
O_2 = Second measurement of the program objective, the dependent variable

The two R's in this design indicate that the clients are to be randomly assigned to each group. The symbol X, which, as usual, stands for the interventive efforts, or the independent variable, indicates that an intervention, or service, is to be given to the experimental group after the pretest (O_1) and before the posttest (O_2). The absence of X in the control group indicates that the intervention is not to be given to the control group. Thus, one group receives the services (the experimental group) and the other group does not receive them (the control group).

Table 8.1 displays results from a program-level evaluation study of this type. If the experimental group is equivalent to the control group, the pretest results should be approximately the same for both groups. Within an acceptable margin of error, 24 can be considered approximately the same as 26. Since the control group has not been given any services, the posttest results for this group would not be expected to differ appreciably from the pretest results. In fact, the posttest score, 27, differs little from the pretest score, 26, for the control group.

TABLE 8.1   Client Outcomes by Group

Group	Pretest (O_1)	Posttest (O_2)	Difference ($O_1 - O_2$)
Experimental	24	68	−44
Control	26	27	− 1

Because the experimental and control groups are considered equivalent, any rival hypothesis that affected the experimental group would have affected the control group in the same way. No rival hypothesis affected the control group, as indicated by the fact that without the intervention, the pretest and posttest scores did not differ. Therefore, it can be concluded that no rival hypothesis affected the experimental group, either, and the difference (–44) between pretest and posttest scores for this group was probably due to the intervention and not to any other factor.

Random Sampling and Random Assignment

Random sampling and assignment procedures are essential to assure that the results derived from a program-level evaluation study apply not only to the clients who actually took part in the program but to a much larger population. This makes it possible to generalize the findings to other program settings or other clients with similar characteristics, provided that the sample—those who are chosen to take part in a study—is representative of the population to whom the findings are to be generalized. A sample may also consist of cases or elements chosen from a set or population of objects or events, but most human service evaluations deal with people, individually or in groups.

Random sampling is the procedure used to select a sample from a population in such a way that the individuals (or objects or events) chosen accurately represent the population from which they were drawn (see Chapter 9). Once a sample has been randomly selected, the individuals in it are randomly assigned either to an experimental or to a control group in such a way that the groups are equivalent. This procedure is known as *random assignment* or randomization.

In random assignment, the word *equivalent* means equal in terms of variables that are important to the evaluation study, such as the clients' motivation for treatment or level of parenting skills.

If the effect of treatment time on clients' outcomes is being evaluated, for example, the evaluation design might use one experimental group which is treated for a comparatively longer time, a second experimental group which is treated for a shorter time, and a control group which is not treated at all. If we are concerned that the clients' motivation for treatment might also affect their outcomes, the clients can be assigned so that all the groups are equivalent (on the average) in terms of their motivation for treatment.

The process of random sampling from a population, followed by random assignment of the sample to groups, is illustrated in Figure 8.1. The design calls for a sample size of one-tenth of the population. From a population of 10,000, therefore, a random sampling procedure is used to select a sample of 1,000 individuals. Then random assignment procedures are used to place the sample of 1,000 into two equivalent groups of 500 individuals each. In theory, Group A will be equivalent to Group B, which will be equivalent to the random sample, which will be equivalent to the population in respect to all important variables studied.

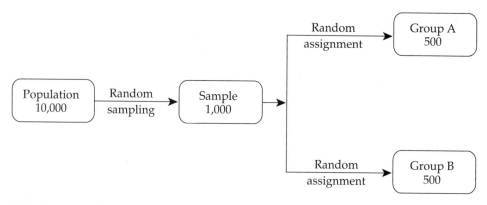

FIGURE 8.1   Random Sampling and Random Assignment Procedures

Matched Pairs

Another more deliberate method of assigning clients or other units to groups involves matching. The matched pairs method is suitable when the composition of each group consists of variables with a range of characteristics.

Sometimes trios and quartets can also be matched if more groups are required, but the matching process grows more complex and uncertain as the numbers in the matched set increase. It is usually not practical to match more than four clients. One of the disadvantages of matching is that some individuals cannot be matched and so cannot participate in the evaluation project. When available clients are few, this can be a serious drawback.

Suppose a new intervention program for depression is being evaluated, and it is important that the experimental and control groups have an equal number of more severely and less severely depressed clients. The clients chosen for the sample are matched in pairs according to level of depression; the two most severely depressed clients are matched, then the next two, and so on. One person in each pair of approximately equally depressed clients is then randomly assigned to the experimental group, and the other is placed in the control group.

An example of this procedure is as follows: A standardized measuring instrument that measures depression is administered to a sample of ten clients. Their scores are then rank ordered, and one of the clients with the two highest scores is selected to be assigned either to the experimental group or the control group. It does not make any difference which group the first client is randomly assigned to, as long as there is an equal chance that the client will go to either the control group or the experimental group. In this example the first person is randomly chosen to go to the experimental group, as illustrated below:

Rank Order of Depression Scores (in parentheses)

First Pair
   (69) Randomly assigned to the experimental group
   (68) Assigned to the control group
Second Pair
   (67) Assigned to the control group
   (66) Assigned to the experimental group
Third Pair
   (65) Assigned to the experimental group
   (64) Assigned to the control group
Fourth Pair
   (63) Assigned to the control group
   (62) Assigned to the experimental group
Fifth Pair
   (61) Assigned to the experimental group
   (60) Assigned to the control group

The client with the highest score (69) is randomly assigned to the experimental group, and this client's "match," with a score of 68, is assigned to the control group. This process is reversed with the next matched pair, where the first client is assigned to the control group and the match is assigned to the experimental group. If the assignment of clients according to scores is not reversed for every other pair, one group will be higher than the other on the variable being matched.

To illustrate this point, suppose the first person (highest score) in each match is always assigned to the experimental group. The experimental group's average score would be 65 ($69 + 67 + 65 + 63 + 61 = 325/5 = 65$), and the control group's average score would be 64 ($68 + 66 + 64 + 62 + 60 = 320/5 = 64$). If every other matched pair is reversed, however, as in the example, the average scores of the two groups are closer together; 64.6 for the experimental group ($69 + 66 + 65 + 62 + 61 = 323/5 = 64.6$) and 64.4 for the control group ($68 + 67 + 64 + 63 + 60 = 322/5 = 64.4$). In short, 64.6 and 64.4 (difference of 0.2) are closer together than 65 and 64 (difference of 1).

Internal and External Validity

In addition to the six characteristics of "ideal" program-level evaluation designs described above, an "ideal" evaluation study must also have both internal and external validity. Internal validity has to do with the provisions of the evaluation design for establishing that the introduction of the independent variable (such as a treatment intervention) alone can be identified as the cause of change in the dependent variable (such as the client's outcome). In contrast, external validity has to do with the extent to which the evaluation design allows for generalization of the findings of the study to other groups and other situations.

Both internal and external validity are achieved in a design by taking into account various threats that are inherent in the evaluation effort. A program-level evaluation design for a study with both types of validity will recognize and attempt to control for potential factors that could affect the study's outcome or findings.

Threats to Internal Validity

In an "ideal" program-level evaluation, the evaluator should be able to conclude from the findings that the intervention (independent variable) is or is not the only cause of change in the program's objective (dependent variable). If a study does not have internal validity, such a conclusion is not possible, and the study is not interpretable (Campbell & Stanley, 1963).

Internal validity is concerned with one of the requirements for an "ideal" evaluation—the control of rival hypotheses, or alternative explanations for what might bring about a change in the program's objective(s). The higher the internal validity of an evaluation study, the greater the extent to which rival hypotheses can be controlled; the lower the internal validity, the less they can be controlled. We must be prepared to rule out the effects of factors other than the intervention that could influence any changes in the program's objective(s). The factors that constitute threats to internal validity are listed in Figure 8.2 and described in this section.

Threats to Internal Validity

1. *History.* Unaccounted-for events that may affect the dependent variable.
2. *Maturation.* Mental or physical changes in participants over the course of the study.
3. *Testing.* Measurement of the dependent variable with a pretest.
4. *Instrumentation.* Lack of validity or reliability in measuring instruments used.
5. *Statistical regression.* The tendency of high or low scores to move toward the mean, or average, score upon retesting.
6. *Differential selection.* Failure to achieve or maintain group equivalence in study participants.
7. *Mortality.* Loss of participants who drop out of a study before it is completed.
8. *Reactive effects.* Reaction of participants to their participation in a study.
9. *Interaction effects.* Interaction among factors that have an effect on one another.
10. *Relations between experimental and control groups.* Control group members are exposed to the intervention through contact with the experimental group members.

FIGURE 8.2   Research Factors that Can Threaten Internal Validity

History

History refers to any event that may affect the program's objective, and that could not be accounted for in the evaluation design. More specifically, it refers to events occurring between the first and second measurement of the program objective (the pretest and the posttest). If events occur that have the potential to alter the second measurement, there is no way of knowing how much (if any) of the observed change is a function of the intervention, and how much is attributable to these events.

Suppose, for example, that the effect of a certain educational program on racial tolerance is being evaluated. A pretest is given before the program is initiated, but before the posttest is administered, an outbreak of racial violence occurs in the community such as the one that happened in Los Angeles in 1992. This sequence of events may well counter the "true" effects of the educational program, so the posttest scores would indicate a lower level of racial tolerance than they would have otherwise. An earthquake, an election, illness, or marriage—any event, public or private—can be an example of this kind of history.

Maturation

Maturation refers to changes, both mental and physical, which take place in clients who participate in an evaluation over the course of the project and which therefore can affect the outcome of the program's objective. Suppose a new interventive technique designed to improve behavior in adolescents who are physically challenged is being evaluated. Since adolescents tend to undergo rapid biological change, changes in behavior noted in the experimental results may be due as much to their maturation as to the treatment intervention.

However, maturation refers not only to physical or mental growth. Over time, as clients grow older and (presumably) wiser, they also become more or less anxious, bored, happy, or rich, and more or less motivated to take part in an evaluation study. These variables and many more can affect the ways in which clients respond when the program objective is measured a second or third time.

Testing

The pretests that are the starting point for some program-level evaluation designs are another potential threat to internal validity. One of the simplest descriptive evaluation designs involves three steps: measuring some program objective, such as learning behavior in school or attitudes toward work; initiating a program to change that variable; and then measuring the attainment of the objective again at the conclusion of the program. This simple design can be written in symbols as follows:

$$O_1 \quad X \quad O_2$$

where:

O_1 = First measurement of the program objective, the dependent variable
X = Intervention, the independent variable
O_2 = Second measurement of the program objective, the dependent variable

Testing can be a threat because taking the pretest can have an effect on posttest scores. Some clients might have a higher score on the posttest, for example, because they recall the questions (or items) on the pretest, or they might have a lower score because their experience with the pretest has made them anxious. In either case, the difference between pretest and posttest scores ($O_1 - O_2$ = difference, or effect of X) may not accurately reflect the effectiveness of the program.

In order to avoid the testing effect, an evaluation design could be used which does not require a pretest (to be discussed shortly). If a pretest must be used, the length of elapsed time between the pretest and the posttest should be considered. A pretest is far more likely to affect the posttest scores when the time between the two is short. The program objectives under study are another factor. The pretest is more likely to affect the posttest when the study is dealing with skill or knowledge levels—factual information which can be easily recalled and tested.

Instrumentation Error

As presented in Chapter 6, a lack of validity or reliability in measuring instruments can invalidate the measurement of program objectives. Instrumentation error may be due to a mechanical device that malfunctions, a measuring instrument that has not been adequately standardized or pretested, or an observer whose observations are inconsistent throughout the course of the project. It may also occur if a measuring instrument that is perfectly reliable and valid in itself is not administered properly.

Statistical Regression

Statistical regression refers to the tendency of extremely low and extremely high scores to regress, or move toward the average score. Suppose Ray, a human service student, has to take a multiple-choice pretest exam in a research course about which he knows nothing at all. There are many questions, and each question has five possible answers. Since he has a 20 percent chance of guessing right on each question, he might expect to score 20 percent on the exam, just by guessing. If he is a bad guesser, he will score lower; if a good guesser, higher. The other members of his class, all of whom are just as confused as he is, take the same exam, and the score for the class averages out at 20 percent.

Suppose, now, that the research instructor separates the low scorers from the high scorers and tries to even out the academic level of the class by giving the low scorers special instruction. In order to see if this has been effective, the entire class then takes another multiple-choice exam.

According to the logic of statistical regression, both the low scorers and the high scorers would move toward the average score. Even without any special instruction and still in their state of ignorance, the low scorers would be expected to score higher than they did before; that is, by moving toward the average, their scores would increase. The high scorers would be expected to score lower than they did before.

It would be easy for the research instructor to assume that the low scores had increased because of the instruction and the high scores had decreased because of the lack of instruction. Not necessarily so, however; the instruction may have had nothing to do with it. It may all be due to statistical regression.

Differential Selection

To some extent, the clients selected for a program-level evaluation study are different from one another to begin with. "Ideal" evaluations require random sampling and random assignment procedures to groups. This assures that the results of a study will be generalizable to a larger population (external validity). The threat to internal validity is failure to achieve or maintain equivalency among the groups, because clients assigned to them are not approximately equal.

This threat is present when the evaluator is working with preformed groups or groups that already exist, such as classes of students, self-help groups, or community groups. Formal case-level designs especially use such groups. When using case-level or program-level evaluation designs, the evaluator does not know whether the preformed groups used are representative of any larger population. Thus, it is not possible to generalize the evaluation's results beyond the clients (or objects or events) that were actually studied. In addition, it is very probable that different preformed groups will not be equivalent with respect to relevant variables, and these initial differences will invalidate posttest comparisons.

Accordingly, preformed groups should be avoided whenever possible. If it is not feasible to do this, rigorous pretesting must be done to determine in what ways the groups are (or are not) equivalent, and differences must be compensated for with the use of statistical methods.

Mortality

Mortality refers to the tendency of clients to drop out of a program-level evaluation study before it is completed. Their absence can have a significant effect on the study's findings.

The clients who drop out may be different from the other clients in some ways. For example, they may have been less motivated to begin with than those who stay in. If considerably more clients drop out of the experimental group than drop out of the control group (or vice versa), the evaluation project may end up with groups that are not as equivalent in variables such as motivation as the pretests indicated. Since dropouts often have such characteristics in common, it cannot be assumed that the attrition occurred in a random manner. An evaluation design that controls for mortality should be considered.

Reactive Effects

Changes in the behaviors or feelings of clients may be caused by their reactions to the novelty of the situation or the knowledge that they are participating in an evaluation study of some kind. The evaluator may wrongly believe that such reactive effects are due to the intervention, the independent variable.

The classic example of reactive effects was found in a series of studies carried out at the Hawthorne plant of the Western Electric Company in Chicago many years ago. Researchers were investigating the relationship between working conditions and productivity. When they increased the level of lighting in one section of the plant, productivity increased; a further increase in the lighting was followed by an additional increase in productivity. When the lighting was then decreased, however, production levels did not fall accordingly but continued to rise. The conclusion was that the employees were increasing their productivity not because of the lighting level but because of the attention they were receiving as subjects in the study.

The term *Hawthorne effect* is still used to describe any situation in which the clients' behaviors are influenced not by the intervention but by the knowledge that they are taking part in a study of some kind. Another example of such a reactive effect is the placebo or sugar pill given to patients which produces beneficial results because they believe it is medication.

Reactive effects can be controlled by ensuring that all clients in a program-level evaluation study, in both the experimental and control groups, appear to be treated equally. For example, if one group is to be shown an educational film, the other group should also be shown a film—some film carefully chosen to bear no relationship to the intervention being investigated. If the study involves a change in the clients' routine, this in itself may be enough to change behavior, and care must be taken to continue the study until novelty has ceased to be a factor.

Interaction Effects

Interaction among the various threats to internal validity mentioned above can have an effect of its own. Any of the factors already described as threats may interact with one another, but the most common interactive effect involves differential selection and maturation.

Consider the example of an evaluator who is studying two groups of depressed clients. The intention was for these groups to be equivalent, in terms of both their motivation for treatment and their levels of depression. However, it turns out that Group A is more generally depressed than Group B. Whereas both groups may grow less motivated over time, it is likely that Group A, whose members were more depressed to begin with, will lose motivation more completely and more quickly than Group B. Inequivalent groups thus grow less equivalent over time as a result of the interaction between differential selection and maturation.

Relations between Experimental and Control Groups

The final group of threats to internal validity has to do with the effects of the use of experimental and control groups which receive different interventions. These effects include diffusion of services, compensation, rivalry, and demoralization.

Diffusion or imitation of services may occur when the experimental and control groups talk to each other about the evaluation's purpose. Suppose a study is designed which presents a new relaxation exercise to the experimental group and nothing at all to the control group. There is always the possibility that one of the clients in the experimental group will explain the exercise to a friend who happens to be in the control group. The friend explains it to another friend, and so on. This might be beneficial for the control group, but it invalidates the evaluation's findings.

Compensatory equalization of treatment occurs when an evaluator or staff member administering the service to the experimental group feels sorry for clients in the control group who are not receiving it and attempts to compensate them. For example, a worker might take a control group client aside and covertly demonstrate the relaxation exercise.

If an evaluation study has been ethically designed, there should be no need for guilt on the part of the practitioner because some clients are not being taught to relax. They can be taught to relax when the study is "officially" over. If the relaxation exercises are found to be helpful to those clients in the experimental group, there is no reason why the exercises cannot be given to the control group at a later date.

Compensatory rivalry is an effect that occurs when the control group becomes motivated to compete with the experimental group. For example, a control group in a program to encourage parental involvement in school activities might get wind that something is up and make a determined effort to participate too, on the basis that "anything they can do, we can do better." There is no direct communication between groups, as in the diffusion of treatment effect—only rumors and suggestions of rumors. However, rumors are often enough to threaten the internal validity of a study.

In direct contrast with compensatory rivalry, demoralization refers to feelings of deprivation among the control group which may cause them to give up and drop out of the evaluation project. In this case, this effect would be referred to as mortality. The clients in the control group may also act up or get angry.

Threats to External Validity

External validity is the degree to which the results of a program-level evaluation study are generalizable to a larger population or to settings outside the evaluative context, situation, or setting. If an evaluative design is to have external validity, it must provide for selection of a sample of clients for the study that is representative of the population from which it was drawn.

Generalizability is difficult to establish in case-level evaluations; we would have to be able to demonstrate that the clients on whom the intervention is to be tested are representative of a larger group of clients to whom the intervention might be applied. Program-level evaluation designs provide a much broader basis for generalization; if two or more groups are used, we must be able to demonstrate that groups formed for the evaluation project are not only representative of a larger population but are equivalent in all important variables. Moreover, it is necessary to establish that nothing happened during the course of the evaluation—except for the introduction of the intervention, the independent variable—to change either the

---

Threats to External Validity

1. *Pretest-treatment interaction.* Relation between participants' reaction to pretest and response to treatment.
2. *Selection-treatment interaction.* Relation between selection of research participants and their response to treatment.
3. *Specificity of variables.* Using variables that are specific only to the research participants or setting.
4. *Reactive effects.* Participants' reaction to knowledge that they are taking part in a study.
5. *Multiple-treatment interference.* Commingling of results of successive treatments.
6. *Research bias.* Tendency of researchers to find results they want or expect to find.

FIGURE 8.3   Research Factors That Can Threaten External Validity

representativeness of the sample or the equivalence of the groups. The research factors whose effects can constitute threats to external validity are listed in Figure 8.3.

Pretest-Treatment Interaction

This threat is similar to the testing threat to internal validity. The nature of a pretest can alter the way clients respond to the experimental intervention, as well as to the posttest. Suppose, for example, that an educational program on racial tolerance is being evaluated. A pretest which measures level of tolerance could well alert the clients to the fact that they are going to be educated into loving all their neighbors. However, many people do not want to be "educated" into anything—they are satisfied with the way they feel and will resist the instruction. This will affect the level of racial tolerance registered on the posttest.

Selection-Treatment Interaction

Selection-treatment interaction commonly occurs when a program-level evaluation design cannot provide for random selection of clients from a population. Suppose we want to study the effectiveness of professional workers who work in family service agencies, for example. If our research proposal was turned down by 50 agencies before it was accepted by the 51st, it is very likely that the accepting agency differs in certain important aspects from the other 50. It may accept the proposal because its workers are more highly motivated, more secure, more satisfied with their jobs, or more interested in the practical application of the study than the workers within the other 50 agencies.

As a result, we would be assessing the workers on the very factors for which they were unwittingly (and by default) selected—motivation, job satisfaction, and so on. The evaluative study may be internally valid but, since it will not be possible to generalize the results to other family service agencies, it would have little external validity.

Specificity of Variables

The threat of specificity of variables has to do with the fact that an evaluation project conducted with a specific group of clients at a specific time and in a specific setting may not always be generalizable to other clients at a different time and in a different setting. For example, it has been demonstrated that an instrument developed to measure the IQ levels of upper-class, white, suburban children does not provide an equally accurate measure of IQ when it is applied to working-class children of racial minorities in the inner city.

Reactive Effects

As with internal validity, reactive effects occur when the attitudes or behaviors of the clients who take part in a program-level evaluation are affected by their knowledge that they are taking part in an evaluation project. As in formal case-level evaluation designs, another threat to external validity is that clients are changed to some degree by the very act of taking a pretest. Thus, they are no longer exactly equivalent to the population from which they were randomly selected, and it may not be possible to generalize the results of the study to apply to that population. Because the pretest affects the clients who are being tested, the results may only be valid for those who were pretested.

Multiple-Treatment Interference

If a client is given two or more treatments in succession, the results of the first treatment may affect the results of the second treatment. A client attending treatment sessions, for example, may not seem to benefit from one therapeutic technique, so another is tried. In fact, however, the client may have benefited from the first technique, but the benefit does not become apparent until the second technique has been tried. As a result, the effects of both techniques become commingled, or the results may be erroneously ascribed to the second technique alone.

Because of this threat, experimental treatment interventions should be given separately if possible. If the design does not allow this, sufficient time should be allowed to elapse between treatments to minimize the possibility of multiple-treatment interference.

Researcher Bias

People who do evaluations, like people in general, tend to see what they want to see or expect to see. Unconsciously and without any thought of deceit, they can manipulate a program-level evaluation study so that the actual results agree with the anticipated results. A practitioner may favor an intervention so strongly that the evaluation design is structured to support it, or the results are interpreted favorably.

If the evaluator knows which individuals are in the experimental group and which are in the control group, this knowledge alone might affect the study's results. Students an instructor believes to be bright, for example, often are given higher grades than their performance warrants, while students they believe to be dull are given lower grades. The way to control for such bias is to perform a double-blind experiment in which neither the evaluation clients nor the evaluator knows who is in the experimental or control group or who is receiving a specific treatment intervention.

Program-Level Evaluation Designs

Examples of simple evaluation designs were introduced in the previous chapter with case-level designs, because they represent a class of designs that is comparatively consistent and uncomplicated. Many of these designs have the same purpose: to evaluate the effects of interventions on clients. Many have the same independent variable—the intervention—and the same dependent variable—the attainment of the practice objective. The study is done at the individual level—a single person, a single couple, a single group, a single family, a single community or a single organization.

Understanding formal case-level designs, therefore, lays a good foundation for understanding more complex program-level evaluation designs that use groups of clients rather than single clients. But only some of the program-level evaluation designs discussed in this chapter are complex; a design that is unnecessarily complex costs more, takes more time, and probably will not serve its purpose nearly as well as a simpler one. In choosing an evaluation design, therefore, the principle of

TABLE 8.2   **Knowledge Levels and Corresponding Evaluation Designs**

Knowledge Levels		Evaluation Designs
1. Exploratory	*a:*	One-group posttest-only
	b:	Multigroup posttest-only
	c:	Longitudinal case study
2. Descriptive	*a:*	Randomized one-group posttest-only
	b:	Randomized cross-sectional survey
	c:	Randomized longitudinal survey
	d:	One-group pretest-posttest
	e:	Comparison group posttest-only
	f:	Comparison group pretest-posttest
3. Explanatory	*a:*	Classical experimental
	b:	Solomon four-group
	c:	Randomized posttest-only control group
	d:	Interrupted time-series

parsimony must be applied: As in formal case-level designs discussed in the previous chapter, the simplest and most economical route to gather the necessary data is the best choice. The order for the lists of group evaluation designs in Table 8.2 goes from simplest to most complex, and the descriptions of the designs in this and the following sections follow the same order.

A simple notation is used to write these designs in symbol form. Only three basic symbols are used:

X = Intervention, the independent variable
O = Measurement of the program objective, the dependent variable
R = Random selection from a population or random assignment to a group

Exploratory Designs

At the lowest level of the continuum of knowledge that can be derived from program-level evaluation studies are the exploratory studies. An exploratory study explores a program's objective about which little is already known, in order to uncover generalizations and develop hypotheses which can be investigated and tested later with more precise and hence more complex designs and data-gathering techniques.

The three examples of exploratory designs given in this section do not use pretests; they measure the program objective only after the introduction of the intervention, or the independent variable.

One-Group Posttest-Only Design

The one-group posttest-only design (Design 1*a*) is sometimes called the one-shot case study or cross-sectional case study design. It is the simplest of all the program-level evaluation designs.

Suppose the effectiveness of a stop-smoking program is being evaluated. Did anyone who completed it actually stop smoking? To answer this question, all that needs to be done is to locate the last group of clients who completed the program and count the number of clients who no longer smoke.

The basic elements of the one-group posttest-only design are illustrated in Figure 8.4. This simple design can also be written as follows:

$$X \quad O_1$$

where:

X = Intervention, the independent variable
O_1 = First and only measurement of the program objective, the dependent variable

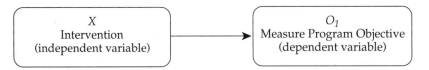

FIGURE 8.4   One-Group Posttest-Only Design

This design only provides for a measure (O_1) of what happens when one group of clients is subjected to one treatment or experience (X). The group was not randomly selected from any particular population, and thus the results of the findings cannot be generalizable to any other group or population. This design will not ascertain whether the value of O_1 indicates any improvement since a pretest was not conducted.

It is safe to assume that all the members of the group smoked before the treatment was introduced, since clients who do not smoke would not enroll in a quit-smoking program. Even if the value of O_1 indicates that some of the group did quit smoking after the treatment, it cannot be determined whether they quit *because* of the intervention (the program) or because of some other rival hypothesis. Perhaps a law was passed to limit smoking in public places, or an ultimatum was issued by the doctor leading the group.

Multigroup Posttest-Only Design

The multigroup posttest-only design (Design 1*b*) is an elaboration of the one-group posttest-only design in which more than one group is used. To check a bit further into the effectiveness of the stop-smoking program, for example, we might decide to locate several more groups who had completed the program and see how many of the clients in each group had stopped smoking. Any number of groups may be used in this design.

This design can be written in symbols as follows:

$$
\begin{array}{lcc}
\text{Experimental Group 1:} & X & O_1 \\
\text{Experimental Group 2:} & X & O_1 \\
\text{Experimental Group 3:} & X & O_1 \\
\text{Experimental Group 4:} & X & O_1 \\
\end{array}
$$

where:

X = Intervention, the independent variable
O_1 = First and only measurement of the program objective, the dependent variable

With this design it cannot be assumed that all four X's are equivalent because all four programs might not be exactly the same; one group might have had a different facilitator, the program might have been presented differently, or the material could have varied in important respects. It cannot be assumed that all the groups were equivalent either; the clients in one group might have been better motivated to stop smoking (on the average) than the clients in the other groups.

It certainly cannot be assumed that any of the groups were representative of the larger population who might wish to stop smoking in the future. Nothing is known about whether any of the clients would have stopped smoking anyway, without the program. Nothing is known as to the extent to which smoking was perhaps reduced, because a pretest was not conducted, and it is not known how heavily the group members smoked before they went through the program.

Longitudinal Case Study Design

The longitudinal case study design (Design 1c) is exactly like the posttest-only design, only it provides for more measurements of the program objective, or the dependent variable. This design can be written in symbols as follows:

$$X \quad O_1 \quad O_2 \quad O_3 \dots$$

where:

X	=	Intervention, the independent variable
O_1	=	First measurement of the program objective, the dependent variable
O_2	=	Second measurement of the program objective, the dependent variable
O_3	=	Third measurement of the program objective, the dependent variable

The basic elements of the longitudinal case study design are illustrated in Figure 8.5. The same design may be called a panel, cohort, developmental, or dynamic case study design.

Suppose, in the example, that the main concern now is the long-term effects of the stop-smoking program. Perhaps the program was effective in helping some clients to quit smoking, but will they stay that way?

The way to find out is to measure the number of cigarettes they collectively smoked at intervals; say the day after the program ended, then a week after that, and then every week for the next six months. If the stop-smoking program is expressed in symbols, as is the longitudinal case study design, the symbols would represent the following elements:

X	=	Stop-smoking program, the independent variable
O_1	=	First measurement of total number of cigarettes smoked per day by all group members, the dependent variable
O_2	=	Second measurement of total number of cigarettes smoked
O_3	=	Third measurement of total number of cigarettes smoked

Notice that in Design 1a, the program objective is measured by counting the number of group members who quit smoking, whereas in Design 1c, the program

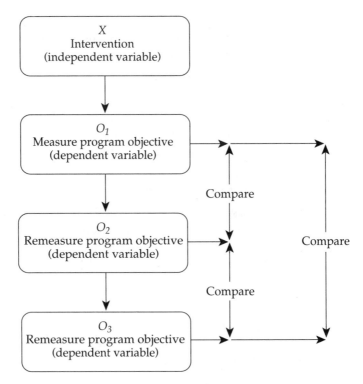

FIGURE 8.5   Longitudinal Case Study Design

objective is measured by counting the total number of cigarettes per day collectively smoked by group members. This demonstrates that a program's objective can be measured in any way that makes the most sense. If we want to know how effective the program is in reducing the number who quit smoking altogether, the number who quit smoking is measured, as in Design 1*a*.

If the goal is to know how effective the program is in making group members as a whole smoke less, the total number of cigarettes they smoke per day can be measured, as in Design 1*c*. In short, two different operational definitions of the program's objective are used: the number of members who quit smoking (Design 1a) and the number of cigarettes smoked (Design 1*c*).

Descriptive Designs

At the midpoint of the knowledge continuum are descriptive designs, which have some but not all of the requirements of an "ideal" evaluation. They usually require specification of the time order of variables, manipulation of the intervention (independent variable), and establishment of the relationship between the intervention and the attainment of the program objectives (dependent variables). They may also control for rival hypotheses and use a second group as a comparison (not a control). The requirement that these designs lack most frequently is random selection of clients from a population and random assignment to groups.

Human service evaluators often are not in a position to assign clients randomly to either an experimental or a comparison or control group. Sometimes the groups to be studied are already in existence; sometimes ethical issues are involved. For example, it would not be ethical to assign clients who need immediate help to two random groups, only one of which is to receive the intervention. Since a lack of random assignment will affect the internal and external validities of the evaluative effort, a descriptive evaluation design must try to compensate for this. The six examples of descriptive evaluation designs presented in this section do this in various ways.

Randomized One-Group Posttest-Only Design

The distinguishing feature of the randomized one-group posttest-only design (Design 2a) is that members of the group are deliberately and randomly selected for it. Otherwise, this design is identical to the exploratory one-group posttest-only design (Design 1a).

The randomized one-group posttest-only design is illustrated in Figure 8.6. In symbols, it is written as follows:

$$R \quad X \quad O_1$$

where:

R = Random selection from a population
X = Intervention, the independent variable
O_1 = First and only measurement of the program objective, the dependent variable

In the example of the stop-smoking group, the difference in this design is that the group does not accidentally assemble itself by participating in a stop-smoking program. Instead, it is randomly selected from a population, say, of all the 400 people who smoke cigarettes in Twin Parks, Idaho (total population 567). These 400 people comprise the population of all the cigarette smokers in Twin Parks. This may seem like an unusually large percentage of smokers in a town this size; it is, as will become apparent later. They also comprise the sampling frame for the study; the use of a sampling frame to select a probability sample will be discussed fully in the next chapter.

The sampling frame of 400 people is used to select a simple random sample of 40 people who smoke cigarettes. The stop-smoking program is administered (X) to these 40 people, and the number of people who quit smoking after the program is determined (O_1). If this design is written for this particular example, the symbols represent:

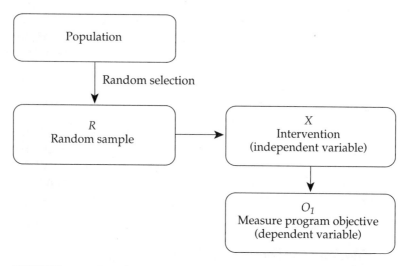

FIGURE 8.6   Randomized One-Group Posttest-Only Design

R = Random selection of 40 people from the population of people who smoke cigarettes in Twin Parks

X = Stop-smoking program, the intervention

O_1 = Number of people in program who quit smoking, the program objective or dependent variable

Assume that the program fails to have the desired effect, and 39 of the 40 people continue to smoke cigarettes after participating in the program. Because the program was ineffective for the sample and the sample was randomly selected, it can be concluded that it would be ineffective for the entire cigarette smoking population of Twin Parks—the other 360 who did not go through the program. In other words, because a representative random sample was selected, it is possible to generalize the results to the population from which the sample was drawn.

Since no change in the program objective occurred, it is not sensible to consider the control of rival hypotheses. The evaluator need not wonder what might have caused the change—X, or an alternative explanation. However, if the program had been successful, it would not be possible to ascribe success solely to the program, because the evaluator would have no idea of what other factors might have contributed to it.

Randomized Cross-Sectional Survey Design

The randomized cross-sectional survey design is one of the two designs that are commonly used with surveys as the data-collection method. It is written as follows:

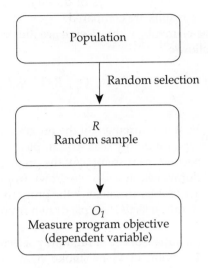

FIGURE 8.7   Randomized Cross-Sectional Survey Design

$$R \quad O_1$$

where:

R = Random selection from a population
O_1 = First and only measurement of the program objective, the dependent variable

The notation RO_1 describes what is done when a survey is carried out. This design is illustrated in Figure 8.7.

For example, suppose a survey is conducted to find out how many people in Twin Parks smoke cigarettes. First, a representative random sample (R) is drawn of all the people in the town. Then personal interviews are conducted to determine how many of the people in this sample smoke cigarettes. The number of cigarette smokers uncovered is the O_1 part of the RO_1 notation; there is no X part in this design. Note that there does not have to be an intervention before a survey can be undertaken. This design is used quite often in needs assessments.

Randomized Longitudinal Survey Design

The randomized longitudinal survey design (Design 2c) is exactly the same as Design 2b, except that the measurement of the program objective is repeated two or more times. Successive surveys of different random samples are conducted, and then the group results are compared.

The basic elements of this design are illustrated in Figure 8.8. In symbols, it is written as follows:

$$R_1O_1 \quad R_2O_2 \quad R_3O_3 \ldots$$

where:

$R_1O_1 =$　First measurement of the program objective (the dependent variable) for a randomly selected sample drawn from a population

$R_2O_2 =$　Second measurement of the program objective for a different randomly selected sample drawn from a population

$R_3O_3 =$　Third measurement of the program objective for a different randomly selected sample drawn from a population

Suppose an initial survey of randomly selected people from Twin Parks uncovers that 99.44 percent of them smoke cigarettes (O_1). Six months later another randomly selected sample is surveyed, with results O_2. In another six months, a

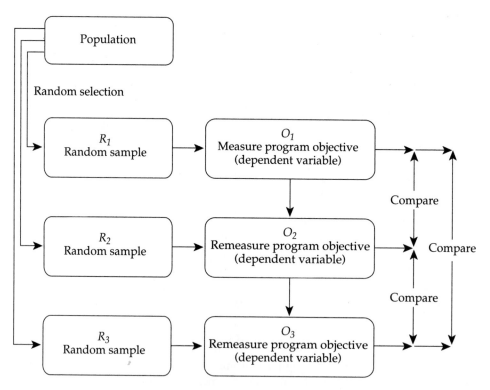

FIGURE 8.8　Randomized Longitudinal Survey Design

third survey is conducted, with results O_3. These results can be used to monitor the cigarette smoking behavior over time of the people in the population.

This design thus provides a description of net change over time. It can be used to monitor the knowledge, behaviors, attitudes, or affects of any population. For the example used here, R_1O_1, R_2O_2, and R_3O_3 would represent the first, second, and third "smoking" surveys of three different randomly selected groups of people in Twin Parks.

One-Group Pretest-Posttest Design

The one-group pretest-posttest design (Design 2*d*) may also be referred to as a before-after design, because it includes a pretest of the program's objective (dependent variable) which can be used as a basis of comparison with the posttest results. This design is illustrated in Figure 8.9 and written as follows:

$$O_1 \quad X \quad O_2$$

where:

O_1 = First measurement of the program objective, the dependent variable
X = Intervention, the independent variable
O_2 = Second measurement of the program objective, the dependent variable

The one-group pretest-posttest design, in which a pretest precedes the introduction of the intervention and a posttest follows it, can be used to determine

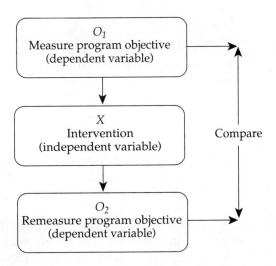

FIGURE 8.9 One-Group Pretest-Posttest Design

precisely how the intervention affects a particular group in relation to program objectives. The design is used often in human service decision making—far too often, in fact, because it does not control for extraneous variables. The difference between O_1 and O_2 on which these decisions are based, therefore, could be due to many other factors rather than the intervention.

In the stop-smoking example, history would be an extraneous variable or threat to internal validity, because all kinds of things could have happened between O_1 and O_2 to affect the clients, such as a new tax on cigarettes which raises the price. Testing also would be a problem; just the experience of taking the pretest could motivate some clients to quit smoking. There also could be other threats or interactions among threats.

Comparison Group Posttest-Only Design

The comparison group posttest-only design (Design 2e) improves on the exploratory one-group and multigroup posttest-only designs by introducing a comparison group which does not receive the intervention but is subject to the same posttest as those who do (the experimental group). A group used for purposes of comparison is usually referred to as a comparison group in an exploratory or descriptive program-level evaluation design and as a control group in an explanatory program-level evaluation design. While a control group is always randomly assigned, a comparison group is not.

The basic elements in this design are illustrated in Figure 8.10. It is written as follows:

$$\text{Experimental Group:} \quad X \quad O_1$$
$$\text{Comparison Group:} \qquad\qquad O_1$$

where:

X = Intervention, the independent variable
O_1 = First and only measurement of the program objective, the dependent variable

In the stop-smoking program, if January, April, and August sections are scheduled and the August sessions are cancelled for some reason, those who would have been clients in that section could be used as a comparison group. If the values of O_1 were similar for the experimental and comparison groups, it could be concluded that the program was of little use, since those who had experienced it (those receiving X) were not much better or worse off than those who had not.

There would not be a real basis for this conclusion, however, because there is no evidence that the groups were equivalent to begin with. Therefore the comparison group cannot be used to control for such threats to internal validity as maturation, testing, and history, since these factors could have affected each group differently.

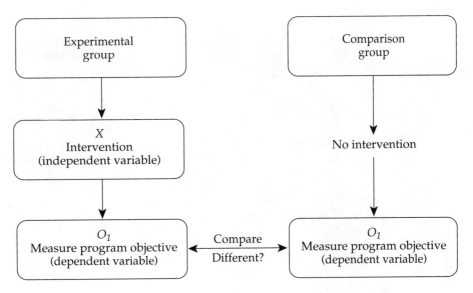

FIGURE 8.10   Comparison Group Posttest-Only Design

Comparison Group Pretest-Posttest Design

The comparison group pretest-posttest design (Design 2*f*) elaborates on the one-group pretest-posttest design (Design 2*d*) by adding a comparison group. This second group receives both the pretest (O_1) and the posttest (O_2) at the same time as the experimental group, but it does not receive the intervention. The elements of this design are shown in Figure 8.11. In symbols, it is written as follows:

$$\text{Experimental Group:} \quad O_1 \quad X \quad O_2$$
$$\text{Comparison Group:} \quad O_1 \quad \quad O_2$$

where:

O_1 = First measurement of the program objective, the dependent variable
X = Intervention, the independent variable
O_2 = Second measurement of the program objective, the dependent variable

The experimental and comparison groups formed under this design will probably not be equivalent, because members are not randomly assigned to them. The pretest, however, will indicate the extent of their differences. If the differences are likely to affect the posttest, the statistical technique of analysis of covariance can be used to compensate for them.

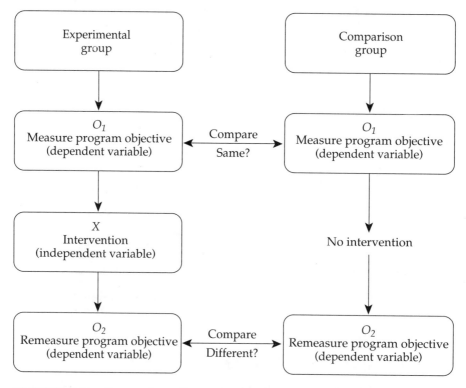

FIGURE 8.11   Comparison Group Pretest-Posttest Design

Explanatory Designs

Explanatory program-level evaluation designs approach an "ideal" evaluation most closely. They are at the highest level on the knowledge continuum, have the most rigid requirements, and are most able to produce results that can be generalized to other clients and situations. Explanatory designs, therefore, are most able to provide valid and reliable evaluation results that can add to our theoretical knowledge base.

The purpose of most explanatory designs is to establish a causal connection between the intervention (the independent variable) and the program objectives (the dependent variable). The attainment of the objectives could always result from chance rather than from the influence of the intervention, but there are statistical techniques for calculating the probability that this will occur (see Weinbach & Grinnell, 1995).

Classical Experimental Design

The classical experimental design (Design 3a), or classical evaluation design, is the basis for all explanatory designs. It involves an experimental group and a control

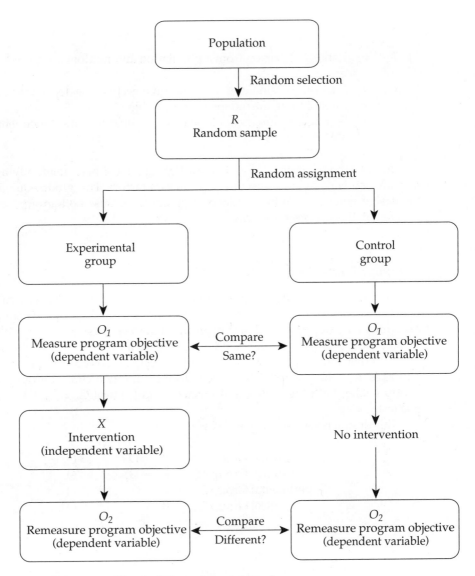

FIGURE 8.12 Classical Experimental Design

group, both created by random sampling and random assignment methods. As Figure 8.12 shows, both groups take a pretest (O_1) at the same time after which the intervention (X) is given only to the experimental group, and then both groups take the posttest (O_2).

This design is written as follows:

Experimental Group: R O_1 X O_2
Control Group: R O_1 O_2

where:

R = Random selection from a population and random assignment to group

O_1 = First measurement of the program objective, the dependent variable

X = Intervention, the independent variable

O_2 = Second measurement of the program objective, the dependent variable

Because the experimental and control groups have been randomly assigned, they are equivalent with respect to all important factors. This group equivalence in the design helps control for extraneous variables, because both groups would be affected by them in the same way.

Solomon Four-Group Design

The Solomon four-group design (Design 3*b*) is a variation of the classical design which involves four rather than two randomly assigned groups. There are two experimental groups and two control groups, but the pretest is taken by only one of each of these groups. Experimental Group 1 takes a pretest, receives the intervention, and then takes a posttest. Experimental Group 2 also receives the intervention but takes only the posttest. The same is true for the two control groups; Control Group 1 takes both the pretest and posttest, and Control Group 2 takes only the posttest.

This design is written in symbols as follows:

Experimental Group 1:	R	O_1	X	O_2
Control Group 1:	R	O_1		O_2
Experimental Group 2:	R		X	O_2
Control Group 2:	R			O_2

where:

R = Random assignment to group

O_1 = First measurement of the program objective, the dependent variable

X = Intervention, the independent variable

O_2 = Second measurement of the program objective, the dependent variable

The advantage of the Solomon four-group design is that it allows for control of testing effects, since one of the experimental groups and one of the control groups do not take the pretest. However, it has the disadvantages that twice as many study clients are required, and it is more work to implement this design than the classical experimental design.

Randomized Posttest-Only Control Group Design

The randomized posttest-only control group design (Design 3*c*) is identical to the descriptive comparison group posttest-only design (Design 2*e*), except that in this explanatory design clients are randomly assigned to groups. This design, therefore, has a control group rather than a comparison group.

The randomized posttest-only control group design usually involves only two groups, one experimental and one control. There are no pretests. The experimental group receives the intervention and takes the posttest; the control group only takes the posttest. The basic elements of this design are illustrated in Figure 8.13.

This design can be written as follows:

Experimental Group: R X O_1
Control Group: R O_1

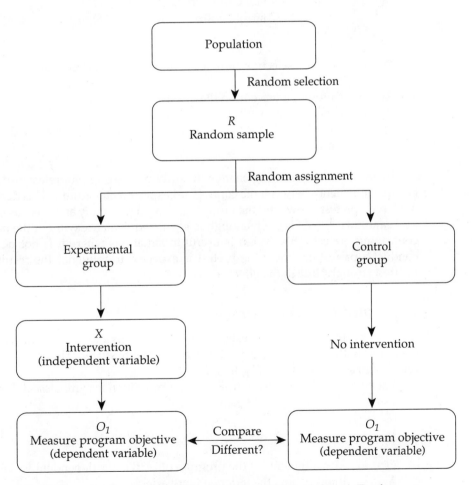

FIGURE 8.13   Randomized Posttest-Only Control Group Design

where:

R =   Random selection from a population and random assignment to group

X =   Intervention, the independent variable

O_1 =   First and only measurement of the program objective, the dependent variable

Suppose we want to test the effects of two different treatment interventions, X_1 and X_2. In this case, Design 3c could be elaborated upon to form three randomly assigned groups, two experimental groups (one for each intervention) and one control group. This design would be written as follows:

$$
\begin{array}{llll}
\text{Experimental Group 1:} & R & X_1 & O_1 \\
\text{Experimental Group 2:} & R & X_2 & O_1 \\
\text{Control Group:} & R & & O_1 \\
\end{array}
$$

where:

R =   Random selection from a population and random assignment to group

X_1 =   Different intervention than X_2, independent variable X_1

X_2 =   Different intervention than X_1, independent variable X_2

O_1 =   First and only measurement of the program objective, the dependent variable

In addition to measuring change in a group or groups, a pretest also helps to ensure equivalence between the control and experimental groups. This design does not have a pretest. However, the groups have been randomly assigned, as indicated by R, and this in itself is often enough to ensure equivalence without the need for a confirming pretest. This design is useful in situations where it is not possible to conduct a pretest or where the pretest is expected to influence the results of the posttest strongly, due to the effects of testing.

Interrupted Time-Series Design

In the interrupted time-series design, a series of pretests and posttests are conducted over time, both before and after the intervention is introduced. The basic elements of this design are illustrated in Figure 8.14.

An interrupted time-series design might be written in symbols as follows:

$$O_1 \quad O_2 \quad O_3 \quad X \quad O_4 \quad O_5 \quad O_6$$

where:

O's   =   Measurements of the program objective, the dependent variable

X =   Intervention, the independent variable

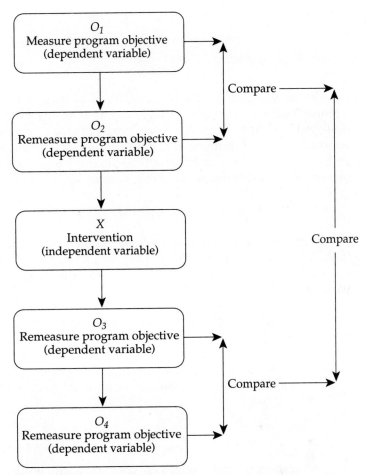

FIGURE 8.14 Interrupted Time-Series Design

This design takes care of the major weakness in the descriptive one-group pretest-posttest design (Design 2d), which does not control for rival hypotheses. Suppose, for example, that a new policy is to be introduced into an agency whereby all promotions and raises are to be tied to the number of educational credits acquired by practitioners. Since there is a strong feeling among some workers that years of experience ought to count for more than educational credits, the agency's management decides to examine the effect of the new policy on morale.

Because agency morale is affected by many things and varies normally from month to month, it is necessary to ensure that these normal fluctuations are not confused with the results of the new policy. Therefore a baseline is first established for morale by conducting a number of pretests over a six-month period before the policy is introduced. Then, a similar number of posttests is conducted over the six months following the introduction of the policy. This design would be written as follows:

$$O_1 \quad O_2 \quad O_3 \quad O_4 \quad O_5 \quad O_6 \quad X \quad O_7 \quad O_8 \quad O_9 \quad O_{10} \quad O_{11} \quad O_{12}$$

The same type of time-series design can be used to evaluate the result of a treatment intervention with a single client, as in the formal case-level designs described in Chapter 7. Such a design might call for a pretreatment baseline to be established (say, O_1 through O_5), and then the intervention would be introduced and measured the same number of times, in order to see whether or not improvement continues. This design would be written:

$$O_1 \quad O_2 \quad O_3 \quad O_4 \quad O_5 \quad XO_6 \quad XO_7 \quad XO_8 \quad XO_9 \quad XO_{10}$$

Alternately, the intervention could be continued for a time and then withdrawn to see if the dependent variable returns to its pretreatment level. If the intervention is continued for XO_5 through XO_8 and then withdrawn, the design would be written:

$$O_1 \quad O_2 \quad O_3 \quad O_4 \quad XO_5 \quad XO_6 \quad XO_7 \quad XO_8 \quad O_9 \quad O_{10} \quad O_{11} \quad O_{12}$$

The treatment intervention will be effective if, after it is withdrawn, the beneficial effects continue and measurement of the program objective indicates that the data points for O_9 through O_{12} maintain the same level as those for XO_5 through XO_8.

Summary

Program-level evaluation designs are conducted with groups of cases rather than on a case-by-case basis. They cover the entire range of evaluation concerns and provide designs that can be used to gain knowledge on the exploratory, descriptive, and explanatory levels. The chapter presented the threats to internal and external validity and demonstrated how these threats can affect various evaluation designs.

The last chapter described how formal case-level evaluations can be used to enhance quality improvement at the line level; that is, it presented various evaluative designs that can be used to evaluate (or monitor) clients' practice objectives. This chapter presented various designs that can be used to evaluate program objectives. Thus, the two chapters complement one another as they both describe how evaluations can be used in the quality improvement process at the case level (practice objectives) and at the program level (program objectives). All of the evaluative designs presented in the last chapter and this one can be used to enhance the delivery of human services.

Most of the designs described in these two chapters can be used in the project and monitoring approaches to quality improvement (see Chapter 3), depending on when the evaluation takes place. Designs that reflect the project approach usually take place after a program is completed, whereas designs that reflect the monitoring approach usually take place while the program is underway.

This chapter has pointed out that if the findings from a program-level evaluation study are to be generalized to other clients, or other settings, the people, objects, or events studied must be representative of the populations to which the results are to be applied. In the following chapter, the concept of generalization is examined further by considering sampling procedures which can be used to make sure that people, objects, or events selected for an evaluation study are representative of the populations from which they were drawn.

Key Terms

Classical Experimental Design: An explanatory research design with randomly selected and randomly assigned experimental and control groups in which the program's objective (the dependent variable) is measured before and after the intervention (the independent variable) for both groups, but only the experimental group receives the intervention.

Comparison Group Posttest-Only Design: A descriptive research design with two groups, experimental and comparison, in which the program's objective (dependent variable) is measured once for both groups, and only the experimental group receives the intervention (the independent variable).

Comparison Group Pretest-Posttest Design: A descriptive research design with two groups, experimental and comparison in which the program's objective (the dependent variable) is measured before and after the intervention (the independent variable) for both groups, but only the experimental group receives the intervention.

Compensation: Attempts by evaluators or staff members to counterbalance the lack of treatment for control group clients by administering some or all of the intervention (the independent variable); a threat to internal validity.

Compensatory Rivalry: Motivation of control group clients to compete with experimental group clients; a threat to internal validity.

Constants: A characteristic that has the same value for all clients in an evaluation.

Control Group: A group of randomly selected and randomly assigned clients in a study who do not receive the experimental intervention (the independent variable) and are used for comparison purposes.

Demoralization: Feelings of deprivation among control group clients which may cause them to drop out of the evaluation study; a form of mortality which is a threat to internal validity.

Dependent Variable: A variable that is dependent on or caused by another variable; an outcome variable which is not manipulated directly but is measured to determine if the independent variable has had an effect. Program objectives are dependent variables.

Differential Selection: The failure to achieve or maintain equivalency among the preformed groups; a threat to internal validity.

Diffusion of Treatment: Problems that may occur when experimental and control group clients talk to each other about a study; a threat to internal validity.

Experimental Group: In an experimental research design, the group of clients exposed to the manipulation of the intervention (the independent variable); also referred to as the treatment group.

External Validity: The extent to which the findings of an evaluation study can be generalized outside the evaluative situation.

Generalizability: Extending or applying the findings of an evaluation study to clients or situations which were not directly evaluated.

Hawthorne Effect: Effects on clients' behaviors or attitudes attributable to their knowledge that they are taking part in an evaluation project; a reactive effect that is a threat to internal validity.

History in Research Design: Any event that may affect the second or subsequent measurement of the program's objectives (the dependent variables) and which cannot be accounted for in the evaluation design; a threat to internal validity.

Hypothesis: A theory-based prediction of the expected results in an evaluation study; a tentative explanation of a relationship or supposition that a relationship may exist.

Independent Variable: A variable that is not dependent on another variable but is said to cause or determine changes in the dependent variable; an antecedent variable that is directly manipulated in order to assess its effect on the dependent variable. Interventions are independent variables.

Instrumentation Error: Any flaws in the construction of a measuring instrument or any faults in the administration of a measuring instrument that affect the appraisal of program and practice objectives; a threat to internal validity.

Interaction Effect: Effects on the program's objective (the dependent variable) that are produced by the combination of two or more threats to internal validity.

Internal Validity: The extent to which it can be demonstrated that the intervention (the independent variable) in an evaluation is the only cause of change in the program's objective (the dependent variable); soundness of the experimental procedures and measuring instruments.

Interrupted Time-Series Design: An explanatory evaluation design in which there is only one group and the program objective (the dependent variable) is measured repeatedly before and after the intervention (the independent variable).

Longitudinal Case Study Design: An exploratory research design in which there is only one group and the program's objective (the dependent variable) is measured more than once; also referred to as a panel design, a cohort design, a developmental design, or a dynamic case study design.

Matched Pairs Method: A technique of assigning clients to groups so that the experimental and control groups are approximately equivalent in pretest scores or other characteristics, or so that all differences except the experimental condition are eliminated.

Maturation: Any unplanned change in clients due to mental, physical or other processes which take place over the course of the evaluation project and which affect the program's objective; a threat to internal validity.

Mortality: The tendency for clients to drop out of an evaluation study before it is completed; a threat to internal validity.

Multigroup Posttest-Only Design: An exploratory research design in which there is more than one group and the program's objective (the dependent variable) is measured only once for each group.

Multiple-Treatment Interference: When a client is given two or more interventions in succession, the results of the first intervention may affect the results of the second or subsequent interventions; a threat to external validity.

One-Group Posttest-Only Design: An exploratory design in which the program's objective (the dependent variable) is measured only once; the simplest of all group evaluation designs.

One-Group Pretest-Posttest Design: A descriptive research design in which the program's objective (the dependent variable) is measured before and after the intervention (the independent variable).

Pretest-Treatment Interaction: Effects of the pretest on the responses of clients to the introduction of the intervention (the independent variable); a threat to external validity.

Principle of Parsimony: A principle stating that the simplest and most economical route to evaluating the achievement of the program's objective (the dependent variable) is the best.

Random Assignment: The process of allocating clients to experimental and control groups so that the groups are equivalent; also referred to as randomization.

Random Sampling: An unbiased selection process

conducted so that all members of a population have an equal chance of being selected to participate in the evaluation study.

Randomized Cross-Sectional Survey Design: A descriptive research design in which there is only one group, the program's objective (the dependent variable) is measured only once, the clients are randomly selected from the population and there is no intervention (the independent variable).

Randomized Longitudinal Survey Design: A descriptive research design in which there is only one group, the program's objective (the dependent variable) is measured more than once, and clients are randomly selected from the population before the intervention (the independent variable).

Randomized One-Group Posttest-Only Design: A descriptive research design in which there is only one group, the program's objective (the dependent variable) is measured only once and all members of a population have equal opportunity for participation in the evaluation.

Randomized Posttest-Only Control Group Design: An explanatory research design in which there are two or more randomly selected and randomly assigned groups; the control group does not receive the intervention (the independent variable), and the experimental groups receive different interventions.

Reactive Effects: An effect on outcome measures due to the clients' awareness that they are participating in an evaluation study; a threat to internal and external validity.

Researcher Bias: The tendency of evaluators to find results that they expect to find; a threat to external validity.

Rival Hypothesis: A theory-based prediction that is a plausible alternative to the research hypothesis and might explain results as well or better; a hypothesis involving extraneous variables other than the intervention (the independent variable); also referred to as the alternative hypothesis.

Selection-Treatment Interaction: The relationship between the manner of selecting clients to participate in an evaluation study and their responses to the intervention (the independent variable); a threat to external validity.

Solomon Four-Group Design: An explanatory research design with four randomly assigned groups, two experimental and two control; the program's objective (the dependent variable) is measured before and after the intervention (the independent variable) for one experimental and one control group, but only after the intervention for the other two groups, and only the experimental groups receive the intervention.

Specificity of Variables: An evaluation project conducted with a specific group of clients at a specific time and in a specific setting may not always be generalizable to other clients at a different time and in a different setting; a threat to external validity.

Statistical Regression: The tendency for extreme high or low scores to regress, or shift, toward the average (mean) score on subsequent measurements; a threat to internal validity.

Testing Effect: The effect that taking a pretest might have on posttest scores; a threat to internal validity.

Study Questions

1. In your own words, briefly describe the six factors that are required for a study to be classified as an "ideal" experiment?

2. What is meant by internal validity in human service evaluation studies?

3. What is meant by external validity in human service evaluation studies?

4. What are the differences between random selection and random sampling?

5. In groups of six, decide on a human service-related problem area. Design three hypothetical studies using one exploratory, one explanatory, and one descriptive evaluation design. For each study determine what data

needs to be gathered. Provide the graphic representation of the study detailing the R's, O's, and X's. Present the three designs to the class with a detailed explanation of sampling procedures.

6. In groups of four, discuss each of the threats to external validity and the threats to internal validity in terms of how you would control for each one. What problems arise when attempting to control for all of the threats to internal and external validity? Present your discussion to the class.

7. Describe thoroughly in your own words the similarities and differences between formal case-level evaluation designs and program-level evaluations. Discuss in detail how they complement one another in contemporary human service practice.

8. Discuss how program-level designs provide data that are more generalizable than those data that are generated from formal case-level designs.

9. In your own words describe what an "ideal" program evaluation is. What is the purpose of conducting one? Why is an "ideal" evaluative study rarely achieved in the human services?

10. Time order of variables is crucial to an "ideal" evaluation, as is the manipulation of at least one independent variable and the establishment of a relationship between interventions and program objectives. Why?

11. "Ideal" evaluations also require the control of rival hypotheses, the use of a control group, and random sampling and assignment. Explain why this is so.

12. In addition to the six characteristics of "ideal" evaluations, an "ideal" evaluation study must have internal and external validity. What is the main difference between internal and external validity?

13. In an "ideal" evaluation, the evaluator should be able to conclude from the findings that the intervention is or is not the only

cause of the change in the program's objective. What factors would threaten the ability of the evaluator to draw such a conclusion?

14. In an "ideal" evaluation, the results are generalizable to a larger group or setting outside of the evaluative context, situation, or setting. Why is generalizability so important to establish in evaluative studies? What factors would threaten the generalizability of the results of a particular study to a large population or group?

15. Why is the principle of parsimony so important in choosing an evaluative design?

16. Why are exploratory designs at the lowest level on the continuum of knowledge that can be derived from evaluation studies? What is meant by an exploratory design?

17. What are the characteristics of a one-group posttest-only design? Can the results of this design be generalized to another group or population? Why or why not? Can a causal relationship between the program or practice objectives and intervention be established with these designs?

18. What are the characteristics of a multigroup posttest-only design? Can we assume that all the groups in the study are equivalent? Can we assume that any of the groups are representative of the larger population? Why?

19. How is the longitudinal case-study design like the one-group post-test-only design? How is it different? What is the advantage of using this design?

20. Why are descriptive designs found at the midpoint on the continuum of knowledge that can be derived from evaluation studies? Explain what is meant by a descriptive design.

21. How is the randomized one-group posttest-only design similar to the exploratory one-group posttest-only design? How is it different? What is the advantage of using the randomized design? What is a major problem in its use?

22. What is the difference between a randomized cross-sectional survey design and a randomized longitudinal survey design? Under what conditions would you choose the use of one design over another?

23. Describe the characteristics of the one-group pretest-posttest design. Why is the design used so often in the human services? What are some of the shortcomings of this design? How is this design different from the comparison group pretest-posttest design?

24. How is the comparison group posttest-only design an improvement over the exploratory one-group and multigroup posttest-only designs?

25. What is the difference between a control group and a comparison group? How does the use of a comparison group affect the evaluator's ability to prove a causal relationship between the intervention and the program objectives?

26. Why are explanatory designs at the highest level on the continuum of knowledge that can be derived from evaluation studies? Explain what is meant by an explanatory design.

27. What is a classical experimental design? How does it fulfill the requirements of an "ideal" explanatory evaluative design?

28. How is the Solomon four-group design a variation of the classical experimental design?

29. Read Case Study A. Given the contents of the case study, construct thirteen individual program-level evaluation designs (listed in Table 8.2) that could be used to evaluate one of the program's objectives. Use X's, O's, and R's in your designs. For each design, list the threats to internal and external validity that would be relevant to the design. Pay particular attention to the program's population when constructing each design. For each program-level design, discuss what case-level design comes closest to it (Chapter 7).

30. Read Case Study B. Given the contents of the case study, construct thirteen individual program-level evaluation designs (listed in Table 8.2) that could be used to evaluate one of the program's objectives. Use X's, O's, and R's in your designs. For each design, list the threats to internal and external validity that would be relevant to the design. Pay particular attention to the program's population when constructing each design. For each program-level design, discuss what case-level design comes closest to it (Chapter 7).

31. Read Case Study C. Given the contents of the case study, construct thirteen individual program-level evaluation designs (listed in Table 8.2) that could be used to evaluate one of the program's objectives. Use X's, O's, and R's in your designs. For each design, list the threats to internal and external validity that would be relevant to the design. Pay particular attention to the program's population when constructing each design. For each program-level design, discuss what case-level design comes closest to it (Chapter 7).

9

USING SAMPLING PROCEDURES

As WE HAVE STRESSED in previous chapters, case-level evaluations (Chapter 7) are used in the quality improvement process in an effort to provide first-rate services to clients who are currently receiving day-to-day services within human service programs; that is, they monitor and evaluate the attainment of client practice objectives. Program-level evaluations (Chapter 8), on the other hand, are used to improve the services and programs an organization offers to its clients; that is, they monitor and evaluate the attainment of program objectives. As we know, most evaluation designs (at the case and program levels) can be used in the monitoring approach to quality improvement and in the project approach to quality improvement, depending on when the design is implemented.

When a human service program's objectives are being monitored or evaluated via group designs, it is sometimes not possible to use all the data (cases) to determine the achievement of program objectives. In addition, it is usually not necessary to use all the data; we can use data from only some of the cases, if we know that the cases we select represent all of the cases. This process is known as sampling.

Closely associated with the formulation of a group evaluation design, as presented in the preceding chapter, is the specification of the sampling plan, or the methods that will be used to ensure that the individuals selected for the sample actually represent the population from which they come. These participants will provide data on the program's objectives to be achieved in an evaluation study.

Ideally, data should be obtained from or about each and every person (or event or object) in a given set. The resulting data would then be descriptive of the entire set. In practice, however, it is rarely possible (or feasible) to obtain data about every single unit; such a process would be too time-consuming and too costly. The common practice, therefore, is to gather data from some units in the set and use these data to describe the entire set.

Thus, *sampling* is the selection of some units to represent the entire set from which the units were drawn. If the selection is carried out in accordance with the requirements of sampling theory, the data obtained from the selected units should quite accurately pertain to the entire set.

Sampling Theory

The logic of sampling theory was introduced in the previous chapter. By way of review, consider the example of an evaluation project that seeks to assess the extent of drug dependence among chronically ill older people in Kansas City. The total set of people is referred to as a population—in this case, the entire group of chronically ill older people in Kansas City. Because it would not be feasible to study the drug dependence of each and every individual in this population, some of the chronically

This chapter has been adapted and modified from Peter Gabor, Sampling. In R. M. Grinnell, Jr. (Ed.), *Social Work Research and Evaluation* (4th ed.). © 1993 F. E. Peacock Publishers. Used with permission.

ill older people in Kansas City are selected for a sample, and data are collected about drug dependency among this group.

These findings are then applied, or generalized, to the population from which the sample was drawn. This procedure can be justified if the sample is representative of the population; that is, if the relevant characteristics of the sample are similar to the characteristics of the population from which the sample is drawn.

Sampling theory provides a method of ensuring that a sample and population will be similar in all relevant characteristics. All that is required is that a sample be chosen using a procedure that provides each member of the population with the same probability of being selected. This procedure is called *probability sampling*. There are two major categories of sampling procedures, probability and nonprobability. In probability sampling, every member of a population has a known probability of being selected for the sample, so it can be established that the sample is representative of the population from which it was drawn. In *nonprobability sampling*, the probability of selection cannot be estimated, and it is difficult to establish the representativeness of the sample in relation to the population.

When a sample is representative of the population, it is possible to generalize findings about the sample to the population from which it was drawn. Studying an appropriately drawn sample of chronically ill older people in Kansas City, therefore, puts evaluators in a position to describe drug dependency in the entire group of chronically ill older people in that city.

The use of sampling techniques is not limited to the study of people. Any population can be described with considerable accuracy through the selection of an appropriate sample. For example, the population may be composed of objects such as case files in an agency. Through the selection of a sample of files, questions relating to all the files in the agency could be answered. Similarly, events and processes such as decision making about foster home placement in a particular county can be the objective of an evaluation study. An appropriately selected sample would yield data about placement decision making in that county.

The Sampling Frame

In selecting a probability sample, the first step is to compile a sampling frame. The *sampling frame* is that collection of units (e.g., people, objects, or events) which has a possibility of being selected. In other words, it is the listing from which a sample is actually selected. Ideally, it would be best to use the population as the sampling frame; however, this is seldom feasible because complete listings of populations rarely exist.

An example could be an evaluation study which tries to ascertain the experiences of human service workers in Phoenix with their supervision. The population of interest in this study is defined as all professional human service workers in Phoenix on January 1, 1995. Ideally, evaluators would like to proceed by drawing a sample from this population. There is no definitive list containing the names of all human service workers in Phoenix, thus the first task is to create a listing of them from which evaluators can subsequently draw the sample. This listing is known as a sampling frame.

A number of strategies can be employed in compiling a sampling frame in this example. One strategy is to obtain lists of workers from all human service agencies and organizations that are known to employ them. Human service workers in private practice listed in the telephone book could then be added to this list. If the task is executed with care, a reasonably complete list of human service workers in Phoenix would result.

However, for a number of reasons, the sampling frame is unlikely to be identical to the population. The lists of workers provided by agencies and organizations may not be up to date: some workers may have been hired since the agency lists were compiled; others might have resigned or found positions in other agencies. Professionals who have recently entered private practice may not be listed in the telephone book, while others who are listed may have left private practice. Some organizations that employ human service workers may have been missed entirely.

In short, the sampling frame and the population are not identical, although it is desirable that the sampling frame approximate the population as closely as possible. Because in practice it is from the sampling frame that the sample is actually drawn, the representativeness of the sample is limited by how closely the sampling frame approximates the population of interest.

Probability Sampling

In probability sampling every member of a designated population has a known probability of being selected for a sample. It is possible, therefore, to calculate the degree to which the sample is representative of the population from which it was drawn. Probability sampling strategies may have just one stage or several stages. Figure 9.1 presents a graphic summary of the examples used to illustrate the three one-stage and one multistage probability sampling strategies discussed in this section.

One-Stage Probability Sampling

In one-stage probability sampling, the strategies or procedures may be classified as simple, systematic, or stratified random sampling. In each case, the selection of the sample is completed in one process.

Simple Random Sampling

In simple random sampling, members of a population are selected, one at a time, until the desired sample size is obtained. Once an individual unit (e.g., person, object, event) has been selected, it is removed from the population and has no chance of being selected again. This procedure is often used in selecting winning lottery numbers.

Single-Stage Strategies

Simple Random Sampling
Assuming a population of 500 and a sampling fraction of 1/5

Population	Random selection	Sample
$N=500$	$\xrightarrow{\text{of 20\% of population}}$	$N=100$

Systematic Random Sample
Assuming a population of 500 and a sampling interval of 5

Population	Select every	Sample
$N=500$	$\xrightarrow{\text{5th person}}$	$N=100$

Stratified Random Sampling
Assuming a population of 500 composed of 450 human service workers and 50 supervisors; stratification on position; sampling fraction of 1/5

Human service workers
$n=450$ → Random selection of 20% workers → Human service workers in sample $n=90$

Population $N=500$

Supervisors $n=50$ → Random selection of 20% of supervisors → Supervisors in sample $n=10$

Final sample $N=100$

Multistage Strategy

Cluster Sampling
Assuming a 3-stage selection

Stage 1 — Residential blocks $N=300$ → Random selection of 17% of blocks → Blocks in sample $N=51$

Stage 2 — List residential units on selected blocks $N=2000$ → Random selection of 20% of units → Units in sample $N=400$

Stage 3 — List single parents in selected units $N=100$ → Random selection of 25% of single parents → Final sample $N=25$

FIGURE 9.1   Summary of Probability Sampling Strategies

For example, the objective of a particular lottery may be to guess six of 50 numbers. The winning numbers are selected by placing 50 balls, numbered 01 to 50, in a bowl and asking a blindfolded person to select, one at a time, six balls from the bowl. Each time a ball is selected, it is set aside and becomes one of the winning numbers; the end result is that six different numbers are selected by chance.

In practice, it is necessary to assign a unique number to each member within the population. As an example, consider a case where the population consists of 500 clients being seen by a family service agency. It is decided that a sample of 100 (a sampling fraction of 1/5 or 20 percent of the population) is required. First, each client is assigned a number from 001 to 500. Next, 100 numbers in the range 001 to 500 are randomly selected. The clients who had been assigned the 100 selected numbers constitute the sample. The selection of numbers can be carried out with the assistance of a computer or by using a published table of random numbers.

A variety of computer programs which generate random numbers is available. Typically, all that is required is entering into the computer the range from within which selections are to be made, as well as the quantity of random numbers required. The computer then generates a list of the required numbers.

Alternatively, a published table of random numbers can be used to select the sample manually. Part of such a table is shown in Table 9.1. The selection process begins with the random selection of a single number anywhere in the table. Suppose the numeral zero in the number 63028 (third column from left, eighth row) is selected in this manner. Actually, three-digit numbers are required for the example,

TABLE 9.1   Partial Table of Random Numbers

68184	44863	98829	56521	74091	09650
60805	90103	61257	12091	45575	22159
04687	39883	11410	77807	62677	75969
22349	59342	51877	24518	06649	65092
21677	91041	92446	78841	05564	32148
67766	15685	90940	76819	96220	59042
11818	90159	14001	68806	61153	08832
85682	40814	63028	56279	72596	10727
76835	09299	31846	37856	66522	01298
50861	16920	13441	55761	61849	66381
97572	70083	38334	74287	67983	57953
91838	95826	26713	73760	38187	04484
77484	95791	70856	79031	10513	63264
92636	30403	65385	08121	11889	80350
07306	16036	39854	31304	43613	56677
34622	21652	04720	30237	57056	92546
88071	06990	71900	30549	01372	34339
38738	11476	17209	68242	03077	57500

(63)028
↑

because the possible range of selection is from 001 to 500. Accordingly, the two digits to the right of the selected number (in this case 2 and 8) will also be used, making the first entry 028. The evaluator also could have decided to use the three digits to the left, in which case the first entry would be 630—too large to fit the 001 to 500 range.

The client who had been assigned the number 028 is the first person selected for the sample. Because the evaluator has planned to move down the table, immediately under 028 the next three-digit number would be 846. This number is out of range, so it is skipped. The next number is 441; the client who had been assigned that number is selected. The selection then continues with client number 334, and so on. At the bottom of the column the evaluator moves either right or left to the next column, according to a preset plan. When all 100 numbers have been selected, the random sample is complete.

Systematic Random Sampling
Conceptually, the selection of a simple random sample is a relatively simple and straightforward process. However, in practice, such a procedure is rarely used, particularly when the population from which a sample is to be selected is fairly large and the random numbers are to be selected one by one, by hand. The procedure can be quite tedious and time-consuming. A more practical alternative is systematic random sampling.

In this procedure, the evaluator determines the total number of units in the list and decides on the size of the sample. Assume that the list is again comprised of 500 clients and the desired size of the sample is 100. Dividing the former by the latter (500/100 = 5), provides the size of the sampling interval, which in this case is five.

Thus, every fifth client on the list will be selected to constitute the sample. The selection process begins by randomly selecting a number from 1 to 5. The number selected designates the first client, and every fifth client is subsequently chosen. Suppose the number selected is 2. In such a case, clients who had been assigned 002, 007, 012, 017, 022 and so forth will be chosen; client number 497 will complete the sample.

In most cases, a systematic random sample is equivalent to a simple random sample. However, it is possible that the sampling frame or list on which the selection is based has a recurring pattern that can bias the sample. For example, professional staff members in a human service agency may be listed on a unit-by-unit basis, with each unit having nine line-level workers and one supervisor. The supervisor is listed as the tenth person in the unit. A systematic sample drawn from such a listing would almost certainly contain a bias. In a sampling plan that calls for names to be selected at intervals of five, the first number chosen would determine if supervisors would be either over-represented or under-represented in the sample. If the first number selected were 1, 2, 3, or 4, no supervisors at all would be included in the sample, even though they comprise 10 percent of the population. If the first number selected is 5, every second person selected for the sample would be a supervisor, and supervisors would be grossly overrepresented.

With systematic random sampling, it is essential to study the list from which the selections are to be made closely to ensure that no underlying patterns that could bias the sample are present. If it can be confirmed that the list is free of recurring patterns, systematic random sampling is an efficient and effective way of selecting a sample from a population.

Stratified Random Sampling

Stratified random sampling is a procedure that can help reduce chance variation between a sample and the population it represents. This procedure may be used when a population can be divided into two or more distinct groups, called strata. The strata are then sampled separately, using simple random-sampling or systematic random-sampling techniques.

In the example above, the population of professional staff members in the human service agency is constituted of 90 percent workers and 10 percent supervisors; of the professional staff complement of 500, therefore, 450 are workers and 50 hold supervisory positions. Theoretically, a 20 percent simple random sample of the professional staff should yield 90 workers and 10 supervisors. However, this will not always happen because although a random sample may be representative of the population, it is not necessarily identical to it. Normal sampling error may result in a sample that is composed of 92 workers and 8 supervisors, or 87 workers and 13 supervisors, or some other combination.

But this population of agency professionals is composed of two groups, or strata: line-level human service workers and supervisors. A separate sample therefore can be drawn from each group, using simple random-sampling or systematic random-sampling techniques. A 20 percent sample can be drawn from each group, resulting in a total sample of 100 people that is composed of 90 workers and 10 supervisors.

Because the same sampling fraction is used for each stratum, the approach is known as proportional stratified sampling. One of the advantages of such a sample is that it perfectly represents the characteristics of the population from which it was drawn in regards to the variable or variables on which the stratification was based. Some sampling error would normally be expected if either simple random sampling or systematic random sampling had been used. Using stratified random sampling can eliminate this source of sampling error.

It is also possible to draw a disproportional sample from the strata. In this procedure, different sampling fractions are used for some or all of the strata. For example, the evaluator might use a 1/5 sampling fraction (a 20 percent sample) when selecting line-level workers but a 3/5 sampling fraction (a 60 percent sample) in the selection of supervisors. This procedure would yield 90 workers and 30 supervisors.

It would make sense to proceed in this manner if one of the objectives of an evaluation was to examine closely some characteristic of the supervisors. Using proportional sampling, only ten supervisors would be available for study. If the subsequent analysis required further division of this group (for example, according

TABLE 9.2   **Data for Disproportional Stratified Sampling for Population of Workers and Supervisors**

	Line-Level Workers	Supervisors
Number in population	450	50
Percent of population	90	10
Sampling fraction	1/5	3/5
Number in sample	90	30
Percent of unweighted sample	75	25
Weighting factor	1	1/3
Number in weighted sample	90	10
Percent of weighted sample	90	10

to educational level, age, or gender), only a small number of supervisors would be left in each group, making such analysis difficult. By sampling disproportionally, the total number of supervisors in the sample is increased, which makes it possible to conduct further detailed analyses.

When strata that have been disproportionately sampled are combined in order to make estimates about the total population, it is necessary to weight each stratum which had been sampled at a higher rate to compensate for the higher rate of selection. If supervisors were selected at three times the rate of workers, an adjustment factor of 1/3 (the inverse of 3 to 1) is used to adjust for the disproportional selection of supervisors. The numbers and percentages of line-level workers and supervisors in the sample then would accurately represent those in the population. Table 9.2 provides a summary of disproportional sampling and the adjustment process in relation to the example in this section.

Multistage Probability Sampling

The single-stage probability sampling procedures described above depend on the availability of a population list or sampling frame from which the sample is to be selected. It is not always possible to compile a sampling frame for the population of interest, however; this is likely to be the case when a population from a city, county, or state is to be sampled. Multistage sampling procedures provide a strategy through which a population can be sampled when a comprehensive list does not exist and it is not possible to construct one. The most commonly used of these procedures is cluster sampling.

Cluster Sampling
Cluster sampling is more complicated than the single-stage sampling strategies; essentially, each stage of multistage sampling is in itself a simple random sample or

a systematic random sample. The stages are combined to build on one another and arrive at a final sample.

For example, suppose evaluators conducting a community needs assessment want to determine the types of family support services single parents need. While many of the agencies and human service workers providing help to single parents undoubtedly have opinions, suppose very little is known about what single parents themselves perceive their needs to be. In fact, it is not even known how many single parents there are in the community. Since no comprehensive list of single parents can be compiled, it is not possible to proceed with a one-stage probability sampling strategy.

A form of cluster sampling known as area probability sampling provides the means to carry out such a study. Stage 1 of this strategy involves listing all the residential blocks, known as clusters, within the community and then drawing a sample from these clusters. Suppose there are 300 residential blocks and the evaluators decide that a sample of 50 (a sampling fraction of about 1/6) will constitute an adequate sample. Fifty blocks are selected, using simple random sampling; next the residential units located on those blocks are to be sampled.

The evaluators also decide that in Stage 2, 20 percent of the residential units located on the blocks selected in Stage 1 will provide an appropriate sample. All the units on the 50 blocks are listed, and 20 percent are randomly selected. Interviewers are assigned to contact the residents in these units to determine if any resident is a single parent. When the number of single parents in the sample has been determined, the incidence of single parenthood in the community can be estimated. Moreover, the evaluators now have a list of single parents, which is required for Stage 3.

In Stage 3, a sample is drawn of the single parents listed. The evaluators may decide, for example, that about 25 percent of the single parents should be interviewed. An alphabetical list of the single parents who were located in Stage 2 is compiled, and, using a systematic random sample strategy, every fourth name is selected for the final sample. In-depth interviews are then conducted with the single parents in the sample to determine the types of community support that single parents generally would like.

Nonprobability Sampling

With nonprobability sampling, the probability of selection cannot be estimated, so there is little or no support for the claim that the sample is representative of the population from which it was drawn. Nevertheless, there are many situations where it is infeasible or impossible to draw a probability sample, and nonprobability sampling is the only alternative. Four types of nonprobability sampling—convenience, purposive, quota, and snowball sampling—are described in this section. Figure 9.2 presents a graphic summary of these strategies.

Convenience Sampling

Sample is composed of nearest and most available participants.

Purposive Sampling

Participants, who are known or judged to be good sources of information, are specifically sought out and selected for the sample.

Quota Sampling

1. Variables relevant to the study are identified (e.g., gender and age).
2. Variables are combined into discrete categories (e.g., younger female, younger male, older female, older male).
3. The percentage of each of these categories in the population is determined (e.g., 35% younger female, 25% younger male, 30% older female, 10% older male).
4. The total sample size is established (e.g., $N = 200$).
5. Quotas are calculated (younger females = 35% of 200 = 70; younger males = 25% of 200 = 50; older females = 30% of 200 = 60; older males = 10% of 200 = 20).
6. The first available participants possessing the required characteristics are selected to fill the quotas.

Snowball Sampling

1. A small number of participants are located in the population of interest.
2. Data are obtained from these participants and they are also asked to identify others in the population.
3. The newly identified participants are contacted, data are obtained, and this group is also asked to identify others in the population.
4. The process continues until the desired sample size is obtained.

FIGURE 9.2 Summary of Nonprobability Sampling Strategies

Convenience Sampling

Convenience sampling, sometimes called availability sampling, relies on the closest and most available subjects to constitute the sample. This procedure is used extensively in human service evaluations.

For example, an evaluator interested in studying the various therapeutic techniques used by human service workers with depressed clients could consider all depressed clients seen at a certain agency within the past six months as the sample for a study that could yield useful data. However, it would be difficult to determine to what degree the clients in the sample are representative of all depressed people receiving treatment in a specific geographic location. It is possible that clients receiving services from this particular agency are different, in important ways, from depressed people receiving services elsewhere. These differences may well affect the nature of the services provided. For this reason, the opportunity to generalize from such a study is limited.

Purposive Sampling

In purposive sampling, also known as judgmental sampling, evaluators use their own judgment in selecting the sample. The basis for selecting such a sample is that it can yield considerable data to answer the evaluative question under investigation.

For example, the purpose of an evaluation may be to examine the workings of new legislation for young offenders. Under such circumstances, it might make sense to interview a small number of youth workers, probation officers, lawyers, judges, and directors of detention facilities who have worked extensively under the new legislation. The people in this sample are used as key informants in an attempt to construct a picture of how the legislation has been implemented.

In other circumstances, the selection is made to choose information-rich cases. For example, one approach to studying the reasons for breakdown in foster care placement for preschool children would be to select a sample of cases where five or more placement changes have taken place. While these cases (it is hoped) would not be representative of foster care cases generally, they could provide clues to the factors involved in placement breakdown.

Quota Sampling

Quota sampling is somewhat analogous to stratified random sampling. Essentially, the strategy consists of identifying variables or characteristics of the sample that are relevant to the study, determining the proportion (quota) of these characteristics in the population, and then selecting participants in each category until the quota is achieved.

As an example, for an evaluation examining the skills practitioners use to establish working relationships with their clients, the evaluator may have a hunch that there are differences in the approaches taken by female and male workers and by older and younger workers. These two variables, sex and age, can be combined into four discrete groups: younger female workers, younger male workers, older female workers, and older male workers.

The percentage of professionals in each of the four categories within the population of interest is then determined. Suppose the evaluator determines that the percentages are 35, 25, 30, and 10 percent, respectively, as indicated in Table 9.3. If a total sample of 200 is required, 70 younger females (35 percent of 200), 50 younger males, 60 older females, and 20 older males will constitute the sample. The final step in selecting a quota sample is to find a sufficient number of workers to fit each of these characteristics.

The main limitation of quota sampling is that considerable discretion is exercised in selecting individuals to fill each quota. In the example, the evaluator might go to two large human service agencies and find sufficient numbers of workers to draw the entire sample. While this would be convenient, the representativeness of such a sample would be questionable. It could be argued, for example, that workers in smaller agencies relate to clients differently than those in larger agencies. A second problem with quota sampling is that to establish the quotas, reasonable

TABLE 9.3   Quota Sampling Matrix: Percentages and Quotas of Sex and Age among Human Service Workers

	Younger ($n=120$)		Older ($n=80$)		Total ($N=200$)	
Sex	Number	Percent	Number	Percent	Number	Percent
Female	70	35	60	30	130	65
Male	50	25	20	10	70	35
Totals	120	60	80	40	200	100

knowledge of the characteristics of the population under study is required. Where precise data about the variables relevant to quota setting are not available, the quotas may not accurately represent the population characteristics.

Snowball Sampling

Snowball sampling is particularly useful when members of a population are difficult to identify and locate. This is often the case when studying people whose behavior is regarded as deviant, illegal, or otherwise meets with social disapproval. For example, it is often difficult to identify members of such populations as teenage prostitutes, homeless people, or intravenous drug users.

The strategy of snowball sampling is to locate a few individuals in the population of interest and ask them to identify other people in the same group. These people, in turn, are asked to identify still other respondents. The cycle continues until an adequate sample size has been achieved. Although this strategy may be the only one through which a sample can be drawn from certain populations, it has the evident drawback that the sample depends entirely on the individuals who are first contacted. If the sampling were initiated with a different set of individuals, the entire sample might be differently constituted. Consequently, the degree to which snowball samples are representative cannot be determined.

Snowball sampling may also be used to locate people with divergent views on a topic, to ensure that the sample represents all segments of a population. This is important in a population where minority opinions might otherwise be disregarded.

Nonsampling Errors

In addition to selecting an appropriate sample, efforts must also be made to reduce nonsampling sources of error. One source of nonsampling error is an inadequate sampling frame, which has already been mentioned. Because the sample is drawn from the sampling frame, if the list does not correspond well to the population of interest, it will be difficult to infer anything about the population from the sample. Other nonsampling errors include nonresponse from participants, field errors, response errors, and coding and data entry errors. While these are not sampling errors, they also affect the accuracy of the data obtained from the sample, and therefore, its representativeness.

Effects of Nonresponse

In making estimates from probability samples, it is assumed that the data have been collected from all the units designated for the sample. In this sense, however, a sample is only a theoretical entity, for seldom can a complete set of data be collected. The sample always includes some individuals who cannot be reached or refuse to respond. A high rate of nonresponse offers a distinct possibility that the sample obtained will be biased, since those who do respond may be in some way different from those who do not.

In a study to examine the frequency of evaluation activities in children's group-care programs in a large state, for example, data are collected by mailing question-naires to the executive directors of a sample of human service agencies offering such programs. Completed questionnaires are returned by 55 percent of the directors sampled. Does the 45 percent nonresponse rate result in a biased sample?

There is no simple answer to such a question, and, unless further data are collected from nonrespondents, it is not possible to answer it with any degree of certainty. Suppose (as is likely the case) that the directors who respond are more interested in evaluation, because there is a high level of such activities in their agencies. Under such circumstances, the sample would be biased, resulting in an overestimation of evaluation activities.

The sample will not be biased by a high nonresponse rate if the reasons for the lack of response are not related to the variables under study. However, because of the potential of nonresponse to bias the sample, every effort should be made to incorporate into the evaluation design factors that will ensure a high response rate.

Field Errors and Response Errors

Other nonsampling errors occur in the field or in participants' responses to inter-views or questionnaires. Ideally, an evaluation design would not allow the field staff much discretion in selecting the sample. If given latitude, they might select for the sample only those files that are well organized and neatly written, those indi-viduals who are easily accessible and nonthreatening, or those housing units that are well maintained and easy to reach.

Interviewers, however, almost always can exercise some discretion in conduct-ing complex interviews, providing prompts, or recording the data. Particularly when the data collection method is observation, the observer can decide what to observe and how to record it.

Field errors resulting from such circumstances can be minimized by ensuring that field staff members are well trained and supervised, and that the procedures they are to follow have been explicitly stated in detail.

Skillfully designed questionnaires and well-trained interviewers also can minimize the impact of response errors. The quality of the data collected will suffer if large numbers of respondents misunderstand questions or are not qualified to answer but provide answers nevertheless. Respondents also may attempt to present themselves (or their opinions) in a socially desirable manner. They may profess views they do not actually hold or deny behaviors or feelings that they believe might be met with disapproval.

Coding and Data Entry Errors

In the final analysis, the best sampling design and the most meticulous data collection will be to no avail if the resulting data are inaccurately coded or entered. The training and supervision of the clerical staff responsible for these functions and judicious use of double coding and double entry procedures enhance the reliability of these procedures.

Summary

Because it is usually not feasible to obtain data from an entire population (of people, things, or events) in which evaluators are interested, sampling procedures are used to select some individuals (or some other units) as representative of the entire population. The two main types of sampling procedures are probability and nonprobability sampling.

The first step in probability sampling is to construct a sampling frame, a list of units from which the sample will be selected. This step is required because a listing of all members in an actual population seldom exists. The sample is then drawn, using either one-stage sampling (with simple random, systematic random, or stratified random sample strategies) or multistage (cluster) sampling. In all forms of probability sampling, random selection procedures are used, all units in the sampling frame have the same known probability of selection, and it is possible to make an estimate of the precision of the sample.

In some situations where probability sampling is not possible, a nonprobability sample may be drawn. The four kinds of nonprobability samples described in this chapter are convenience, purposive, quota, and snowball sampling. Such samples may provide data that would otherwise be inaccessible, but these approaches are less powerful than probability sampling because various selection biases in them cannot be ruled out. In addition, it is not possible to estimate the precision of the sample.

Care should be taken in the design to minimize nonresponse, an inadequate sampling frame, field and response errors, and coding and data entry errors.

The next chapter describes the process of how to select and implement some of the exploratory and descriptive designs that were presented in Chapters 7 and 8.

Key Terms

Area Probability Sampling: A form of cluster sampling that uses a three-stage process to provide the means to carry out a study when a comprehensive list of a population cannot be compiled.

Cluster Sampling: A multistage probability sampling procedure in which a population is divided into groups or clusters and the clusters, rather than the individuals, are selected for inclusion in the sample.

Convenience Sampling: A nonprobability sampling procedure that relies on the closest and most available participants to constitute a sample.

Field Error: A type of nonsampling error in which field staff show bias in their selection of a sample.

Multistage Probability Sampling: Probability sampling procedures used when a comprehensive list of a population does not exist and it is not possible to construct one.

Nonprobability Sampling: Sampling procedures in which all of the persons, events, or objects in the sampling frame have an unknown, and usually unequal, chance of being included in a sample.

Nonsampling Errors: Errors in study results that are not due to sampling procedures.

One-Stage Probability Sampling: Probability sampling procedures in which the selection of a sample from a population is completed in one single process.

Probability Sampling: Sampling procedures in which every member of a designated population has a known chance of being selected for a sample.

Purposive Sampling: A nonprobability sampling procedure in which individuals with particular characteristics are purposely selected for inclusion in the sample; also known as judgmental or theoretical sampling.

Quota Sampling: A nonprobability sampling procedure in which the relevant characteristics of a sample are identified, the proportion of these characteristics in the population is determined, and participants are selected from each category until the predetermined proportion (quota) has been achieved.

Response Error: A type of nonsampling error in which the participants of an evaluation present themselves differently than they actually are, perhaps in a manner that is socially desirable.

Sample: A subset of a population of individuals, objects, or events chosen to participate in or to be considered in a study; a group chosen by unbiased sample selection from which inferences about the entire population of people, objects, or events can be drawn.

Sampling Frame: A listing of units (people, objects, or events) in a population from which a sample is selected.

Sampling Theory: The logic of using methods to ensure that a sample and a population are similar in all relevant characteristics.

Simple Random Sampling: A one-stage probability sampling procedure in which members of a population are selected one at a time, without chance of being selected again, until the desired sample size is obtained.

Snowball Sampling: A nonprobability sampling procedure in which individuals selected for inclusion in a sample are asked to identify additional individuals who might be included from the population; can be used to locate people with divergent points of view.

Stratified Random Sampling: A one-stage probability sampling procedure in which the population is divided into two or more strata to be sampled separately, using random or systematic random sampling techniques.

Systematic Random Sampling: A one-stage probability sampling procedure in which every person at a designated interval in the population list is selected to be included in the study sample.

Study Questions

1. Discuss how sampling theory is helpful to the process of human service evaluation.

2. Discuss the purpose and the use of sampling frames in the human services.

3. Discuss the issues of generalizability in the human services.

4. What are the differences between probability and nonprobability sampling? What are the advantages and disadvantages of each? Justify your answer by using the points outlined in this chapter.

5. List and discuss the different types of probability sampling procedures.

6. Discuss the procedure of generating a random sample.

7. Discuss how sampling errors vary with the size of a sample.

8. List and discuss the various forms of nonsampling errors.

9. What suggestions could you provide to minimize nonsampling errors?

10. In groups of four, design an evaluation study of your human service program. Discuss what random sampling procedures could be used. Decide on the sampling procedure you would use and how you would collect the data. How does your study compare with those of the other groups in the class. Discuss the problems associated with random sampling and possible solutions to the problems.

11. In groups of four, design an evaluation study that concerns all the students of your university or college. Decide on a sample size and discuss how you could use the different nonprobability sampling methods to obtain your sample. Present your study to the class.

12. Your student association embarks on an evaluation project seeking to assess the extent of program satisfaction among students in your state. What is the population in this case? Is it possible to study the satisfaction of all the students in this population?

13. What method could your student association alternately use? What are some of the advantages of using this alternate method?

14. Your student association decides to conduct their evaluation using a probability sample. Why? How would they go about selecting the sample? How would they ensure that this sample is representative of its intended population?

15. Why is simple random sampling considered a one-stage probability sampling method? How could your student association conduct a simple random sampling of its population?

16. Why would your student association likely not use a simple random sampling technique when drawing the sample? What would be a more practical alternative?

17. Under what circumstances could your student association use a stratified random-sampling procedure in drawing their sample? How would they develop a sample using this technique? What are the advantages of using this technique?

18. How would your student association draw a disproportional sample from its population? Under what circumstances would they proceed in this manner?

19. A form of cluster sampling known as area probability sampling provides your student association with a means to carry out their study. How does it draw a sample using this sampling method?

20. Suppose it is impossible for your student association to draw a probability sample for their study and nonprobability sampling is their only alternative? What does this method entail?

21. How would your student association draw their sample using convenience sampling? The president of your student association cautions against the use of this approach. Why?

22. Under what conditions could your student association decide to utilize a purposive sampling method?

23. Under what conditions would your student association decide to utilize the quota sampling method? What does this strategy consist of? What are the limitations of using this approach?

24. Would your student association likely use a snowball sampling approach? Why or why not?

25. Your student association enjoyed the ability to draw a probability sample. How would the effects of nonresponse affect the results?

26. How can organizers of evaluations minimize the impact that field and response errors can have on sample precision?

27. Why is it important for evaluators to hire competent data entry personnel?

Part IV

DECISION MAKING

Chapter 10
Implementing Quality Improvement Designs

Chapter 11
Decision Making to Improve Quality

Part IV focuses mainly on the monitoring approach to quality improvement as discussed in Chapter 3. The monitoring approach is highlighted in this section because, for most human service practitioners, it is more practical and feasible to implement than the project approach to quality improvement. It is an approach that can be readily implemented as an integral part of day-to-day service provision.

Chapter 10 describes both case-level and program-level designs that can be used in the monitoring approach to quality improvement and provides several examples of how they can implemented. A key feature of this chapter is a discussion of how data from case-level designs, used with client practice objectives (Chapter 7), can also be incorporated into group-level designs that are used with program objectives (Chapter 8). Chapter 11 presents a description of how case- and program-level data can be analyzed and interpreted in making decisions in the quality improvement process.

10

IMPLEMENTING QUALITY IMPROVEMENT DESIGNS

CHAPTERS 7 AND 8 discussed basic case-level and program-level evaluation designs. In this chapter, we will consider in more detail how these designs can be used in the quality improvement process.

Chapter 3 presented two complementary approaches to evaluation: project and monitoring. Each approach has an important role to play in the quality improvement process, but there are some key differences between them as well. The project approach is undertaken on a one-shot basis, tends to involve descriptive and explanatory designs, and is most useful for purposes of knowledge-building. The monitoring approach is a continuous process of evaluation that relies on exploratory (and sometimes descriptive) designs and is most closely associated with the quality improvement process.

In this chapter, our emphasis will be on the monitoring approach, as it has been throughout this book, because this approach is practical to implement and can be used to collect some very valuable data. As we shall see in this chapter, the designs associated with the monitoring approach can be used both at the case level, to monitor a client's progress toward attainment of practice objectives, and at the program level, to monitor the attainment of program objectives.

Fundamental Purposes of Evaluation

Before we focus on evaluation designs used in the quality improvement process, it is worth reviewing two fundamental purposes of evaluation: building knowledge and aiding decision making. We will also consider how evaluation designs used in the quality improvement process contribute to those purposes.

Building Knowledge

Traditionally, the primary purpose of an evaluation has been to determine how effectively a program is meeting its objectives. If the program treats alcoholics, for example, one program objective may be to help clients abstain from alcohol. Others may seek to improve clients' functioning in such areas as employment, parenting, and personal relationships. A traditional project-type outcome evaluation will determine the proportion of clients who abstained from alcohol after completing the program, or by how much the functioning level of clients increased in the various areas. In other words, the evaluation asks whether human service workers' activities were successful in obtaining the desired program objectives. To take it one step further, an evaluation asks: Does the service cause the desired results?

This kind of causal knowledge is obviously important. If certain techniques are known to be effective in one case, the same techniques can be effectively utilized somewhere else. However, as previously discussed, causal knowledge is usually obtainable only by using explanatory designs. But these designs can be disruptive; they often involve the random assignment of clients to groups, with all the ethical difficulties associated with this procedure; they are time-consuming, complex, and expensive.

Because of their associated difficulties, evaluations involving explanatory designs have traditionally been carried out only periodically, as major, one-shot projects. This periodic project approach itself creates difficulties. As discussed in Chapter 3, staff may perceive the evaluation process to be judgmental, irrelevant to their work, or even harmful to their clients, with the result that workers may not cooperate fully and may even withhold or distort data in an effort to present the program in a more favorable light.

A dilemma thus presents itself. Knowledge is essential if human service programs are to be improved and their clients better served. The traditional project approach to knowledge building, which works well in a laboratory, is often not practical in an agency setting. The setting is of primary concern—it is the place where the clients, the service interventions, and the data are most readily to be found, and it is the place where the knowledge must be applied.

Exploratory and some descriptive evaluation designs provide an answer to this dilemma. Observing the effect of a certain treatment technique on one client, or a group of clients, may reveal nothing more than that a particular program objective improved to a certain degree. No claim is made that the treatment caused the improvement. However, if the same treatment is used again with a different client or a different group and improvement again occurs, it becomes somewhat more likely that the treatment had something to do with the improvement. Success with a third client or group increases the likelihood, success with a fourth client or group increases it more, and so on.

Causality is never experimentally established, but it is indicated more and more strongly as client follows client and the individual results are considered together. Probability builds on probability, and, over time, a causal relationship between a treatment and an apparent effect becomes increasingly likely. Knowledge obtained in this way is not *certain*, but, neither is knowledge obtained through explanatory designs. It is enough that a probability is sufficiently high to suit the purpose at hand.

These approaches to evaluation can be best implemented through monitoring, which is a continuous process of checking, adjustment, and rechecking. The monitoring approach to quality improvement involves the continuous collection, analysis, and synthesis of data, performed as an integral part of normal program operations. Through monitoring, data are collected routinely, without disruption of service.

Another aspect of knowledge building through monitoring should not be forgotten. Traditional project-type explanatory design methods often require that the program be held stable until the evaluation has been concluded. In other words, staff are not permitted to introduce an innovation—perhaps inspired by preliminary evaluation results—until the evaluation is officially over. Because an evaluation may not again be undertaken for a considerable period of time, the innovation, if introduced afterwards, is unlikely to be tested. In contrast, the monitoring approach to quality improvement allows innovations to be introduced immediately. Data on the innovation are collected along with all other data, making comparisons possible. Knowledge building occurs, not in relation to a static program, but in relation to a dynamic program in the process of improving.

Aiding Decision Making

Decision making commonly occurs at three levels: (1) at the case level, in relation to individual clients or a group of clients; (2) at the program level, in relation to the program as a whole; and (3) at the top administration level, where organizational and funding decisions are made.

At the Case Level

Decisions concerning clients should be made on the basis of solid information, derived from data that are as accurate as possible. Very often, decisions must be made quickly. It is therefore important that the human service professional always have at hand current, comprehensive, and accurate data about the client's situation. The traditional project approach to quality improvement is not designed to provide these kinds of data. As we have seen, the results of a traditional project-type evaluation may not be relevant to program staff and, in some cases, may not even be shared with them. Even if the results are relevant, by the time they are made available, they are out of date: Considerable time necessarily elapses between data collection and release of the evaluation report. Traditional evaluation methods have little utility in providing practitioners with timely feedback on clients.

The monitoring approach to quality improvement is precisely designed to provide such feedback. The human service worker is very likely to know the current level of Aldo's problem with peer relations if the last measurement was made a few days ago, during the last session. Furthermore, the worker will have a record of changes in the level of Aldo's problem (practice objective). Is it going up or down, remaining at the same level, or fluctuating continually? If it is fluctuating, is there perhaps a relationship between the highs and lows and events in Aldo's life? Is the problem greater, for example, every time his parents visit him at the group home or in the community?

Data collected through monitoring will provide the worker with information on which to base client-related decisions. Each such decision will in turn lead to the collection of more data that, properly analyzed and synthesized, will yield more information to form the basis of future decisions. Data gained in this way are never a substitute for the practitioner's own judgment, but they can guide his or her decisions and provide a method whereby decisions, once made, can be evaluated.

In sum, the monitoring approach to quality improvement provides four advantages at the case level that the project approach does not: (1) it yields current, comprehensive, and accurate data to guide decision making; (2) it allows practitioners to evaluate their decisions in a timely fashion so that their interventions can be continued, discontinued, or changed where indicated; (3) it permits workers to evaluate the effectiveness of their own practices continually; and (4) measurement results can be readily shared with the clients, enabling them to see clearly the progress they are making.

At the Program Level

At the program level, both the project and monitoring approaches to quality improvement can provide valuable data for administrators. However, the philosophical differences between the two approaches tend to give rise to important differences in what is evaluated and how it is evaluated.

Monitoring is intended to provide ongoing feedback to staff and administrators about the program's functioning so that it can be improved. "Functioning" naturally includes all aspects of the program: how effectively and efficiently it is achieving its goal via the attainment of its objectives, how well it is meeting community needs, and the activities or processes by which both these things are accomplished. The monitoring approach allows links to be established between community needs, program process, and program results or outcome so that all facets of the program can be considered as a whole.

In contrast, the project approach tends to focus on one aspect of the program at a time. This aspect may be needs or process, but more commonly it is outcome: how effectively or efficiently the program meets its objectives. It is quite possible for outcome to be considered without reference to the process by which it was obtained. In other words, an evaluation may reveal that a program is meeting its objectives, but remain entirely mute on what it is that staff members are doing to achieve this success.

Consider a jobs program to help the unemployed that was originally designed to teach job-search techniques to groups through a 10-session combination of lectures, discussions, films, and role-plays. Suppose that, after finding that few program graduates obtained jobs, the staff revised the program to include, for every case, identification of potential employers and individual coaching for job interviews for as long as required. This revised program achieved success, but in a project evaluation the success was ascribed to the original program because the evaluation did not include a consideration of process. Had the same evaluation been undertaken using a monitoring approach, revisions to the program would automatically have been considered. In addition, exploratory designs could have been used, arriving at results for the program as a whole through the aggregation of case-level data. Exploratory designs commonly used in monitoring will be discussed more fully later in this chapter.

At the Administrative Level

Higher level administrators, faced with budget restrictions, often are interested in comparing similar programs. They want to know which programs are most effective in order to replicate them where they are needed. In addition, funding for successful programs may be increased at the expense of less effective ones, which may be cut back or terminated altogether.

Such program decisions will usually be based, at least partly, on evaluations of programs. Whether or not decision makers want programs to be evaluated by an outside person, who will of necessity use the project approach to quality improvement, depends on what documentation of effectiveness the program itself can present. If this documentation is of poor quality or nonexistent, an outside evaluator will almost certainly be brought in. If, however, program staff have been using the monitoring approach to quality improvement and have amassed evidence of their effectiveness, outside intervention becomes less likely. Management will have all the data required for decision making already at their fingertips.

The topic of decision making raises the issue of accountability. From an ethical standpoint, human service workers are accountable to themselves and their clients: They need to be able to demonstrate to their own and the clients' satisfaction that they are providing the best possible service. Workers are also accountable to their supervisors, who bear some responsibility for activities undertaken within an agency. Supervisors are accountable to program administrators, who are accountable to funders, who must account, in turn, for the money they spend.

Concern about accountability at every level has risen enormously over the last ten years. Growth in the number of government-operated and -funded human service programs, coupled with economic woes, has made it imperative that programs be able to demonstrate their effectiveness. At the same time, the rising consumer movement has drawn attention to the impact of programs on users and has required that programs be accountable to the people they serve. These combined influences have made accountability a present-day survival issue; the only way to really be accountable is through the quality improvement process.

Approaches to quality improvement are also undergoing a change. The traditional project approach is slowly giving way to the more practical monitoring approach, in which data are continuously collected, synthesized, and analyzed to provide solid information on which professionals can base their practice decisions. No one set of data can provide the level of probability that an "ideal" experiment would; but all the data, together, amount to a formidable body of evidence. It is as though a rock that was formerly attacked with a sledgehammer is now being worn away, slowly but inexorably, by a persistent trickle of data.

Uses of Monitoring

Before we discuss some of the evaluation designs commonly employed in the monitoring approach to quality improvement, it may be helpful to examine in more detail what monitoring can do. We will consider precisely how the monitoring approach serves each of its purposes: to provide empirical data for both case-level and program development decisions, to provide concurrent feedback to improve the effectiveness and efficiency of service, and to provide data to meet accountability demands.

Providing Empirical Data for Case-Level Decisions

Empirical data means data derived from observation or measurement, as opposed to data derived from inference or theory. For example, suppose that Ms Tran's mother has recently died. Because Ms Tran was close to her mother, we may theorize that she will be depressed immediately after the death and will grow less depressed as time goes by. These predictions of changes in Ms Tran's depression level are theoretical assumptions based on general human experience of death.

Suppose also that a professional sees Ms Tran a few days after the death and again at intervals, and that changes in Ms Tran's body language confirm that the depression is lessening with time. The worker's observations comprise empirical data, because they reflect what the worker actually saw as opposed to what the worker theorized would occur. Nevertheless, they are *subjective* empirical data, as the worker may have seen what he or she expected to see. Ms Tran's reports that she is growing less depressed also comprise empirical data, and are also subjective because Ms Tran may have persuaded herself that she is feeling what she thinks she ought to feel.

If Ms Tran completes a standardized measuring instrument to measure her depression on a weekly basis, the changing scores will also provide empirical data, but of a more objective nature, as standardized instruments are carefully designed to measure the magnitude of problems. The practitioner's observations, Ms Tran's statements, and the measuring instrument's scores provide three sets of empirical data, of varying objectivity, that may confirm the assumption that depression over a death lessens with the passage of time.

A word should be said here about the notion of objectivity as it applies to empirical data. The concept of empirical data, or data derived from observation, is drawn from the physical sciences, where objectivity is easier to come by than it is in the social sciences. A scientist in a laboratory who sees a solution turn blue will find it difficult to deny its blueness, even when theory suggests that it ought to be red. Of course, there are various shades of purple that might be interpreted as blue or red— objectivity is rarely simple, even in a laboratory—and the scientist's observation, taken by itself, may lead to error. However, blueness and redness can be translated into radiant energy of different wavelengths which can be objectively measured. The objectivity here stems from the fact that no person, and hence no human judgment, is involved in the measurement; the energy impinges upon the instrument and the instrument records the result.

Human service workers seeking objectivity are not so fortunate. The things we need to measure—people's attitudes, affects, or behavior—are infinitely more complex than radiant energy. And the instruments we use to measure them—questionnaires, rating scales, inventories, and checklists—must be completed by people and scored and interpreted by people. Objectivity is not possible in the social sciences in the same way as it is in the physical sciences, although explanatory evaluation designs have done much to increase the probability that results will be objective. And if pure objectivity is not possible, it follows that empirical data will not be purely objective.

The words *empirical data* have come to be associated with objectivity because empirical data in the physical sciences are usually objective. There is a kind of magic to the word *empirical*. It connotes not just data derived from experiment or observation but data that are reliable and authoritative, to be believed and acted upon. In the social sciences, this is only partly true because observational or experimental data are not purely objective: they are just *more* objective than data drawn from inference or theory. This is why data should be drawn from more than one source if at all possible. Agreement between two sets of empirical data makes objectivity more likely; three sets are better yet.

Even with these caveats, empirical data are a better guide to decision making than supposition, inference, or theory. A worker who just supposes that Ms Tran is depressed about her mother's death is in a very poor position to help if Ms Tran is, in fact, secretly relieved that her mother can no longer influence her life. Ms Tran may, understandably, be reluctant to confide this to a practitioner who expects depression. The worker's supposition, reinforced by Ms Tran's lack of forthrightness, may lead to an inappropriate service plan, such as participation in a bereavement group where Ms Tran, surrounded by the genuinely bereaved, may develop feelings of guilt because she does not feel the anguish others do. In the human services, assumptions are dangerous.

The professional's first task, then, is to determine whether Ms Tran actually is depressed; if she is, about what; and if she is not, just what the problem is. Once the problem has been identified, its level can be measured, in several different ways if possible. The initial measurements provide a baseline.

The baseline measures serve two purposes. First, they identify areas of concern and provide a starting point from which the worker can negotiate with the client about the problem to be addressed first. Second, they indicate the problem level before intervention, and if the problem level is changing, show the direction of change. Such data are obviously helpful in deciding how to proceed with services. If the data show that the problem is improving without intervention, the worker may decide to leave well enough alone or possibly focus on another problem while continuing to monitor the progress of the first. If the problem is worsening, immediate intervention may be needed. If the problem is stable, a strategy for improvement can be formulated, with the client's assistance.

While services are underway, measurements of the problem level can be made at regular intervals. If improvement is continuous, the practitioner can conclude that the intervention strategy is successful. If the problem remains the same or worsens, the worker may try a different strategy. When sufficient improvement has been made, additional measurements before termination can establish that the improvement is being maintained. Preferably, there will also be a follow-up period in which the worker sees the client at increasingly longer intervals, each time measuring the problem level to test for relapse.

During the entire course of assessment, treatment, termination, and follow-up, there are decisions to be made. Should this problem be addressed before that one? Should this service be continued or should another be tried? Should the client perhaps be referred to another professional or program? Is the client ready to terminate? Will additional services be needed months or years after official termination has occurred? Monitoring client progress at the case level provides sound data for answering these questions.

Note that nowhere during this process is the treatment openly credited with bringing about the improvement. Naturally, the practitioner will be interested in whether the treatment or something else caused the improvement, but from the point of view of helping the client, it is more important to know whether any improvement has occurred. Exploratory designs, such as those discussed later in this chapter, are usually adequate for monitoring practice objectives. These designs yield empirical data that, although they say nothing about causality, can guide the professional in deciding whether to continue, modify, completely change, or terminate services.

Providing Empirical Data for Program-Level Decisions

Decisions at the program level often involve changing activities or process in order to obtain improved results. The most obvious results to be considered are the results of treatment, that is, client outcomes expressed in statistical form. For example: Did a satisfactory proportion of clients terminate successfully, as planned, after reaching the program objective? What proportion of clients terminated unilaterally? What proportion of cases are in the inactive file? What is the average cost per client?

Empirical data can provide the answers to these questions. If the results are satisfactory, the program can continue as before; if not, reasons can be postulated and remedies devised and implemented. Collection of further data will then tell administrators whether the remedies worked.

The postulation of reasons for unsatisfactory performance is never a simple matter. Perhaps the eligibility criteria fail to distinguish clients who are unlikely to benefit from the program from those who will benefit. Perhaps the line-level workers are insufficiently trained, or the service models are inadequate. Perhaps the population being served is particularly mobile, never staying in one area long enough to benefit from a long-term program. It is almost impossible to identify the reason(s) for poor performance unless there are data immediately available. What are the eligibility criteria, and how are they applied? What characteristics distinguish persons who are accepted into the program from those who are rejected? What qualifications do the human service workers have, and what training did they undertake last year? What are the common interventions in use? Did clients who terminated unilaterally stop coming because they were dissatisfied, or because they moved out of the area?

An efficiently operated program will have a data-collection system capable of answering these questions. It is not enough to know what client outcomes are; it is necessary to know what process leads to the outcomes, both in theory and in practice. If certain assessment procedures are supposed to be undertaken, are they carried out in practice as designed? If referrals are to be handled by a special intake worker, does the secretary or someone else handle them when the worker is unavailable?

A project approach to quality improvement may not uncover discrepancies between theory and practice, especially if staff are fearful of an unfavorable result and fail to volunteer information. In contrast, monitoring activities try to improve the program on a day-to-day basis. If no provision has been made for the intake worker's unavailability, for example, this fact will quickly become apparent to an administrator, who can take steps to resolve the problem.

Ongoing monitoring of activities allows administrators to know what the program process really is, so that they can relate the program's outcomes to the activities producing those outcomes. For example, empirical data may reveal that clients who terminate successfully from a family support program take an average of two years to reach their practice objectives. Other data may show that 50 percent of clients terminate unilaterally after six months without reaching their practice objectives, and further, that this 50 percent participate only for as long as court orders require them to attend. On the basis of these data, administrators may decide to shorten and compress the program, so that clients can reach at least some of their practice objectives in a six-month period. Alternatively, they may decide to petition the courts to increase the mandatory period of treatment. Whatever they decide, the decision could not have been made if data had not pointed out the problem. Routine monitoring can provide data useful not just for problem solving but also for problem identification.

To summarize, then, program administrators have a responsibility to ensure that their programs provide effective and efficient services to their clients. They cannot fulfill this responsibility unless they have access to comprehensive, accurate, and timely data about the results the program is achieving and the process by which those results are achieved. This information is obtained through the analysis and synthesis of raw, empirical data: facts such as the number of clients presently being served or the assessment procedures being used. These data will both point to problem areas and guide the formulation of solutions, with the result that the program, continually monitored, will continually be improved.

Providing Concurrent Feedback to Improve Services

It was earlier stressed that the data used to guide decision making at both the case and program levels must be current. Data taken from an evaluation conducted three years ago are of limited value: Needs, concerns, communities, resources, and intervention techniques all change too fast.

For example, routine monitoring of client demographic characteristics may show that the proportion of males being referred to a sexual abuse treatment program is increasing. This increase may necessitate changes in the program, such as the provision of support groups for male survivors, specific training programs for staff, or the recruitment of additional male staff members. If client demographic characteristics are not routinely monitored, the increase in the number of male survivors referred may not be formally recognized for some years. Changes to the program will not be made, and males may for some time be inadequately served.

The monitoring approach to quality improvement provides continuous feedback about who is being served, by what methods, by whom, how effectively, and how efficiently. On the other hand, the project approach provides only periodic feedback, which may not cover all program areas and is current only at the time it is produced.

Continuous timely feedback is just as vital at the individual level. If no client returns to a particular practitioner more than twice, for example, the supervisor must know quickly so that remedial action can be taken. Rapid feedback is also necessary in order to determine whether the problem has been solved: Has the supervisor's training succeeded in teaching the practitioner how to engage new clients?

Providing Empirical Data to Meet Accountability Demands

As mentioned earlier, over the last two decades accountability has become a major concern for human service programs. Increasingly, accountability must be demonstrated by the provision of verifiable information drawn from empirical data. For example, funders will want to know whether a program is serving community needs. Such needs may be assessed in part through requests for service from community members, which are reflected in referrals to the program. A growing population of seniors will result in more referrals of seniors, who will require additional distinctive services geared to their special needs. Is a family violence program that formerly focused on child protection now taking steps to counsel seniors who have been abused? What steps? With what results? How many seniors?

Results or outcomes are, of course, of particular interest, but it is not results in isolation that interest funders: It is results in relation to the program's objectives. Whereas human service programs in past years have tended to have fuzzy, unmeasurable objectives, programs nowadays are required to specify precisely what they aim to achieve so that the degree to which they have achieved it can be measured. This is one strength of the monitoring approach: Specification of concrete, measurable program and practice objectives is part of the process, as is specification of objectives for various program components.

Precise specification of practice objectives is also of primary importance at the case level. If one of the practice objectives of treatment is, say, to reduce Mr. Sharma's anxiety, the practitioner must know to what level the anxiety should be reduced before Mr. Sharma is likely to function adequately. Standardized measuring instruments with clinical cutting scores are helpful here. Specific practice objectives whose achievement can be documented through empirical data allow workers to demonstrate accountability to themselves, their clients, and their supervisors. In turn, the documentation of clients' practice objectives provides a means by which the program can demonstrate accountability to its funders.

Monitoring Designs at the Case Level

The monitoring approach to quality improvement, as we have seen, can involve the continual collection of data with respect to all aspects of a program: needs, process, outcome, and efficiency. The designs to be discussed in this section are, however, concerned solely with evaluating client outcome, that is, evaluating the degree of attainment of practice objectives.

Exploratory Designs

The three exploratory designs most commonly used to monitor individual cases are: B designs, $B_1B_2B_3$ designs, and BCD designs.

B Designs

It often happens that a client is in a state of crisis and the practitioner acts immediately, judging that it would be harmful to the client to postpone intervention until baseline data have been collected. Nor can a retroactive baseline be established if the client is in no condition to provide reliable data about the history of the presenting problem. Even if the client is not in crisis, there may not be time, in a short-term program, to collect baseline data.

Nevertheless, the worker needs to have an idea of what the problem level is to begin with, and one measurement made before intervention is better than none. Subsequent measurements during the intervention will serve the four purposes described earlier: they provide data to guide decision making at both the case and program levels; they provide concurrent feedback to improve the effectiveness and efficiency of service delivery; and they provide data to meet accountability demands.

The process of continually measuring the effects of a single intervention is known as a *B design*. Measurement is continued until the data show that the problem has disappeared or has stabilized at an acceptable level.

For example, a client who is unemployed may lack assertiveness in job-search situations. The practitioner can measure the initial level of the problem on a standardized measuring instrument and begin to implement an intervention package, consisting of instruction, discussion, videotaped role-plays, and regular homework assignments. After a number of sessions and measurements, the client may resolve the problem by achieving an increased (improved) score on the instrument and by finding a job. Figure 10.1 shows the client's scores on the instrument plotted over time.

Four points should be noted from this example. First, the worker is not relying entirely on one measure of progress. The instrument is the only paper-and-pencil instrument used, but other sources of data have also been employed. There is a visual record of increased assertiveness obtained from the taped role-plays. Written resumes, assigned for homework, may now include relevant experiences that the client had previously not thought worth mentioning. Discussion of the client's job-search efforts may indicate a new willingness to question prospective employers.

The client's reports on job interviews may reveal an increasing number of assertive statements. The worker's own impression may be that the client is more assertive. And of course, success in obtaining a job is another indicator that assertiveness has increased to an adequate level. No matter how good the indicator,

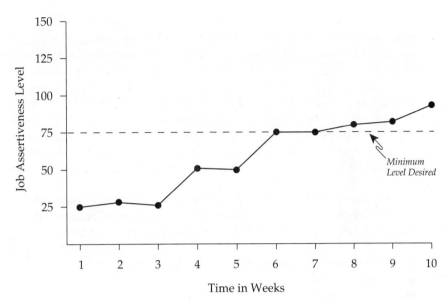

FIGURE 10.1 *B* **Design: Job Assertiveness Levels over a 10-Week Period**
(Note: high scores = high assertiveness levels)

or how valid, reliable, and sensitive the instrument, it is always best to obtain data in as many ways and from as many sources as possible.

Second, as Figure 10.1 shows, change is occurring in the desired direction. This trend toward increased assertiveness tells the worker that the intervention is working and ought to be continued.

Third, by the the sixth week the problem appears to have been resolved, as 75 is the minimum desirable level on this instrument (see Figure 10.1). Nevertheless, the practitioner continues to make measurements for four more weeks to ensure that gains are being maintained. A stable or improving level of achievement tells the worker that no further intervention is necessary and services may be terminated.

Fourth, the *B* design provides no evidence at all that the intervention *caused* the increased assertiveness. If the same intervention is used with a different client and achieves the same result, it becomes more likely that the intervention caused the result. If it works with a third client, the likelihood increases further. This is the principle behind the aggregation of client data for the purpose of program evaluation, to be discussed in Chapter 11. However, at the case level the purpose of monitoring is not to establish causality, but to track the client's progress (or lack of progress) so that the decision to continue or change the intervention will be a rational one, based on empirical data.

$B_1B_2B_3$ *Designs*
Chapter 7 discussed a descriptive design for case-level evaluation called the $AB_1B_2B_3$ design. The letter code indicates that this design involves an *A* or baseline phase followed by three variations of a *B* or interventive phase. The $B_1B_2B_3$ *design* is simply

the $AB_1B_2B_3$ design without the A phase. There is now no baseline with which to compare the results of the B interventions, but nevertheless, repeated measurements during the first intervention will tell the professional to what degree the problem is being resolved. If it is not being resolved at all, the worker will probably want to try a different intervention; that is, the B design will give way to a BC design, in which one intervention is followed by a second, different intervention.

If, however, the B intervention is somewhat successful—if the problem diminishes but nonetheless persists—a variation of B may be tried. Perhaps the intervention is needed more often or in greater amounts, or an additional element is needed. The original B intervention now becomes the B_1 phase, and the variation becomes B_2.

For example, the nonassertive job seeker introduced earlier may require twice the number of weekly appointments, or more role-plays, or more detailed feedback from the worker about the body language displayed on videotape. The intervention itself has not changed, but its intensity has. If measurements during the more intensive intervention show that success is being achieved, the worker may then want to reduce the intensity, moving into a B_3 phase by setting appointments only monthly. Figure 10.2 shows the client's assertiveness scores, plotted against time through the B_1, B_2, and B_3 phases. In this figure, success is achieved in the B_2 phase, and the B_3 phase is a maintenance phase, where the purpose is to ensure that improved assertiveness is not fleeting and to work toward termination. The B_3 phase need not be a maintenance phase, however; it can be a different modification of the original intervention.

It will now be obvious that these designs are not premeditated: A worker does not think, at the beginning of treatment, "With this client, I will implement a $B_1B_2B_3$ design." Instead, the design evolves to follow the client's need, remaining at B if the intervention works, becoming B_1B_2 if it works somewhat, and becoming BC or BCD if different interventions are needed. The point of a monitoring approach is that repeated measurements of the problem level show the practitioner whether and to what extent changes are taking place, so that future interventive decisions can be guided by these data.

BC *Designs*

The *BC design* is one in which there is no A or baseline phase but only two consecutive and different intervention phases, B and C. The C phase may be initiated because the B intervention was unsuccessful, or it may be designed to ensure that the gains achieved in B are maintained. Figures 10.3 and 10.4 show C phases following on an unsuccessful and a successful B intervention, respectively. In both cases, the C phase represents a different intervention, not some variation on B (e.g., Figure 10.2).

To use the nonassertive client seeking a job as an example, the practitioner may have first tried a counseling approach focused on the client's childhood, drawing out instances where nonassertive behavior was rewarded and assertive behavior punished, on the assumption that the problem would disappear once its cause was

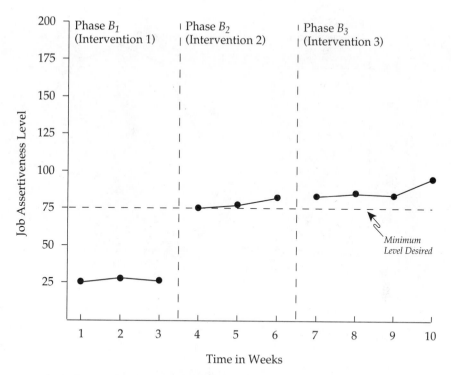

FIGURE 10.2 $B_1B_2B_3$ **Design: Job Assertiveness Levels over a 10-Week Period**
(Note: high scores = high assertiveness levels)

understood. The results of this *B* intervention, plotted in Figure 10.3, showed that the hoped-for resolution was not occurring. The worker therefore decided to try a new intervention, ignoring the client's childhood and focusing instead on teaching assertive behavior appropriate to a job-search situation. The results of this different intervention are plotted in the *C* phase of Figure 10.3 and show that the client's assertiveness level markedly improved. In Figure 10.4, the *B* intervention succeeded as the client reached the desired level of assertiveness. The *C* phase, in this case, becomes a maintenance phase.

An extension of the *BC* design is the *BCD design*, in which there are three consecutive and different interventions but no baseline phase. Neither this nor the *BC* design gives any evidence of causality, as the results may have been due to any number of extraneous factors rather than to the intervention; it is impossible to tell which was the cause. Furthermore, a positive result obtained in the *C* phase may have been due to the combined effects of the *B* and *C* interventions—and possibly extraneous variables as well. The picture grows more confused as more interventions are added; in the end, all one can say with confidence is that change has occurred.

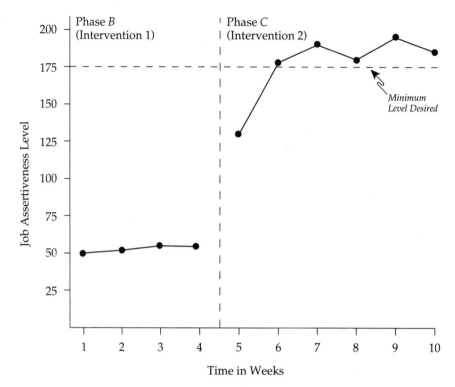

FIGURE 10.3 *BC* **Design: Unsuccessful** *B* **Intervention followed by a Successful** *C* **Intervention**
(Note: high scores = high assertiveness levels)

Descriptive Designs

Descriptive designs can also be used in case-level evaluation (see Chapter 7). These designs—*AB*, *AB₁B₂B₃*, *ABC*, and *ABCD*—all have an *A* or baseline phase with which the results of subsequent phases can be compared. They can be used to monitor the clients' progress in the same way as can exploratory designs, and they have the added advantage of providing some limited evidence of causality due to the baseline phase.

Monitoring Designs at the Program Level

Descriptive and explanatory designs for evaluating program outcomes were discussed at some length in Chapter 8. Recall that many of these designs involve two groups: an experimental group and a comparison group. For example, the comparison group pretest-posttest design—a descriptive design—may be symbolized by the following notation:

$$\text{Experimental Group:} \quad O_1 \quad X \quad O_2$$
$$\text{Comparison Group:} \quad O_1 \quad \quad O_2$$

where:

O_1 = First measurement of the program's objective, the dependent variable
X = Intervention, the independent variable
O_2 = Second measurement of the program's objective, the dependent variable

This notation indicates that an initial measurement of the problem level, O_1, is made for both experimental and comparison groups. An intervention, X, is given only to the experimental group, and then a second measurement of the problem level, O_2, is made for both groups. The assumption underlying this design is that, because the experimental and comparison groups are similar, extraneous variables will affect them in the same way.

If the O_1 and O_2 scores for the comparison group are similar, showing that no extraneous variables were involved, then the difference between the O_1 and O_2

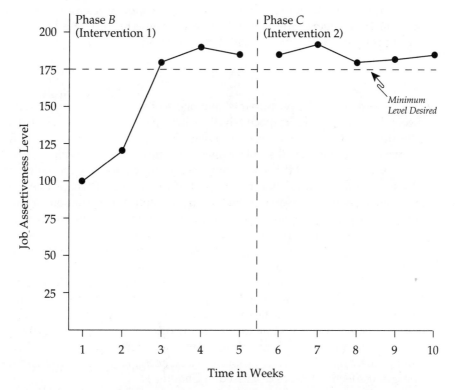

FIGURE 10.4 *BC* **Design: Successful *B* Intervention followed by a Successful *C* Intervention**

(Note: high scores = high assertiveness levels)

scores for the experimental group can be attributed to the intervention. If there is a control group instead of a comparison group, the control group is more nearly equivalent to the experimental group, and the evidence for causality is thus stronger. Designs with comparison or control groups are powerful because they allow changes to be attributed to the intervention. Unfortunately, in many evaluation situations, it is not possible to implement them. Consequently, designs that do not use comparison or control groups are more frequently employed in program-level monitoring. Two examples of these designs are the one-group pretest-posttest design with follow-ups and the one-group posttest-only design with follow-ups.

One-Group Pretest-Posttest Design with Follow-Ups

Many human service programs offer group services in which all clients are working toward the same group program objective. For example, suppose that a program objective for a parenting group is to develop more realistic expectations of preschool children in such areas as toilet training and self-care. The group leader obtains or develops an instrument to measure parental expectations, and this instrument is administered to all group participants during the first group session. The program or intervention is then implemented over the next few weeks, and the instrument is administered several times after the intervention. This design is known as the one-group pretest-posttest design with follow-ups, and is written as:

$$O_1 \quad X \quad O_2 \quad O_3 \quad O_4 \quad \ldots$$

O_1 and O_2 are the participants' average scores, or mean scores, on the first and second measurements, respectively. The difference in means from O_1 to O_2 indicates the amount of change that has taken place from pretest to posttest. The worker has no way of knowing whether this change was due to group activities or to extraneous factors. Let us say that the scores show increasingly realistic expectations. This is no cause for self-congratulation on the part of the worker. Perhaps one of the group members was visited by her mother, received intensive instruction on toilet training of preschool children, and passed this information on to other group members over coffee. The one-group pretest-posttest design with follow-ups is thus a descriptive design, in that the observed result cannot be attributed to the intervention. However, the effects of the intervention can be monitored over time.

The data can be used to determine whether group activities are effective enough to warrant their continuance within a program. If the difference between the pretest and posttest results is satisfactorily large, the group will probably be run again for other clients, using the same format. If the difference is smaller, group facilitators may consider changing some of the activities for the next group of clients. Pretest and posttest data for several groups can also be aggregated to provide a measure of program effectiveness, as discussed in Chapter 11.

Had the measuring instrument been administered at intervals during the group cycle, these additional results would have allowed the practitioner to know how the group was progressing during the intervention. If attitudes were not changing in the desired direction, the program could have been modified, perhaps by presenting different material, or presenting material in a different way. Modifications could also have been made if attitudes were changing in the right direction but not by a sufficient amount.

In sum, the pretest (O_1) and posttest (O_2) measurements are the only measurements needed to evaluate the intervention because they show the degree to which the group has achieved its mutual program objective. However, additional measurements, taken after the second measurement, would enable facilitators to check the group's progress and monitor the effects of the intervention over time.

One-Group Posttest-Only Design with Follow-Ups

Where it is not possible to obtain a measure of problem level before group services begin, the worker may have to be content with an intervention followed by several measurements. This design is known as the one-group posttest-only design, and is written as:

$$X \quad O_1 \quad O_2 \quad O_3 \quad O_4 \quad \ldots$$

where:

X = Intervention, the independent variable
O's = Repeated measurements of the program's objective, the dependent variable

Again, because there is no pretest or pre-intervention measurement, it is not possible to determine whether change has taken place within the group. But the leader can determine the level reached by the group after the intervention. If the worker uses a standardized measuring instrument, which often specifies the score at which a problem can be considered to be resolved, the O_1 measurement will tell the worker whether the group as a whole still has a significant problem after the intervention.

Here again, the O's are the only measurements necessary to evaluate the group's attainment of its program objective. However, repeated measurement during the group cycle allows the worker to monitor the group over time after the intervention.

Criteria for Selecting Evaluation Designs

An evaluation design is a process used to evaluate some aspect of a program. In other words, the design is intended to elicit data that are required in making some decision. Selecting a design involves considering what decision is to be made—what the purpose is—and what data are required to meet it. We have already seen that the major purposes of evaluation are to build knowledge and to aid decision making. We have also seen that the monitoring approach to quality improvement can meet these purposes by providing continuous empirical data to aid in case-level and program-level decision making. In addition, it establishes accountability and provides growing amounts of exploratory data that together aid in building knowledge.

Design Selection at the Case Level

The particular design selected depends on what the evaluative purpose is, what data are needed to fulfill it, how quickly the data are needed, and what data-collection methods are practical under the circumstances.

A practitioner serving a client in crisis may select an exploratory B design, intervening immediately and then taking as many measurements as possible to guide the intervention process. The B design may evolve into a BCD design or a $B_1B_2B_3$ design, or even a B_1AB_2 design if for some reason the intervention is discontinued and the problem returns to its initial level.

If the client is not in crisis, the worker may choose a descriptive AB design. This is the most sensible choice, as it provides the worker with a number of baseline measures against which to compare the results of the intervention. Again, the basic AB design may evolve into an ABC design, an $ABCD$ design, an $AB_1B_2B_3$ design, or an $A_1B_1A_2B_2$ design, depending on the success of the intervention and the client's circumstances. For example, a professional working with an aggressive client may begin by taking baseline measurements (A phase) and then initiate an insight-oriented approach to counseling (B phase). If measurements of aggression show that exploration is ineffective in this case, the worker may decide to adopt a behavioral approach instead (C phase). A design that began as a simple AB has now become ABC. If the behavioral approach also proves to be ineffective, the worker may design a different service package altogether, which will constitute a D phase.

Alternatively, if the behavioral approach is successful, the D phase might consist of a maintenance phase introduced as a prelude to termination. It may also happen that the insight-oriented approach adopted with this client is only partly successful; that is, measurements may show that the aggression level is decreasing but not to a sufficient degree, or not sufficiently fast. In this case, the worker may schedule more frequent sessions so that more material can be covered in a shorter time. The B phase counseling approach now becomes B_1, and the more frequent treatment is B_2. If a further element is needed—perhaps a greater intensity in sessions—this further variation becomes B_3; or B_3 may consist of a maintenance phase, as before.

$A_1B_1A_2B_2$ designs, in which a successful intervention is withdrawn, most often occur by accident. For example, suppose that a client who is successfully undergoing treatment for alcohol abuse withdraws from the program for a time to attend to a family emergency. By the time the client re-enters the program, all the original gains have been lost and the alcohol abuse has reverted to its initial level. The same treatment, applied successfully for the second time, constitutes the second B phase (B_2) in the $A_1B_1A_2B_2$ design.

Occasionally, an $A_1B_1A_2B_2$ design may be selected deliberately to test a hunch. Imagine that a worker and the staff of a nursing home disagree on the best way to prevent a nursing home resident from hoarding towels. The resident is clever about stealing towels from bathrooms, cupboards, and trolleys and ends up every night with 30 towels or more stored in various places in his bedroom. The A, or baseline, phase is fairly steady at a count of 30 towels hoarded daily. The worker suggests giving the resident as many towels as he wants every morning for a two-week period, taking none away, and counting the number in the bedroom every night. By the end of the two weeks, the resident has begun to throw the massed towels out of his room, retaining a nightly average of only five. The B phase intervention has thus been successful in substantially reducing the number of towels hoarded.

So far, we have described an AB design. Now, in order to find out if the problem reoccurs when the intervention is removed, the worker asks the staff to stop giving the resident towels. Soon, the stealing and hoarding behaviors begin again, until the resident once more has a nightly count of more than 30 towels. When the staff begin to give out towels for the second time, the stealing stops and the number of towels hoarded drops to five. The AB design is thus repeated, producing an $A_1B_1A_2B_2$ design and some evidence that the intervention caused the result.

$A_1B_1A_2B_2$ designs are not often used purposefully because of the ethical difficulties involved in removing a successful intervention. However, as illustrated above, certain circumstances can warrant selection of this design. Similarly, circumstances might warrant the selection of a $B_1C_1B_2C_2$ design. Perhaps a practitioner who is implementing a largely unsuccessful B phase intervention asks a colleague for advice and is doubtful about the colleague's suggestion. The colleague, who has met this same problem before, suggests that the proposal be implemented as a C phase; the worker's B intervention should then be repeated and, finally, the C intervention should be tried again. Comparison between the results of the first and second B (B_2) and C (C_2) interventions will indicate, to both practitioners, which intervention works the best, possibly to the benefit of future clients.

Selection of a design at the case level depends on both the particular situation of the client and the uses to be served by the evaluation. Case-level evaluation has three possible uses: (1) to guide the intervention process by providing ongoing measures of the problem level; (2) to provide data to be aggregated for a program evaluation; and (3) to provide data that generates knowledge used in improving the program and enhancing the practitioner's skill. Generally, data that contribute to knowledge will need to be obtained from explanatory designs, purposefully selected and followed: for example, A_1BA_2, $A_1B_1A_2B_2$, B_1AB_2, and $B_1C_1B_2C_2$. Data to be aggregated for program evaluation will preferably come from explanatory or descriptive designs; and data to be used for monitoring progress will often be exploratory, but may be descriptive as well.

Design Selection at the Program Level

Program-level evaluation has two main uses: to increase knowledge in the human services field and to provide data on which various program development and management decisions can be based. Designs used to increase knowledge will usually be explanatory. Designs used for decision making are far more variable, and depend on what decision is to be made. A summative-type decision, concerning the fate of the program, will normally require causal data derived from explanatory evaluation designs. However, if the context of the program is such that clients cannot be randomly assigned to groups and no control groups can be obtained, descriptive designs may have to suffice. Data used in monitoring program success should preferably be obtained through descriptive designs but may be obtained through exploratory designs, as these latter are so much easier to implement.

In sum, designs at both the program and case level are selected with regard to the evaluation purpose and the data needed to fulfill that purpose. If the purpose is to aid decision making, the data collected must be relevant to the decision, must be current, and must be provided in time to assist the decision. Because the timeframe for decision making is often short, it is sensible, wherever possible, to collect the data ahead of time. At the case level, for instance, a practitioner knows that decisions will constantly have to be made about whether to continue, vary, or change the present service package. If data on the problem level have already been collected, the decision can be made quickly. If there are no data, the worker will have to either defer the decision, with possible harm to the client, or make the decision without benefit of data.

At the program level, it is less easy to anticipate what decisions will have to be made and, therefore, what data will be needed. At the same time, it is often difficult to put off making the decision until the relevant data have been collected. The reasonable solution is to establish a data system whereby data related to needs, process, and outcome are routinely generated and analyzed. This topic will be covered in Chapter 12.

An additional point to be considered is that the design chosen must be capable of being implemented in the particular circumstances and with the particular client or group. At the case level, for example, an *AB* design cannot be selected if the client is in crisis, because there is no time to collect the baseline data before beginning the intervention. At the program level, an explanatory design cannot be selected if it is not possible to assign clients randomly to groups.

To put the point rather more succinctly, important criteria in selecting a design for evaluation include the following: (1) implementation of the design must be feasible in the particular circumstances, (2) the design must provide data appropriate to the decision to be made, (3) the design must provide current data, and (4) the design must provide data within the timeframe allowed for decision making.

Summary

This chapter has presented the ways in which monitoring can be used in case- and program-level evaluations. It also discussed the way in which monitoring is used to fulfill one of the fundamental purposes of evaluation, decision making at the case, program, and top administrative levels. The next chapter advances the discussion by investigating how the monitoring procedures presented in this chapter can be used to help make decisions in the quality improvement process.

Key Terms

Empirical Data: Isolated facts presented in numerical or descriptive form that have been derived from observation or testing, as opposed to data derived from inference or theory.

Evaluation Design: A process used to evaluate some aspect of a program; intended to elicit data that are required in making some decision.

Study Questions

1. What are the characteristics of the monitoring approach to quality improvement?

2. How do monitoring evaluation methods aid practitioners in making case-level decisions? Which of these benefits, if any, applies to Case Study A?

3. What suggestions can you offer that would change Case Study A to a true explanatory design? What would be the advantages and disadvantages of such changes? How would the design changes affect the nature of the data obtained?

4. Knowledge building is an important feature of monitoring evaluations. In your opinion, what knowledge did practitioners gain in Case Study A that would assist them in case planning? What knowledge did program administrators gain?

5. In your own words, briefly describe the characteristics of empirical data. Do the data in Case Study A have any empirical characteristics? If so, which ones?

6. Basing your answer on the data collection system and the evaluation design used in Case Study A, would you say the program is equipped to make decisions that could lead to improved client outcomes? Why or why not?

7. In your opinion, how can data on children's aggression scores, such as those presented in Case Study A, be used to provide evidence of program accountability at the program and funder levels?

8. What strategies could a crisis worker, utilizing only *B* designs, employ to examine the effectiveness of his or her interventions?

9. Working in groups, select a human service program that is familiar to all members of the group. Discuss the types of decisions to be made at the case level, program level, and administration level. Develop an evaluative design that would best suit each level of decision making. Are the designs different or the same for each level? What are the advantages and disadvantages of using the same evaluation design for all levels of decision making? Present your findings to the class.

10. Suppose you are asked to develop an evaluation design to determine the effectiveness of the classroom instruction you are receiving in this course. In groups of four, develop a design that includes baseline data collection. What type of data would you collect? What problems would you encounter in trying to collect data before the class (i.e., the intervention) begins? Discuss your design with the class.

11. Make a case where you argue that the benefits of monitoring approaches can make contributions to program-level decision making.

12. A fellow employee questions whether monitoring approaches to evaluation can help in case-level decision making. How do you respond?

13. Administrators at your agency have many complex program-level decisions to make. How do you convince them that empirical data gathered through ongoing evaluation

are necessary and beneficial toward this end? Provide a clear human service example in your discussion.

14. Some skeptical staff members wonder how current, continuous evaluation data will help to improve services at the agency. How do you respond?

15. You know that administrators and workers alike at your agency are consumed with accountability concerns. What will you include in your presentation that will alleviate some of these concerns?

16. Your presentation includes a demonstration of how easy it is for practitioners to monitor their individual cases. You present the *B* design. What do you tell the staff about it? (Be sure to include when it is used, what purposes it serves, and the benefits and limitations of its use.)

17. Under what circumstances would you recommend that fellow workers try the $B_1B_2B_3$ changing intensity design? How does this design assist the practitioner?

18. Under what circumstances would you recommend that workers use the *BC* or *BCD* designs? Why do these designs not permit any attribution of causality?

19. Your presentation also includes a discussion of descriptive designs and how they can be used to monitor the progress of clients. How are they different from explanatory designs?

20. You remind agency staff that descriptive designs can be used to evaluate not only case outcomes but program outcomes as well. Describe the comparison group pretest-posttest design to the group. Explain how data generated by this design can be used in program-level decision making. How would additional measurements beside the pre- and posttest improve service to the clients?

21. You next present the one-group posttest-only design. Under what circumstances would you use this design? What are the advantages and disadvantages of using this design?

22. Explain how workers can select an evaluation design at the case level.

23. Explain under what circumstances a *B* design will be selected. What about an *AB* design? An *ABC* design? An $A_1B_1A_2B_2$ design? A $B_1C_1B_2C_2$ design?

24. You remind fellow workers that selection of a design at the case level depends not only on the particular situation of the client but the uses served by the evaluation effort as well. What are the uses of case-level evaluation? How do these uses guide the selection of a design?

25. Reread Chapter 7 on case-level evaluations. As you know, all exploratory, descriptive, and explanatory case-level evaluation designs can be used in the monitoring approach to quality improvement, depending on how often it is utilized in measuring a client's practice objective. Discuss how each one of these designs can be utilized in a monitoring approach to quality improvement. What type of information is provided by each of the designs and what decisions can be based on each design? Which designs are the most suitable for monitoring purposes? Why?

26. Reread Chapter 8 on program-level evaluations. As you know, all exploratory, descriptive, and explanatory program-level evaluation designs can be used in the monitoring approach to quality improvement, depending on how often it is utilized in measuring a client's practice objective. Discuss how each one of these designs can be utilized in a monitoring approach to quality improvement. What type of information is provided by each of these designs and what decisions can be based on each design? Which designs are the most suitable for monitoring purposes? Why?

11

DECISION MAKING TO IMPROVE QUALITY

PREVIOUS CHAPTERS HAVE INTRODUCED the different types of case- and program-level evaluation designs that can be used in the monitoring approach to quality improvement. This chapter explores more fully how they can be used in the decision-making process.

The Decision-Making Process

Ideally, all professional decisions should be arrived at via a rational process based, in part, on the collection, synthesis, and analysis of empirical data. Suppose, for example, that a human service worker must decide whether to terminate services, and that the termination criteria are relatively straightforward. A client can be terminated in two simple ways: when the program objectives have been met, and when it becomes apparent that the program objectives are not going to be met and a referral might be in order. Notice that a client is not terminated on the attainment of practice objectives but on the attainment of program objectives.

On the face of it, this termination decision should pose no problems. The worker and client could jointly decide at the beginning of treatment what the practice objectives are to be in an effort to meet program objectives. A measuring instrument—or, preferably, a number of measuring instruments—is chosen, and it is decided, for each instrument, what score or rating will constitute an acceptable level of improvement for each practice objective. When the program objective is reached, the client can be terminated. The entire process is rational and objective, based on empirical data supplied by standardized measurement.

The same rational process should apply toward a program in reference to its maintenance objectives and goal. Suppose that an administrator of a sexual abuse treatment program has to change the program's eligibility criteria to include male offenders, who are not currently being served. This directive came from the program's major funding source. Thus, the program's goal has to be modified to reflect these current realities. The program's administrator and the funding source have to consider various factors. Are adequate services for male offenders provided by other human service programs in the community? Will extra funding be available, or will service to offenders mean reduced services for other types of clients? Are there presently workers whose qualifications and experience would enable them to serve offenders? Is there enough physical space to avoid such difficulties as offenders sharing the same reception area with female survivors of sexual abuse?

Though complex, these questions can be largely resolved on the basis of empirical data. Possibly, the issue has arisen because male offenders are constantly being referred to the program and cannot easily be redirected elsewhere, indicating that a gap in service exists in the local community. The extent of the gap can be assessed through data on the number of referrals (1) received by the program, (2) successfully redirected, and (3) refused without being redirected. In a similar way, data can be employed to assess how much the new service would cost, given existing staff and facilities, and through what channels the funding might be obtained. In theory, then, the decision will be rational, based on empirical data showing the extent of the need and the feasibility of providing the service.

As stressed throughout this book, few decisions are made in the human services solely on the basis of empirical data. Contextual variables must also be considered. In addition, empirical data are often incomplete, missing, or unavailable. Thus, subjective data based on the professional's impressions, past experiences, values, and intuition also play a part in decision making. Empirical data guide the decision-making process—they do not rule it.

For instance, the program administrator cited above may find that routine monitoring procedures have provided the data needed to demonstrate a service gap to current (e.g., United Way) and potential (e.g., Justice Department) funding sources. If funding is available, but not in an amount sufficient to provide what the program administrator considers satisfactory service, the administrator then has three choices: (1) provide no service until more funding can be acquired; (2) provide as good a service as possible at the given level of funding; or (3) draw small amounts of resources from other programs within the agency, hoping the services to other clients in the other programs will not suffer.

Empirical data are useful here to only a limited degree. Data can tell the administrator what resources could be siphoned off from other programs within the agency and how that would affect service to their clientele. The actual decision, however, requires a value judgment. Should other services be reduced in order to provide a service to young offenders? Is an inadequate service better than no service, or is it advisable to wait until an appropriate level of additional funding can be acquired? Is it ethically acceptable to deny services in the short term in order to provide better services in the long term? Data cannot answer these questions; all program administrators must make their own ethical and political judgments.

The need for judgment also arises when the information synthesized from the data is uncertain or incomplete. For example, it may not be possible to assess with any accuracy the effect of a small withdrawal of resources from other programs, or data on the services provided by these programs may be missing or outdated. We will have more to say on the subject of uncertain or incomplete data later in this chapter.

Even when the data yield information that appears to be certain and complete, the decision is usually not based solely on empirical data. To return to our earlier example of a human service professional deciding whether to terminate with a client, the data may indicate unequivocally that the program objective for a particular client (and thus the client's practice objectives as well) has been reached and maintained over time, and that the client is therefore ready to be terminated. The worker may nonetheless have a feeling or intuition that this client is not ready to be terminated. This feeling may be founded on experience with previous clients in similar situations or on the rapport that the worker has built with this particular client.

There are many workers who have a healthy respect for data but who will, nevertheless, follow their instincts over the data when the two conflict. The decision to follow a feeling may or may not be sensible; it depends on the circumstances. The data may not show the result that the worker expects to see, and the expectation may be so firmly fixed in the worker's mind that the data are disregarded. Here, following intuition is not sensible; valid and reliable data should not be discarded just because they fail to confirm a hypothesis.

Nevertheless, empirical data do have their limitations. A series of measurements can show how the level of a practice objective has changed in the past, what it is at present, and how it is likely to change in the future, *assuming* that all relevant factors remain the same. These measurements on the practice objective will not show the possible effect of Mr. Jackson's upcoming court appearance, a factor which the practitioner should take into account when deciding whether to end services to Mr. Jackson.

Decision making, then, is based partly on empirical data, some of which may be missing, ambiguous, or contradictory, and partly on subjective data. Subjective data include clinical impressions, professional judgments based on past experiences, and intuition. Both empirical data and subjective data have strengths and limitations; a professional who is familiar with these strengths and limitations will be better equipped to know when and to what degree each can be relied on in decision making.

Empirical and Subjective Data in Decision Making

This section provides more detail on the use of empirical and subjective data in human service practice and evaluation, and present some advantages and limitations.

The Use of Empirical Data

The main advantage of empirical data as a decision-making tool is its relative precision and objectivity. If, for example, professional human service workers are under the impression that the time they devote to community relations is more than adequate, but the data show that 90 percent of community requests for program representatives are refused, there is little more to say on the issue. Faced with these data, the workers will probably devote more attention to community matters.

At the case level, assume that a worker's clinical judgment is that the self-esteem problems of children in group treatment for acting out behavior are diminishing, and that empirical standardized measurement confirms her impression: The self-esteem problem scores of group members have declined from an initial average of 65 to a current average of 45—a reduction of 20 points in the desired direction. The higher the score the higher the self-esteem problem. Because empirical data and subjective data both point to the same tentative conclusion (a decrease in the children's self-esteem), the worker can have more confidence that she has correctly analyzed her clients' problems.

In this situation, empirical measures do have some advantages over subjective judgments: They not only confirm that self-esteem problems are diminishing, but also indicate to what degree. The empirical data show that the improvement has been modest and that, on the average, group members are still scoring over the desired clinical cutting score of 30. Empirical measures thus permit a more accurate understanding of the current status of clients' practice objectives. In short, empirical measures complement subjective measures.

In regard to accountability at both the case and program levels, workers, supervisors, administrators, and funders require precise and objective data to satisfy themselves that a program's objectives are being achieved. Assessment based only on the line-level workers' or program administrators' impressions and intuition will not usually suffice as there is no way to verify their validity and reliability. Empirical data will considerably strengthen the contention that program objectives are being achieved.

Limitations

Empirical data have four main limitations in decision making: (1) They may be incomplete or missing altogether; (2) they may not be available when the decision has to be made; (3) they may be uncertain or ambiguous, allowing conflicting interpretations; and (4) they may not take all pertinent contextual factors into account.

The monitoring approach to quality improvement can address the problems of incomplete, missing, and currently unavailable data. In general, both program administrators and line-level workers know what kinds of decisions they normally make and what empirical data are needed for each of these decision-making points. They can therefore take steps to ensure that all the data they routinely require are collected in time to assist with decision making. Each worker's case files should contain complete and current data on clients' progress toward practice and program objectives and the allocation of the worker's time to direct client service, advocacy for clients, training, administration, and community projects. At the program level, the management data system (to be discussed in the following chapter) should provide complete and current data regarding such matters as caseload numbers, staff training, volunteer recruitment, community involvement, intake, assessment, treatment, and termination procedures.

Of course, no data collection system is perfect. There will be times when the data needed for decisions are not there, or only partly there, or will be there next week. In these cases, it is sometimes possible to extrapolate: that is, fill in missing data points from known data, or continue a line on a graph, *assuming* that the trend will be the same in the future as in the past. If it is not possible to obtain the needed data in this way, the decision will have to be made on the basis of whatever empirical data are available, supplemented by the decision maker's judgment and intuition.

Uncertain or ambiguous data are more difficult. For example, weekly measurements of Ms Furuto's depression level may yield scores that do not fall neatly into any clear pattern. Looking at the points on the graph for the last two months, the worker may at first conclude that her depression is lessening: Five of the eight points seem to lie close to a gentle, declining slope. But three points that do not fit the line at all show elevated levels of depression.

A closer look at the graph gives a different impression. The downward slope, if it is a slope at all, in fact is more level than not; and those three anomalous points, which show an alarming increase in depression, might well be more representative of Ms Furuto's problem level. Unsure, the practitioner turns to other data sources. Ms Furuto's partner reports that she is going out more and taking more interest in family matters—support for the conclusion that the depression is lessening. Ms Furuto herself reports that she is having fewer crying spells—more support—but she has also recorded in her journal that the disturbance in her eating and sleeping patterns is as serious as ever.

This is another case in which the worker's judgment comes into play. Different ways of measuring the same practice objective provide mutual confirmation when they show the same result. When they show conflicting results, the worker must first seek possible reasons for the discrepancies. Perhaps some stressor events in Ms Furuto's social environment can explain the spikes in the depression scores. Or, possibly, there is some inconsistency in the way Ms Furuto has been recording impressions in her journal. In short, the worker must rely on judgment in evaluating the reliability and validity of the various sources of data. What is important is that all sources of data are taken into account, empirical and subjective, so that a well-founded decision becomes more likely.

At the group level, different conclusions may be drawn from the same data set, depending on the particular statistical methods chosen to analyze the data. Suppose, for example, that an evaluation study is conducted to examine changes in the self-esteem of young people who have participated in an agency's self-esteem building groups. It is found that, on the average, little change takes place between the beginning and the end of the self-esteem programs. However, a slightly more detailed analysis may yield different results. If the data for preadolescent and adolescent youngsters are separated, it may be found that preadolescents improve their self-esteem to a considerable degree, whereas the self-esteem of adolescents actually declines.

The choice of analysis is thus no insignificant theoretical exercise: The ramifications can be far-reaching. If decisions are taken on the basis of the first analysis, the entire program might be revamped; if on the basis of the second analysis, the services offered to adolescents might be revamped but the services offered to preadolescents left intact.

In sum, the results obtained from any evaluation design are only as good as the design itself, and the interpretation given to the data is only as good as the method of analysis selected: Without thoughtful attention, data collection and analysis can become an excellent illustration of the saying "Garbage in, garbage out." The practitioner, then, should at one and the same time be trusting and not too trusting of the way things seem to be. *Judicious skepticism* is a professional asset.

The Use of Subjective Data

Human service workers sometimes assume that logic and intuition are naturally antithetical processes: that a person possessing one must lack the other. In fact, all people of normal intelligence are capable of both logical thought and intuition. Indeed, it may be argued that intuition *is* logical thought, the result of data subconsciously assimilated and processed. Most competent professionals assimilate data continuously throughout contact with clients, noting the client's stance, gait, gestures, voice, eye movement, and set of mouth. Some of this is consciously noted; some filters through subconsciously and emerges later as a clinical impression or intuition.

One of the limitations of empirical data, stated above, is that they may not take all pertinent factors into account. Any factor to do with a program, or a client's life for that matter, is affected to various degrees and in various ways by a myriad of other factors. At the program level, for example, funding is affected by community needs, the program's effectiveness and efficiency in meeting these needs, the state of the economy, and various other personal, political, and social factors.

At the case level, the wisdom of terminating Ms Birkey depends not only on the level of her problem but also on her life situation and overall emotional and physical condition. Predictable future events and the worker's caseload also enter the picture, together with the possible effects of termination on Ms Birkey. The termination decision is based on all available data concerning these factors and the worker's judgment as to the relative importance of each.

However, for some factors no empirical data may exist. Clinical intuition alone can tell the worker that Ms Birkey's court appearance, scheduled for next month, will considerably reduce the present level of the achievement of her practice objective, necessitating further intervention. Thus, as we have stressed throughout this book, subjective data complements empirical data.

Limitations

The chief drawback to subjective data is that impressions and intuition often spring to the mind ready formed, and the process by which they were formed cannot be examined. Perhaps the practitioner's intuition about the traumatic effects Ms Birkey's court appearance sprang from numerous bits of information about Ms Birkey and the court process, absorbed over time and subconsciously integrated. But perhaps less relevant bits of information were also integrated: the worker's own negative court experience years ago, or the worker's personal dislike for the current district attorney. Intuition may thus be tainted by personal bias, of which the worker may be unaware and against which there is little defense.

It is reasonable to assume that, of the various data contributing to an intuition, some will be accurate and relevant, some will be less relevant, and some will be in error. The same is true of empirical data: a wrong box mistakenly checked on a self-administered questionnaire, for example, will lead to a wrong result. The difference between empirical data and subjective data lies in the fact that errors in the former are open to inspection and discovery where errors in the latter are not (Taylor, 1993).

Let us examine this last point more closely. If there are ten empirical data points on a graph, and nine of them fit on a straight line but the tenth is a long way off, we should consider the possibility that the tenth point is in error and should be disregarded. But with subjective data, the tenth point will not be clearly atypical and may be more likely to be considered meaningful and may not be disregarded. The resulting intuition may thus give as much weight to erroneous or irrelevant data as to data that are relevant and accurate.

Further, human beings tend to place inordinate faith in their intuitive judgments (Grinnell & Siegel, 1988). A worker who has made an intuitive decision will probably have a comfortable feeling of certainty regarding it. Yet, empirical data, even those obtained from the most rigorous experimentation, do not provide certainty. In fact, the more rigorous the evaluation study, the more likely it is that the evaluator will qualify the study's findings, warning that they are only to be accepted until more data can be gathered by future evaluation efforts (Reid, 1988, 1993).

The feelings of certainty that accompany an intuitive decision can be dangerous. A human service worker who is certain, and comfortable in the certainty, may be very reluctant to take notice of empirical data that refute the intuition. Sometimes the empirical data will be ignored altogether; sometimes the worker will "reinterpret" the data in a way to justify the intuitive decision previously made. In either case, the decision is made without taking all data fully into account, with the probable result of a lower quality decision.

If empirical data relevant to a decision are not immediately available, the probability that they will be discounted is even higher. Urgent decisions may well be made at once based only on impressions, global judgments, and intuition. If the decision can be delayed, the practitioner may decide to delay it, resolving not to think about it again until all the "facts" are in. Even so, random thoughts are hard to control and it is likely that the worker *will* think about it, weighing the facts that are known, applying intuitive perceptions, perhaps even reaching tentative conclusions without the benefit of the data still to be collected. Clearly, then, it is important to have empirical data ready at hand. The best way that this can be accomplished is through a well thought out continuous data collection procedure.

To recapitulate the foregoing, although it would be desirable to base all decisions on logically analyzed empirical data, complete, air-tight information on all factors affecting a given decision is seldom available in the human services. Nevertheless, decisions do have to be made; consequently, empirical data are often supplemented by more subjective types of data such as the worker's clinical impressions, global judgments, experiences, and intuition. Ultimately, the practitioner will have to use judgment in reconciling all these sources of data in order to arrive at an understanding of the situation.

It is important not only to consider all sources of data but also to be aware of the strengths and limitations of each of those sources. Quality decisions are usually the result of explicitly sifting through the various sources of data and choosing those sources in which it is reasonable to have the most confidence under the circumstances.

Having considered the two primary types of data used in decision making, we now turn to the decision-making processes relevant at the case and program levels.

Case-Level Decision Making

If case-level decisions of highest quality are to be reached, the professional human service worker should know what types of decisions are best supported by empirical data and what types will likely require the use of subjective data.

A helping relationship with a client is a process, passing through a number of stages that follow logically one from the other. There are essentially six such stages: engagement, problem definition, practice objective-setting, intervention, discharge, and follow-up. In practice these phases are not likely to follow this tidy sequence (Grinnell, Rothery, & Thomlison, 1993; Duehn, 1985). Engagement, for example, occurs most prominently at the beginning of the relationship, but it continues in some form throughout the process. Problem definition is logically the first consideration after engagement, but if it becomes evident during intervention that the client's problem is not clearly understood, the problem definition and objective-setting phases will have to be readdressed. Nevertheless, discernible phases do exist. The following example will illustrate the types of decisions that are normally made in each phase.

The Engagement and Problem Definition Phases

Suppose that a doctor has told Mr. Ramos he must quit smoking. This is a concrete problem, readily defined, and decisions about it can be made largely on the basis of empirical data. Mr. Ramos reports that he smokes about 45 cigarettes a day, and his practice objective (in this case it will also be a program objective) is to reduce this number to zero. If the worker believes that Mr. Ramos's self-reports will be accurate, the helping process will be merely a matter of gathering the baseline data, initiating an intervention, and monitoring Mr. Ramos's progress by having him count the number of cigarettes he smokes each day (an *AB* design as presented in Chapter 7). If the intervention is successful, Mr. Ramos will be terminated when he has reached his objective and maintained his nonsmoking behavior over a reasonable period. We do not suggest, of course, that quitting smoking is easy; but merely that a concrete simple observable objective (smoking in this case) lends itself to decision making, largely on the basis of empirical data.

When the problem is more abstract, subjective data will come more prominently into play. Suppose that a married couple named the Wrights come to a family service agency to work on their marriage problems and have been assigned a worker named Maria. From Ms Wright's point of view, the problem is that her partner does not pay enough attention to her. In the worker's judgment, Ms Wright's perception is a symptom of another problem that has yet to be defined. However, the client's perception is a good starting point, and the worker may attempt to objectify and quantify Ms Wright's statement. In what ways, precisely, does her partner not pay enough attention to her? Ms Wright obligingly gives numbers: Her partner has not gone anywhere with her for the past three months, but he regularly spends three nights a week playing basketball, three nights at the local bar, and one night at his mother's.

Mr. Wright, protestingly brought into the session, declares that he spends most nights at home and the real problem is that his partner is lazy and argumentative. Further enquiry leads Maria to believe that Mr. Wright spends more nights away from home than he reports but fewer than his partner says; Ms Wright, feeling herself unloved, most likely is argumentative; and the basic problems are actually poor communication and unrealistic expectations on the part of both. A host of other problems that surfaced subtly during the enquiry cannot be addressed until the communications problem has been solved; communication, therefore, should be the initial target of the intervention—the first practice objective. A second practice objective could be to reduce the Wrights' unrealistic expectations of each other. Let us consider that the Wrights have these two practice objectives that are specifically geared toward the program objective, "to increase their marital satisfaction." These two practice objectives are "to increase the Wrights' communication patterns," and "to reduce the Wrights' unrealistic expectations of each other." Maria believes that the attainment of these two practice objectives will increase their marital satisfaction—the main purpose why the Wrights are seeing a professional human service worker. Remember, the Wrights want a happier marriage—that is why they sought out services—they did not seek out help with their dysfunctional communication patterns and unrealistic expectations of one another. Thus, to increase their marital satisfaction becomes the program objective and communications and expectations become the two practice objectives.

So far, Maria's conclusions have been based on her own impressions of the conflicting data presented by the Wrights. Unless the problem is straightforward and concrete, as it was in the case of the cigarette-smoking Mr. Ramos, the problem-defining phase often depends more on the worker's judgment, experience, and intuition than it does on empirical data. Even when paper-and-pencil instruments, such as those presented in Chapter 5, are used to help clients identify and prioritize their problems, the choice of the problem to be first addressed will largely be guided by the worker's intuition and judgment. Once intuition has indicated what the problem *might* be, however, the magnitude of the problem can often be measured empirically.

In the Wrights' case, Maria has tentatively decided to formulate a practice objective of increasing the Wrights' communication skills. In order to confirm that communication skills are problematic, she asks Mr. and Ms Wright each to independently complete a 25-item summated standardized measuring instrument containing such items as "How often do you and your spouse talk over pleasant things that happen during the day?" with possible responses of "very frequently," "frequently," "occasionally," "seldom," and "never." This standardized instrument has a range of 0 to 100, with higher scores showing better communication skills. It has a clinical cutting score of 60, indicating effective communications above that level, and it has been tested on people of the same socioeconomic group as the Wrights and may be assumed to yield valid and reliable data.

The introduction of the measuring instrument at this stage will serve two basic purposes. First, the scores will show whether communication is indeed a problem, and to what degree it is a problem for each partner. Second, the scores will provide a baseline measurement that can be used as the first point on a graph in whatever case-level design Maria selects. In the Wrights' particular case, the instrument also serves a third purpose: to engage Mr. Wright in the therapeutic process.

Maria has had no trouble engaging Ms Wright. Mr. Wright, however, is a different matter. Reluctant from the start to be involved in counseling, he is no more inclined to trust Maria's perceptions than he was his partner's. Maria's clinical intuition tells her that if she spends the session talking in generalities, Mr. Wright will not come back. What he needs is evidence, preferably in the form of hard facts, that she knows what she is doing. Mr. Wright needs, in short, precisely the same thing as her supervisor and the program's funders need: empirical data.

Maria scores the results of the communication inventory in Mr. Wright's presence and informs him that effectively communicating couples usually score a minimum of 60, whereas he has scored 50 and Ms Wright has scored 40. Mr. Wright, who has known for a long time that he and his partner have not been communicating, is visibly impressed and murmurs that he has "10 points left to go." This is only the second time he has spoken in the session, as Maria immediately points out, whereas during the same hour Ms Wright has made a dozen statements to him starting with an accusatory "you," and perhaps 20 to the worker starting with a complaining "he." At no time has she started a sentence with "I."

Mr. Wright looks at Maria with a new respect. He is prepared to be instructed on the matters of "I" statements and active listening; he will participate in role-plays, and he is willing to record, every day for a week, his own "I" statements, those of his partner, and the content of any conversation lasting for at least five minutes. The standardized measuring instrument, in this case, has enabled Maria to confirm her intuition that communication is a problem and to measure the level of the problem; it has provided her with a way to monitor changes in the level of the practice objective in the weeks ahead; and it has helped her to engage Mr. Wright in the helping process by gaining his confidence.

The Practice Objective-Setting Phase

In the Wrights' case, the program objective is to increase their marital satisfaction. One way to increase their marital satisfaction (program objective) is to have them communicate better as measured by a communications inventory (practice objective). Thus, one of many practice objectives could be to increase the couple's communication skills to a minimum score of 60, the clinical cutting score on the communication inventory. The practice objective-setting phase in this example thus relies heavily on empirical data: A specific practice objective is framed in terms of a change from a clinically significant level to one that indicates the absence of a clinically significant problem.

The same process applies in cases where the measuring instrument selected is less formal and precise. For example, Maria may ask each partner to complete a self-anchored rating scale indicating his and her level of satisfaction with the degree of communication achieved. The range on this instrument could be from 1–6 with higher scores indicating greater levels of satisfaction. If Mr. Wright begins by rating his satisfaction level at 3 and Ms Wright indicates hers at 2, the practice objective chosen may be to achieve a rating of at least 4 for each partner. Here again, practice objective-setting is based on empirical data collected at the beginning of the intervention.

The Intervention Phase

The selection of the intervention strategy itself will be based on data only to a limited degree. Perhaps Maria has seen previous clients with similar practice objectives and also has empirical evidence, via the professional literature, that a specific intervention has been successful before. But even though the intervention is chosen on the basis of data accumulated from previous research studies and past experience, each intervention is tailored to meet the needs of the particular client, and the decision about what strategy to adopt and how to implement it is largely based on subjective data—the worker's experience and clinical judgment.

Although empirical data may play only a part in selection of the intervention strategy, once that strategy is selected, its success is measured on the basis of consistently collected empirical data. Ideally, data will be collected using a number of different measures. In the Wrights' case, the scores from repeated administrations of the communication inventory will comprise one set of empirical data for one particular practice objective. Frequency counts of specifically selected behaviors may comprise another set: for example, a count of the number of conversations daily lasting at least five minutes, or the number of "I" statements made daily by each partner. In addition, Maria may develop her own form for rating the communication skills demonstrated during interviews: appropriate eye contact, voice modulation, body language, listening skills, and so forth. These sets of data together will provide considerable information about whether and to what degree progress is being made.

Maria is also likely to come to a more global opinion about how the couple is doing. This opinion will be based on a variety of observations and impressions formed as she works with the two. The process by which such an opinion is formed is intuitive and may, depending on the worker and the circumstances, be quite accurate. However, the method by which it is arrived at is idiosyncratic and is, therefore, of unknown validity and reliability. For this reason, relying on clinical impressions exclusively is inadvisable. On the other hand, as we saw in Chapter 6, empirical measurements are also not immune to problems of validity and reliability. The best course is a middle one: Determination of client progress should be based on a combination of empirical data and subjective data. Where empirical data and clinical impressions lead in the same direction, Maria can proceed with considerable confidence that she has a clear and accurate picture of the client's progress. Where empirical data and clinical impressions diverge, Maria should first attempt to determine the reasons for the difference and ensure that she has a good understanding of her clients' problems and needs.

When Maria is satisfied that she has an accurate grasp of client progress, she is ready to proceed to decisions about intervention. These decisions, as the following sections will show, are guided by changes in the practice objective, of which there are three types: (1) deterioration or no change, (2) insufficient or slow change, and (3) satisfactory amount of change.

Deterioration or No Change

Suppose that Ms Wright, who scored 40 on the first administration of the communication inventory, scores 41 on the second, 43 on the third, and 42 on the fourth (see Figure 11.1). In addition, Mr. Wright scores 51, 53, and 52 respectively. How would Maria analyze and interpret such data?

First, Maria will want to consider what the other available sources of data indicate. Let us assume that, on a self-anchored communication satisfaction scale, Ms Wright still rates her satisfaction at 2 and that, during the treatment interviews, she avoids eye contact with Mr. Wright and tries to monopolize the worker's attention with references to "he" and "him." In this situation, the data all seem to point to the same conclusion: There has been virtually no change or progress. Under

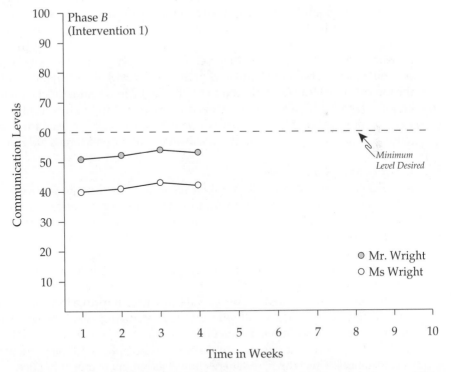

FIGURE 11.1   *B* Design: The Wrights' Communication Levels over Time Indicating No Change
(Note: high scores = high communication levels)

such circumstances, it is reasonable to place considerable reliance on data obtained from the communication inventory.

As Figure 11.1 also indicates, the slope of the line connecting the measurement points is virtually flat—that is, stable, indicating neither major improvement nor deterioration. Moreover, the level of the problem is well below the desired minimum score of 60. Such data would normally lead Maria to conclude that a change in the intervention is warranted and perhaps a *BC* design should be used.

Here is where qualitative considerations may enter the decision-making process. For example, Maria may be aware of disruptions in the lives of Mr. and Ms Wright. Perhaps Mr. Wright received a lay-off notice during the second week of the intervention. Maria may now need to consider whether the effects of the intervention might not have been counteracted by these adverse circumstances. Ultimately, she will need to decide whether to continue the intervention in the hope that, once the couple has dealt with the shock of the impending lay-off, the intervention will begin to have the desired effect.

It is also possible that the intervention is known to have a delayed impact. This characteristic could have been determined from the professional literature or from Maria's previous experience with the intervention. Under such circumstances it may, again, be reasonable to maintain the intervention for some time longer and see whether movement toward the practice objective begins.

How long it is sensible to continue an intervention in the absence of documented progress is a matter best left to Maria's judgment. As long as there is reason to believe that an intervention may yet have the desired impacts, she is justified in pursuing that intervention. However, if there is no evidence of change for the better, the intervention strategy will need to be changed. Here again, the data will provide empirical evidence supporting the need for a change in the intervention, but they will not indicate what future intervention strategies might be used instead. Formulation of a new intervention strategy will again call upon Maria's judgment.

Insufficient or Slow Change

Insufficient or slow change is a familiar scenario in the human services. A gradual but definite improvement in the communication inventory scores indicates that Mr. and Ms Wright are slowly learning to communicate. However, their marriage continues to deteriorate because their communication skills are still at a low level; progress needs to be more rapid if the marriage is to be saved. It must be remembered that marital satisfaction is the program objective and communication is the practice objective.

In general, many clients improve only slowly or improve in spurts with regressions in between. The data will reflect what is occurring: what the problem level is and at what rate and in what direction it is changing. However, no data can tell a worker whether the measured rate of change is acceptable in the particular client's circumstances. This is an area where clinical judgment comes into play.

The worker may decide that the rate of change is insufficient, but just marginally so; that is, the intervention is successful on the whole and ought to be continued, but at a greater frequency or intensity. Perhaps the number of weekly sessions can be increased, or more time can be scheduled for each session, or more intensive work can be planned. In other words, a *B* design will now become a B_1B_2 design (as illustrated in Figure 11.2) or, if baseline data has been collected, an *AB* design will become an AB_1B_2 design. If, on the other hand, the worker thinks that intensifying the intervention is unlikely to yield significantly improved results, a different intervention entirely may be adopted. In this case, the *B* design will become a *BC* design (illustrated in Figure 11.3), or the *AB* design will become an *ABC* design.

Sometimes improvement occurs at an acceptable rate for a period and then the client reaches a plateau, below the desired minimal level; no further change seems to be occurring. The data will show the initial improvement and the plateau (see Figure 11.4), but they will not show whether the plateau is temporary, akin to a resting period, and further improvement will occur in time; or whether the level already achieved is as far as the client can go. Again, this is a matter for clinical judgment. The worker may decide to continue with the intervention for a time to see if improvement begins again. The exact length of time during which perseverance is justified is a judgment call. If the client remains stuck at the level reached beyond

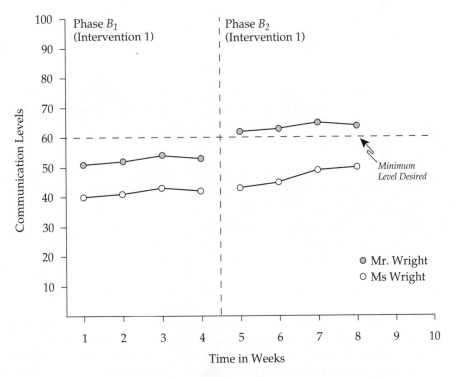

FIGURE 11.2 B_1B_2 **Changing Intensity Design: The Wrights' Communication Levels over Time Indicating Insufficient Change at B_1 followed by a More Intensive B_2**
(Note: high scores = high communication levels)

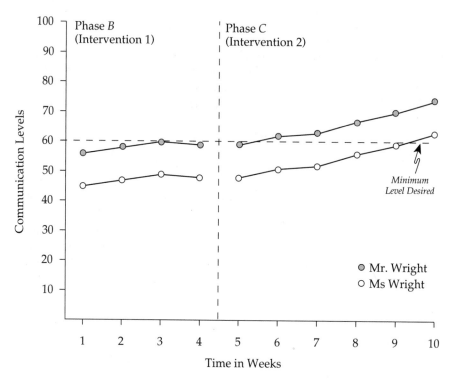

FIGURE 11.3   **BC Design: The Wrights' Communication Levels over Time Indicating Insufficient Change at the *B* Intervention Followed by a *C* Intervention**
(Note: high scores = high communication levels)

that time, the worker will have to decide whether to apply the intervention more intensively, try a new intervention or be content with what has been achieved.

Satisfactory Change

Frequently, it is hoped, the empirical data will show an improvement. At times the improvement will be steady and sustained, and at other times an overall trend of improvement will be punctuated with periods of plateau or even regression. This latter scenario is illustrated in Figure 11.5. Essentially, continuation of the intervention is justified by continuing client progress, although Maria may wish at times to make minor modifications in the intervention.

It is important to keep in mind that not all case-level designs permit the worker to conclude that the intervention has caused the change for the better (see Chapter 7). In the case of many designs that are likely to be used in the monitoring of human service interventions, it is only possible to conclude that the client's practice objective has changed for the better. This is the situation in the design shown in Figure 11.5. From a service perspective, however, evidence that the client is improving is sufficient justification for continuing the intervention; it is not necessary to prove that the intervention is *causing* the change.

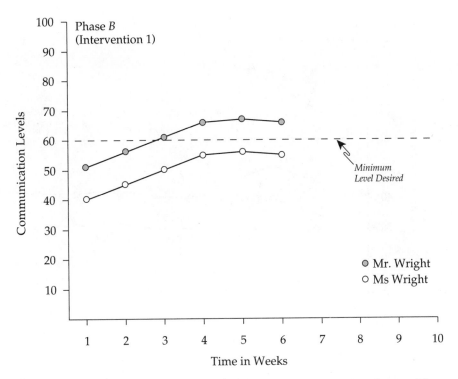

FIGURE 11.4   *B* **Design: The Wrights' Communication Levels over Time Indicating an Initial Improvement Leveling off to a Plateau**
(Note: high scores = high communication levels)

When the data show that the client has reached the program or practice objective, the worker will, if possible, initiate a maintenance phase, perhaps gradually reducing the frequency of contact with a view to termination but trying to ensure that the gains achieved are not lost. If other practice objectives need to be resolved, the maintenance phase for one objective may coincide with the baseline or interventive phase for another. It is quite possible to engage in a number of case-level designs at the same time with the same client; because client practice objectives are usually interrelated, data obtained in one area will often be relevant to another.

The maintenance phase is also important, ensuring that the practice objective really has been satisfactorily resolved. Assume that data show a steady improvement, culminating at a point within the target range (as in Figure 11.3). *One* measurement below the minimum desired level means only that the practice objective was not at a clinically significant level when *that* measurement was made. Subsequent measurements may show that a significant problem still exists. A number of measurements are required before Maria can be confident that the practice objective has stabilized at the minimal level. Similarly, where the trend to improvement included plateaus and regressions, measurements must continue beyond the achievement of the objective to ensure that the practice objective has indeed stabilized in the desired level and direction.

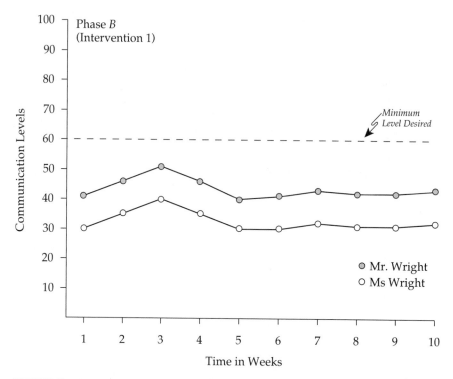

FIGURE 11.5   *B* **Design: The Wrights' Communication Levels over Time Indicating Improvement with Periods of Plateaus and Regressions**
(Note: high scores = high communication levels)

The Termination and Follow-Up Phases

Once it is decided that the program objective (not the practice objective) has been totally accomplished, the next step is termination and follow-up. The termination decision is straightforward in theory: When the data show that the program objective has been achieved by the client, via the attainment of practice objectives, and the program objective level is stable, the client can be terminated (see Figure 2.2). In reality, however, other factors need to be taken into account, such as the number and type of support systems available in the client's social environment and the nature and magnitude of possible stressor events in the client's life. The worker must carefully weigh all the factors, including information yielded by empirical data, in making a decision to terminate.

Ideally, the follow-up phase will be a routine part of the program's operations. Follow-up measurements always pertain to program objectives, not practice objectives. However, many human service programs do not engage in any kind of follow-up activities, and other programs conduct follow-ups in a sporadic or informal way. If the program does conduct routine follow-up, decisions will already have been made concerning how often and in what manner the terminated client should be contacted. If no standardized follow-up procedures are in place, the human service worker will have to decide whether follow-up is necessary and, if so, what form it should take.

Data can help to decide whether a follow-up is necessary. If data reveal that a client has not reached a program objective, or has reached it only marginally, a follow-up is essential. If the data show a pattern of improvement followed by regression, a follow-up is also indicated, to ensure that regression will not occur again.

The follow-up procedures that measure program objectives may be conducted in a number of ways. Frequently used approaches include contacting former clients by letter or by telephone at increasingly longer intervals after termination from the program. A less frequently used approach is to continue to measure the program objectives that were taken during the intervention period. For example, as the Wrights are terminated, Maria could arrange to have them complete, at biweekly intervals, the Marital Satisfaction Scale (not the communications inventory) that they completed on a weekly basis while receiving services. Maria could mail the scales to the Wrights, who, because they have already completed them numerous times, should have no problem doing so during follow-up. The inclusion of a stamped, self-addressed envelope can further encourage them to complete this task. In this manner, Maria can determine empirically whether marital satisfaction gains made during treatment are maintained over time.

At a minimum, collecting data during follow-up results in a *BF* design as illustrated in Figures 11.6 and 11.7. If an initial baseline phase had been utilized, the result would be an *ABF* design. Where follow-up data indicate that client gains are being maintained, a situation illustrated in Figure 11.6, termination procedures can be completed. Where follow-up data reveal a deterioration after termination, illustrated in Figure 11.7, Maria is at least in a position to know that her clients are not doing well. Under such circumstances, complete termination is not warranted. Instead, Maria should consider whether to resume active intervention, provide additional support in their social environment, or offer some other service. The follow-up data will not help Maria to decide what she should do next, but they will alert her to the need to do something.

It should be noted that Figures 11.6 and 11.7 provide data for marital satisfaction scores (the lower the score the better the marital satisfaction) and do not represent the couple's communication scores as in Figures 11.1–11.5 (the higher the score the better the communication). This is because follow-up data are always concerned with program objectives (in this case, marital satisfaction), not practice objectives (in this case, communication, and expectations of one another).

Program-Level Decision Making

The primary purpose of the monitoring approach at the program level is to assess the program in an ongoing manner so that the services provided can be continually

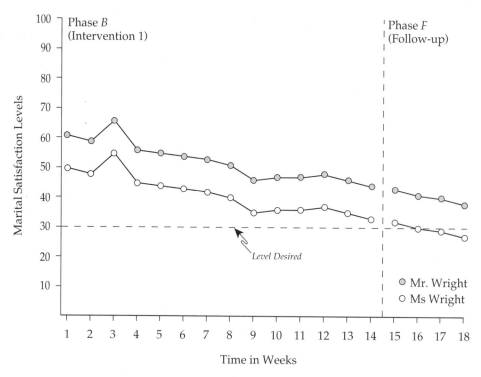

FIGURE 11.6   *BF* **Design: The Wrights' Marital Satisfaction Levels during Treatment (***B***) and after Termination (***F***) Indicating Maintained Improvement after Termination**
(Note: low scores = high satisfaction levels)

developed and improved. The program may be assessed in various ways. Success rates may vary with problem type. A particular program may achieve good success with children who have family-related problems but less success with children whose problems are primarily drug-related.

Or perhaps good results are achieved with one type of client but not another: A drug rehabilitation program may be more successful with adults than it is with adolescents. Or, again, a particular program within an agency may achieve its program objectives better than another program within the same agency. For example, a child welfare agency may successfully operate an adolescent treatment foster care program but have less success with its adolescent group care program. If several residential programs are operated, one may achieve its program's objectives to a higher degree than another (e.g., Figure 4.5). Finally, the agency must be considered as a whole. How successful is it when all of its programs are assessed together? What might be done on a general organizational level to improve the agency's effectiveness and efficiency?

Measurement and comparison of outcomes can be readily achieved through the collection and analysis of empirical data. The kinds of data collected and analyses

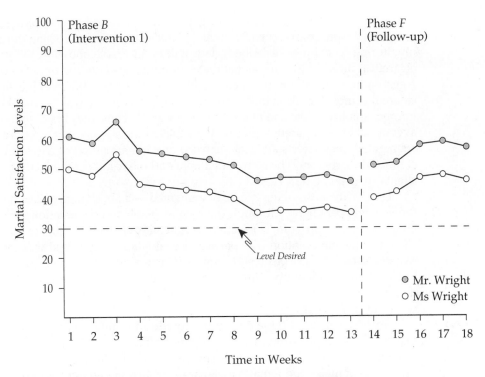

FIGURE 11.7 *BF* **Design: The Wrights' Marital Satisfaction Levels during Treatment (*B*) and after Termination (*F*) Indicating Deterioration after Termination**
(Note: low scores = high satisfaction levels)

performed will depend on the program being considered. Essentially, evaluation of outcome may be conducted with regard to similar problems and cases, the program, or the entire agency. Each of these will be considered in turn.

Problems and Cases

Many human service agencies offer services to people with a variety of needs: pregnant teens, disabled seniors, preadolescents with self-esteem problems, couples seeking help with their marriages, and people who are trying to stop smoking. The agency will be interested in knowing, and is usually required by funders to document, to what degree its programs are helping people with particular types of problems.

From a program perspective, the results achieved by any one client, satisfactory or not, do not say much about the effectiveness of the program as a whole. Program effectiveness can be determined only by examining data from groups of clients, often using simple aggregation methods that will be described shortly.

Assume, for example, that during a six-month period of a smoking cessation program, the program served 80 clients, 40 male and 40 female. Using the case-level monitoring techniques described, data will be available showing the number of cigarettes smoked by each client at the beginning and at the end of the intervention. Aggregating the individual client results indicates that the average number of cigarettes smoked daily at the beginning of the intervention was 34, and the average number smoked at the end of the program was 11. Thus, the clients smoked on the average 23 fewer cigarettes after they completed the stop-smoking program. These aggregated data, after statistical analysis, provide a method of assessing the outcome of the program. The aggregated data and the results of the analysis for all 80 clients are presented in Table 11.1.

The decline in smoking can be documented as a net change of 23 cigarettes, on the average, per client. Although the data available in this situation permit documentation of the program's objective, or outcome, it is not possible to attribute this change to the intervention. The particular evaluation design used was the descriptive one-group pretest-posttest design, and, as we saw in Chapter 8, such descriptive designs do not support inferences about causality. Nevertheless, this type of design enables program administrators and professionals to document the overall results of their programs.

Further analysis of these data may provide additional and more specific information. For example, suppose that program staff had the impression that they were achieving better results with female smokers than with male smokers. Aggregating the results of males and females as separate groups would permit a comparison of the average number of cigarettes each group smoked at the end of the program. The data for this analysis are presented in Table 11.2. Note that the average number of cigarettes smoked at the beginning of the program was exactly the same for the males and females—34. Thus, it could be concluded that there were no meaningful differences between the males and females in reference to the average number of cigarettes they smoked at the start of the intervention.

As Table 11.2 shows, at the end of the program males smoked an average of 18 cigarettes daily and females an average of 4 cigarettes. On the average, then, females smoked 14 fewer cigarettes per day than did males. Essentially, this analysis confirms workers' suspicion that they are obtaining better results with female smokers than with male smokers.

TABLE 11.1   Average Number of Cigarettes Smoked at the Beginning and End of the Smoking Cessation Program ($N = 80$)

Beginning	–	After	=	Difference
34		11		23

TABLE 11.2 **Average Number of Cigarettes Smoked at the Beginning and End of the Smoking Cessation Program by Sex (N = 80)**

Sex	Beginning	–	After	=	Difference	N
Males	34		18		16	40
Females	34		4		30	40
Totals	34		11		23	80

The information obtained via the simple analysis presented above provides documentation of program outcomes, a vitally important element in this age of accountability and increased competition for available funding. There is, however, a further advantage to compiling and analyzing evaluation data. By conducting regular analyses, human service program administrators and workers can obtain important feedback about program strengths and weaknesses. These data can be used to further develop services. For example, the data discussed above may cause the program to be modified in ways that would improve effectiveness with male clients while maintaining effectiveness with female clients. This would not only improve services to the male client group but would also boost overall program outcomes.

Program

A program is a distinct unit, large or small, that operates within an agency. For example, a treatment agency may comprise a number of treatment programs, or a child welfare agency may run a treatment foster care program, and a residential child abuse treatment program as part of its daily operations. The residential program itself may comprise a number of separate homes for children of different ages or different problem types (e.g., Figure 4.5).

Both of these programs should be evaluated if the agency as a whole is to demonstrate accountability and provide the best possible service to its clientele. A thorough evaluation will include attention to needs, process, and outcomes as well as efficiency. However, since the greatest interest is often in outcome, this section will focus on outcome evaluation, where the question is, "To what degree has a program succeeded in reaching its program objectives?"

If this question is to be answered satisfactorily, of course, the program's objectives must be defined in a way that allows them to be measured. Let us assume that one of the objectives of the residential child abuse treatment program is to enable its residents to return to home. The degree of achievement of this program objective can be determined through a simple count—What proportion of the residents returned home within the last year?

If the agency includes several programs of the same type, in different locations, lessons learned from one can be applied to another. In addition, same-type programs will have the same program objectives and the same ways of measuring them, so that results can be aggregated to provide a measure of effectiveness for the entire agency. If the programs are dissimilar—for example, a treatment foster care program and a victim-assistance program—aggregation will not be possible, but separate assessment of program outcomes will nevertheless contribute to the evaluation of the agency as a whole.

Agency

Outcome evaluation, whether in respect to an agency, a program, or a case, always focuses on the achievement of objectives. How well has the agency fulfilled its mandate? To what degree has it succeeded in meeting its goal, as revealed by the measurement of its program objectives? Again, success in goal achievement cannot be determined unless all of the agency's programs have well-defined, measurable program objectives that reflect the agency's mandate.

As seen in Chapter 4, agencies operate on the basis of mission statements, which often consist of vaguely phrased, expansive statements of intent. The mission of a sexual abuse treatment agency, for example, may be to ameliorate the pain caused by sexually abusive situations and to prevent sexual abuse in the future. Although, there is no doubt that this is a laudable mission, the concepts of pain amelioration and abuse prevention cannot be measured until they have been more precisely defined.

This agency's mandate may be to serve persons who have been sexually abused and their families living within a certain geographical area. If the agency has an overall goal of "to reduce the trauma resulting from sexual abuse in the community," at least the mandate is reflected and measurement is implied in the word *reduced*. The concept of trauma still needs to be operationalized, but this can be accomplished through the specific, individual practice objectives of the clients whose trauma is to be reduced—the primary trauma for a male survivor may be fear that he is homosexual, whereas the trauma for a nonoffending mother may be guilt that she failed to protect her child.

If logical links are established between the agency's goal, the goals of the programs within the agency, and the individual practice objectives of clients served by the program, it will be possible to use the results of one to evaluate the other. Practice objective achievement at the case level will contribute to the success of the program, which will in turn contribute to achievement of the agency's overall goal.

Using Outcome Monitoring Data in Program-Level Decision Making

Just as the program outcome for any client may be acceptable, mixed, or inadequate, program-level evaluation results can also be acceptable, mixed, or inadequate, reflecting the degree to which its program objectives have been achieved.

Acceptable Results

Before a result can be declared "acceptable," it is necessary to define clearly what counts as an acceptable result for a specific program objective. Let us return to the example of the residential program, where one of its program's objectives was to enable residents to return home: If 90 percent of residents succeed in making this move within six months of entry into the program, has the program's objective been achieved to an acceptable degree? What if 80 percent of residents return home within six months and a further 10 percent return home within a year? Or suppose that 100 percent return home within six months but half of the adolescents eventually return to the program? Evidently, an acceptable result is largely a matter of definition. The program administrators and sponsors must decide what degree of objective achievement can reasonably be expected given the nature of the clientele, the resources available, and the results of similar programs. For example, is the degree of success shown in Tables 11.1 and 11.2 acceptable? If the program comprises a number of subprograms, the same decision will have to be made with regard to each.

Once the standards for an acceptable level of achievement have been set, evaluation will then be a matter of comparing actual outcomes against these standards. Where standards are met, program personnel can, with some degree of confidence, continue to employ existing procedures and practices. If a monitoring approach to evaluation is used and outcomes are analyzed on a regular basis, workers will be able to see not only whether program objectives are being achieved to an acceptable degree, but also whether the level of achievement is rising or falling. Any persistent trend toward improvement or decline is worth investigating so that more effective interventions and processes can be reinforced and potential problems can be detected and resolved.

Mixed Results

Occasionally, the results of an outcome evaluation will show that the program is achieving its objectives only partially. For example, a program may be successful in helping one group of clients but less successful with another. This was the situation in the smoking cessation program presented above: Female clients were being helped considerably, but male clients were obtaining much less impressive results (Table 11.2). Similarly, an evaluation may reveal seasonal variations in outcomes: At certain times of the year a program may achieve its objectives to an acceptable degree, but not at other times. Clients in farming communities, for instance, may be able to participate in the program in the winter more easily than during the growing season, when they are busy with the tasks of farming. This factor alone may result in reduced achievement at both the case and program levels. It is also possible, and an evaluation may show, that one program within an agency is achieving its objectives to a greater degree than another similar program.

In such situations, human service administrators will undoubtedly wish to adjust practices and procedures so that the under-performing components of a program can be upgraded. In making any adjustments, however, care must be taken not to jeopardize those parts of the program that are obtaining good outcomes. In the case of the smoking cessation program, for example, the workers may be tempted to tailor several sessions more to the needs of male clients. Although this may indeed improve the program's performance with male clients, the improvement may come at the expense of effectiveness with females. A preferable strategy would be to form separate groups for males and females during some parts of the program, leaving the program unchanged for female clients but developing new sessions for male clients to better meet their needs. Of course, it is impossible to predict in advance whether changes will yield the desired results, but ongoing monitoring will provide feedback about their efficacy.

Inadequate Results

One of the strengths of a program-level monitoring system is that it takes into account the entire program process, from intake to follow-up. A low level of program objective achievement is not necessarily attributable to the interventions utilized by the workers with their clients. It is possible that the problem lies in inappropriate eligibility criteria, unsatisfactory assessment techniques, inadequate staff training, or a host of other factors, including unforeseen systematic barriers to clients' involvement in the program.

If an outcome evaluation shows that results are unsatisfactory, further program development is called for. To diagnose the problem or problems, the program administrator and workers will want to examine data carefully concerning all the stages that lead up to intervention as well as the intervention process itself. Once they have ideas about the reasons for suboptimal performance, they are in a position to begin instituting changes to procedures and practices—and monitoring the results of those changes.

Summary

One of the most important reasons for monitoring is to obtain timely data on which further decisions about intervention plans or program development can be based. At the case level, the worker will continually monitor changes in the client problem; at the program level, data relating to needs, processes, and outcomes can help staff make informed decisions about program modifications and changes. The next chapter looks at how data systems can be designed to collect monitoring data and synthesize them into a suitable form to be used for decision making.

Key Term

Subjective Data: Isolated facts, presented in descriptive terms, that are based on impressions, experience, values, and intuition.

Study Questions

1. Explain the difference between empirical and subjective data. Discuss how a human service worker would use both types of data to make case-level decisions for the six clients in Case Study C.

2. In your own words, briefly outline the limitations of empirical data. Compare your list with those identified in this chapter. Were there any limitations of empirical data present in Case Study C? If so, what were they?

3. In your own words, briefly outline the limitations of subjective data. Compare your list with those identified in this chapter. Were there any limitations of subjective data present in Case Study C? If so, what were they?

4. What is meant by the phrase "Garbage in, garbage out" in monitoring evaluations? What suggestions can you offer for workers to avoid the "Garbage in, garbage out" scenario?

5. Using the six clients in Case Study C as an example, describe in detail the six stages of helping as outlined in the chapter. Identify the monitoring evaluation elements that could have been used as decision-making criteria at each stage.

6. Suppose a worker intuitively feels that her client is at risk for experiencing more serious episodes of loneliness. What suggestions can you offer to assist the worker in obtaining empirical data to support her subjective conclusion?

7. How could follow-up have been incorporated into Case Study C? What additional information would a follow-up period have provided for the worker? What practical problems might the worker have experienced if a follow-up period was used? In your opinion, would the benefits of a follow-up period in Case Study C have outweighed the problems? Why or why not?

8. In reference to Case Study C, what additional information would a worker need in order to claim program-level success? Justify your answer.

9. What is meant by the "clinical significance" of data? How does the clinical significance of data affect decision making for human service workers?

10. What options for program development might an administrator have when program results prove to be inadequate? What ethical considerations must be addressed?

11. In groups of four, agree on a human service problem and the criteria for client termination. Identify four different methods of measuring the problem that will assist you in deciding whether or not the client is ready for termination. To what degree will the information obtained from each of these methods be consistent? Will the decision to terminate client services tend to rely more on empirical or subjective data? Present your findings to the class.

12. In groups of five, develop a hypothetical human service program, complete with a mission statement, a goal, objectives, activities, and measurements of the program objectives. Choose an exploratory design to monitor and appraise case-level client outcomes, and identify the type of data to be collected for various practice objectives. Suppose the data obtained indicate mixed results. What adjustments would you make to the interventions to increase client success? Review your list of adjustments and prioritize them according to order of implementation. Present your discussion to the class.

13. Human service decision making is based upon two different types of data. What are

they? As you briefly describe each type, explain how they guide the decision-making process.

14. What are the advantages of using empirical data in decision making? Justify your response. Be specific and clear. Use a human service example throughout your discussion.

15. What are the limitations of using empirical data in decision making? Justify your response. Be specific and clear. Use a human service example throughout your discussion.

16. Under what conditions do workers use subjective data in decision making? When is the use of subjective data useful to the decision-making process? Justify your response. Be specific and clear. Use a human service example throughout your discussion.

17. Identify and discuss the major drawback to using subjective data in decision making. Justify your response. Be specific and clear. Use a human service example throughout your discussion.

18. How do practitioners make decisions at the case level? How are the highest quality decisions reached? Justify your response. Be specific and clear. Use a human service example throughout your discussion.

19. What phases exist in a helping relationship in which decisions have to be made?

20. You are currently working with a client named Jennifer who wants to lose weight. You also see her mother, Irene, who is having problems with her boss at work. What types of decisions do you make with each of these clients in the engagement and problem definition phase of intervention? On what types of data are these decisions based? Justify your response. Be specific and clear.

21. Define a practice objective for Irene. To what degree does this phase rely on empirical data? Justify your response. Be specific and clear.

22. In what way are your intervention strategies with clients like Jennifer and Irene based on

empirical data? Justify your response. Be specific and clear.

23. How would your success with Irene be measured on the basis of consistently collected data? On what basis should you determine Irene's progress? Justify your response. Be specific and clear.

24. You realize your intervention decisions regarding Irene are based on her progress and your interpretation of her progress. How would you interpret a deterioration or no change in Irene as she works toward her practice objective? How would you interpret an insufficient or slow change in Irene's progress? Justify your response. Be specific and clear.

25. What kind of data would you take into account when deciding when Irene should be terminated? How can data aid your decision about whether to follow up with Irene? Justify your response. Be specific and clear.

26. What is the purpose of using a monitoring approach to quality improvement at the program level? How can program progress be assessed? Justify your response. Be specific and clear.

27. What kinds of data must be collected and analyzed when measuring the outcomes of a particular program? How is an evaluation of program outcomes conducted? Justify your response. Be specific and clear. Use a human service example throughout your discussion.

28. Suppose a program-level evaluation indicated *acceptable* results. How would such a result affect staff and administrative behavior? Justify your response. Be specific and clear. Use a human service example throughout your discussion.

29. Suppose a program-level evaluation indicated *mixed* results. How would such a result affect staff and administrative behavior? Justify your response. Be specific and clear. Use a human service example throughout your discussion.

30. Suppose a program-level evaluation indicated *inadequate* results. How would such a result affect staff and administrative behavior? Justify your response. Be specific and clear. Use a human service example throughout your discussion.

31. In your own words, discuss in depth why program objectives are measured at follow-up and not practice objectives. What is the rationale behind this? What are the limitations of follow-up data if practice objectives are not being measured? Under what circumstances would the measurement of practice objectives be justified for follow-up data? Justify your answer. Use one common human service example throughout your discussion.

32. How would you determine the success of the smoking program via the data contained in Tables 11.1 and 11.2? Do you feel the program achieved its program objective of reducing the smoking behavior of its clientele to zero? Discuss in detail. Justify your response.

33. Table 11.2 presents a breakdown by sex of the data contained in Table 11.1. Construct five hypothetical tables that are similar to Table 11.1 using the variables age, referral source, ethnicity, extent of previous smoking behavior, and socioeconomic status. What would these other tables tell you in reference to the stop-smoking program? Discuss in detail. Justify your answer.

34. Reread Chapter 7 on case-level evaluations. As you know, all exploratory, descriptive, and explanatory case-level evaluation designs can be used in case-level decision making. Discuss how each one of these designs can be utilized in a monitoring approach to quality improvement by highlighting what case-level decisions can be made with each design. Provide one common human service example throughout your discussion.

35. Reread Chapter 8 on program-level evaluations. As you know, all exploratory, descriptive, and explanatory program-level evaluation designs can be used in program-level decision making. Discuss how each one of these designs can be utilized in a monitoring approach to quality improvement by highlighting what program-level decisions can be made with each design. Provide one common human service example throughout your discussion.

36. As we have seen in this chapter, some standardized measuring instruments are constructed where a higher score means there is *more* of a problem than a lower score (e.g., Figures 11.6 and 11.7, marital satisfaction levels). Some are designed where a higher score means that there is *less* of a problem than a lower score (e.g., Figures 11.1 through 11.5, communication levels). Discuss the implications that these two kinds of instruments have for you in reference to interpreting scores from them. Go to the library and find an example of each. Give each one to your classmates.

Part V

IMPLEMENTATION

Chapter 12
Data to Information

Chapter 13
Creating a Quality Improvement System

Chapter 14
Ethics and Accountability

Chapter 15
Evaluation and Quality Improvement in Action
YVONNE UNRAU

There are a number of important considerations in implementing evaluations that pertain to the quality improvement process. If evaluation activities are to become an integral part of service provision, a data system that can collect the appropriate data and organize it into meaningful information must be established (Chapter 12). Moreover, establishing a continuous, internal evaluation system requires the involvement of committed, knowledgeable staff members. Thus, a key consideration in implementing evaluations is the establishment of an organizational environment that will encourage and support evaluation activities (Chapter 13).

Underlying all implementation decisions is a requirement that evaluations be conducted in a manner that meets ethical standards, in order to safeguard from harm participants and others affected by the results of evaluations (Chapter 14).

The final chapter is an applied summary that provides a concrete example of the application of all the material presented in the previous fourteen chapters.

12

DATA TO INFORMATION

A HUMAN SERVICE AGENCY is a complex organization that can contain numerous interlinking parts. A treatment program may have set procedures for client intake, assessment, intervention, termination, and follow-up. Other types of programs within the same agency may offer other sets of activities, each of which will also be undertaken according to set procedures. For example, an educational program may operate a library and organize workshops, seminars, and presentations for lay persons and professionals. A program for adolescents with developmental disabilities may run a number of residential programs which include an educational component.

The procedures just listed above all have to do with client-related activities, but there are also procedures for staff-related activities, volunteer-related activities, community-related activities, and fund-raising activities, to list only a few. For example, procedures will regulate how staff are selected and trained; how volunteers are recruited, selected, trained, supervised, and acknowledged; and which fund-raising activities are undertaken using which methods.

Monitoring can also involve another set of procedures. These define what data are collected when, where, in what manner, and by whom; who will collate and interpret them; and how, and in what form, the results will be disseminated. Most importantly, the monitoring system must be designed in such a way that data collected at any stage are demonstrably relevant to the decisions to be made. For example, data collected by front-line human service workers should bear upon, in the first instance, decisions they are required to make. In other words, the data collected by workers should guide clinical decision making.

The important point here is that data are not collected indiscriminately in the hope that they will somehow be useful. Only the needed data are collected, usually starting at the case level. Subsequently, as has been shown, data may be aggregated to assist in decision making at two other levels—the program and agency. It is astonishing to see how many programs collect data that have nothing to do with decision making of any kind: They just collect data and hope that someday it will be useful to someone, somewhere, somehow. This kind of thinking is wrong and perhaps unethical, as it is inappropriate to collect data from a client that will not be used to make a decision of some kind, either immediately or in the long term.

Staff Roles in Developing a Monitoring Capacity

As will be discussed in Chapter 13, it is very important that monitoring be carried out within an organizational culture that acknowledges that *all* human service programs fall short of perfection. The purpose of monitoring is not to assign blame; it is to better serve clients by identifying strengths and limitations, so that the former can be reinforced and the latter corrected. The monitoring approach to quality improvement allows shortcomings to be identified not only by supervisors or administrators, but by the line-level workers themselves, allowing them to be more fully accountable for their own practice effectiveness.

Data obtained through monitoring will also allow supervisors and administrators to scrutinize information derived from the data more closely, bringing to light deficiencies and opportunities for improvement that might previously have been overlooked. However, this greater accountability can only be attained if line-level workers, supervisors, and administrators approach monitoring with a positive attitude, viewing the process as the best means of improving client services.

Establishing and maintaining a monitoring system (see Chapter 13) requires the full cooperation of all program staff, from administrators to direct service workers. The line-level workers will have to collect most of the data. If some form of monitoring had been employed in the past, probably additional or different data will now have to be collected, involving a change in the procedures to which the workers are accustomed. New client intake and progress forms may be developed and a computerized data system may be installed.

Management, for its part, must play a major role in providing funds for the implementation of a monitoring system, in addition to providing worker training and continual support. The design and implementation of the monitoring system will cost money; computer hardware and software must be purchased and consultation fees must be paid. It will also cost money to train the workers and support staff as well; this is a vital component on which management should resist the temptation to skimp. Training is particularly necessary if the new system introduces computerization.

Establishing an Organizational Plan for Data Collection

As discussed, the data collected in a monitoring system must be pertinent to the decisions to be made immediately, as well as throughout the client's progress within the program. For example, certain data will be required at client intake in order to decide whether or not to accept the referral. Once accepted, the client may go through a formal assessment procedure, at which point further data will likely be required. Obviously, data collection must meet case-level decision-making needs. Less obvious, but equally important, is that the system be designed with a view to the subsequent aggregation of case-level data so they can be converted to program-level data later on.

At both the case and program levels, the data required for ongoing monitoring depend on the kinds of clients served and the kinds of activities the program conducts. In a treatment program, data may be required to facilitate client intake, assessment, intervention, termination, and follow-up. In a child welfare program, data on neglect or abuse may be required. In an educational program, data may be required to assist in the purchase and dissemination of materials and the development of workshops, seminars, and presentations. Data collection must be well thought out and organized so that all the required data are collected at the most convenient time and in the most appropriate form.

Case-Level Data Collection

Perhaps the best way to decide what data are needed at the case level is to follow a client through the program by way of a client flowchart. Figure 12.1 presents a flowchart illustrating the sequence of events in a child protection program.

The beginning of the process is the referral. Suspected abuse may be reported by a variety of sources, from teachers to neighbors. All referrals are immediately directed to the Intake Unit. If the call comes during office hours, an intake worker takes the information; after hours, the call is routed to an emergency worker. Because every allegation of child abuse must be looked into, at this point the two most relevant pieces of data are the age and place of residence of the alleged victim.

Within a short period, an intake worker will normally contact the referring source as well as the family to verify the complaints and to obtain further details. Based on this information, the worker decides whether a full investigation is warranted. If so, an investigating worker will likely interview the alleged victim and will probably interview the alleged offender, family members, school teachers, and relevant others.

As with every activity, each interview will have a specific purpose. The purpose of interviewing the alleged victim will be fourfold: to verify that the alleged abuse has in fact occurred, to ensure the immediate safety of the child, to determine whether treatment is needed, and if so, what treatment would be best, and to inform the child and others connected to the case about what will happen next. The investigating worker will conduct this interview on the basis of data collected by the intake worker and will need information in the following general areas: the specific circumstances of the alleged abuse, the specific circumstances in which it was disclosed, data about the child, and data about the family. The intake form thus must be designed to incorporate all these different data needs.

From a case-level perspective, then, the data collected at intake can serve two broad purposes: to ensure that the alleged victim is a child resident within the program's catchment area and to fulfill the investigating worker's data needs. It is worth noting here that, since a monitoring system is intended to provide needed and timely data to staff members, and since workers themselves know best what data they need to help them in their decision making, the most effective forms are ones designed by workers rather than by consultants from outside the program.

When the investigation is complete, the data are used to assess the degree of continuing risk to the child. On this basis, the worker determines whether an out-of-home placement is required. In any event, continuing cases are transferred from the Intake Unit to the Family Services Unit, where a worker is assigned to the family to coordinate protection and treatment functions. The worker will then conduct a full assessment based on the data provided by the investigating worker as well as any additional data collected. The purpose of assessment is to determine the child's present level of functioning in relevant areas so that an appropriate intervention plan can be established. In other words, data collected during assessment will be used in making decisions about the client's case plan.

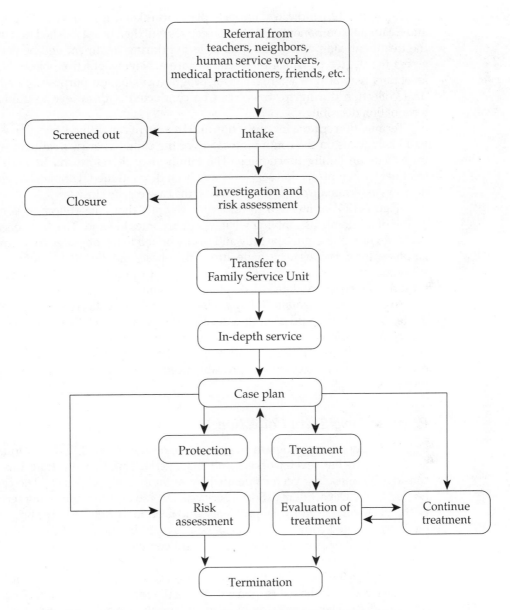

FIGURE 12.1   Client Flowchart for a Child Protection Program

As Figure 12.1 indicates, the case plan formulated may have both protection and treatment components. Practice objectives will then be established in relation to the treatment component, and data collected during treatment will be needed to assess the degree to which interventions are achieving practice objectives. Case-level data may also be aggregated for program evaluation purposes. In addition, data collection during treatment can be conducted with an eye to guiding the termination decision.

Termination criteria for protection and treatment can differ. Protection workers will likely focus on the continuing safety of the child, whereas treatment workers may focus on family functioning. The family may therefore still be undergoing treatment when protection services have been discontinued. Ultimately, when the decision to terminate all services is made, the case can be closed.

Figure 12.1 is intended to underline the fact that data collection is never a matter of randomly assembling whatever data comes to hand. The data collected in each program phase must be fully and firmly linked to the objectives of the particular phase, the decisions to be made during the phase, and the informational needs of subsequent phases. Insufficient data will lead to poor decision making; overly profuse and irrelevant data will result in confusion and unnecessary costs.

To ensure that adequate links exist between the data collected and the decisions made, the workers could compile a decision data chart which lists, in chronological order, the decisions to be made, the data needed to make each decision, and the actual data collected. If there is a discrepancy between what is needed and what is being collected, the workers will probably need to consider revising data collection protocols.

Program-Level Data Collection

Data collection at any program stage must be designed to fulfill the informational needs of both line-level workers and managerial staff. To illustrate this point, consider a counseling center operated by a family service agency. The center is funded by the Department of Social Services (DSS) to provide counseling services to DSS clients with psychosocial problems who need more help than the brief, instrumentally oriented counseling that can be provided by the DSS. Figure 12.2 shows part of an intake form that new clients might complete in the center's office while they are waiting for a first interview.

Note that the form has lines on the righthand side that workers can use to computer-code the clients' responses. Where the form asks the reason for seeking services, if the client responds by, say, circling Number 1, the code for marital problem, "1" would then be entered on the appropriate line at the right.

An intake form such as the one illustrated in Figure 12.2 could be the first document in the client's file (Mindel, 1993). Of course, different programs will need different or additional data. A job-training program, for example, will likely ask about jobs previously held, previous income, reason for present unemployment, and participation in other job-training programs.

Name: _____   __ __ __ __ __ __

Current Address: _____

_____

_____ **Zip Code** _____

Home Telephone Number: _____   __

TYPE OF SERVICE SOUGHT (please circle one number)   __

1. Individual counseling
2. Couple counseling
3. Family counseling

SEX (please circle one number)   __

1. Male
2. Female

BIRTH DATE _____   __ __

REFERRAL SOURCE (please circle one number)   __

1. Self
2. Friends, family
3. Physician
4. Clergy
5. Department of Social Services
6. Other agency
7. Other (specify) _____

REASON FOR SEEKING SERVICES (please circle one number)   __

1. Marital problems
2. Family problems
3. Problems at school
4. Problems at work
5. Parent-child problems
6. Health problem
7. Substance abuse
8. Personal adjustment problems
9. Other (specify) _____

FIGURE 12.2   Excerpts from an Intake Form

An individual intake form provides beginning data for a case record, but it is not very useful for program evaluation purposes unless it is part of a summary. Figure 12.3 provides four basic and simple tables from a monthly intake report on the counseling service compiled by aggregating the data from 200 individual client intake forms for the month of October 1995.

Figure 12.3 shows at a glance that 200 new clients were accepted into the program during the month of October, 63 percent of whom were referred by DSS. The program is thus able to document the degree to which it is achieving one of its mandates: providing services to clients referred by DSS. Equally important, if referrals from DSS begin to decline as the months go by, the director will be able to spot this trend immediately and take steps to better meet its mandate, or perhaps to negotiate an adjustment of this mandate if new circumstances have arisen. The general point of importance is that monitoring provides ongoing feedback that helps to ensure continuing achievement of a program's mandate—to see clients referred by DSS.

Contrast this with the situation of a program that undertakes biannual, project-type evaluations. By the time data indicating a problem with the DSS referrals are received, the problem will have had a long time to get firmly established, and is likely to be a very serious one. In all likelihood, the program's reputation among the DSS workers will have suffered. DSS may even have concluded that because this program is not providing adequate service, alternative services should be sought out.

The intake report also provides other useful data. Tables reporting the frequency distribution of the sex and age of new clients provide the data required to ensure that the program is attracting the type of clients for whom it was established. Assume that one of the program's maintenance objectives is to attract 100 adolescents and young adults during October 1995. Figure 12.3 indicates that 54 percent of new clients are 29 years of age or under. This kind of data indicates that the workers are on the right track. If, on the other hand, the program's thrust was to provide services to a large number of senior citizens, data revealing that only 5 percent of new clients are 60 years of age or over would be cause for concern (Figure 12.3). A program director is unlikely to undertake extensive changes on the basis of data for one month, but if several consecutive monthly reports indicate that older people constitute only a small percentage of new clients, the program director may well conclude that a problem exists and needs to be addressed immediately.

The course of service provision can be followed by completing a client contact form after each session, such as the one illustrated in Figure 12.4. The client identification number (e.g., 144277) allows the data from this form to be collated with data from the intake form and other contact forms prepared for this client. The data provided on this form may subsequently be used to monitor the effects of the intervention(s).

Some of the most important data on this form concern program outcome. For this program, the program objective is to "increase the functioning levels of the clients." First, the client's functional level (recorded as "6" in Figure 12.4) represents the worker's rating of the client's overall level of functioning at the beginning

Sex of Clients		
Sex	*Number*	*Percent*
Male	90	45
Female	110	55
Totals	200	100

Age of Clients		
Age Ranges	*Number*	*Percent*
10–19	30	15
20–29	78	39
30–39	42	21
40–49	28	14
50–59	12	6
60 +	10	5
Totals	200	100

Referral Sources of Clients		
Sources	*Number*	*Percent*
Self	8	4
Friends, family	12	6
Physicians	8	4
Clergy	10	5
DSS	126	63
Other agencies	28	14
Other	8	4
Totals	200	100

Reasons Clients Requesting Services		
Presenting Problems	*Number*	*Percent*
Marital problems	18	9
Family problems	40	20
Problems at school	28	14
Problems at work	12	6
Parent-child problems	30	15
Health problems	20	10
Substance abuse	22	11
Personal adjustment problem	20	10
Other	10	5
Totals	200	100

FIGURE 12.3   Excerpts from a Monthly Intake Report for October 1995 (from Figure 12.2)

of services. The scale has a range from 1 to 9, with higher numbers representing higher levels of functioning. Three points on the scale have been defined:

1. = totally dependent
2.
3.
4.
5. = minimally autonomous functioning
6.
7.
8.
9. = autonomous functioning

Clients may be considered for discharge at level 5, but will ideally attain level 7, 8, or 9 before service is terminated.

Client's Name: *Jane Harrison*   **Date:**   *29*   *11*   *95*
                                                         DD   MM   YY

Client Identification Number   *1 4 4 2 7 7*

Program Objective (Increase Client's Functioning Level)   *6*

Practice Objectives:

	Objective	*Measuring Instrument*
1.	*39*	**ISE**
2.		
3.		

Disposition (circle one only)

(1.) Continuing service
2. Referred   Where _____
3. Closed

(1.) Joint decision
2. Client decision
3. Worker decision

FIGURE 12.4   Excerpts from a Client Contact Form

Scores from up to three standardized measuring instruments to measure practice objectives can also be recorded on this contact form. In Figure 12.4, the current week's score on a measuring instrument that measures self-esteem, 39, is recorded for one of the practice objectives which is considered to be directly related to this client's overall functioning. These data, pertaining to client practice objectives, can be used to follow changes in identified practice objectives during the course of the intervention and, as well, can be aggregated into monthly summaries and other reports, as we discussed in Chapter 11, and presented at the bottom of Figure 12.6.

Aggregated reports may be prepared by clerical staff who may not take confidentiality as seriously as the workers within the program. Thus, it is important that forms passing beyond the practitioner's control not contain any data that would enable another person to identify the client. All the data needed by others can be provided in the form of numbers and computer codes, as illustrated in Figure 12.5.

The client's identity, information about the disposition of the case, the client's functional status, and measurement scores of the practice objectives are indicated by

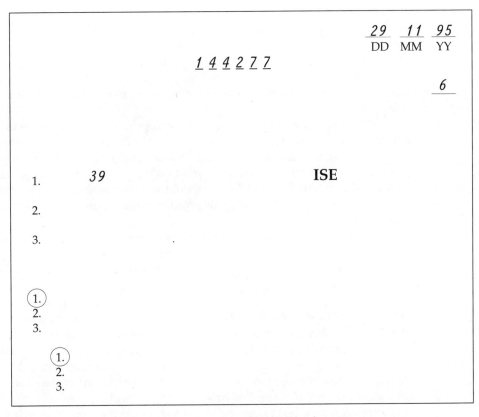

FIGURE 12.5 Excerpts from a Data Analysis Form (from Figure 12.4)

numbers. Data processing clerks will not know who the client is, and need not even know the codes for the variables. The forms shown in Figures 12.4, and 12.5 can be printed and bound together in a manner that makes it possible to complete both forms simultaneously with just a moment's work.

Figure 12.6 provides excerpts from a summary report of cases closed in the counseling unit in the month of October 1995. These data are the result of aggregating data from the client's intake and termination forms. Aggregating data in this manner provides information that is very useful in understanding program functioning.

We can readily see, for example, that over a third of the clients who terminated (36 percent) did so unilaterally. Depending on program norms and expectations and past experience, this may be considered problematic. If the data are further analyzed to learn more about the termination problem, program staff can determine whether unilateral termination is characteristic of any particular client group, such as males, older clients, or clients with a specific practice objectives. Such data are invaluable in diagnosing the problem and deciding on program adjustments and modifications. Data from subsequent reports will then shed light on the success of the measures adopted.

The summary report also provides data about program outcomes. Examining the data on client functioning levels at intake will tell management whether they are successfully targeting the clientele whom the program is intended to serve. And functioning levels at termination provide a profile of how well client problems had been resolved by the time of termination. As can be seen in Figure 12.6, the average functioning level of the 50 clients who terminated in October 1995 went up by one point, from 4.7 to 5.7.

As the data show, 78 percent of the clientele leave the program at or above the minimally autonomous functioning level of 5. However, only 24 percent of clientele attain the most desirable levels of 7, 8, or 9 at discharge. Contextual data, such as the practice objectives established and previous results, would be required to fully interpret these data. Nevertheless, it would not be unreasonable to conclude that, although the service is achieving acceptable results, there is room for further improvement.

Data pertaining to specific client practice objectives also provide useful information. Comparing the average practice objective score at the beginning with the average score at termination for a group of clients provides data about net change achieved with respect to each practice objective.

Of course, these data in themselves do not tell the whole story. They are indicators, and very useful indicators, but their full interpretation requires careful attention to contextual variables and issues. For instance, it is possible that the more modest results achieved with clients experiencing marital and family problems is attributable to factors other than the way in which the program is designed and delivered. It may be that two of the more experienced workers have been on leave for the past several months. Perhaps one of these positions was covered by temporarily reassigning a less experienced worker, while the other one was left vacant. Thus, during the preceding several months fewer marital counseling and family

Cases Terminated

Method of Termination	Number	Percent
Mutual consent	25	50
Client decision	18	36
Worker's decision	7	14
Totals	50	100

Client Functional Levels (Program Objective)

	Clients at Each Level			
	Beginning		Termination	
Functioning Level	N	Percent	N	Percent
1. Totally Dependent	0	0	0	0
2.	1	2	1	2
3.	2	4	0	0
4.	20	40	10	20
5. Minimally Autonomously	18	36	7	14
6.	6	12	20	40
7.	3	6	8	16
8.	0	0	3	6
9. Autonomously	0	0	1	2
Totals	50	100	50	100
Averages	4.7		5.7	

Average of Clients' Practice Objectives

Practice Objectives	Beginning	Termination	n
Self-Esteem	61	42	12
Peer Relations	57	37	4
Depression	42	27	4
Marital Satisfaction	51	48	6
Clinical Stress	47	41	9
Alcohol Involvement	40	31	4
Partner Abuse	52	42	1
Sexual Satisfaction	66	60	5
Anxiety	52	41	5
Total			50

Note: All practice objectives measured by Hudson's Scales as reported in Nurius and Hudson, 1993. High scores = higher level of problem.

FIGURE 12.6   Excerpts from a Monthly Summary Report Form of Closed Cases for October 1995

therapy hours have been delivered, by less experienced staff; this could obviously have affected client outcomes. In general, interpreting the information obtained through monitoring always requires consideration of contextual variables and cannot be done purely on the basis of raw data.

In addition, the last section of Figure 12.6 only represents the average scores for practice objectives at the beginning and end of treatment. The figure does not indicate how long, on the average, the clients received the services. For example, the 12 clients who had a self-esteem practice objective may have been in the program six months whereas the six clients who had a marital satisfaction practice objective may have been in treatment for only three months. Thus, the dimension of time has not been taken into account in an effort to try to obtain as true a picture as possible. It should also be pointed out that the practice objectives listed in Figure 12.6 could also be program objectives if the client was being seen only to work on one, and only one, of these objectives. For example, if a client only wanted to reduce depression, then the program objective would be "to reduce depression to a score of 30 or less." As mentioned earlier, practice facilitative objectives (subobjectives) that are believed to relate to the program objective of depression would have to be formulated.

Staff members may react to summaries such as the one shown in Figure 12.6 in a number of ways. They may resent the fact that their work is being scrutinized, particularly if the monthly summary has been newly instituted. Where the results suggest that there is room for improvement (which is usually the case), they may be uncertain of their own competence and, perhaps, somewhat afraid of management's reaction. Alternatively, or perhaps in addition, they may be alerted to the fact that they need to develop different treatment interventions which would hopefully improve the achievement of the program's objective and/or practice objectives.

Which one of these feelings will predominate depends to some extent on the way the monitoring system was introduced to the practitioners. Workers who were consulted about the system's development, informed about its advantages, and involved in its application are more likely to regard the monthly summary as useful feedback. Staff who were neither consulted nor involved are likely to regard it with apprehension and resentment.

Equally important in shaping attitudes to monitoring is how the agency's administration uses, or abuses, the data generated. If the data are used in a judgmental, critical manner, staff are likely to remain skeptical and defensive about the monitoring process. Where the data are regarded as useful feedback and are used in a genuine, cooperative effort to upgrade and further develop services, workers will likely welcome such reports as tools that can help them improve their practices.

These considerations suggest that managers should view such data as a means of assisting them in identifying areas for improvement and in identifying the causes of problems and difficulties. Obviously, this approach is far more likely to evoke a positive response than one in which data are used to reveal staff inadequacy. Management's responsibilities do not, however, end here. To foster a truly positive environment for monitoring, managers should not only be concerned with pinpointing potential trouble spots, but should also be committed to supporting the workers' efforts to improve program effectiveness.

Manual Data Management and Analysis

Today, many human service programs use computerized data systems, more commonly (and incorrectly) called computerized management information systems. As we have stressed in previous chapters, data are isolated facts; information results from synthesis and interpretation of the facts. Thus, the computerized systems generate and display *data,* they do not generate and display *information.*

But there are more ways than one to collect data. Some agencies use manual methods, and some use a combination, processing certain data by hand and other data by computer. In this section we investigate manual data management, which, like every other system, has advantages and limitations.

Advantages

Perhaps the major advantage of manual data management is the degree of control it allows. Workers who manage their own data control access to that data, perhaps to the point of leaving highly sensitive material in handwritten form rather than having a secretary type it. Data that are not on the computer cannot be disseminated through a computer network and cannot be obtained, perhaps accidentally, by someone who is not entitled to them. Workers who manage their own data may therefore be more confident that client confidentiality is not breached.

A second advantage, the ready availability of material, depends on the organizational skills of the practitioner. A piece of paper properly filed in the worker's own filing cabinet may be more accessible than the same data held in a central computer's memory. In addition, data prepared by workers for their own use can be organized according to personal preferences rather than according to a standard format. Important data can be highlighted in red rather than entered in a form, and the analysis can be tailored to the specific interests of the worker. Interpretations can be written in the margins. However, it should be noted that computer and manual data management systems are not mutually exclusive. Most human service workers will keep their own notes whether or not the agency has a computerized system, and these narrative descriptions will always be a valuable source of data, and thus, of information.

Limitations

The disadvantages of manual data management mirror the advantages of computerized data management. One of the main limitations is that it is difficult to access other people's data for the purposes of aggregation or comparison. One worker may not record the same data as another, even in relation to the same program or practice objective; the data may be missing or incomplete; and even if the relevant data are recorded, they may be in the wrong format—one person may record raw pretest and posttest scores where another enters difference scores (pretest score − posttest score = difference score). Data for computer use, by contrast, must be collected and entered using a standard format, even though the format selected may not be the one preferred by the individual practitioner.

A second problem is that only a limited volume of data can be collected, analyzed, and processed manually. Particularly at the program level, it would be an enormous task to manually organize the vast amounts of data that will likely be available. Yet at the program level, data are useful in decision making only when they are presented in summary form, as shown, for instance, in Figures 12.3 and 12.6. Manually integrating the raw data into a summary form is likely to be very time-consuming and labor-intensive; it is the kind of task that is likely to be postponed or omitted when the workload becomes heavy. As well, more sophisticated forms of statistical analysis are not feasible using manual methods, and manual analysis is always subject to computational errors. Thus, the results of manual analysis may be neither accurate nor timely.

The Use of Computers

Computers can be used to advantage in both case- and program-level monitoring. Computer programs now exist that greatly facilitate the tasks of monitoring, and with the cost of desktop computers ever declining, their use in evaluation has become widespread (Nurius & Hudson, 1993).

Case-Level Monitoring

Human service workers who regularly use case-level designs to monitor clients' progress tend to make extensive use of paper-and-pencil measuring instruments to measure practice objectives. Many of the instruments are self-administered; the client fills them out without the aid of the worker. However, blank instruments must be stocked, retrieved, administered, and scored, and the results then need to be graphically displayed so that they can be easily understood by the practitioner and client.

Instruments originally designed to be self-administered can be administered by computers, into which clients can directly enter their responses. Administering instruments by computer greatly facilitates the tasks of case-level monitoring: The computer can keep the required instruments in files, ensuring that they are always at hand; it can be programmed to accept only valid responses to questions, thereby limiting entry errors; and it can check for the consistency of a client's response between two questions, giving the client an opportunity to change a response that contradicts a response to a similar previous question.

After the instrument has been administered, the computer can instantly provide a score, retrieve previous scores, and draw a graph of all scores to date. Not only can the computer perform the scoring and graphing tasks with greater accuracy than a human, but the results are immediately available. If a practitioner asks a client to complete an instrument at the start of a session, the results will be available for that session. Many standardized measuring instruments have computerized versions available.

Of course, some clients will want nothing to do with computers, and others will enjoy working with them. Still others, particularly adolescents raised on video games, may be more comfortable with the computer than they would ever be with the human service worker. Technology may seem cold and hard, but it is also nonjudgmental, and its very impersonality can seem an advantage to a young person who does not trust adults. Interaction takes place on a limited and concrete level, but it is still interaction; and an adolescent who will not be honest with a worker may be quite prepared to be forthright with a computer.

Some computer programs have been written to help organize other tasks of case management. Workers can enter their case notes into the computer and use it as a filing system. Data on a client can be entered after every contact so that when a report about that client is needed for a case conference, the relevant entries are already assembled in a file. Some computer programs also have provisions for editing contact notes and compiling them into progress reports. Finally, there are computer programs that help with a variety of other tasks, such as keeping timesheets, maintaining billing data, and writing form letters (Nurius & Hudson, 1993).

Program-Level Monitoring

At the program level, computers have a multitude of uses. One of their special talents is the ability to perform the same computation, using different data sets, over and over again without error, boredom, or fatigue. Documents such as monthly summaries need only be set up once. Subsequently, a worker only has to enter the data for the current month and instruct the computer to calculate, format, and print.

Similarly, statistical software packages allow a frequently used analysis to be set up so that only the data have to be entered; the computer will conduct the calculation. There is a magical quality to this which can be dangerous: It allows staff members who know little about statistics to produce a document full of impressive but inappropriate numbers. Nevertheless, many statistical calculations are prohibitively time-consuming when done by hand, and a statistical analysis program, in educated hands, can prove to be an invaluable benefit.

The aggregation of case-level data can also be accomplished by computers. For example, suppose that a client named Beulah entered the program in September and her functioning level was rated at level 4. When terminated in October, her functioning level was rated at level 8. For the purposes of program evaluation, she is one of the 20 clients who began at level 4 and one of the 3 clients who ended at level 8 (see Figure 12.6). Similarly, suppose another client, named Bob, started in April at level 7 and was terminated in October at level 9. He is one of the 3 clients who started at level 7 and the only client who ended at level 9. It must be noted that the length of service for each client varied. All they have in common in Figure 12.6 is they all were terminated in October 1995.

As Figure 12.6 shows, analysis has been also conducted to determine the average functional status of all clients terminated in October—the program objective. As is shown, this group of clients had entered the program with an average functional status of 4.7 and left it with an average functional status of 5.7 (an increase of 1.0 in functioning level). In program evaluation terms, a one-group pretest–posttest design has been implemented.

Similarly, the computer can assist with the aggregation and analysis of other case-level monitoring data. In this agency, workers routinely use standardized measuring instruments to track changes in clients' practice objectives. As shown in Figure 12.6, the computer has selected all clients who had practice objectives related to self-esteem and were terminated in October 1995 and calculated the average initial and final self-esteem scores for all those clients. There were 12 clients terminated in October who had self-esteem practice objectives, and the average score for the group declined from 61 at the beginning of service to 42 at termination. Further analysis can be conducted to determine whether this is a statistically significant decline. Again, a one-group pretest–posttest design has been implemented and provides useful data.

Report Writing

Computers are particularly helpful in producing reports. Sophisticated word-processing programs now in common use make it relatively easy to turn out a professional-looking document. The computer will also generate tables and figures with minimal effort on the part of the writer. For example, this entire book, including all tables and figures, was drafted, written, edited, re-edited, formatted, and printed on computers.

Many of the reports generated by human service programs are written to conform to a standard format and are disseminated to the same people (in addition to stakeholders) at regular intervals. Once programmed to set out the report on the printed page, the computer will set it out in the same way every time. Computer technology allows workers to produce regular, custom-made reports tailored to the specific needs of various stakeholders—staff members, management, funders, and the general public—and highlighting areas of interest specific to each group.

Summary

The development of a monitoring capacity in an existing human service program requires the full cooperation of both line-level workers and management. Administrators must be prepared to provide training, support, and resources in addition to demonstrating that the monitoring system is intended to improve the program, not to assign blame.

At the case level, data can be useful in making a variety of decisions. Whenever possible, these data should also be collected in a manner that allows aggregation for the purposes of program evaluation. Staff agreement on the measurement devices to be used for specific problem types will facilitate the aggregation process. Staff must decide, at both the case and program levels, what data are needed, when they will be collected, in what format, and by whom. The development of appropriate forms will guide data collection and ensure that the data are recorded in a consistent, standard format.

Both computerized and manual data management techniques will probably be used, although computers are increasingly becoming the method of choice. Computers can be used at the case level for administering instruments, scoring, and graphing results; and at the program level for aggregation, statistical analyses, and routine administrative functions. Word-processing capabilities facilitate the writing of reports at every level.

Key Terms

Assessment: A professional activity that occurs prior to the intervention phase and investigates a client's present level of functioning in relevant areas so that an appropriate intervention plan can be established.

Computerized Data Systems: An automated method of organizing single units of data to generate summarized or aggregate forms of data.

Contextual Data: Empirical or subjective data that reflect the circumstances of the problem and help to explain the outcome or score.

Decision Data Chart: A chart that lists, in chrono-

logical order, decisions to be made, the data needed to make each decision, and the data actually collected; used to ensure that adequate links exist between the data collected and the decisions made.

Flow Chart: A diagram of client service delivery in which symbols are used to depict client movement throughout the service delivery system.

Manual Data Management: Noncomputerized method of organizing single units of data to generate summarized or aggregate forms of the data.

Study Questions

1. Referring to Figure 12.1, construct a hypothetical client path flowchart for the six clients in Case Study C. Identify possible criteria used at each decision-making point in the flowchart. Explain how the flowchart can be used as a tool to ensure effective client service.

2. The six graphs depicted in Case Study C present data on individual client scores for two practice objectives. Organize all of the six clients' scores into a summary chart for each practice objective. What additional data are made available by the development of the summary chart?

3. What are the advantages of obtaining continuous program data through monitoring

methods over collecting data on a biannual or annual basis?

4. Identify five possible contextual variables that may have influenced client progress in Case Study C. Do the contextual data provide you with a greater understanding of the clients' situation? Why or why not?

5. Review the data presented for the six clients in Case Study C and construct a data decision chart. In your opinion, did a link exist between the data collected and the decisions made? Explain your answer.

6. In your own words, identify the strengths and limitations of using manual data management systems in human service organiza-

tions. Compare your list to the advantages and disadvantages outlined in this chapter.

7. In your own words, identify the strengths and limitations of using computer data systems in human service organizations. Compare your list to the advantages and disadvantages outlined in this chapter.

8. In groups of four, develop a client flowchart for students applying to your human service program. Does the construction of a flowchart bring clarity to the application process? Why or why not? Identify problem areas in the flowchart and develop alternatives to enhance the efficiency of the application process. Present your chart and discussion to the class.

9. How would a director of a human service agency design a monitoring system for the agency?

10. The director acknowledges that the agency's programs fall short of perfection. However, the director emphasizes the development of a monitoring capacity at the agency. How will this affect development of the agency's programs?

11. Your director asks for your input as your agency establishes an organizational plan for data collection. Before you respond, you consider what kind of data should be collected. When should the data be collected? What kinds of decision-making needs should the data meet? You consider the kinds of clients you serve and the kinds of activities your program conducts. How do all these considerations affect the design of a data collection system?

12. Refer to the client flowchart depicted in Figure 12.1. How could this flowchart assist you as a worker in deciding what data are needed at the case level for ongoing monitoring?

13. Explain in detail how the flowchart can be used to ensure effective client services.

14. Explain in detail how you could ensure that adequate links exist between the data collected by your program and decisions made on behalf of clients.

15. Why is an individual intake form not very useful for program evaluation unless it is part of a summary report? Discuss in detail.

16. What are the advantages of obtaining continuous program data through monitoring methods over collecting data on a biannual or annual basis?

17. What additional data are made available by the development of an intake report? Discuss in detail. Use a human service example throughout your discussion.

18. How does the completion of a client contact form enable the worker to provide more effective client service? Discuss in detail. Use a human service example throughout your discussion.

19. How can a client contact form be designed to ensure client confidentiality? Discuss in detail. Use a human service example throughout your discussion.

20. How can client contact forms contribute to understanding program functioning? How can an understanding of program functioning contribute to improved outcomes for clients? Discuss in detail. Use a human service example throughout your discussion.

21. Do the data provided by a summary report such as that depicted in Figure 12.6 tell the whole story of the client problem and the effect a program can have on that problem? Why or why not?

22. Under what circumstances would staff members react to summary reports in a positive way? What are management's responsibilities in fostering a positive attitude toward monitoring among the staff? Discuss in detail. Use a human service example throughout your discussion.

23. Computerized data management is becoming popular in the human services. Some agencies, however, still use manual methods to collect data. Why? Discuss in detail.

24. What are some limitations of manual data management? Discuss in detail. Use a human service example throughout your discussion.

25. How can computer data systems be used to advantage in case-level monitoring? Discuss in detail. Use a human service example throughout your discussion.

26. How can computer data systems be used to advantage in program-level monitoring? Discuss in detail. Use a human service example throughout your discussion.

27. How can computers aid workers in the preparation of reports? Discuss in detail. Use a human service example throughout your discussion.

28. Read Case Study A. Construct a hypothetical client flowchart (e.g., Figure 12.1) for the program. Discuss in detail how the program used a computerized data system that produced the tables and figures represented in the case study. Discuss how the program used case-level data to form program-level data. Given the contents of the case study, construct a hypothetical Client Intake Form (e.g., Figure 12.2) a Monthly Intake Report (e.g., Figure 12.3), a Client Contact Form (e.g., Figures 12.4 and 12.5), and a Monthly Summary Report (e.g., Figure 12.6). Using your imagination, construct other forms that you feel could help the program in the quality improvement process. State explicitly how each form would benefit case- and/or program-level decision making. Do not construct a form that will not be useful in the decision-making process.

29. Read Case Study B. Construct a hypothetical client flowchart (e.g., Figure 12.1) for the program. Discuss how the program could have used case-level data to form program-level data for each of the three outcome measures. Given the contents of the case study, construct a hypothetical Client Intake Form (e.g., Figure 12.2), a Monthly Intake Report (e.g., Figure 12.3), a Client Contact Form (e.g., Figures 12.4 and 12.5), and a Monthly Summary Report (e.g., Figure 12.6). Using your imagination, construct other forms that you feel could help the program in the quality improvement process. State explicitly how each form would benefit case- and/or program-level decision making. Do not construct a form that will not be helpful in the decision-making process.

30. Read Case Study C. Construct a hypothetical client flowchart (e.g., Figure 12.1) for the program. Discuss how the program could have used case-level data to form program-level data for both outcome measures. Given the contents of the case study, construct a hypothetical Client Intake Form (e.g., Figure 12.2), a Monthly Intake Report (e.g., Figure 12.3), a Client Contact Form (e.g., Figures 12.4 and 12.5), and a Monthly Summary Report (e.g., Figure 12.6). Using your imagination, construct other forms that you feel could help the program in the quality improvement process. State explicitly how each form would benefit case- and/or program-level decision making. Do not construct a form that will not be helpful in the decision-making process.

13

CREATING A QUALITY IMPROVEMENT SYSTEM

THE PRECEDING CHAPTERS have discussed the importance of evaluation and quality improvement in human service agencies. If a commitment to quality improvement is to be created and maintained, it will be necessary for the organization to establish policies and procedures with regard to evaluation in general. Once these are in place, specific planning can be undertaken with respect to continuous program monitoring and the more major project evaluations that will be necessary. Evaluation planning will naturally be followed by implementation of the agreed-upon procedures and dissemination of the results in the form of oral presentations and reports.

This chapter presents some considerations for trying to promote a quality improvement system within an organization by taking into account (1) the agency's policies and procedures in reference to evaluation, (2) the specific planning of evaluations within an agency, (3) the implementation of evaluative findings, and (4) the writing of evaluation reports.

General Policies and Procedures

An organization's commitment to the quality improvement process should begin with its highest authority. The governing body should create an overall mandate committing the organization to excellence in services and hence to an ongoing process of quality improvement. Within this overall framework, policies and procedures covering evaluation should be developed and documented.

The first consideration will probably be whether or not the program is evaluable in its present form. As Chapter 4 asked, Has the agency developed a program model which describes all program elements and illustrates the logical links between the program's objectives, the activities undertaken to reach the objectives, and the resources necessary to undertake the activities? Does the program model also link the specific, measurable program objectives to the agency's mission statement, or its broadly stated overall goal? If the agency operates more than one program—if it is an agency serving children, for example, comprised of investigation, treatment, and educational program components—does the model link the specific objectives of the various components both to each other and to the agency's overall goal?

Agency policy may require that such a model be developed. It may also provide for periodic review of the model to ensure that the specified program objectives, activities, and resources reflect current reality. Available resources may change over time: New perceptions and changing community needs may necessitate revisions to eligibility criteria, treatment interventions or program objectives. Agency reorganization may require that different links be developed between the program components.

Once the agency itself and its programs are evaluable, the next consideration may concern what form of evaluation is to take place. Is it to be a monitoring or project approach to quality improvement, or some combination of the two? Is it to focus solely on outcomes or include those activities by which the outcomes are achieved? Will its primary function be to satisfy funders that program objectives are being met or to provide data to staff for decision-making and program improvement purposes? Who will be involved in it? Who will be responsible for it? What proportion of the agency's budget should be allocated to it?

The answers to these questions will likely revolve around the purpose and importance of evaluation as perceived by the agency's administrators. If they view evaluation as a foible of funders, they may make it a policy that an outcome-only evaluation is to be conducted every five years, by executive staff, at minimum cost, and the data are to be channeled through the executive and board to the funders. They may even establish an unwritten policy to ignore the whole business until an evaluation is thrust upon them from without.

Conversely, if they look upon evaluation as a useful tool for program improvement, they may make it a policy that evaluation studies are to be continuous, inclusive of all program elements, conducted by and shared with line-level staff, and presented to outside stakeholders on a regular basis. They may make additional provision for more sophisticated, more intrusive evaluations to be conducted periodically, and they will allocate proportions of the budget to both types of evaluative effort. Responsibility for evaluation will be assigned to a senior staff position; and the policy will provide, as all good policies should, for regular review of the policy.

Policy on all these points may be general or specific. For example, it may be left to the senior staff person in charge of evaluation to decide on the nature and extent of line-level involvement. On the other hand, the involvement may be specified, down to the function, composition and procedures of line-level advisory committees. Similarly, policy with regard to periodic evaluations may merely state that these should be undertaken, or it may state that project approaches to quality improvement should be conducted once every three years, or as appropriate, under specified terms and conditions.

If several programs fall under the same administrative umbrella, it may also be necessary, as a matter of policy, to ensure that all are being evaluated in a compatible manner so that data from individual programs can be aggregated into an evaluation of the agency as a whole. This will involve a consideration, for each program, of what data should be collected, with what instruments, how, where, when, how often, and by whom. It may also involve establishing links between the kinds of data collected by the various programs. For example, a child protection agency providing abuse prevention education to children in local schools may wish to evaluate its educational program partly through data gained by its investigation program. What proportion of children who have been sexually abused who were interviewed by investigating human service workers have taken the agency's child abuse prevention course? What differences, if any, exist in the situations, attitudes, and behaviors of children who have taken the course, compared with children who have not? Evaluative linkages of this kind can be established in many agencies operating similar programs.

In sum, policy will cover, generally or in detail, the evaluability of the agency and its various programs, the nature, purpose and frequency of evaluative efforts, the roles and responsibilities of staff members with regard to evaluation, and the proportions of the budget to be allocated to the evaluative endeavor. Once policies are in place, attention can be given to more specific evaluation planning.

Planning Evaluations

Specific planning is necessary both for program monitoring and for project-type evaluations. In both cases, major factors to be considered in planning include the stakeholders, measurement of program objectives and data-collection methods, staff involvement, and the reporting and utilization of results. However, planning for routine monitoring involves slightly different considerations than planning for a project-type evaluation. Similarly, plans for routine monitoring will vary depending on whether the monitoring is to cover only program outcomes or all aspects of program operations. Factors important in planning will be discussed first for monitoring approaches and then for project-type approaches.

Stakeholders

The first concern in planning is to identify the program's stakeholders as presented in Figure 1.1. Who has instigated the evaluation, for what purpose, what data will be required from which program components, and what use will the stakeholder make of these data?

In Program Monitoring
In many human service programs, outcomes are of more interest to stakeholders than the practitioners' activities that produced the outcomes; and the major focus of monitoring is therefore outcome evaluation. Outcome evaluation will usually have a number of stakeholders: program staff, who want some measure of the effectiveness of their efforts so that they can reinforce strengths and attend to weaknesses; funders, who have to make decisions about the allocation of scarce resources to competing programs; community groups—ethnic or religious groups, for example—who want to be assured that their needs are being met; and government officials or researchers who want to replicate the program or compare its results with those of other similar programs.

Each of these stakeholders will require essentially the same data—the degree to which the program is meeting its objectives—but they may want the data to be differently presented so that different aspects are emphasized. For example, the staff of a drug rehabilitation program may want complete data on the degree of achievement of *every* program objective, although funders may be most interested in the results of a new program—to control substance abuse in pre-adolescent populations, for example. Funders might also be especially interested in a program's efficiency.

Ethnic or religious community groups may have their own agendas. Native American groups may want to know what percentage of the program's clients are

Native Americans and what impact the program has on the ability of these clients to function in the areas of employment and family relations. A religious group who defines success as "abstinence" rather than "reduced use" may want to know what percentage of the program's clients abstain from drug use after going through the program. Researchers may want to know whether the program is more effective for Hispanics than it is for Asians, whether women derive more benefit than men, or whether adolescents are engaged as effectively as adults.

In some agencies, monitoring will focus not only on outcomes but on the major sets of activities through which the outcomes are achieved—intake, assessment, and treatment, for example. The stakeholders here will be program staff themselves, and also administrators and researchers who want a more definitive idea of the factors contributing to the program outcomes. The emphasis for these stakeholders will be upon the program's structure and logic: the essential links between the program's objectives, the activities employed to achieve the objectives, and the resources needed to undertake the activities.

For example, program staff may want to be assured that the program's eligibility criteria reflect current community needs. Administrators may be interested in the relationship between increased staff training and a reduction in the number of clients who terminate unilaterally after one or two treatment sessions. Researchers may want to be sure that treatment activities are linked not only to program objectives but to the characteristics of the clients receiving the services.

In Project Evaluations

Project evaluations may be conducted in addition to routine program monitoring. The purpose may be to identify and resolve problems within the agency or merely to satisfy stakeholders that program objectives are being achieved and operations are proceeding smoothly. The stakeholders here will be the board of directors and funders, and the data required may have to do with outcomes, process, or both.

It is more common, however, for periodic evaluations to be initiated by persons outside the program. The stakeholder may be a funder who requires specific data for research or decision-making purposes. Such a stakeholder may be willing to cooperate with program staff insofar as cooperation facilitates the evaluation effort. At the same time, the stakeholder may be more concerned with the validity, reliability, and generalizability of the findings than with the degree of disruption caused to program operations.

For example, if the evaluation's purpose is to obtain generalizable results, comparison or control groups will have to be incorporated into the evaluation design. Executive staff may then find themselves in the position of balancing the data needs of the stakeholder against the well-being of program clients. Confidentiality may be a particular concern since data about program clients will be directly available to non-program personnel.

The different data needs of the various stakeholders will all have to be taken into account when measurement is being debated. The next factors to be considered in evaluation planning will therefore have to do with the measurement of program objectives and methods used to gather data on them. What will be measured, how, when, where, how often and by whom will it be measured, and how will the data be recorded and analyzed?

Selection of Program Objectives and Measurement Methods

The second important factor in planning for evaluation is the selection of program objectives, the methods to be used to measure them, and the types of data analyses to be performed.

In Program Monitoring

The primary purpose of outcome evaluation, monitoring or project, is to determine the degree to which program objectives have been achieved. Consider, as an example, a drug rehabilitation program whose sole objective is to reduce drug use by program participants. The obvious measurement is the reduction of drug usage—the amount and frequency of drugs consumed. These might be measured every session through client self-reports and staff assessments, entered on self-anchored scales. However, client self-reports may not be reliable. Assessment by an experienced staff member may be more reliable but cannot be completely objective in that a person delivering a program usually has a vested interest in its success. Staff members casting around for reliable and objective measurement methods may decide that reduced drug use will be indicated by improved functioning in such areas as work and leisure activities, money management, parenting, family and peer relationships, and so on; and that these can be measured by standardized measuring instruments.

However, standardized instruments take time to administer and score, and they cannot be completed as often as rating scales, particularly if a number of them are being used. Their validity here is in question also, since improved functioning in any area is not addressed directly in program activities and it is by no means certain that a client's improved functioning—if it occurs—will result in reduced drug use.

On the other hand, improved functioning may be a concern to some program stakeholders and it may be argued that the objectives of the drug rehabilitation program should have to do not only with reduced drug use but with the quality of life of the rehabilitated user. Staff may decide to contact other drug rehabilitation programs to see what measures are in common use, or they may decide to add program objectives dealing with improved functioning and to revise group activities to address these objectives.

Measurement should cover all objectives, reflect program activities, and relate to the data needs of stakeholders. When deciding on measurement methods, the following criteria should be taken into account: The method for measuring each objective should yield valid, reliable data; multiple measurements should be used for every objective whenever possible, particularly for those objectives deemed the most important; the method should stipulate who will make the measurement, where, and when; instruments should be easy to administer and score and lend themselves to frequent use; the data obtained for each program or program component should be compatible with data obtained for other components so that aggregation is possible; and attention should be paid to the program's existing data system so that the new data obtained can be easily integrated with the old.

If a program has a large number of related program objectives, it may be necessary to prioritize them so that more attention is given to measuring the most important. For example, a treatment foster care program may have one main program objective: to enable foster children to move to a less restrictive environment on termination. Less restrictive environments may include living with natural parents or relatives, adoption or permanent foster care. It will not be difficult to determine the percentage of children who did move to one of these environments as opposed to the percentage of children who moved to a more restrictive environment, such as a group or residential home, a psychiatric facility, or detention center.

In order to achieve this main program objective, the program may set a number of practice objectives: increasing natural family involvement, where appropriate; improving foster parents' skills; maintaining good relationships with community and professional groups; ensuring recognition of children's ethnic heritage; improving children's functioning in such areas as school attendance and grades, peer and family relationships, anger management, running away, substance abuse; and so on. The degree of achievement of each of these practice objectives can also be measured, but it might be decided that some are of more concern than others and deserve more emphasis. For example, native groups may want definitive evidence that children's ethnic heritage is being preserved.

In Project Evaluations

Many of the same concerns that apply to program monitoring also apply to project evaluations. However, there may be differences, particularly with regard to the intrusiveness of the measurement methods selected. The criterion that measuring instruments should be easy to administer and score may no longer apply since lengthier, more complex instruments are often necessary to achieve the degree of accuracy required. The data collected in these evaluations cannot always be designed to fit the existing data system since the program's data system may be of little interest to an external stakeholder.

The evaluation will no longer extend over an indefinite period but will be time limited, so that planning will need to include schedules for completion. The measurement plan should identify the program objectives to be measured, the measurement method, and, where appropriate, the particular programs or program components in which the measurements will occur. For example, in a foster care program, one program objective of interest may be foster parent satisfaction, to be measured by means of a questionnaire. Completion dates can then be set for the design of the instruments and the measurement of each objective in each component.

Planning will also include data analysis techniques and completion dates, together with an estimate of the resources needed to complete the work. Approval of the plan by the program's director usually signifies a commitment to provide the needed resources.

Staff Involvement

The third factor to be considered in evaluation planning is the degree to which program staff will be involved in the planning stage itself, the implementation of the plan, and the utilization of the results.

In Program Monitoring

Before decisions can be made about what specific program objectives to measure— or anything else—decision-making procedures have to be in place. Policy may have dictated that line-level staff are to be included in evaluation decision making, particularly since they will have to collect and possibly interpret the data. However, the policy statement may not have been specific about the exact responsibilities of each staff position with regard to the evaluative effort. In a small agency, it may be decided that evaluation planning will be conducted at staff meetings, with all staff involved, and everyone will have input into what program objectives should be measured and how they will be measured. Each staff member will then be separately responsible for collecting appropriate data from his or her own clients or groups.

In a larger agency, advisory committees may be formed comprising senior staff, supervisors, and line-level representatives. Supervisors will then carry the responsibility for ensuring that appropriate data are collected by all workers in a particular department or group. The personal responsibility of workers may extend to analyzing and interpreting the data since there must be a logical link between data-gathering procedures and data-analysis techniques. The best person may therefore be the worker who gathers the data although, in some agencies, data analysis and interpretation will fall to a specific person or department entrusted with the task.

In Project Evaluations

Staff involvement in project evaluation may be much the same as in program monitoring, *if* the evaluation is being initiated internally to obtain data required by agency personnel. Periodic evaluations of this kind may be undertaken by staff themselves or by a hired consultant, selected from those who respond to the agency's Request for Proposal (RFP). Prior to engaging a consultant, staff will usually decide on their data needs and perhaps identify the methods they think might be used to collect the data on program objectives. They will also decide on the criteria to be applied in selecting the consultant—professional qualifications, work experience in the field, and so forth—and will follow these criteria closely when making contract commitments.

The RFP will need to include information on the exact nature of the work to be done, the timeframe envisioned and the recompense to be paid; these matters must also be decided in advance. In some cases, the timeframe might allow for the consultant to be available after the work has been completed to discuss the findings and recommendations with agency staff. Some consultants do not feel that utilization of evaluation results by the program has anything to do with them. Others perceive utilization as part of the evaluation process and gladly take the opportunity to present their findings personally.

Before the contract is awarded, roles and responsibilities must be defined in order to ensure that technical expertise is provided by the consultant, but control over the timing and quality of all stages of the work remains with the agency. Adherence to a clear, comprehensive contract can ensure that the program's data needs are satisfied through an evaluation process that is minimally intrusive and technically sound.

If the project evaluation is initiated by stakeholders external to the program, the situation is liable to be very different, particularly with regard to the role of program staff in decision making. Decisions about what program objectives will be measured and how they are to be measured will often be made by the stakeholder, or by a consultant hired by the stakeholder. Senior staff will usually be consulted, but line-level staff may have little input, and in some cases may not even be apprised of the results.

The relevance of program objectives being measured may not be apparent to program staff; indeed, the selected program objectives may not even be relevant to staff, only to the stakeholder. Wherever possible, measurement will probably be undertaken, or at least supervised, by the stakeholder or consultant on the assumption that evaluative measurement is more objective if it is not made by the person who delivers the program. There is a great deal of truth to this but it does mean that program activities are likely to be substantially disrupted since measurement may be planned without regard to the normal flow of the program.

Implementation of Evaluation Plans

Evaluation planning is based upon a theoretical program model which links resources, activities, and objectives. This model specifically describes the resources used, the activities undertaken, and the program objectives to be achieved. However, theory often differs from practice and it cannot be assumed that procedures are followed as written. For example, the purpose of developing eligibility criteria is to accept into the program only those clients who are likely to benefit from the services provided. An evaluation may determine that the program's eligibility criteria are adequate for this purpose, but that they are not being rigorously applied by intake staff. The fact that treatment outcomes are poor may have nothing to do with treatment activities but very much to do with inappropriate clientele selection.

If one of the purposes of the evaluation is to determine the effectiveness of the treatment interventions in producing the desired outcomes, the conclusion may be drawn erroneously that the services are ineffective. Similarly, if staff are not adhering to the written schedule of service activities, conclusions may be drawn about the effectiveness of interventions which have never, in fact, been employed. Evaluators, therefore, should identify the assumptions underlying the evaluation design and include the testing of these assumptions in the evaluation plan. If the assumptions are found to be incorrect, the plan may have to be substantially revised. In the worst case, the study may have to be abandoned.

A word may be said here about the usefulness of the monitoring approach as preparation for a narrowly focused, more sophisticated project study. Routine monitoring procedures will compare theory with practice, allowing project studies to be based on actual activities and thus to produce valid results. In addition, the project study may be conducted in less time and at less cost since testing of the underlying assumptions will no longer be necessary.

Factors other than wrong assumptions may also interfere with the smooth implementation of the evaluation plan. For example, different raters may erroneously ascribe different values to identical client characteristics or interviewers may deviate from the interview schedule or bias answers by faulty presentation of the questions. These measurement errors can be largely eliminated through quality control procedures which should be included in the evaluation plan. Nevertheless, the discovery of such errors may mean that some of the work has to be done again, disrupting the planned timeframe for data collection, data analysis, and compilation of findings.

It is not uncommon for the amount of time actually needed for each evaluation stage to be underestimated. An accumulation of missed completion dates may negate or severely diminish the usefulness of the study, particularly if a decision based on the study has to be made before the findings are presented. Should the eventual findings contradict the decision, both the stakeholder and the consultant may find themselves in difficult positions.

In sum, implementation of the evaluation plan is theoretically just a matter of doing as decided. In practice, erroneous assumptions, measurement errors, lack of cooperation by staff or clients, or gaps and errors in the plan itself may all lead to delays or, in the worst case, compromise the usefulness or validity of the findings.

Reporting and Utilizing Results

The implementation of evaluation planning is followed by reporting and consideration of how findings will be used. In the monitoring approach, evaluation activities are ongoing and regular reporting of findings is appropriate. These reports may be quite informal and their content tailored to the interests of the audience. Reporting in a project evaluation situation is likely to be a more formal and detailed process. Ideally, the schedule and focus of the reports will be determined by a prior agreement between the program and the one who is doing the evaluation.

In Program Monitoring

The results of ongoing evaluation are often presented to workers on a monthly basis, since one of the goals of program monitoring is continuous review and improvement of the program. The format in which the findings are presented—that is, the design of the reporting form—needs to be carefully planned so that the significance of the results is clear. Qualitative descriptions will need no explanation, but numerical results at first may need to be accompanied by an interpretation. Once staff have become accustomed to the monthly format, explanations will no longer be necessary.

However, continued discussion will be necessary if monthly evaluation reports are not to be filed and rapidly forgotten. Supervisors may prefer to discuss results pertaining to worker performance with the individual workers concerned, but results with broader implications will need to be considered at general staff meetings. Perhaps a particular treatment intervention is proving less effective than expected, or a measurement method is perceived by workers as intrusive, and steps must be taken to change the strategy or measure the objective in a different way.

Planning will also be needed with respect to reports to other stakeholders, if these are to be sent out on a regular basis. Reports to people outside the program will need to be more detailed and descriptive than reports issued to workers, since external stakeholders will be less familiar with program activities and procedures. Emphasis will also need to be given to the particular stakeholder's area of interest, with findings and conclusions clearly stated and substantiated. In addition, it may be necessary to indicate the limitations of data collection and analysis procedures, including any implications affecting confidence in the results.

In Project Evaluations

Documentation for an evaluation will include not only formal reports to the client, but also working files, which should be adequately labeled and easily accessible. These files will contain such things as notes on planning activities, the documentation on which the evaluator's understanding of the program's structure and logic is based, interview notes, data reliability checks, and any documentation relating to significant decisions about the planning or implementation of the study.

Intermediate reports will review progress, including accumulated costs, and will bring to the client's attention any discrepancy between the evaluation plan and the actual implementation. For example, quality control procedures may have revealed a problem with inter-rater reliability, and the evaluator may propose to use a third rater, thus increasing the time and cost needed for data collection.

The final report may begin with a description of the structure, the logic of the program, and the purposes and terms of reference of the study. Any assumptions made will be included, together with steps taken to test the assumptions and the possible effects of the assumptions on the study's findings. Confidentiality considerations will be addressed, with a description of the procedures undertaken to ensure the confidentiality of all respondents.

The methodology of the study may then be described, including measurement procedures and any significant differences between the design as planned and the design as implemented. Limitations of data collection and analysis procedures will be identified and discussed including any implications affecting the use of the findings. The report should be completely clear on the degree of confidence that can be placed in the findings and on their generalizability to other populations or programs. Care must be also taken to ensure that all issues raised by the stakeholder during the course of the evaluation have been addressed in the findings, particularly the purposes which the study was originally commissioned to fulfill.

If draft copies of the data, analysis, and findings are submitted to agency staff for comment before the final report is written, differences of opinion may emerge between the staff and the evaluator. Such differences may be included in the report, ensuring that sufficient information is provided to allow the stakeholder to make an independent judgment about the relative merits of the various interpretations. All of the findings will be clearly and completely presented in the summary, together with recommendations for utilization. If the report is of a technical nature, an additional nontechnical summary may be needed for readers without a technical background.

The evaluation is not complete until the final report has been accepted by the stakeholder. Many would argue that the evaluation is not complete until the stakeholder has developed action plans through which the findings will be utilized.

Summary

Evaluation begins with policies that establish the agency's commitment to evaluative practice and define roles, responsibilities, and procedures related to both program monitoring and project evaluation. Since no program can be evaluated until it is evaluable, policy may include the development of a theoretical model. Such a model would describe program elements and define the various ways in which resources, activities, and program objectives are linked together, within and between programs and program components.

Once policies are in place, evaluation plans can be developed for program monitoring and project studies. Major elements in these plans will be the stakeholder, the measurement of program objectives and methods, the degree of staff involvement, and the reporting and utilization of results. Attention will also be paid to such concerns as client confidentiality, quality control, timelines, cost estimates, and the validity of the underlying assumptions.

Implementation of the evaluation plan will be straightforward in theory but probably much more difficult in practice. It may be found that project studies progress more smoothly, faster, and at a lower cost in agencies that routinely monitor their activities.

Documentation and reporting will begin at the planning stage and continue throughout the evaluation until the final report is accepted by the stakeholder. Formal reports will usually be supplemented by working files, containing progress and administrative notes and documentation supporting the evaluator's understanding of program operations. Since findings of evaluation studies are not always utilized by the stakeholder, the evaluator may be concerned with facilitating utilization. This may be accomplished in part by a balanced, competent, and timely presentation of findings and a willingness on the part of the evaluator to meet with the stakeholder later for purposes of clarification and consultation.

Study Questions

1. Who are the principal stakeholders interested in the results of evaluations? What specific interests will these stakeholders have in the program monitoring process? What specific interests will these stakeholders have in project evaluations?

2. What are the major considerations in selecting the program objectives to be evaluated? Do the considerations differ for program monitoring and project evaluations?

3. What are the criteria for selecting measurement methods? Why are these criteria important?

4. What involvement should line-level staff have in evaluations? Is their role different in program monitoring and project evaluations?

5. What are some considerations in ensuring that an external evaluation consultant is effectively utilized?

6. Why is it important to examine how well program theory is put into practice?

7. Describe the features of a good report summarizing the findings of program monitoring. What are the uses of such reports within and outside the program?

8. Describe appropriate reporting procedures in project evaluations.

9. You are an executive director of a large family service agency. Using the contents of the previous 12 chapters, write a 20-page essay on how you would go about creating a quality improvement system within the agency by addressing all of the topics covered within the previous chapters, such as measuring program and practice objectives (Chapters 4–6), case- (Chapter 7) and program-level evaluations (Chapter 8), sampling (Chapter 9), management data systems (Chapter 12), etc. Be as creative as you wish.

10. Read Case Study A. Using the contents of the case study (client population, contextual variables, ethical, legal, social, and political constraints), develop hypothetical policies and procedures that the staff could have used to create a quality improvement system within the program. In reference to planning evaluations, list the various stakeholders of this program. Discuss in detail how program monitoring would be of interest to each stakeholder. Discuss how project outcome evaluations would be of interest to each stakeholder. Given the contents of the case study, discuss additional hypothetical program objectives that you feel could be formulated and thus evaluated. How would you measure each program objective? For each program objective, list the various practice objectives that are directly related to it. How would you measure each practice objective? How do you feel the program's director involved the line-level staff in measuring the program's objectives? Discuss what kind of monthly report each stakeholder should receive in reference to the attainment of program and/or practice objectives. When the author left the agency, the monitoring approach to quality improvement was halted. Why? What do you think went wrong? How do you feel this could have been prevented, given the contents of this chapter?

14

ETHICS AND ACCOUNTABILITY

EVALUATIONS WITHIN HUMAN SERVICE organizations are activities subject to political pressures and economic and professional considerations, among other social forces. These influences can distort the process of evaluation and nullify its benefits. Against these influences are counterpoised ethical and professional standards, which ensure that the evaluation contributes to the well-being of clients and to the effective functioning of programs.

The Many Faces of Interventions and Programs

In this book, evaluation has been described as a method of determining the degree to which interventions or programs meet their goals, via the assessment of program objectives. It might be inferred from this that an intervention or program exists as a single, fixed entity and evaluative methods merely reveal and record this state, much like a camera capturing the image of a static object.

A little reflection will reveal that interventions and programs do not have one external, objective character—they present more than one face to the world. For example, an intervention with a nine-year-old girl may result in less disruptive behavior in the classroom. However, the client's self-esteem may actually be lowered as a result, owing to her perception, reinforced by other children in the classroom, that she has been singled out for special, negative attention. In addition, her negative behaviors may now be manifested in the community, to the great consternation of her peers and their parents.

However, the client's parents, as yet unaware of trouble in the community, are pleased with the results of the intervention in school because they are no longer receiving complaints from her teacher. The intervention does not have one outcome, but rather a multiplicity of outcomes; different conclusions will be reached concerning the effectiveness of the intervention depending on what questions are asked and of whom.

Similar considerations apply at the program level. Consider the image a program projects in the community. Data on how the program is perceived may be gathered from various sources: community groups, physicians, police, teachers, and neighbors in the immediate area of the facility, among others. Because different people or groups experience the program differently in different contexts, their perceptions, though equally valid, are likely to be varied. The program does not have one image in the community; it has a number of different images—which ones are captured by the evaluative process depends on who is asked.

The point here is that a human service program does not exist in a single, concrete state, as a monolith. It exists in many states, or is multifaceted, and the particular state revealed by an evaluation depends on the purpose and focus of the evaluation and the methodology employed. Evaluators must choose the program objectives to be studied, the sample to be selected, the methods to be used to collect data on the program objectives, timing, and methods of data analysis, and how to interpret and disseminate the findings. The choices made will influence and sometimes dictate the results of the evaluation, and evaluators have considerable latitude in making these choices. A few examples will illustrate how technical decisions can influence and even determine evaluation outcomes.

Selection of Practice and Program Objectives

At the case level, the selection of practice objectives seems relatively straightforward when they are directly related to program objectives, but the choice of practice objectives can influence the outcomes recorded in an evaluation. In the case of the nine-year-old girl discussed above, it may be relatively simple to achieve a decrease in disruptive classroom behaviors. It may well be more difficult to increase her self-esteem or other aspects of her functioning. Depending on the practice objectives actually selected, the results of the intervention provided may indicate success, minimal progress, or possibly even deterioration of her practice objectives.

At the program level, the selection of program objectives is somewhat more complicated. In the simplest of terms, the purpose of an outcome evaluation is to determine the degree to which a program is meeting its objectives. These objectives are usually expressed in terms of outcome criteria: numbers and demographic characteristics of people served, improvement in family functioning, decrease in the prevalence of sexual abuse, and so forth. For example, suppose that a community health care center is set up to serve residents without health insurance who would otherwise be unable to obtain health care. Client intake records show that the center's clientele do not have insurance. In other words, the center is properly serving the people it was designed to serve. But no Asians come to the center even though many Asians without insurance live in the community. If one of the program's objectives is expressed simply in general terms of improving the health of community residents who have no insurance, then the program may be meeting this objective. But if the objective is more specific, requiring that a certain proportion of people from each major racial and ethnic group be served, the program will be failing to meet its objective. The same health center may be deemed successful or not depending on how its program objectives are written.

To complicate matters, many programs do not have specific objectives. How can a program be evaluated if its program objectives are missing? What is to be measured in such a situation? If it lacks specific program objectives, a program can be in real trouble when it comes time for an evaluation, as evaluation sponsors and outside evaluators will proceed on the basis of what they think the program's objectives should be. And their opinion can easily be influenced by their own interests as well as by convenience, feasibility, and political considerations. In short, the program objectives selected may not accurately reflect what the program is trying to achieve, and so the evaluation will almost certainly be negative.

Timing of Data Collection

The timing of data collection can also have a considerable effect on evaluation outcomes. At both the case and program levels, different conclusions may be drawn about client status if progress is measured at the time of termination as opposed to some time after termination. In the case of group care programs for children, for example, deterioration and regression often take place subsequent to termination, because fewer social supports are available in the post-termination environment. Measures taken at the time of termination as well as at follow-up are both legitimate reflections of outcomes, but because they may show different results, the evaluator should let the question that is to be answered dictate the timing of data collection.

Sample Selection

Evaluation results may be influenced considerably by sample selection. For example, if all clients complete a self-administered "satisfaction with services measuring instrument" at termination, clients who have dropped out of the program previously—and who are presumably dissatisfied—will not be included. Thus, the results will reflect more satisfaction with the program than is really the case (Gabor, 1993).

Data collection methods, too, can influence sample selection and thus results. If follow-up data are collected by telephone, former clients who do not have telephones or who have moved out of the area may be difficult to reach. Usually, such clients are not doing as well as clients who are available through local telephone calls. Thus, follow-up data collected by this method may tend to overstate the level of functioning of former clients (McMurtry, 1993).

Interpretation of Results

The degree to which a program achieves its objectives is a measure of its effectiveness or success. However, it is often a matter of opinion whether a particular program's outcome should be deemed "successful." Suppose that 60 percent of the graduates of a job-training program find employment. This figure may be interpreted as indicating success, in that *fully* 60 percent of graduates find employment; or it may be taken to indicate failure, in that *only* 60 percent of graduates find work.

Moreover, such data as the percentage of former clients who find employment represent only a part of the picture. Relevant contextual factors should be considered, such as the stability of the employment, the income earned by clients, and the level of job satisfaction experienced by clients. External factors, such as the level of unemployment in the area, should also be taken into account. Evaluation provides the data but cannot interpret it. The way in which the data are interpreted is a process known as *valuation*. Because criteria for success are seldom predefined, evaluators often play an influential part in the valuation process too; and depending on the judgment of an evaluator, the same result may be classified as either a success or a failure (Weinbach & Grinnell, 1995).

Evaluation as a Social Activity

To synthesize what was previously discussed, the essence of evaluation is to provide an accurate picture of interventions and programs and their outcomes. However, interventions and programs are complex entities, and different pictures may be obtained depending on the program objectives examined, the timing of the data collection, the sample selected, the data collection methods utilized, and the manner in which the results are interpreted (Borowski, 1988). Those responsible for conducting evaluations, whether at the case or the program level, have considerable latitude in how they conduct their studies.

It goes without saying that evaluators should be technically competent and act in a reasonable and ethical manner. They have a responsibility to collect data that fairly represent interventions, programs, and their outcomes. Moreover, they are responsible for conducting the appropriate statistical analyses and for contributing to appropriate interpretation of the data.

The opportunity to influence evaluation outcomes through technical decisions underlines the crucial importance of competent, ethical evaluation practice, an issue to be discussed in the following two sections (Schinke, 1985; Schinke & Gilchrist, 1993).

Ethical Standards for Evaluations

A variety of ethical codes applicable to evaluation and research have been published. Although the ethical guidelines in existence have been written specifically to apply to program evaluations, many of the provisions apply to case-level evaluation as well. Most of the ethical guidelines and principles found in the published codes can be organized around the following themes: purpose of the evaluation, informed consent, confidentiality, evaluation design, and dissemination of results.

The Purpose of the Evaluation

The purpose of the evaluation should be clearly spelled out to all those who are asked to participate, as well as to those who will be directly affected by the evaluation results (Tripodi, 1985). Purpose includes information about who initiated and is funding the evaluation and the types of decisions to be based on the evaluation results. This is a time for clarity and frankness. If the purpose is to obtain precise and objective data that can help in making decisions about funding, this should be clearly spelled out at this stage. If specific aspects of program functioning are of concern and it is hoped that evaluation data will shed light on relevant procedures and practices, this, too, should be explicitly stated.

Although this guideline may seem obvious, it is frequently violated: Evaluations are conducted ostensibly to obtain data for program development, but it subsequently turns out that they were really intended to provide data for a funding decision. It is clearly unethical to engage in an evaluation with a hidden agenda.

Informed Consent

Informed consent means that the client, or the evaluation subject, has voluntarily agreed to participate in a study, knows what will happen during the study, and fully understands the possible consequences. This applies equally to evaluations conducted at the case level and the program level.

Again, this provision seems self-evident, but there are well-known instances in which relevant information has been withheld from participants for fear that they would decline to participate or that their knowing the true purposes of the evaluation would compromise the reliability of measurements.

Participants should also be informed that they can withdraw at any time without penalty, and evaluators should recognize that, even when so assured, many clients do not feel free to do so. This is particularly likely to be true of children, as well as residents in group homes, institutions, hospitals, prisons, and senior citizens' homes. In such settings, it is the evaluator's responsibility to ensure that the consent obtained has not been coerced, either explicitly or implicitly.

Confidentiality

Confidentiality is of paramount importance in the human services, and applies to evaluations at both the case and program levels. The utmost care must be taken to preserve the promised anonymity and to keep confidential data out of the hands of unauthorized persons. As soon after data collection as practical, the identities of participants should be disguised by use of codes that make it impossible to associate specific data with any particular client (e.g., Figure 12.5). Assigning codes will also provide an additional level of protection during the computer analysis phase of the study. The master codebook, listing clients and their assigned codes, should be kept under lock and key, and preferably in a different location from the data.

The Evaluation Design

The selection of an evaluation design inevitably raises ethical concerns.

It was pointed out in Chapter 7 that the most powerful case-level evaluation designs involve the withdrawal of successful interventions and that such withdrawal may well be to the detriment of the client. Under some circumstances, it may be possible to implement these designs without harm to clients. For example, when a client leaves town for a period of time, there may be no alternative but to discontinue the intervention. However, arrangements can be made to continue measuring the practice objective, and when the client returns the intervention can be reintroduced. This would result in a powerful $A_1B_1A_2B_2$ design that could support claims about the causal link between the intervention and client outcomes (Thyer, 1993).

But in most cases there is no clinical justification for withdrawing the intervention, and to discontinue a successful intervention solely for the purpose of implementing a powerful explanatory evaluation design would be unethical. Thus, practitioners are ethically constrained, in most cases, to forego the inferentially powerful withdrawal designs. A less powerful and less ethically contentious exploratory or descriptive design should be implemented; if that is not a viable alternative, the evaluation should not be carried out at all.

Similarly, at the program level, evaluators may be asked to carry out a study that, in practice, cannot be ethically implemented. For instance, some evaluation questions require the implementation of an explanatory design, but under many circumstances, random assignment to experimental and control groups is neither ethically justifiable nor operationally feasible. At other times, those commissioning the study impose unrealistic deadlines that may result in substandard work. It can be tempting to undertake such projects, particularly if they are lucrative, but ethical evaluators will resist the temptation.

Dissemination of Results

The final stage of an evaluation is disseminating the information obtained from the collected data. This stage consists of all activities needed to ensure that evaluation results are made available to all involved persons.

At the case level, human service workers will have up-to-date information about the evaluation because they will have been responsible for data collection. Most clients will undoubtedly express an interest in what the data are showing, and it is usually appropriate to share this information with them. Indeed, progress (or lack of it) will be a continuing topic of discussion between worker and client, and should enhance honesty and openness between them. In general, the process of dissemination at the case level is an informal one and does not involve written reports.

Dissemination becomes a more formal activity at the program level. If an organization is using the monitoring approach to quality improvement, dissemination will be part of the system design. Decisions will undoubtedly have been made about the manner in which, and how often, results will be aggregated. Data can then be compiled and analyzed and reports issued periodically. It is particularly important that these periodic reports not be reserved for senior management, but be made available to the workers whose original data have been aggregated. Ideally, these reports should be viewed as ongoing feedback. By disseminating reports widely within the organization when they become available, senior management can help create an environment in which the reports are viewed as encouraging and informing the ongoing development of the programs.

In project evaluations, reports will usually not be compiled until the latter stages of the project. Again, it is important to disseminate these reports as early and as widely as possible. In particular, evaluators have a responsibility to ensure that all of the clients who participated in the evaluation and were promised copies of reports are provided with them.

Generally, wide dissemination of information developed through evaluation can foster openness, honesty, and a constructive climate for further evaluation work. In our society information is power, and information provided by an evaluation can empower those who receive it—and disempower those who do not. That, in a phrase, is why ethical considerations must govern the dissemination of evaluation results.

Professional Standards for Evaluations

It is important not only that evaluations be carried out in an ethical manner, but also that they be competently conducted and meet existing professional standards. The most commonly accepted standards in the field are those issued by the Joint Committee for Standards on Educational Evaluation. These standards were developed over a five-year period in the late 1970s and reflected the participation of 12 professional organizations and hundreds of professional evaluators.

The Joint Committee identified four criteria against which evaluation practice should be judged: utility, feasibility, fairness, and accuracy. Although the committee's standards were written specifically as guidelines for program-level evaluation, they have considerable applicability to case-level evaluation practice as well. The four criteria, which overlap to some degree with the ethical precepts outlined above, are discussed below.

Utility

The provisions relating to utility attempt to ensure that evaluations are carried out only if they will be of potential use to one or more of the program's stakeholders who make decisions about the program in one way or another. In other words, evaluators are required to establish links between evaluation results and the decisions that will be based on those results. Thus, data obtained from an evaluation should be relevant to decision makers and should be reported in a manner that decision makers can understand.

At the case level, the client and the line-level worker are, in most cases, joint decision makers. Because workers are usually the people who carry out case-level evaluations, they will be able to decide on the type of data to be gathered, the method of analysis, and the way in which evaluation results will impact clinical decision making. However, the standard of utility also makes the worker responsible for ensuring that the client finds the data useful and understandable. This standard, then, implies that the results of clinical evaluation should be used for clinical decision making.

At the program level, evaluation results are usually documented in a report, which normally also provides recommendations. To ensure that the evaluation has utility, the evaluator is responsible for determining beforehand, with as much clarity as possible, the decisions that are to be based on the evaluation results. The evaluator is also responsible for reporting results in a manner that can inform the decisions to be taken. It is obviously important that the report be comprehensible to decision makers. Moreover, the evaluator's task is not limited to publishing the findings; the evaluator must also explain the results to decision makers.

When drafting recommendations, it is important that evaluators keep in mind the social, political, economic, and professional contexts within which recommendations will be implemented. Recommendations that follow logically from the findings but have little chance of being implemented—for example, changes that would require a 50 percent increase in the program's budget—may not meet the criterion of utility. The challenge for the evaluator is to provide recommendations that can result in improvement *within existing constraints*.

Feasibility

The second criterion identified by the Joint Committee was feasibility. An evaluation should not be conducted if it is not practical to implement the study or possible to carry it out within the budget and timeframes available. The issues gathered together under the standard of feasibility concern the selection of evaluation designs, a topic discussed earlier in relation to ethical evaluation practice.

At the case level, feasibility requires that the evaluation design selected should be compatible with service considerations. Although it might be desirable from the perspective of science to implement an explanatory case-level design involving a withdrawal phase, it may be inadvisable (not to mention unethical) to do so. A less intrusive design will likely be a more practical alternative.

At the program level, the questions to be answered may call for an explanatory design requiring random assignment of clients to experimental and control groups. But it may not be possible to implement such a design without considerable disruption to service provision. Perhaps the evaluation questions can be answered through a exploratory or descriptive design; if not, the study will have to be abandoned or refocused. Similarly, funding considerations or deadlines may limit the evaluation questions that can be addressed or the evaluation designs that can be implemented.

Fairness

The third criterion identified by the Joint Committee was fairness: An evaluation should not be undertaken if it cannot be conducted ethically and fairly. As ethical issues were discussed earlier in this chapter, here we consider only the issue of fairness. The concept of fairness implies that a reasonable, balanced picture of the program will be presented. This balance also applies to competing interests regarding the program; evaluators should avoid, or extricate themselves from, any position in which they are vulerable to undue influence from any group of stakeholders. As well, to the best of their ability, evaluators should ensure that the results are appropriately used.

Accuracy

The fourth criterion identified by the Joint Committee was accuracy. This has to do with the technical adequacy of the evaluation process and involves such matters as validity and reliability, measurement instruments, samples, and comparisons. The evaluator is also responsible for making clear any shortcomings in the methodology, and the limits within which the findings can be considered to be accurate.

Although it is the evaluator's responsibility to ensure technical adequacy, this standard does not imply that the evaluator should unilaterally make design and data collection decisions. Rather, it is important that those who will use the evaluation findings participate in these decisions and so come to understand the strengths and limitations of the data.

Uses and Misuses of Evaluations

Although ethical and competent evaluation practices are indispensable in ensuring that the evaluation process benefits clients and programs, they are in themselves insufficient to ensure that the evaluation results are appropriately used. How evaluation results are used depends, to a large degree, on the organizational context as well as on the larger political and social environment.

Misuse of Evaluations

Misuse of evaluations is a chronic and recurring problem in the human services. Some less credible purposes to which evaluations have been put are justification of decisions already made, public relations, performance appraisal, and fulfilling funding requirements.

Justifying Decisions Already Made

Perhaps the most frequent misuse of evaluation is to justify decisions made in advance of the evaluation.

At the case level, for example, a practitioner may have decided, if only at the subconscious level, that a youngster in treatment foster care should be referred to a group-care program. The worker may then select an indicator that is likely to show that the youngster's functioning is highly problematic and use these data to justify the previously taken decision.

At the program level, an agency executive director may already have decided that a certain program should be reduced in size. The executive board may then commission an evaluation in the hope that the results will show the program to be ineffective. Inevitably, any evaluation will uncover *some* shortcomings and limitations, and the executive director can then use these to justify the decision to reduce program size. Similarly, outside funders who have already decided to cancel funding for a program may first commission an evaluation in the hope that the results will justify the decision.

Public Relations

Another frequent misuse of evaluation is to distract attention from negative publicity. From time to time, incidents occur that bring an organization unwelcome publicity; for example, a worker in a group home may be indicted for sexual abuse of residents, or a preschooler may be returned from a treatment foster home to her natural home and be subsequently physically abused. These types of incidents inevitably attract intense media scrutiny.

Some programs will immediately commission a large-scale evaluation and then decline any further comment, pending the outcome of the evaluation. Although an evaluation may be an appropriate response in many such situations, it is even more important to take immediate steps to study the specific incident in detail and adjust procedures and practices to ensure it will never again occur. But where an evaluation is commissioned merely to distract attention, much of the time, effort, and resources invested in that study will be wasted, as there is unlikely to be any genuine interest in the results: The evaluation is a mere diversion.

Performance Appraisal

Another serious misuse of evaluation occurs when it is used for purposes of staff performance appraisal. For example, data relating to client progress may be scrutinized to document a worker's performance in terms of the attainment of clients' practice objectives. Similarly, data may be aggregated across the caseload of a worker and the resulting information used for performance appraisal. At the program level, the contents of an evaluation report may be used to evaluate a supervisor or manager. In all these cases, the evaluation results are likely to be used for political purposes, to "get" someone.

Such uses of evaluation are likely to be destructive, as staff members will undoubtedly become defensive and concentrate their efforts on ensuring that evaluation data show them in a good light. These defensive efforts may well detract from the accuracy and relevance of data, to the detriment of clients and program functioning. Performance appraisal and program evaluation are two distinct processes, with different purposes; both will be compromised if the two are not kept separate.

Fulfilling Funding Requirements

Funders are increasingly requiring evaluation as a condition of funding, particularly of new, innovative, or demonstration programs. Staff members who are trying to set up a new program—or maintain an old one—may see the evaluation component as a ritual without relevance to them, designed only to placate funders. They may thus incorporate an elaborate evaluation component into proposals, or graft evaluation activities onto an existing program, obediently jumping through hoops in order to satisfy funders. It is, of course, a serious misuse (not to mention a waste of time, effort, and resources) to undertake evaluations only to obtain funds, without any thought of using the data to improve interventions and programs.

Appropriate Uses of Evaluations

As discussed in previous chapters, evaluation data may be used appropriately to guide internal and external decision making.

Internal Decision Making

The primary internal use of evaluation data is as feedback. Findings provide information about the degree to which the objectives of clients and programs are being met. Because these data are available in a timely fashion, workers and managers can continually monitor the impacts of their decisions, and where required, make adjustments to activities and program components.

At the case level, evaluation data can provide an empirical basis for clinical decision making. As has been described throughout this book, selected practice objectives are measured repeatedly while the client is receiving service. These data are then used as feedback on client progress and become an important consideration in decisions to maintain, modify, or change interventions.

At the program level, managers are interested in a broader picture of program functioning. The monitoring approach, based on the collection of case-level data, allows an organization to gather data continuously about various program components, practices, and procedures. The principal internal use for such data should be developmental. The process is essentially as follows: Data are aggregated periodically, providing ongoing feedback about the functioning of various aspects of the program. Where the program is not performing as desired, managers have the opportunity to make changes in structures, procedures, and practices. Subsequent data should then provide information about the impact of these changes. In this manner, managers can continually fine-tune and improve the program.

External Uses

External uses of evaluation data usually involve funders, policymakers, researchers, and other stakeholders. Appropriate uses include demonstration of accountability, program and policy decision making, and knowledge building.

Human service programs are in a general sense accountable to their clients, to the community, and to various professional organizations. Specifically, they are almost always accountable to funders and program sponsors. Accountability generally requires that a program demonstrate that its goal is consistent with community needs and that services are being provided effectively and efficiently. One of the most common uses of evaluation is to account for program activities and program results.

At the policy level, it is sometimes necessary to make decisions between various ways of meeting particular social needs. Or, policymakers may decide to encourage the development of programs that are organized along certain models. Currently, for example, in many jurisdictions specialized treatment foster homes are being encouraged and group-care facilities for young people are being discouraged. At other times, funders will face decisions regarding funding for a specific program. In all three cases, evaluation data can provide program level information on which such decisions can be based.

Knowledge building for human service professions is another way in which evaluation results may be used. Each completed evaluation study has the potential of adding to our knowledge base. Indeed, at times evaluations are undertaken specifically for the purpose of acquiring knowledge: Because evaluations are conducted in field settings, they are a particularly useful method for testing the effectiveness of intervention and program models.

Evaluations for external purposes are usually initiated by people outside the program, typically funding bodies such as the United Way. They are often also externally conducted by evaluation specialists on a project basis. When evaluations are externally imposed and externally conducted, there is a higher potential for abuse of the evaluation process and misuse of the results. An effective safeguard is provided when program staff and management are involved in all decisions relating to the planning and execution of the evaluation.

An alternative to the externally conducted project evaluation is available to agencies that establish internal evaluation systems. As discussed in the last chapter, the data collected through such systems can often satisfy many of the needs of external stakeholders.

Establishing a Constructive Context for Evaluations

Organizations have considerable control over the context they create for evaluation. This is fortunate, for the context of an evaluation determines, to a large degree, whether it will be used or misused. Admittedly, organizations have little control over the external environment in which evaluations are conducted, but organizations that establish effective internally driven evaluation systems will be in a good position to ensure that even externally imposed evaluations are not misused.

The establishment of a constructive context for evaluation begins with a commitment to internal, continuous, self-directed evaluation. To accomplish this, the following practices need to be adopted: continuous data collection, use of evaluation data as feedback for developmental purposes, involvement of staff in evaluation tasks, and provision of resources necessary to support the evaluation effort.

Continuous Data Collection

This book has focused on continuous collection of evaluation data through monitoring, as contrasted with periodic data collection through project-type studies. There are two major advantages to continuous data collection: It is not intrusive because it is an integral part of program operations, and the data are likely to be used because they are relevant and current.

Use of Evaluation Data as Feedback to Improve Services

Evaluation data provide, ultimately, information about the degree to which interventions and programs are achieving their objectives. However, in the monitoring approach, data are gathered specifically to provide ongoing feedback so that interventions and programs can be improved. Data are collected on an ongoing basis and are available at regular intervals; staff members can then use these data to fine-tune interventions and program components. The judgmental element of evaluation should be entirely absent, because the purpose of monitoring is not to assign blame: It is to improve interventions and programs so that clients can be better served.

Involvement of Staff

The most constructive environment for evaluation is created through a participatory approach. Direct service staff members should be involved with supervisors and managers at every stage of designing and implementing the evaluation system. This will ensure that data are useful at both the case and program levels.

Dissemination of Results

The information obtained from an evaluation should be shared early and widely. It is important to create a blame-free environment in which problems are identified and addressed without fault being assigned. The open availability of evaluation results can help to foster an environment in which staff members welcome the continuous feedback generated by evaluation.

Summary

This chapter presented various considerations, or constraints, that must be taken into account when evaluating a human service program. Because interventions and programs are complex entities, evaluation outcomes can be influenced through technical processes such as sample selection data collection methods and statistical analysis. Consequently, ethical and professional standards for conducting evaluations are important; in this chapter we outlined major ethnical guidelines for evaluation research. Moreover, we introduced four criteria by which evaluation practice should be judged: utility, feasibility, fairness, and accuracy.

Key Terms

Accuracy: A standard of evaluation practice that requires technical adequacy of the evaluation process; includes matters of validity, reliability, measurement instruments, samples, and comparisons.

Fairness: A standard of evaluation practice that requires evaluations to be conducted in a fair and ethical manner; includes the dissemination of evaluation results.

Feasibility: A standard of evaluation practice that requires evaluations to be conducted only under conditions that are practical and economically viable.

Informed Consent: Procedures in which clients, or evaluation subjects, are told in advance about the major tasks and activities they will perform during an evaluation study; clients then participate in the evaluation study only if they are willing to engage in these activities.

Performance Appraisal: The process of evaluating the efficiency and effectiveness of a staff person's work; a possible misuse of evaluation practice.

Utility: A standard of evaluation practice that requires evaluations to be carried out only if they are considered potentially useful to one or more stakeholders.

Study Questions

1. Select one of the case studies included in this book. Assess the evaluation procedures of the case study according to the standards for evaluation practice in the areas of utility, feasibility, fairness, and accuracy. Explain your answer in detail.

2. In your own words, list the factors that can influence evaluation outcomes. What strategies can you offer to minimize the bias that these factors may introduce into evaluation outcomes?

3. Discuss the process of obtaining informed consent from a client. What level of detail would you use to explain the client's participation in the evaluation? Would your approach to receiving informed consent from a client be formal or informal? Explain your answer in detail.

4. Discuss the differences between internal and external uses of evaluation data. Provide a specific example of each.

5. Many workers fear and resist program evaluation as a formal part of client service. What strategies can you suggest to increase their level of comfort with the notions of accountability and evaluation?

6. What strategies can you suggest to minimize the misuse of program evaluation in human service agencies? Explain your answer in detail.

7. In groups of four, create a code of ethics to guide human service workers in conducting evaluations. Develop brief guidelines focused on the following themes: purpose of evaluation, informed consent, evaluation design, and dissemination of results. Compare your code of ethics with the published version in your field.

8. In groups of five, choose a program-level human service intervention. Clearly identify a purpose, or reason, for evaluating the intervention. How does defining the purpose of the evaluation affect the choice of evaluation design, sampling procedures, data collection, data analysis, and dissemination of results? What other purposes of evaluation can you identify? How do different purposes influence the design and procedure of the evaluation?

9. A co-worker maintains that evaluation of interventions and programs always produce the same result. Comment.

10. You argue that the selection of objectives affects the outcome of an evaluation at the case and program levels. Outline the main points of your argument.

11. You also maintain that the timing of data collection may also affect evaluation outcomes. How do you support your position?

12. You argue that sample selection and interpretation of results affect evaluation outcomes. Why?

13. Given that evaluation is a social activity, why is ethical evaluation practice so important?

14. Ethical guidelines and principles for human service workers indicate that the purpose of the evaluation should be clearly spelled out for all those who participate. Why is this important?

15. Ethical guidelines also require informed consent for participation in evaluations. Why?

16. How is confidentiality a paramount component of ethical evaluation? How can the confidentiality of participants be ensured? Discuss in detail. Provide a human service example throughout your discussion.

17. How do ethical considerations affect the selection of evaluation designs at the case and program level? Discuss in detail. Provide a human service example throughout your discussion.

18. How do ethical considerations affect the dissemination of results at the case and pro-

gram level? Discuss in detail. Provide a human service example throughout your discussion.

19. In a county agency, an evaluation has been commissioned to justify decisions about budget cuts that have already been made. In what ways is this an inappropriate use of evaluation? Discuss in detail. Provide a human service example throughout your discussion.

20. How can an evaluation be used to distract attention from negative publicity? Discuss in detail. Provide a human service example throughout your discussion.

21. How can evaluation data be used appropriately to guide internal decision making? Discuss in detail. Provide a human service example throughout your discussion.

22. How can evaluation data be used appropriately to guide external decision making? Discuss in detail. Provide a human service example throughout your discussion.

23. The establishment of a constructive context for evaluation begins with making a commitment to internal, continuous, self-directed evaluation. What practices must be adopted to accomplish this? Discuss in detail. Provide a human service example throughout your discussion.

24. Read Case Study A. How would you rate this program's monitoring system in reference to the professional standards for evaluation: utility, feasibility, fairness, and accuracy? Why? Justify your response. Do you feel the monitoring approach that was utilized in this program was ethical? Why or why not? Discuss how the data that were collected in this program could be misused. How would you go about preventing the misuse of the data that were collected?

25. Read Case Study B. How would you rate this program's monitoring system in reference to the professional standards for evaluation: utility, feasibility, fairness, and accuracy? Why? Justify your response. Do you feel the monitoring approach that was utilized in this program was ethical? Why or why not? Discuss how the data that were collected in this program could be misused. How would you go about preventing the misuse of the data that were collected?

26. Read Case Study C. How would you rate this program's monitoring system in reference to the professional standards for evaluation: utility, feasibility, fairness, and accuracy? Why? Justify your response. Do you feel the monitoring approach that was utilized in this program was ethical? Why or why not? Discuss how the data that were collected in this program could be misused. How would you go about preventing the misuse of the data that were collected?

15

EVALUATION AND QUALITY IMPROVEMENT IN ACTION

YVONNE UNRAU

As has been established throughout this book, the quality improvement process should be an ongoing commitment in human service organizations that aspire to excellence. The evaluation approaches described in this book provide the means for implementing an ongoing quality improvement system. Both monitoring and project approaches to quality improvement provide a sound basis for decision making. The monitoring approach has been emphasized in this book because of its feasibility in providing data for decision making at both the case and program levels, while the project approach primarily informs program-level decision making.

This chapter relates the key concepts presented in this book to an actual human service program, demonstrating how the main concepts can be employed in practice. The human service program described is a family preservation program. This case example is only one illustration of how a program can deliver services and, at the same time, implement a quality improvement system.

Organization of Services

Figure 15.1 provides a general program description of the case example used in this chapter, including information on the general parameters of the Family Preservation Program at the ABC Family Service Agency.

As can be seen from Figure 15.2, the Family Preservation Program is one of three programs offered by the ABC Family Service Agency. Using the criteria identified in Chapter 4, we know that the other two programs offered by the agency (the Teen-Parent Educational Program and the Family Crisis Support Program) differ from the Family Preservation Program in terms of program goal, organizational structure, client population, referral sources, funding, and staffing. Given the family-oriented nature of the agency, it is reasonable to assume that these other two programs also serve families but focus on a different population need or social problem.

Figure 15.2 depicts the organizational structure of the ABC Agency's program services. The agency's mission and goal statements, situated at the top of the figure, guide the development of each of its three programs. Each program is represented by a pyramid which aids in the construction of a schematic program representation. The Family Preservation Program pyramid is magnified to illustrate the levels of program elements needed for service conceptualization. In addition, a continuum of case-level to program-level evaluation is shown on the left to demonstrate that continuity exists between service conceptualization and subsequent evaluation activities. It is useful to keep this structure in mind since each of the program elements described in this chapter is explained in relation to the Family Preservation Program as depicted in Figures 15.1 and 15.2.

The Program

The Family Preservation Program is one of three programs offered by the ABC Family Service Agency. The scope of the program can be described using the program characteristics outlined in Chapter 1.

First, the *boundary:* The program serves clients residing in a major midwestern city.

Second, *size:* The program is open to families who have been investigated by the Department of Child Welfare for suspected physical abuse. As a result, one or more children have been identified as at risk for removal from the home. The program employs one supervisor and three family preservation practitioners. Each practitioner carries a caseload of five families.

Third, *duration:* The service is short and intensive. Service spans 10 to 12 weeks during which workers meet with each family approximately 10 hours per week. Typically, more time is spent with the family during the first part of the intervention. The worker reduces the number of service hours as termination approaches. Over the course of intervention, each family receives an average of 90 service hours.

Fourth, *complexity:* Program services are marked by a community-based practice approach. Program practitioners work under the legal direction of the Department of Child Welfare. Family counseling, individual parent training, and community networking are common treatment approaches.

Fifth, *clarity of program goals:* Goals remain somewhat broad, given the vast range of problems that lead to the occurrence of physical abuse within a family.

Finally, *innovation:* Innovation of intervention services is a primary feature of the program as much is yet to be learned about treatment of parents who abuse their children. Practitioners utilize a range of established and innovative intervention techniques.

Need for Evaluation

The need for evaluation in the Family Preservation Program is linked to the program staff's desire to claim effective services. Incorporating evaluation into program services aids the program and field in the following four ways:

Increasing Our Knowledge Base
There is much to be learned about parents who physically abuse their children. Evaluation practices in the Family Preservation Program can contribute to further understanding of the phenomenon of child abuse. Specifically, assessing the home-based nature of program services can help answer important questions such as: Should children at risk for physical abuse be removed from their parents' care? Can parents who physically abuse their children learn alternative strategies for disciplining their children?

Guiding Decision Making
Many stakeholders use evaluation results to make decisions about the Family Preservation Program. Day-to-day decision making occurs for program administrators, practitioners, and clients alike. Decision making for policymakers, funders, and the general public is more likely to occur annually. Ultimately, all stakeholders are interested in knowing how effective and efficient the program is in helping parents who abuse their children and in preserving these high-risk families.

Demonstrating Accountability
Ultimately, the Family Preservation Program must demonstrate evidence of effectiveness to continue receiving funds legitimately.

Satisfaction that Goals Are Being Achieved
Being responsible professionals, the practitioners employed by the Family Preservation Program want to know whether or not clients are benefiting from the services received. Additionally, by monitoring client progress, workers and clients can assess whether the treatment approach is worth the time, effort, and money spent.

FIGURE 15.1   Case Example: The Home-Based Family Preservation Program

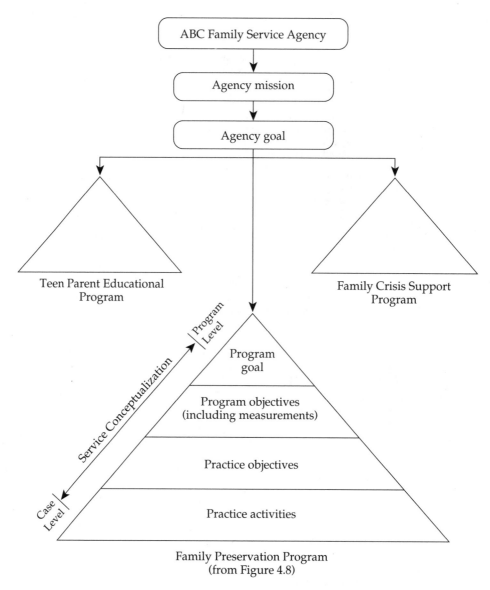

FIGURE 15.2   Simple Organizational Chart of ABC Family Service Agency

Program Goal

The position of the goal at the top of the Family Preservation Program pyramid in Figure 15.2 illustrates its twofold purpose. First, the program goal serves as a focal point or navigational tool, steering the entire scope of program operations in a specified direction. Second, the goal functions as an umbrella under which all other program elements are logically subsumed. The ensuing detail of successive program elements (e.g., program objectives, practice objectives, activities) must logically fit within the context of the stated goal. The program goal for the Family Preservation Program is:

> To preserve family units where children are at risk for out-of-home placements owing to problems with physical abuse. The program aims to strengthen interpersonal functioning of family members through intensive home-based services.

The program goal may at first sight appear to have more utility for program-level evaluation than for case-level evaluation. However, the goal serves an important function in guiding day-to-day practitioner activities. Goals that are vague or are not used for guidance can quickly lead to inappropriate case-level activities. For example, suppose workers in the Family Preservation Program neglected to use the above-stated goal as a navigational tool. How would they determine the suitability of the clients referred? What source would they use to limit the range of services they offer to clients? How would innovative interventions be assessed for fit within the program? Likely, each individual worker could answer each of these important questions. However, a program must have a common frame of reference to determine whether or not *all* the services it renders are rightfully administered and effective.

Losing sight of the program goal can also have serious implications for a program's development. The goal statement allows one to generate several subpopulations (e.g., emotionally disturbed children, single parents) within the target population and a host of social problems thought to be associated with child abuse (e.g., poverty, isolation). Practitioners may be inclined to address these additional needs by initiating other services, such as prevention or community education. These added services are excessive when one considers the limits of the program's goal.

Although it can be argued that such services are needed, it is difficult to imagine how only three workers in one program (see Figure 15.1) could effectively accomplish these additional unmandated tasks while continuing to provide quality services directed to the program's stated goal. Such a drastic deviation in worker activities can, in fact, undermine efforts to show program accountability in services aimed specifically at family preservation. Alternatively, when practitioners adhere to the prescribed purpose of the program, focused data are made available for stakeholders as they consider program decisions.

Program Objectives

From a client-focused perspective, program objectives are the intended and measurable results that all clients in a program strive to achieve. Program objectives identify the general intervention approach offered to clients at the program level. Each program objective is logically linked to the stated program goal.

In Figure 15.2, the program objectives are situated directly beneath the program goal because they aim to delineate the goal into measurable terms. Program objectives capture the essence of the overall practice approach adopted in working with a particular client group. They indicate whether clients will work on aspects of knowledge, skills, or affects related to their particular problem area.

Program objectives are based on theoretical or empirical knowledge and thus serve as the foundation of a program's service delivery system. Defining the theoretical basis of a program is a prerequisite to subsequent evaluation activity (Posavac & Carey, 1992). Generally, program objectives are academically constructed. They aim to define testable assertions on which a program is based. In other words, each program objective assumes that without the aid of the program's services, clients will not show improvement on the objective targeted (Patton, 1986).

As a result, the number of program objectives for any one program is finite. That is, what counts as a realistic number of program objectives will depend on the scope of a program's service structure and the availability of resources. A practitioner who has a caseload of 100 and sees clients twice a month will likely tackle fewer program objectives than a practitioner who has a caseload of 20 and sees clients weekly. The process of defining program objectives compels us to be realistic about what we hope to accomplish with our clients in the time available to us.

Undoubtedly, the goal of the Family Preservation Program could be achieved by various different intervention approaches. The stated goal of the program is complex; it focuses on eliminating child abuse, strengthening family functioning, and preserving high-risk family units. Given the broad nature of this goal and the service structure of the program, the following seven program objectives are believed to be related to the program's goal:

1. To increase positive social supports for parents
2. To increase problem-solving skills for family members
3. To increase parents' use of noncorporal child management strategies
4. To increase communication skills between family members
5. To increase parental cooperation with case-planning services pertaining to child abuse
6. To increase parental acceptance of the child at risk for physical abuse
7. To reduce stress for parents

It is important that program staff collectively agree on the listed program objectives, as it is these objectives for which the program will specifically be held accountable. Selection of program objectives involves careful consideration of the amount of resources available and the manner in which resources will be organized (Kettner, Moroney, & Martin, 1990). Because the program lasts for 10 weeks, the timeframe for each program objective is implicitly set. That is, workers and clients plan to tackle all relevant client-relevant program objectives during the 90 service hours offered over a 10- to 12-week period.

The first three program objectives are displayed in Figure 15.3, which provides a condensed illustration of the program's services. A document such as the one

---

Family Preservation Program

Program Goal

To preserve family units where children are at risk for out-of-home placements owing to problems with physical abuse. The program aims to strengthen interpersonal functioning of family members through intensive home-based services.

Program Objectives

1. To increase positive social supports for parents.

   Literary Support: A lack of positive social support has been repeatedly linked to higher risk for child abuse. Studies indicate that parents with greater social support and less stress report more pleasure in their parenting roles.

   Sample of Activities: Referral to support groups; evaluate criteria for positive support; introduction to community services; reconnecting clients with friends and family.

   Measuring Instruments: Client log; Provision of Social Relations

2. To increase problem-solving skills for family members.

   Literary Support: Operationally, problem-solving is a tool for breaking difficult problems into manageable pieces. Enhancing individuals' skills in systematically addressing problems increases the likelihood that they will successfully tackle new problems as they arise. Increasing problem-solving skills for parents and children equips family members to handle current problems, anticipate and prevent future ones, and advance their social functioning.

   Sample of Activities: Teach steps to problem-solving; role play problem-solving scenarios; supportive counseling.

   Measuring Instruments: The Problem-Solving Inventory

3. To increase parents' use of noncorporal child management strategies.

   Literary Support: Empirical research suggests that deficiency in parenting skills is associated with higher recurrence of abuse. Furthermore, parents who demonstrate a high need for control and resort to excessive discipline tend to use more abusive discipline strategies.

   Sample of Activities: Teach noncorporal discipline strategies; inform parents about the criminal implications of child abuse; assess parenting strengths; provide reading material about behavior management.

   Measuring Instruments: Self-report log of child management strategies used; checklist of discipline strategies; does child remain at home?

FIGURE 15.3   Program-Level Documentation of Family Preservation Program (from Figure 15.2)

Family Preservation Program	Family X	Family Y
Program Objectives and Measurements	**Practice Objectives and Practice Activities**	**Practice Objectives and Practice Activities**
Objective 1: To increase positive social supports for parents.	*Practice Objective 1a:* To increase Ms X's knowledge about available positive social supports.	*Practice Objective 1a:* To increase Mr. and Ms Y's knowledge about available positive social supports.
Measuring Instruments: a. Client log b. Provision of Social Relations	*Activities:* Provide a list of support groups; assess Ms X's personal support network; assist Ms X in evaluating existing supportive resources.	*Activities:* Assess available supports in the local community; teach Mr. and Ms Y how to establish new supports; refer parents to educational group for parent's with young children.
	Practice Objective 1b: To increase Ms X's use of available social supports.	*Practice Objective 1b:* To increase Mr. and Ms Y's ability to discriminate between negative and positive social supports.
	Activities: Assist Ms X in organizing her time to include aspects of social support; refer to parent support group; discuss how use of social support might alleviate current life stressors.	*Activities:* Assess Mr. and Ms Y's ability to differentiate positive and negative support (e.g., neighbor's advice); discuss strategies for Mr. and Ms Y to increase positive support.
Objective 2: To increase problem-solving skills for family members.	*Practice Objective 2a:* To improve Ms X's abilities in use of a problem-solving method.	*Practice Objective 2a:* To increase Mr. and Ms Y's abilities in use of a problem-solving method.
Measuring Instrument: Problem-Solving Inventory	*Activities:* Teach steps to problem-solving; role-play problem-solving situations; coach Ms X as she problem solves with Billy.	*Activities:* Teach steps to problem-solving; role-play problem-solving scenarios; discuss benefits of using a systematic problem-solving approach.
	Practice Objective 2b: To increase Ms X's ability to generate options under stressful conditions.	*Practice Objective 2b:* To increase Mr. and Ms Y's ability to recognize a problem.
	Activities: Apply problem-solving to job finding; explore the nature of Ms X's main coping strategies; discuss how different coping techniques can produce different outcomes; reframe perspective on the problem.	*Activities:* Discuss Mr. and Ms Y's criteria for determining a problem; teach how adults and children can interpret problems differently; create hypothetical problem situations and discuss possible consequences.
Objective 3: To increase use of noncorporal child management strategies.	*Practice Objective 3a:* To increase Ms X's repertoire of noncorporal discipline strategies.	*Practice Objective 3a:* To increase Mr. and Ms Y's repertoire of noncorporal discipline strategies.
Measuring Instruments: a. Self-report journal b. Checklist of discipline strategies c. Does child remain at home?	*Activities:* Teach noncorporal discipline strategies; assess parenting skills for strengths and weaknesses.	*Activities:* Teach noncorporal discipline strategies; assess parenting skills for strengths and weaknesses.
	Practice Objective 3b: To increase Ms X's parenting skills under stressful conditions.	*Practice Objective 3b:* To establish a method whereby Mr. and Ms Y can evaluate good child discipline strategies with Sally.
	Activities: Inform Ms X about legal issues related to child abuse; provide reading related to single parenting; generate strategies for disciplining Billy under stressful conditions; evaluate Ms X's level of expectation for Billy's behavior.	*Activities:* Discuss views on discipline; inform Mr. and Ms Y about legal issues related to child abuse; coach Mr. and Ms Y in using new parenting techniques.
	Practice Objective 3c: To increase Ms X's feelings about her ability to discipline Billy.	
	Activities: Construct a self-anchored scale for monitoring; assess parenting skills for strengths and weaknesses; teach alternative discipline strategies.	

FIGURE 15.4   Case-Level Documentation of a Family Preservation Program

presented in Figure 15.3 is a useful tool for communicating the nature of a program's services to the various stakeholder groups as identified in Chapter 1. Figure 15.4 provides an example of case-level service conceptualization related to each of the first three program objectives. This case-level document shows how all client service delivery stems from the stated program objectives. Because program objectives are measured, the figure also gives examples of measuring instruments.

Practice Objectives

Practice objectives are developed for case-level functions within a particular program. Referring back to Figure 15.2, it is possible to visualize practice objectives as falling between the levels of program objectives and practice activities. The location of practice objectives in the pyramid illustrates their function in integrating the theory-base of program objectives with the action-orientation of practice activities. As mentioned, the development of program objectives is primarily an academic exercise based on literature reviews and professional deliberation. In contrast, practice objectives are constructed in consultation with each client.

Practice objectives must not only be logically linked to the program objectives, they must also fit with each client's specific situation. An inadequate link between a practice objective and program objective may result in an intervention plan that does not have program sanction or does not logically fit within the parameters of the program's goal. Furthermore, each practice objective must be agreeable to the client. The absence of client consent can obstruct the client's participation in the intervention and ultimately lead to a poor client outcome.

If all clients in a target group were alike, then it would not be necessary to conceptualize the program's services beyond the objectives. However, in the practice arena, clients present problems in a multitude of ways. For example, suppose the following two families are referred to the Family Preservation Program by Child Welfare Services.

Family X:
Family X was referred to the Family Preservation Program as a result of Ms X, a single mother, repeatedly striking her 10-year-old son Billy with a broom handle. The school nurse noted welts and bruises on Billy's arms and back and immediately notified the Department of Child Welfare. The investigative intake worker determined that Ms X was currently facing a great deal of financial stress, as she had recently lost her job. In her efforts to stay employed and take care of Billy, Ms X feels that she has no time for a social life and has no one to turn to for help. Just prior to the beating, Ms X caught Billy stealing $20 from her purse.

Family Y:
Family Y was referred to the Family Preservation Program as a result of a second-degree burn to the hand of 2-year-old Sally. The investigative social worker observed that Mr. and Ms Y appeared somewhat cognitively delayed. They explained that Sally did not obey their instruction to stop

playing by the stove. Acting on the advice of a neighbor, Mr. *Y* briefly touched Sally's hand to a heated stove element in an effort to teach her not to touch hot things in the future. Mr. and Ms *Y* stated that they were trying to teach their child a lesson, not harm her. In fact, they did give Sally proper medical attention for her burn.

The specific characteristics that differentiate Families *X* and *Y* are referred to as contextual variables. Although both families are legitimate candidates for the program's services (i.e., they fall within the program's goal and could benefit from the outlined seven program objectives), they clearly require different intervention strategies.

The case-level illustration (Figure 15.4) denotes how the hierarchical organization of program services can accommodate the unique service needs of each client. As all clients in the program must work toward one or more of the stated program objectives, common practice objectives can develop. For example, Figure 15.4 shows Clients *X* and *Y* as both working to improve their problem solving ability (Program Objective 2). On the other hand, individualized practice objectives are also included. For example, Ms *X* has a greater need to learn about problem-solving related to stressful situations (Practice Objective 2b); Mr. and Ms *Y* require more skill in recognizing problem situations (Practice Objective 2b).

The utility of the case-level document presented in Figure 15.4 is most evident when the tasks of treatment planning, monitoring client change, and case supervision are considered. Applied to one family, Figure 15.4 illustrates a format for a treatment plan. The practice objectives articulate the direction of client change, and the activities specify the action that needs to be taken. Detailing the intervention plan within the context of the program objectives and measurements permits logical monitoring of the treatment intervention and client outcomes. For example, if the practitioner can provide evidence that clients have increased their available positive social support over the course of the intervention (Program Objective 1), outcomes for that objective can be considered successful.

Achievement of any one practice objective does not indicate, or even suggest, that the overall treatment intervention is successful or that the corresponding program objective has been met. However, a systematic approach to conceptualizing human services can begin to clarify the complex nature of the helping process. Furthermore, it provides guidelines for monitoring client change and for directing discussion in supervision.

Activities

This text defines activities as actions or behaviors that move a client and practitioner toward the accomplishment of program and practice objectives. Practice activities are represented in Figure 15.2 by the broad base of the pyramid, reflecting the large range of intervention techniques available to front-line practitioners. Practice activities are placed below practice objectives because they are directly guided by the specifications of the latter. For instance, if the practice objective is to increase Ms *X*'s ability to praise her son, activities may include teaching Ms *X* how to offer praise, practicing expressions of praise, and providing a list of praise statements. This practice objective would exclude such actions as counseling Ms *X* about dissatisfaction with her boyfriend.

Practice activities are concrete in that when they occur, we are able to describe them. Teaching, engaging in role-plays, and providing information are concrete activities that are simple to observe and easy to describe. Other activities, such as paradoxical interventions and metaphoric counseling techniques, may be less obvious to an observer; but when asked, the worker sometimes is able to articulate the procedure or process. Activities may range from something as simple as providing a client with reading material to something as complex as facilitating a parent support group. Regardless of their level of complexity, activities have describable qualities that give other professionals an understanding of how to repeat them.

In terms of service conceptualization, practice activities offer us a great degree of creativity. Because they are not directly evaluated, their selection is not constrained by an evaluation design. Thus, in developing a schematic representation of service, we can creatively generate innovative activities to achieve our stated practice objectives more effectively. As the list of possible practice activities is endless, we need only articulate those thought to be instrumental in achieving a practice objective. Figure 15.4 provides a list of practice activities that correspond to various practice objectives developed for Families *X* and *Y*.

Although practice activities primarily serve case-level functions, they are also included in a program-level document such as the one presented in Figure 15.3. The purpose of including a sampling of practice activities in the program description is to communicate the nature of the program's approach to service delivery. At the case level, the articulation of practice activities is useful in assessing how effective they are in working toward the practice objectives on a case-by-case basis. As previously mentioned, practice activities that demonstrate reliable effectiveness may merit replication or adaptation to other client situations.

Creating Practice Objectives

The process of service conceptualization guides the construction of an effective and efficient service plan for each client. Practice objectives are developed within the parameters of the program objectives and the contextual variables of each client's situation. If too much emphasis is placed on program objectives, we run the risk of providing "cookie cutter" services. That is, we apply the same practice objectives to all clients regardless of their individual situations. On the other hand, if client contextual variables are overemphasized, workers may find themselves providing services in areas that go beyond the program's mandate.

For example, working in a family's home, a family support worker may observe excessive corporal punishment, in addition to witnessing marital discord, drug use, family isolation, or illiteracy on the part of a parent. Although one cannot rule out the possibility of a relationship between these social problems and child abuse within the family, the worker must determine which factors contribute most to the risk of physical abuse.

Staff members in the Family Preservation Program have a considerable task ahead of them if they try to achieve all seven program objectives with each client during the 10- to 12-week treatment period. Each worker must assess related problems for their impact on the target problem of child abuse within the family. For example, it may be that Mr. and Ms Y are heavy drug users, which interferes with their ability to improve social supports, learn new child management strategies, and so forth. If this is the case, a facilitative objective (e.g., to stop drug abuse) must be set before program treatment can be initiated.

Developing and Defining Practice Objectives

Practice objectives are at the heart of quality improvement at the case level. As a result, careful attention must be given to their development and definition. In the Family Preservation Program the client is the family. Therefore, the worker's initial task is to work with family members to determine what their understanding of the problem is. Because a major focus of the program is parents' physical abuse of their children, the onus of defining the problems rests primarily with the parents. Most parents will not openly state that they are physical abusers; the frustrations with discipline will more likely be expressed through discussion of other life problems. For example, Ms X may talk about her recent job loss or Billy's stealing behavior. In contrast, Mr. and Ms Y do not recognize the harm they have done; consequently, they do not feel they have a problem.

However defined, the practitioner begins with the problem that is most salient to the client. It is likely that the initial problems raised by a client will be facilitative or instrumental. For instance, Ms X, having recently lost her job, feels she cannot concentrate on problems with Billy until she has some assurance about her financial situation. Clearly, securing finances is a priority for Ms X. If the worker hopes to make gains with Ms X's parenting strategies, attention must also be paid to her unemployment situation. The intensity of the home-based service approach in the Family Preservation Program makes it possible to attend to instrumental and practice objectives concurrently. For example, the worker may offer to drive Ms X to the unemployment office (an instrumental objective). Having taken some action to deal with Ms X's first concern of employment, the worker can begin to explore Ms X's relationship with Billy.

When establishing practice objectives with a client, the worker can offer a great deal of encouragement by focusing on the client's strengths. In so doing, the practitioner can convey that clients have already made some significant gains. For example, suppose the worker notices that Mr. and Ms Y consistently verbalize how much they care for Sally. At the same time, the worker observes that Sally receives very little physical affection from her parents. In fact, on a rough count, the worker notes that Sally receives about eight corrective touches (e.g., slap to the wrist, spank on the bottom) to one affectionate touch (e.g., pat on the head, hug). The worker can suggest that Mr. and Ms Y do very well in verbalizing their positive feelings for Sally. As evidence of their achievement, the worker can repeat phrases or words used by Mr. and Ms Y to communicate caring messages to Sally. Having established a sense of accomplishment in this regard, the worker can suggest increasing positive physical contact. As a result, a practice objective of increasing daily positive physical contact between Sally and her parents can be established.

Note that the established practice objective fits within the context of two of the seven program objectives: the third, increasing parents' use of noncorporal child management strategies, and the sixth, increasing parental acceptance of the child. The process of further establishing the practice objective involves such tasks as refining terms and specifying responsibilities, timeframes, and methods of monitoring. For instance, the worker and Sally's parents must agree on what counts as "positive physical contact," when such contact should be given, where, and by whom. To measure this practice objective, the worker could simply ask Mr. and Ms Y for self-reports, observe parent-child interactions, or develop a tabulation sheet by which Mr. and Ms Y can monitor their own behaviors.

Measurement

Program objectives such as the three listed in Figure 15.3 are broad enough to encompass a wide range of practice objectives and activities. Finding a standardized measuring instrument to measure the complexity of each objective validly and reliably can hence be difficult. Chapter 6 discussed the important features of good measuring instruments, which include validity, reliability, sensitivity, non-reactivity, and utility.

Given the hectic pace of most human service programs, utility is an extremely important consideration in selecting a measuring instrument. Refer back to Figure 15.3 for instruments that measure the program's three objectives. Two standardized instruments are listed as well as other measuring strategies, such as client log and checklists. As mentioned in Chapter 5, measurement of practice objectives is often more rudimentary than measurement of program objectives. The amount of client change in reference to a practice objective is more often determined by inference and judgment rather than by relying on data derived from a standardized measuring instrument. That is, we sometimes have a sense that a change has occurred but cannot clearly articulate the basis for our belief. Delineating practice objectives and activities via the methods described in this book provides a means to translate intuitions into a more explicit and objective process.

To ensure reliability of data collection for program-level measures, workers in the Family Preservation Program are trained to administer measuring instruments in a manner that does not bias client responses. Measuring instruments are administered after clients agree to participate in the treatment process and before any formal intervention begins. Like all other components of services offered by the Family Preservation Program, measuring instruments are administered in the clients' home.

Although the techniques used for measuring program objectives and practice objectives may sometimes be similar, the purpose of the measurement is different for each. Measurement of program objectives determines the overall effectiveness of a program's approach: Are program results favorable at the level of the entire client group served? Conversely, practice objectives are independently measured for each individual client: Is the specific intervention working with this specific client?

In certain circumstances, practice objectives can also be measured at the program level. Such an opportunity arises when a practice objective is common to a group of clients in the program. When this occurs, data collected for a single client can be grouped with the data from other clients and this aggregated data allows us to examine client group-trends within the program.

For the most part, practice objectives are measured for case-level purposes. That is, measures of practice objectives are used to inform the client and the worker about any changes, which may or may not be a result of the intervention. Recall that practice objectives always relate to a client's knowledge, affects, or behaviors concerning a particular problem. It is therefore possible to monitor the presence (or absence), the magnitude, the duration, and the frequency of any of these three types of practice objectives. Establishing measures makes monitoring of practice objectives easy for clients. Furthermore, if practice objectives are defined so as to maximize success, clients can expect to feel a great deal of accomplishment.

Case-Level Evaluation

The majority of this chapter has so far been devoted to explaining the process of conceptualizing and evaluating service delivery from a practice perspective. Most human service workers have specialized knowledge in a particular practice area, but few couple practice expertise with research "know-how." Yet a commitment to the quality improvement process requires that practitioners be knowledgeable about evaluation methods, particularly those that are practice based.

The process of service conceptualization presented throughout this book provides the basis for developing practice-based evaluation. Service conceptualization provides practitioners with a framework for easing into evaluation designs. The terminology of *program goal*, *program objectives*, *practice objectives*, and *activities* can permit one to use evaluation procedures without losing sight of the program's purpose.

Informal Evaluation

Because the Family Preservation Program is contracted to provide services through the Department of Child Welfare, informal evaluations such as case conferences and private consultations with the child welfare worker are a regular part of its service activities. These case conferences are typically scheduled near the beginning and end of the 10-week intervention period. The initial case conference provides the Family Preservation worker with an overview of the family's problems as viewed by the child welfare worker. The final case conference provides an opportunity for the Family Preservation worker to comment on the client's progress and develop follow-up plans with the child welfare worker.

Collaboration with one or more professional helping systems is not uncommon for Family Preservation workers. Often, client problems spill over into other areas of the client's life, such as employment, school, family, and health care. For the Family Preservation worker it is particularly important to establish a clear line of communication with the child welfare worker, who wields the decision-making power to remove a child from a home. The detail of the program's service conceptualization can facilitate such communication. Program-level documentation (see Figure 15.3) can be offered to other helping professionals to avoid duplication of services across helping systems. Case-level documentation (see Figure 15.4) cannot be freely distributed, owing to issues of client confidentiality, but it can be used to guide discussion at case conferences.

The informal nature of the case conference provides a forum for generating tentative hypotheses about major family concerns. In most cases, such information provides the program worker with a starting place for work with the family. The worker must first check these areas of concern with the family and then develop a strategy to examine and treat the identified problems more objectively.

Formal Evaluation

The primary purpose of a case-level evaluation design is to provide the worker with concrete data to make intervention decisions on a case-by-case basis. Data obtained in the initial case conference can be explored to confirm any clinical hunches. Ideally, an explanatory case-level design should be used to evaluate the intervention for each client (to be discussed later). However, like life itself, evaluation designs must also be flexible. The contextual variables of the client situation will often dictate the most viable evaluation design. A worker has the choice to initiate, remove, or reinstate observation or intervention periods within a case-level design; however, the contextual variables of a client's situation greatly influence the nature of such decisions. In planned interventions, the worker may have more opportunity to select a design, but in crisis interventions, the evaluation or practice design is established by default.

Design Selection: Planned Intervention
Family Preservation workers use case-level designs as a method of monitoring client practice objectives. In cases where a practice objective and a program objective are the same, the worker uses the same instrument to measure both. In such cases the measuring instrument may be administered more frequently, perhaps at two-week intervals.

Factors that will influence the choice of design are the family's ability to measure their own practice objectives, availability of family members, and opportunity to manipulate a single intervention. Furthermore, the worker must orient the client to the terminology and procedures of evaluative practice. By stating the goal of the program, the worker helps clients to understand that services are specifically intended to enhance positive family functioning and prevent the removal of one or more children. The worker can explain to parents that it is important that they understand the intervention process and participate in monitoring their own results. The data collected from this formal evaluation procedure are presented at the case conference at the end of the intervention, where the child welfare worker and the Family Preservation worker decide upon the degree of risk still remaining in the family.

The intensity of home-based family services compels a practitioner to initiate several different intervention strategies concurrently. As mentioned previously, in the process of tackling a facilitative objective, the worker may also begin to work on a particular practice objective. Given that several important clinical activities are happening at once, it is even more important that the worker be clear about the specific interventions being used. In most cases, the worker will rely on a simple *AB* design, in which phase *A* reflects the initial assessment and observation period of family members and Phase *B* launches the intervention process. The *B* phase, however, is more typically a package of interventions rather than a discrete intervention technique.

Consider Ms *X*, who is interested keeping Billy at home. Rather than expressing this desire in terms such as, "I want to preserve my family unit" (e.g., the program goal), Ms *X* is more likely to say, "I want to feel proud of being a single mom." Further conversation with Ms *X* reveals that feeling proud means feeling she is doing a good job of raising Billy and using appropriate discipline. As Ms *X* explains her needs, the worker can reflect on several of the program's objectives as an anchor in determining how to tackle this problem with Ms *X*. The two decide to formulate a practice objective about discipline: to increase Ms *X*'s feelings about her ability to discipline Billy. This practice objective fits with the program objective to increase noncorporal child management strategies.

Because Ms *X* has expressed a desire to feel better about her parenting abilities, she and the worker develop a self-anchored scale to provide her with a means of evaluating her feelings as they relate to her interactions with Billy. Figure 15.5 shows a graph of Ms *X*'s feelings about her parenting ability during a baseline (*A*) and an intervention period (*B*). The graph shows that Ms *X* consistently scored low during the four days of baseline. After the onset of intervention, Ms *X* reported a general improvement in her self-reported discipline scores. The significance of this improvement is realized by reviewing the criteria for each level of the self-anchored scale.

Ms *X* determines that she feels best about her ability to parent when she is calm, able to notice Billy's strengths, and able to communicate clearly with Billy. When she feels this way, she scores herself a 7. At the other extreme, she does not feel good about her ability to parent when she is yelling at Billy or physically disciplining him;

in these instances, she scores a 1. Together, Ms X and the worker define discrete criteria for each level of the scale, as follows:

1. Very angry at Billy, yelling at Billy, use of physical discipline (hitting, holding Billy's arm, smacking Billy on the head)
2. Angry at Billy, yelling at Billy, threatening to hit Billy
3. Frustrated with Billy, raising voice, threatening to take away privileges (no follow-through)
4. Somewhat calm, able to send Billy to his room and call for support
5. Calm, able to send Billy to his room and remain calm
6. Somewhat encouraged, able to empathize with Billy, listen to Billy
7. Encouraged, able to notice Billy's strengths, clearly communicate with Billy, follow through with alternate discipline strategies

Thus, Ms X can easily score her feelings, at scheduled times each day, about her ability to parent. Note that although Ms X is measuring her feelings about parenting, these feelings have been operationalized to include behavioral indicators. Hence the worker and Ms X can be confident that any change in feeling also produces a corresponding change in interaction between Billy and his mother.

The limitation of using an *AB* design is that the practitioner cannot determine what factors directly contribute to the change in Ms X's feelings. Such data could be obtained if the worker used a more systematic approach at the onset of intervention. For example, after the initial baseline period, the worker could choose to use only supportive counseling techniques. Intuitively, the worker is examining Ms X's

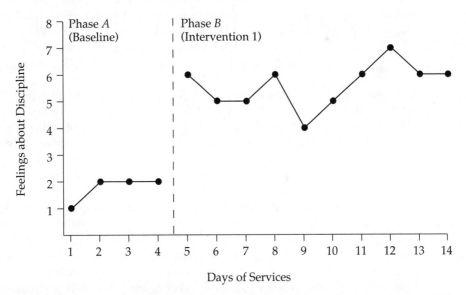

FIGURE 15.5 *AB* **Design: Ms X's Feelings about Ability to Discipline Billy (Average Score per Day)**

(Note: high scores = high feeling about discipline)

affects in relation to the amount of support she feels. If affects, as measured on the self-anchored scale, show no change, then the worker introduces a second intervention phase, such as teaching alternate discipline strategies. By delaying the beginning of the teaching intervention, the worker has effectively developed an *ABC* design. No matter what design used, however, the worker has a structure for continuous feedback that can contribute to the client's understanding of the situation and the worker's decisions about services.

Design Selection: Crisis Intervention

When a client situation involves a crisis, intervention must begin immediately, thus forming a *B* design. Such a design, exploratory in nature, generates data about whether or not the client shows change over time, but it does not tell the worker whether change was caused by the intervention because no initial measurements were taken.

For example, suppose Family *X* was referred to the program on an emergency basis. When the human service worker arrives at the family home, she witnesses Ms *X* and Billy in a hostile argument. When the worker enters the home, Ms *X* begins to sob uncontrollably while Billy darts from the house screaming, "I hate you and I'm not coming back."

Clearly, the worker does not have time to record any baseline data of family interactions, nor would it be appropriate to administer any standardized measuring instruments at this time. The worker immediately shifts to setting instrumental and facilitative objectives to get this family into a state of readiness for treatment. First, the worker must calm Ms *X* so that she and the worker can begin to deal with Billy's running away. Recall that the Family Preservation Program is associated with the Department of Child Welfare; Billy's safety hence becomes the main priority. Second, the Family Preservation worker and Ms *X* must develop a strategy to get Billy to return and stay at home so that efforts to improve the mother–son relationship can begin.

Once instrumental and facilitative objectives have been met (e.g., Billy has returned home and Ms *X* is receptive to intervention), the worker then has the opportunity to explain the intervention process to the family. At this point, the time for collecting pretest measures or establishing a true baseline phase (*A*) has passed. The worker's initial contact with the family has been primarily reactive. That is, the worker has relied on previous practice experience and general practice knowledge to help the family through the period of crisis.

Although formal measuring instruments were not used, this initial period of contact gave the worker a chance to assess contextual variables, such as Ms *X*'s willingness to accept help and patterns of communication between Ms *X* and Billy. Because the worker has already intervened in the family's situation, any initial measures will be biased by the previous interactions. Consequently, intervention begins with an intervention phase (*B*). Throughout the crisis period, the worker collects data by which to generate tentative hypotheses about how the family functions. One hypothesis put forth to Ms *X* is that she does not cope well under stress. After discussing stress and coping techniques, the worker and Ms *X* agree to generate individual practice objectives that deal with stress-related situations (Program Objective 7).

In this instance, the worker might use a standardized measurement that measures stress. Figure 15.6 presents a graph of Ms X's stress scores during the intervention phase. Notice that at the onset of intervention, Ms X recorded a high stress score during the first week of treatment. However, in the second and third weeks, Ms X recorded a considerable decline in her stress scores (Phase B_1). Although the scores show a general decline in stress during the B_1 phase, the worker cannot be sure whether this decline was caused by the selected intervention or whether it is simply the calm after the storm.

At this point, the worker may wish to withdraw the intervention for a brief period of time, thus creating a B_1AB_2 design and providing herself and the client with more confidence in the efficacy of the selected practice activities. Figure 15.6 shows that Ms X's stress scores increase when the intervention is withdrawn (Phase A) and, once again, show a decline when treatment is reintroduced (Phase B_2). Thus, change in Ms X's stress scores can be attributed, with some degree of confidence, to the specific intervention used.

Whatever the level of design utilized, a practitioner using monitoring evaluation methods can generate highly useful data, so long as he or she remains aware of the limits of the type of data gained from each design. For instance, a worker who has the opportunity to employ an explanatory A_1BA_2 design can feel confident that the observed effects were caused by the intervention. However, a worker who can employ only a B design can still generate data relevant to the selection of future intervention strategies.

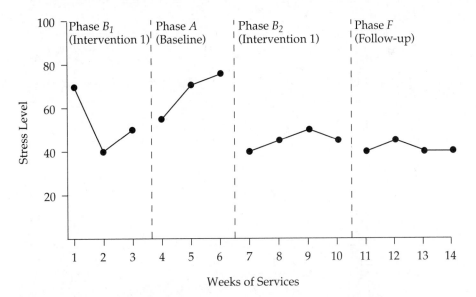

FIGURE 15.6 B_1AB_2F **Design: Ms X's Stress Levels over Time**
(Note: high scores = high stress levels)

Program-Level Evaluation

Whereas case-level evaluation produces data that are largely used to direct intervention planning, program-level data are concerned more with the overall effectiveness of program services on clients. Data obtained from program-level evaluations make a more solid contribution to our knowledge base because they offer measurements on a group of clients rather than on a single client.

Nevertheless, the options for design selection are similar. A program may begin with designs of an exploratory nature to generate ideas for further testing, and later move to more sophisticated research designs. The Family Preservation Program applies program-level evaluation in two ways: aggregated case-level designs, and group designs.

Aggregated Case-Level Designs

Single-case evaluation of clients with common practice objectives can be aggregated to examine service outcome across a group of clients. For example, suppose the program supervisor observes that in the past several months ten clients have formulated a practice objective relating to their feelings about ability to discipline. Furthermore, clients have used a self-administered 7-point self-anchored scale (higher scores indicate improvement) as a measuring instrument. In reviewing client files, the supervisor notes that in all ten cases, workers primarily used teaching and counseling techniques with each client. By grouping individual client outcome scores, the supervisor can assess the general change across the ten clients for the stated practice objective. The results are presented in Figure 15.7, where a

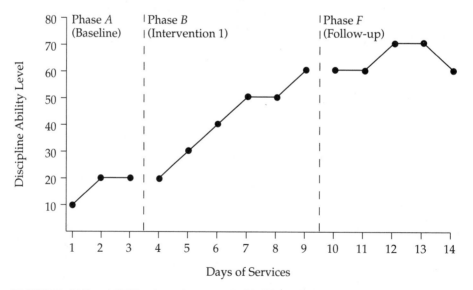

FIGURE 15.7   *ABF* Design: Average Self-Report Levels of Ability to Discipline Child over Time (*N* = 10)
(Note: high scores = high discipline levels)

general increase in scores suggests that teaching and supportive counseling are related to improvement as measured by the self-anchored scale for the ten clients included.

Group Designs

To measure program effectiveness, pretest and posttest scores on each program objective were gathered (refer to Figures 15.3 and 15.4). The overall change scores of all clients on the program objective of problem-solving skill show the general effectiveness of program services. The graph presented in Figure 15.8 shows the overall change in client scores from beginning to end of intervention for the dimension of problem solving. The graph only provides outcome data of the "overall" program effect on the 40 parents. Notice that the parents' average pretest score on the Problem-Solving Inventory was 100 and their posttest average score was 150. On this scale, higher scores indicate improvement. Thus, as a group, parents increased their problem-solving ability by 50 points. The same procedure could be used for the children as well.

Data on program objectives become more meaningful when considered in conjunction with data on the rates of family preservation. Figure 15.9 displays the percentage of families remaining together during and after the program's interven-

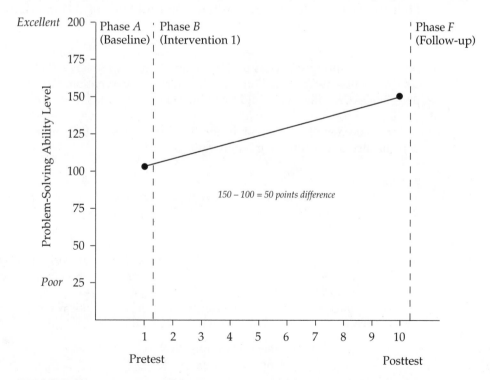

FIGURE 15.8 Pretest and Posttest Scores of Client's Problem-Solving Skills over Time (*N* = 40)

(Note: high scores = high problem-solving ability)

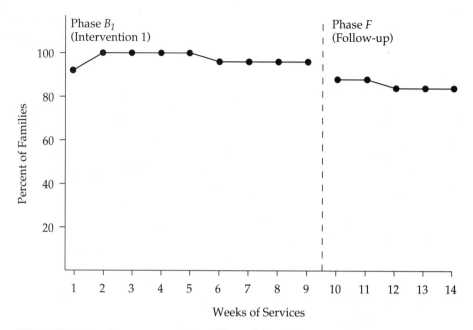

FIGURE 15.9   Percentage of Families with Child Living at Home during and after Intervention

tion (that is, during Phase *B* and follow-up). Figure 15.9 shows that 92 percent of children were residing at home at the start of intervention. At six weeks, the percentage of families with children living at home dropped to 96 percent. A further decline is shown at the end of the ten-week intervention where 88 percent of children successfully remained at home. After 14 weeks, the program reports 84 percent success in preserving family units served.

Testing Ideas

To test particular notions or trends that appear to arise from the grouped case-level data, different kinds of group designs can be employed. For example, suppose an administrator reviews the practice objectives of all clients served in the past six months. She notices that a large number of clients participated in the program's self-help support group. Single-case evaluations show that the majority of clients who participate in weekly support group meetings over six weeks display greater improvement than those who do not.

An explanatory design is initiated in an effort to confirm the effects of the support group. The design notation would be:

$$
\begin{array}{lcccc}
\text{Experimental Group:} & R & O_1 & X & O_2 \\
\text{Control Group:} & R & O_1 & & O_2
\end{array}
$$

To implement the design, workers randomly assign the start dates to clients. Those who begin earlier (the experimental group) participate in the support group. Clients with delayed starting dates form the control group, as they do not receive support group treatment for a three-week period. After six weeks, pretest and posttest scores of the two groups are compared to determine if there are clinical or statistically significant differences in client outcome. If clients who participate in the support group consistently show improvement over those who do not, then more confidence can be placed in the support group as a form of intervention.

Alternatively, if the group design proves to be unfeasible, the effectiveness of a support group can be tested at the case level and then aggregated to assess group change. Similar data can be derived from the aggregate results of an $A_1B_1A_2B_2$ case-level design. By withdrawing the support group intervention, one can compare single client scores across time. The advantage of a case-level design is that it allows the practitioner to determine who should participate in the group, as opposed to having participation determined by random selection.

Sampling

Sampling procedures in human service programs require even more flexibility than the construction of evaluation designs. In the human services, a convenience sample is often the only available sampling technique. Earlier in this chapter we mentioned that all clients in the Family Preservation Program are referred by the Department of Child Welfare. One would hope that the client referral process involved matching client need with the program's services. It is more likely, however, that clients are referred on the basis of availability of program openings. Regardless of which is the case, we can be certain that client referrals to the program are not random. We can also be certain that clients are drawn from a sampling frame of child welfare clients (see Table 9.1).

The clients referred to the program by Child Welfare constitute the sampling frame from which to examine the program's effects. How representative the sample is of the larger population of families involved with Child Welfare is generally not known. The representativeness of the sample can be determined by collecting sample demographic data, such as family composition, socioeconomic status, and age of family members, and comparing these data with a matched set of demographic characteristics from the Child Welfare population at large.

Sampling procedures can also be used within the program. Possibilities include randomly assigning clients to a worker, randomly assigning the order of intervention phases, or creating matched pairs of clients to compare variations of an intervention approach. Practitioners must, however, be cautious about generalizing findings from evaluations within the program to the population at large, as the overall program sample is biased.

Implementing Quality Improvement Designs

The utilization of evaluation procedures within the Family Preservation Program can bolster the program's credibility. Data generated by integrating evaluation and practice activities become an important resource for furthering knowledge and for making decisions within the various stakeholder groups.

Increasing Our Knowledge Base

The data generated in the program support the approach of preserving family units where children are at risk for physical abuse. Program results do not suggest that all children should remain in potentially abusive situations. Rather, the program offers cautious optimism that home-based intensive family services are effective in strengthening family ties and reducing the risk of child physical abuse. Program results also suggest that some parents who abuse their children are capable of learning alternative disciplining strategies. Such data are particularly useful to community education programs that aim to dispel myths about intrafamilial child abuse.

In addition to adding to knowledge about child abuse in families, the data raise further questions for exploration. For example, what family characteristics are associated with successful program outcomes? What types of intervention strategies are most effective? The quality improvement system employed by the program provides a basis for exploring these questions.

Guiding Decision Making

Program data can also be disseminated to various stakeholders to encourage informed decision making. Policymakers and funders, who probably have little direct contact with the program, can be provided an annual report presenting the program's results. Program successes can be highlighted to justify increased funding requests to expand or reinforce existing services. In instances where program results do not show great promise, program data can be used to identify areas for further program development. In this way, policymakers can be assured that monies are not spent on ineffective client services.

Program results can also be used to educate the general public about the program's services. Specifically, the positive effects of the program can be used in educating the public about providing services to parents who abuse their children. Successful program results can challenge popular notions, such as all children who are abused need to be rescued from "evil" parents.

Executive directors also require data for informed decision making. Access to empirical data can enhance an executive director's credibility in claiming overall program success. Furthermore, because the data have been collected by front-line workers, executive directors can feel assured that they have a comprehensive understanding of their programs' operations.

The use of data for decision making between practitioners and clients is a continual process. The ongoing feedback generated by monitoring evaluation procedures assists workers in developing service plans best suited to the individual client. Rarely does the feedback explain which intervention produced which outcome. Rather, the data are used to maximize the opportunity for improved client outcomes. For example, suppose the worker used relaxation exercises to reduce Ms X's stress level, but the measuring instrument shows no change on her stress scores. Furthermore, Ms X states that she feels uncomfortable using the relaxation techniques. Basing her decision on the feedback from the measuring instrument in addition to Ms X's comments, the worker could abandon the intervention and begin something new.

Decision Making

Most data generated from evaluation procedures in the Family Preservation Program are obtained through monitoring approaches and are exploratory in nature. Therefore, data are most appropriately used to make informed client-level decisions. That is, the data collected can strengthen knowledge obtained through practice experience and insight. Furthermore, the data provide an objective yardstick to assess the outcomes of the decisions made.

Because the data generated from the Family Preservation Program are client-based, decisions made from those data maintain a client focus. Consequently, all levels of decision making must consider the impact on direct client service delivery. Maintaining a client perspective becomes particularly important when decisions are made by stakeholders not directly related to the program.

Ethical Evaluation

When asked, most clients will agree to participate in a process that contributes to the overall effectiveness of the services they receive. However, it is essential for workers to receive written informed consent from all clients who are administered standardized measuring instruments. In the Family Preservation Program, such written consent is obtained from clients at the beginning of intervention, when the overall program approach is explained. Those who agree to full participation in the program sign a statement of informed consent. Clients have the option to decline participation on any or all standardized measurements by recording such exemptions on the consent form. The option to decline can be used at any point of program services. Clients are not, in any way, bound by the original agreement made when signing consent forms.

Summary

This chapter presented a concrete example of how one home-based family preservation program utilizes the material contained in the previous 14 chapters of this book. The chapter demonstrated via this example how the evaluative process helps human service professionals to obtain data for the purpose of quality improvement—the ultimate goal of *Evaluation and Quality Improvement in the Human Services.*

Part VI

CASE STUDIES

Case Study A
*Monitoring Practice on the Agency Level:
An Application in a Residential Care Facility*
RAMI BENBENISHTY

Case Study B
*Empirical Support for the Effectiveness of Respite Care
in Reducing Caregiver Burden: A Single-Case Analysis*
CHERYL A. RICHEY   VANESSA G. HODGES

Case Study C
*The Effectiveness of Outreach Counseling and Support
Groups for Battered Women: A Preliminary Evaluation*
ALLEN RUBIN

Part VI contains three excellent case studies that directly relate to the human service field. Many of the study questions at the end of each chapter use one or more of them. These cases demonstrate how the monitoring approach to the quality improvement process can be easily incorporated in day-to-day practice activities. In addition, they clearly illustrate how the concepts presented in this book can be used in evaluation studies at the case and program levels.

CASE STUDY A

Monitoring Practice on the Agency Level: An Application in a Residential Care Facility

RAMI BENBENISHTY

Source: R. Benbenishty, *Research on Social Work Practice,* 1(4), pp. 371–386. Copyright © 1991 by Sage Publications, Inc. Reprinted by permission of Sage Publications, Inc.

FISCHER (1981) CLAIMED that social work is undergoing a "paradigm shift," moving from the old ways of relying on "theoretical understandings, for the most part not empirically based" (p. 200), to a new approach: "empirical social work." Although not everyone concurs with Fischer's views (e.g., Gordon, 1983), it is evident that throughout the range of social work activities we see more reports on attempts and methodologies to improve systematic monitoring and evaluation of practice. As experience accumulates, it seems that we are now in a better position to appreciate both the great potential in systematic and empirical monitoring of practice and the many serious difficulties it faces when applied as an integral part of everyday practice. This article reports on an application of a monitoring system designed for residential care. The application is reported in order to illustrate the needs, possibilities, and dilemmas involved in such endeavors rather than to propose this system as a technology to be adopted "as is" or to present findings evaluating the outcomes of residential treatment.

The discussions on monitoring and evaluating practice focus on two directions: monitoring on the level of the individual client and program evaluation. Thus attempts are being made to develop single-case designs and to help individual practitioners use them to monitor and evaluate their interventions (e.g., Gambrill & Barth, 1980; Levy, 1983). A notable example is Hudson's (1987) work on the Client Assessment System, a computerized package to assist practitioners in monitoring individual clients. Parallel attempts are aimed at evaluating the overall effectiveness of agencies and of social programs (e.g., Austin et al., 1982; Brawley & Martinez-Brawley, 1988; Patton, 1978).

Benbenishty (1989a) proposed an approach that combines these two approaches and used this hybrid to monitor practice on the agency level. The heart of this approach is using simple single-subject designs to monitor intervention with each individual client while using the same instruments and language throughout the agency, thus allowing the aggregation of the information on the agency level.

This approach can be used in many agencies. For example, Benbenishty (1988) monitored task-oriented family interventions in a social agency in Israel. Each individual practitioner used single-case designs to monitor the intervention with each of the families in the caseload. The data from all practitioners were aggregated to create a data base describing the agency as a whole and to produce outputs relevant to all practitioners in the agency (Benbenishty & Ben-Zaken, 1988). This type of monitoring on the agency level seems to be especially useful in settings in which the clientele is relatively homogeneous and the practitioners are more interdependent in terms of sharing information. Residential care agencies for children seem to be in a special need for an approach that combines individual monitoring and agencywide accumulation of data.

Most residential care facilities have the policy that children's stays should be temporary and last only long enough to bring about changes that allow a long-term placement, preferably in a permanent home. Thus it is very important to monitor each child closely and regularly to assess progress and suitability of more desired settings. Furthermore, in most residential care facilities for children, the policy is of "therapeutic milieu." Consequently, many people are involved simultaneously with the same child, each taking care of different aspects of the child's life. There is a need, therefore, for a shared language among these different workers, each of them privy to only a few aspects of the child's life in care.

Residential care settings take a great responsibility over the children's lives. Therefore, they are (and should be) under heavy scrutiny by the public and the legal system that demand to know why the children are in care, what is being done for them, and how well they progress. This demand for accountability requires these agencies to know exactly the children's situation and what is being done for them and to document this information meticulously (cf. Paul, Mariotto, & Redfield, 1986). Moreover, taking into consideration the high turnover among staff members, it is also clear that the documentation should allow the assessment of change even if and when the workers who originally made these assessments have left the agency. On the basis of this analysis, we developed a monitoring system to respond to the need of practitioners in a residential care facility for children to assess the children's situation regularly, to document the information, and to share it with other practitioners in the agency and with outside systems.

Monitoring System at Methodist Children's Village

Methodist Children's Home Society (MCHS) is a comprehensive child welfare agency that provides residential treatment, educational daycare, and adoption, foster care, and pregnancy counseling services. The residential program, which is the focus of this article, provides treatment to 50 to 55 children who live on the grounds in a "village" of eight cottages. The children range in age from 6 to 13 years, and about 80 percent are boys. Treatment for the children is provided in each cottage by a team of childcare workers and the cottage supervisor. The monitoring system was designed mainly to support the clinical work of the six to seven caseworkers and their supervisors. The project lasted about 14 months and was terminated when the author left MCHS.

The monitoring system had several elements, some of which were implemented and others planned but not implemented within the timeframe of the project. For the purposes of this illustrative article, only the most important element of this system, a behavior checklist used to describe the children's behavior problem while in care, will be discussed (the interested reader is referred to Benbenishty, 1989b, for more details on other elements of the system).

MCHS was involved in a joint venture with a university to develop several practice aids to support their work. At the first stage of the project, the author was introduced to the staff as a university faculty member who was interested in aiding workers to develop procedures to monitor their practice. The author presented his approach in general terms and received the staff's consent to suggest a monitoring approach designed for their practice needs. After several group discussions, interviews with each of the caseworkers, and an extensive review of the literature, two alternative instruments were suggested to the workers: Quay and Peterson's (1983) Revised Behavior Problem Checklist (RBPC) and the Child Behavior Checklist

(CBCL; Achenbach & Edelbrock, 1978, 1983). The workers chose the Child Behavior Checklist as the main instrument.

The CBCL was developed originally for parents to report on their children's social competencies and behavior problems within the past six months. The 118 behavior problem items form (for boys 6 to 11 years old) 10 scales: Schizoid-Anxious, Depressed, Uncommunicative, Obsessive-Compulsive, Somatic Complaints, Social Withdrawal, Hyperactive, Aggressive, Delinquent, and Other). Items and scales may also be combined to describe higher-order domains of internalizing and externalizing problem behaviors. Achenbach and Edelbrock (1983) conducted extensive studies to validate this checklist (for a recent study and a review, see Jones, Latkowski, Kircher, & McMahon, 1988).

The checklist was modified to suit the needs of the agency. These modifications were necessary because the children were not residing at home and because the intended use was for frequent assessments done as an integral part of clinical work and not as part of a one-shot research endeavor. At MCHS, each worker used the behavior problem part of the checklist at the end of each month to describe the child's behavior in the past month. Their reports were based on their observations and on consultation with other staff members working with the child, especially cottage supervisors. It should be noted that whereas in some cases the cooperation between the social worker and the cottage supervisor was excellent and the forms were completed as part of routine mutual briefings, in other cases strife between factions of team members did not allow good cooperation among them in this task.

As mentioned, the checklist was modified for use by the workers and not by the parents and was completed every month instead of every six months. Therefore, the preface to the list of items had to be modified accordingly. After three months of use, the checklist was modified even further by deleting those items that formed the scales of Obsessive-Compulsive, Somatic Complaints, and Other (all graphs presented later exclude these scales to preserve uniformity). This modification was done to facilitate completion of the scale and on the basis of the workers' requests and of the preliminary analysis that showed little frequency of these items. Completion of the checklist took from 5 to 15 minutes per child, except in cases in which a lengthy discussion about the child was prompted by the joint work on the checklist. All these changes in the checklist made validity and reliability findings reported in the literature not directly relevant to the present study. Future applications should collect reliability and validity data relevant to the revised application of the CBCL or any other instrument used to monitor practice.

The completed forms were submitted to the author at the end of each month and then fed to a personal computer. The file was then processed by two separate programs: Lotus 1-2-3 and SPSS (Nie, Hull, Jenkins, Steinbrenner, & Bent, 1975). The statistical package of the SPSS program was used to compute the scores on the various scales and to create a data base that accumulated over time. The author has used the data in extensive statistical analyses, combining the data from the checklist with additional data from the children's files. The Lotus spreadsheet program was used mainly to graph the information processed by the statistical program. All programming and analyses were done by the author and did not require extensive programming experience or skills. Processing of the monthly reports and the printing of the reports and graphs lasted from 1 to 3 days, using the computing resources of the University of Michigan and the author's personal computer.

The information culled from the checklist was processed and reported back to the workers. In the following sections, the various reports are presented separately for each level of analysis. Samples of these reports are provided here to illustrate the great potential in processing information collected regularly by practitioners as part of their everyday professional work.

Analyzing Data Regarding the Individual Child

The Problem Profile

The workers used the checklist to report on the child's problems. The computer programs scored the checklist on the basis of the CBCL manual. For each scale, the mean score of the items checked in that scale as problematic was computed. A "Total" scale was added for the mean of all items in the checklist. For ease of interpretation, the mean was transformed from the original scale of 0–2, to a scale of 0–200, by multiplying the raw score by 100.

A bar graph was generated, describing the "problem profile" of the child in the past month. The height of the bars in the graph represented the scale score. This graph allowed the staff to see the areas in which the child had greater or fewer problems. It should be emphasized that this graph does not compare the child with any preestablished norms but rather compares the scores across the various problem areas.

Figure A-1 presents a problem of a child in his first month at MCHS. It can be seen that most of the child's problems were related to being aggressive, hyperactive, and delinquent. There were fewer problems in what are considered the "internalizing" scales (e.g., Depressed, Uncommunicative). In addition to this information, workers were given the *national norms* on the various scales (taken from Achenbach & Edelbrock, 1983). Thus they could compare the score of a specific child on a scale with what is considered "normal" or "clinical" for each scale. Keeping in mind the modifications in the present application, this information aided in interpretation of the scores.

Time Series of Problem Profiles

The child's scores for the past several months were graphed to allow identification of trends over time. Figure A-2 presents a picture of a child's scores on the problem scales for a 5-month period. Changes can be seen following the month of April. There was a considerable increase in problems in May, whereas in June there was a return to levels similar to the February–April period. Caseworkers could then interpret the graph, trying to identify the significant events that could explain these changes.

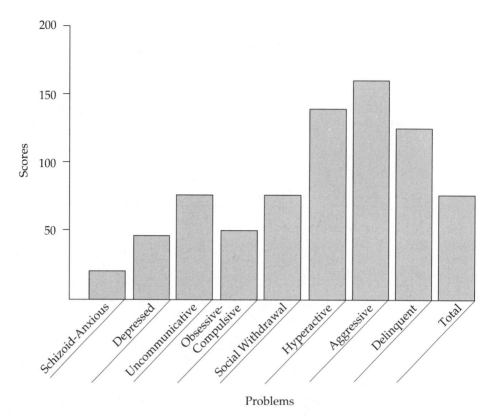

FIGURE A-1   Problem Profile: Johnson S.—February

Because the composite scales combine many items and form a score that cannot be directly interpreted in clinical terms (Achenbach & Edelbrock, 1978), some workers felt they should get information that is closer to the "raw data." Thus in addition to graphing the scores on the composite scales, the workers were given the list of all items on the checklist with the scores for each month. (Because the *raw scores* were provided, no transformation was needed for this output.) Table A-1 is an excerpt of a listing of a child's scores on several items for a period of six months.

Table A-1 illustrates the use of time-series data regarding specific behaviors. It can be seen that for certain behaviors, there were no problems at all during that period (e.g., "overeating" and "overtired"); in others, the problems seem to have subsided (e.g., "refuses to talk" and "sets fires," whereas other problems persisted for the whole period (e.g., "teases a lot" and "trouble in sleep").

Analyzing Data across Groups of Children

The system generated outputs that presented the scores of each individual within a group of children. This presentation allows a *comparison* between each child and a

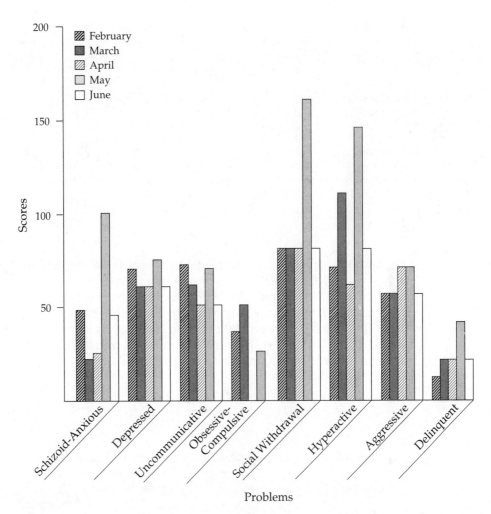

FIGURE A-2   Changes over Time: Robert R.—February to June

relevant reference group drawn from the MCHS population. When the scores of all the children on a certain scale (or on the total score) in MCHS are rank ordered, it is possible to identify which children seem to have more problems and which seem to have fewer (see Table A-2).

The upper part of Table A-2 presents a listing of the children, rank ordered according to their scores on the "Total" scale in a specific month. The lower part of the table presents a listing of the children rank ordered according to the *degree of progress* in their total score in the previous five months. Such reports can help identify those children who are extreme in their scores in order to help treatment planning. For instance, if a child is found in one of the extremes of the list month after month, it may trigger a discussion as to whether the child should remain in the facility.

TABLE A-1   Changes over Time: J. R., February–June 1987

	February	March	April	May	June	Sum
Trouble in sleep	2	2	2	2	2	10
Refuses to talk	2	2	1	1	0	6
Overeating	0	0	0	0	0	0
Sets fires	2	1	0	0	0	3
Overtired	0	0	0	0	0	0
Teases a lot	2	1	2	1	2	8

Note: Scale was scored 0 = *not true*, 1 = *somewhat or sometimes true*, 2 = *very true or often true*.

In addition, graphs also presented scores for all the children in a worker's caseload. This helped in setting priorities and in caseload management. Similarly, a graph describing all the children in the same cottage helped in identifying children who exhibited behavior that was very different from the other children in the same cottage. This type of analysis should be used cautiously. On one hand, it helps the practitioner gain perspective and see how extreme a certain client behavior is. On the other hand, it may focus attention on certain children and single them out as being the "toughest" children.

TABLE A-2   Rank Ordering of Children on Aggression

Name	Aggression Score
David R.	20
Dan M.	22
Sam J.	22
Jane L.	130
Moses A.	135
Danya L	138

Name	*Improvement in Aggression Score (February–June)*
Sam J.	–58 (improvement)
Rick F.	–55
Sandra M.	–50
Johnson K.	0 (no change)
Sara K.	+20
Danya L	+25
Albert F.	+40 (deterioration)

Analyzing the Aggregated Data

The system generated outputs that aggregated data and described groups of children. First, the village as a whole was described. This allowed identification of the more prevalent problems in the agency. For instance, the analysis showed that the problems "argues a lot," "demands attention," "disobedient at home/MCHS," and "disobedient in school" were the most frequent. In terms of the composite scores, it was possible to describe the profile of the "average child" in MCHS and to compare it with children outside of the facility to whom the CBCL was administered by others (this comparison could be done only tentatively due to the revisions introduced in this application).

Moreover, the aggregated data allowed a sophisticated statistical analysis to identify profiles of children in terms of their behavior problems. In a cluster analysis conducted on the data, it was found that most of the children shared a similar problem profile, and the differences between the two clusters of children related more to how severe the problems were rather than to a different profile of problems. Hence Cluster 1 consisted of children with fewer problems than children in Cluster 2. Figure A-3 presents the mean profiles for the two clusters of children.

From Figure A-3 it can be seen that the two problem profiles differ mainly in the "externalizing" subscales of Social Withdrawal, Hyperactivity, Aggression, and Delinquency. The children in Cluster 2 had more problems in these scales.

The data were also aggregated by cottages, thus allowing a comparison across cottages in terms of specific problem areas or in terms of the overall degree of problem behavior. Figure A-4 is a graph that was presented to the supervisors of the cottage personnel and to other members of the clinical leadership. This figure indicates which cottages have a concentration of children with a specific problem (aggressive behaviors in this example) and which cottages have children with fewer problems. It can be seen that Cottage A has a very high mean score on the aggression scale, whereas Cottage F has far fewer problems of aggression than the rest. In some instances, such a report may have direct impact on changes in allocation of children to cottages. It may also have effects on identifying training goals for each team of workers, according to the needs that are more pertinent to the specific cottage.

In addition to these almost automated reports, the monitoring system produced more complex, comprehensive, and integrative reports. The children's files were analyzed and translated into computerized records. This allowed statistical analyses that examined sources for variance in the children's scores on the CBCL and in the changes that occurred during the child's stay. Thus, for instance, a significant association was found in an interesting direction: Whereas children of delinquent mothers showed mean progress of 12 points on the total CBCL score, it was only 3 points for the others, and whereas the 10 children of delinquent fathers progressed 14 points on average, the rest had only 2 points of mean progress. These specific findings may not be clinically useful, but they exemplify the potential to identify patterns in the data that may be useful in diagnosis, in assessment of prognosis, and

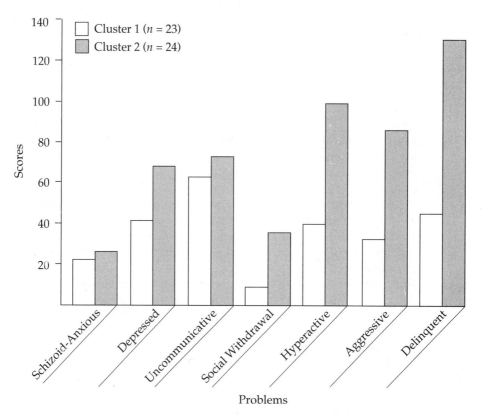

FIGURE A-3   Comparing Clusters of Children

in the long run, in planning of interventions based on child characteristics and background on entry into care.

Discussion

This article has reported on systematic monitoring of children in residential care. It illustrates the range of possibilities that opens up when all the staff members of an agency use the same monitoring instrument systematically and the data are processed, aggregated, and charted to aid in practice. It is sometimes surprising to see how rich and informative the products of such a monitoring system can be, particularly when acquired with relatively limited effort on the part of the workers.

As shown in the previous sections, the data collected can yield many important outputs that should, and can, be integrated into the workers' clinical judgment. Furthermore, the *process* involved in participation in systematic monitoring was very important. Workers were required to be constantly aware of and update many aspects of the child's life. They had to increase their cooperation with other staff

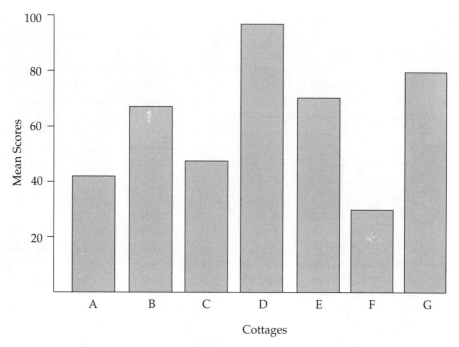

FIGURE A-4   CBCL across Cottages: Aggression Scale—June

members in order to get a more accurate and comprehensive picture of the child. They also had to search for more varied and timely information in order to interpret and to understand the child's situation and changes in his or her behavior as reflected in the charts.

The project reported here indicated not only the potential in such endeavors but their pitfalls and possible dangers. To make monitoring an integral part of practice, it was important to find an instrument and procedures that would not demand too much of the practitioners. The CBCL seemed to be an excellent choice. In the present context, however, the CBCL had its limitations (as any other single instrument would). One shortcoming was that it was seen by the workers as too long and thus had to be shortened. But, as mentioned, this modification made available normative and psychometric data not directly relevant. Future applications should directly assess the inter- and intraworker reliability in the use of the instrument.

Another limitation was that the composite scales in the checklist are empirically, not clinically, based. Consequently, certain items are associated with scales that seem to be unrelated to their content. For instance, the items "poor school work" and "poorly coordinated and clumsy" belong, according to the CBCL manual, to the Hyperactive Behavior Scale.

While the author did try to explicate the rationale and details of the instrument, it was very difficult for the workers to keep in mind all the limitations while interpreting the findings. In a number of cases, the author felt that for the sake of brevity and simplicity, fewer warnings and reservations should be voiced. This decision, however, may have compromised the validity of some of the workers' interpretations.

The difficulty in weighing the relative importance of the reports of a monitoring system against the limitations of the instrument being used is exacerbated by the use of computers. Computers can produce very impressive statistics and charts. These products may be based on data of varied quality, including unreliable and invalid data. Recipients of the computer output cannot assess the quality of the input that was the basis for the output. Thus we have identified what might be termed *the illusion of accuracy*. A checklist may have been completed mindlessly or by someone who does not know the child well, but the computer graph indicates that the score on a certain scale is 75.5, creating the impression that some accurate assessment has taken place.

Our informal attempt to assess the overall cost-benefit balance of this project yielded a mixed picture. On the positive side, the investments in using the checklist were relatively minor—completing the checklist took from 5 to 15 minutes per child and the analysis required relatively little time and personnel. The products of this monitoring system were varied, rich, and timely. Several workers were very content with their participation in the project and felt that they were being rewarded adequately for their effort by the outputs of the system. In fact, at a certain point in the project, the author became aware of complaints that participation in the project required too much work and suggested that the checklist be completed every three months, instead of every month. Other workers, however, said that the information provided every month was very useful and any change in frequency of reports would reduce their relevance.

In contrast to this encouraging response, some of the workers have voiced their opposition to the project repeatedly. These negative reactions were much more moderate as the project proceeded and some of its benefits to the workers became more visible. Nevertheless, one staff member maintained a negative reaction throughout the project, only two were very positive, and the rest were rather lukewarm or indifferent to the project.

When the author had to leave the agency, the project was immediately terminated. This lack of continuity is a clear indication of a very tenuous acceptance of the system. Reasons for difficulties in acceptance can be traced to tensions among professional and administrative staff, intensive turnover in key positions in the agency, and lack of support by the facility's administrative director. Still, the fact that social workers did not choose to demand the project's continuation implies that problems in integration have deeper roots.

Difficulties in acceptance seem to be directly related to the changes in traditional practice introduced by the project. Throughout the project, it was clear that the periodic use of the checklist was not accepted by some staff members as an integral part of practice. The reports produced by the author were considered interesting and relatively relevant but did not become an indispensable element of most of the workers' clinical judgment and decision making. One of the reasons might have been the focus of the checklist on observable behaviors whereas some of the workers were much more interested in intrapersonal dynamics and the motives and reasons for the child's behaviors.

One way of dealing with the difficulties in integration of such a monitoring system into daily practice is to make it more comprehensive and to address as many information needs as possible (Benbenishty, 1989a). Additional instruments can be used for standardized intake, to describe the interventions, to monitor goal attainment, and to cover other aspects of the child's life (e.g., content of symbolic play, defenses, and coping style). Such a system can provide more of the information deemed relevant by the workers. The problem is, of course, that such a system demands much deeper commitment and investment of the practitioners and administrators of the agency.

Our general conclusion from this experience is that there are clear benefits to implementing a clinical information system to monitor practice. Such a system, however, should be more comprehensive at the outset, covering as many practice-relevant areas as possible. To help the assimilation of this system, more support and legitimacy should be provided by the administrative and clinical leadership. Work routines should be modified in a cooperative effort by the clinical leadership and the social workers. These routines should get full support from the administration and become an accepted and required mode of operation. Practitioners who consider working in such agencies would be able to judge in advance whether they accept the practice orientation and values underlying this empirical approach to monitoring.

In fact, the optimistic conclusion that monitoring systems can be integrated to practice was the basis for our continuing efforts to design systematic monitoring for other agencies as well. Benbenishty and Oyserman (in press) developed a national monitoring system to cover all foster care in Israel. The design and implementation of this system has been influenced to a large extent by the experience in the project described here and is being disseminated throughout the Israeli foster care system.

References

Achenbach, T. M., & Edelbrock, C. S. (1978). The classification of child psychopathology: A review and analysis of empirical efforts. *Psychological Bulletin, 85,* 1275–1301.

Achenbach, T. M., & Edelbrock, C. S. (1983). *Manual for the child behavior checklist and revised child behavior profile.* Burlington: University of Vermont, Department of Psychiatry.

Austin, M., Cox, G., Gottlieb, N., Hawkins, J., Kruzich, J., & Rauch, R. (1982). *Evaluating your agency's programs.* Beverly Hills, CA: Sage.

Benbenishty, R. (1988). Assessment of task-oriented family interventions with families in Israel. *Journal of Social Service Research, 11,* 19–43.

Benbenishty, R. (1989a). Combining the single-system and group approaches to evaluate treatment effectiveness on the agency level. *Journal of Social Service Research, 12,* 31–47.

Benbenishty, R. (1989b). Designing computerized clinical information systems to monitor interventions on the agency level. *Computers in Human Services, 5,* 69–88.

Benbenishty, R., & Ben-Zaken, A. (1988). Computer-aided process of monitoring task-centered family interventions. *Social Work Research and Abstracts, 24*(1), 7–9.

Benbenishty, R., & Oyserman, D. (in press). A

clinical information system for foster care in Israel. *Child Welfare.*

Brawley, E., & Martinez-Brawley, E. (1988). Social programme evaluation in the USA: Trends and issues. *British Journal of Social Work, 18,* 391–431.

Fischer, J. (1981). The social work revolution. *Social Work, 26,* 199–206.

Gambrill, E., & Barth, R. (1980). Single case designs revisited. *Social Work Research and Abstracts, 16*(1), 15–18.

Gordon, W. (1983). Social work revolution or evolution? *Social Work, 28,* 181–185.

Hudson, W. W. (1987). *The clinical assessment system.* Tallahassee, FL: Walmyr.

Jones, R., Latkowski, M., Kircher, J., & McMahon, W. (1988). The Child Behavior Checklist: Normative information for inpatients. *Child and Adolescent Psychiatry Journal, 27,* 632–635.

Levy, R. (1983). Overview of single-case experiments. In A. Rosenblatt & D. Waldfogel (Eds.), *Handbook of clinical social work* (pp. 583–602). San Francisco: Jossey-Bass.

Nie, N., Hull, C., Jenkins, J., Steinbrenner, K, & Bent, D. (1975). *Statistical package for the social sciences* (2nd ed.). New York: McGraw-Hill.

Patton, M. (1978). *Utilization-focused evaluation.* Beverly Hills, CA: Sage.

Paul, G., Mariotto, M., & Redfield, J. (1986). Assessment purposes, domains, and utility for decision making. In G. Paul (Ed.), *Assessment in residential treatment settings* (pp. 1–26). Champaign, IL: Research Press.

Quay, H., & Peterson, D. (1983). *Interim manual for the Revised Behavior Problem Checklist.* Coral Gables, FL: University of Miami Press.

Empirical Support for the Effectiveness of Respite Care in Reducing Caregiver Burden: A Single-Case Analysis

CHERYL A. RICHEY   VANESSA G. HODGES

Source: C. A. Richey and V. G. Hodges, *Research on Social Work Practice*, 2(2), pp. 143–160. Copyright © 1992 by Sage Publications, Inc. Reprinted by permission of Sage Publications, Inc.

PEOPLE ARE LIVING LONGER, resulting in increasing numbers of older citizens. In the United States the proportion of people aged 65 years and over has doubled since the beginning of this century and is expected to triple within the early part of the next century (Siegel &Taeubex, 1982). In 1980, the elderly represented slightly over 11 percent of the population (American Association of Retired Persons, 1986). With greater life expectancies, percentage increases have been particularly marked among the old-old (75 and over); a group especially vulnerable to ill health and consequent dependency (Archbold, 1983). Furthermore, demographic trends suggest that the majority of older persons will continue to be women, resulting in an aged population that is primarily a female society (Hooyman, 1987).

These population trends, along with the policy shifts of deinstitutionalization and diversion (Briar & Ryan, 1986), raise serious questions regarding society's continuing ability and willingness to address the needs of its older members and their home-based caregivers. Indeed, the increase in the proportion of older persons coupled with a decline in federal funds for formal, comprehensive programs has led to forecasts of increasing demands on the family to provide support services for their older members (Stoller, 1983). As a result, parent-caring, the provision of needed services to functionally impaired elderly parents, is increasing proportionately with the number of frail elderly in the population. Contrary to popular belief, the immediate family remains the major source of support for dependent older persons (Lang & Brody, 1983). Further, women, who themselves may be 60 or 70 years old, constitute about 80 percent of the family members providing support for elderly relatives (Brody, 1985).

Despite the positive rewards of caregiving, for example, facilitating a comfortable and loving environment for one's mother, achieving one's personal standards of familial or intergenerational duty, or developing closer, more intimate family relationships (cf. Hooyman & Lustbader, 1986), taking care of a chronically ill or incapacitated elderly person is nevertheless a progressively difficult, all-consuming activity. Enormous effort is required to feed, dress, and bathe another adult, who may be unresponsive or even hostile to such assistance. These physical caregiving tasks do not include the additional responsibilities that come from providing close supervision and interpersonal stimulation to the elder.

The demands, stress, risks, and costs associated with caregiving have been discussed by many authors (e.g., Biegel, Sales, & Schulz, 1991; Cantor, 1983; Johnson, 1983; Montgomery, Gonyea, & Hooyman, 1985; Moroney, 1980; Pearlin, Mullan, Semple, & Skaff, 1990; Pruchno & Resch, 1989; Sheehan & Nuttall, 1988; Soldo & Myllyluoma, 1983; Zarit, Reever, & Bach-Peterson, 1980). Caregiver burden, although defined and measured somewhat differently across studies, is generally accepted as a multidimensional concept, which can be divided into two broad categories. The first category, termed "objective burden," "caregiving impact" (Poulshock & Deimling, 1984), or "primary stress" (Pearlin et al., 1990), involves strain associated with caregiver responsibility for providing personal care and for managing specific tasks related to activities of daily living (ADL) and supervision of family members who are extremely confused or tend to wander as a result of their disability. These effects largely focus on the concrete or instrumental impact of caring on caregivers' daily lives, including family relationships and social activities. The second broad category of burden identified as "subjective burden" (Poulshock & Deimling, 1984) or "secondary stress" (Pearlin et al., 1990) involves caregivers' perceptions, appraisals, and interpretations of their experiences as tiring, difficult, or upsetting, which can be influenced by such feelings as low self-esteem, loss of self, and role strain.

Caring for severely impaired older parents often begins when the caregiver is herself in middle age or early old age, thus marking the beginning of another "caregiving career" (Briar & Ryan, 1986, p. 23). For example, a recent study of 50 caregivers and their frail relatives reported that 48 percent of the caregivers were adult daughters, and the mean caregiver age for the entire sample was 60.34 years (Marks, 1988). In a British study of 41 adult daughters caring for mothers on a coresident basis, 44 percent reported beginning their full-time caring responsibilities when they were between 50 and 59 years old (Lewis & Meredith, 1988). Like child rearing, meeting the dependency needs of a parent is extremely demanding physically and psychologically. Unlike child rearing, in which the child's physical and emotional dependence gradually diminishes, parent-caring demands continue or increase over time (Archbold, 1983).

Indeed, the toll of caregiving appears high. Whether propelled by love, concern, and/or guilt, caregivers frequently provide nonstop care, without respite, until they become emotionally, financially, or physically impaired themselves (Briar & Ryan, 1986). Cantor (1983) observed that family supports tend to erode and strain on the giver tends to increase over time, especially when the older family member suffers from severe, chronic conditions. Numerous studies now document caregiver feelings of burden and stress (Archbold, 1983; Arling & McAuley, 1983; Cantor, 1983; Clark & Rakowski, 1983; Pearlin et al., 1990; Pruchno & Resch, 1989; Stoller, 1983). Caregivers themselves often report feeling physically and emotionally drained (Poulshock & Deimling, 1984). Over 80 percent of the caregivers surveyed in one study reported role stress, and half saw their stress as a serious problem (Johnson, 1983).

Other hazards of parent-caring that have been identified by caregivers include decreases in their own independence and mobility, for example, limited opportunities to pursue activities outside the home, such as shopping, maintaining social contacts, and engaging in recreational or cultural events (Moroney, 1980). Some have suggested that the most prevalent and most severe impact of family caregiving is this restriction of freedom for the caregiver (Archbold, 1983; Cantor, 1983). Not surprisingly, one effect of these restrictions for caregivers of the elderly is feeling entrapped (Moroney, 1976).

Because family members providing continuous care make numerous personal sacrifices, it is not uncommon for intense, negative emotional reactions to develop, including bitterness about their situation (Doll, 1976) and resentment, hostility, and even violence toward the elderly person (Clark & Rakowski, 1983; Hickey & Douglass, 1981). When physical, economic, or emotional burdens reach intense levels, the caregiver's recognition of and sensitivity and responsiveness to the needs of a frail elder are greatly reduced. Thus adult caretakers, overtaxed by caregiving demands, may be at greater risk for elder neglect and abuse (Hickey & Douglass, 1981).

Although there is increasing recognition of the multifaceted burden that accompanies in-home caregiving, ways to reduce the burden have not received commensurate attention (Gallagher, 1985; Zarit, Reever, & Bach-Peterson, 1980). Several authors have urged that research and service agendas include a systematic examination of the effects of respite or substitute care and other support services with high-risk, highly stressed family caregivers (Briar & Ryan, 1986; Zarit, Todd, & Zarit, 1986). Respite care has been defined as temporary care of a disabled person that provides relief to the primary caretaker or individual responsible for ongoing patient well-being (Bader, 1985; Salisbury & Intagliata, 1986). The most fundamental purpose of respite care is to provide rest for caregivers (Foundation for Long Term Care, 1983; Montgomery & Prothero, 1986). Respite services are generally short-term and time-limited, and can include companionship, homemaking services, and total personal care. Location of respite services also varies, based on client needs and agency capacity. Some services are provided in the family home, whereas others are provided in hospitals or community care facilities.

Respite care has a brief but important history in maintaining chronically ill and disabled family members in their family homes. Formal respite services were first provided in the 1970s for deinstitutionalized developmentally disabled children (Cohen, 1982). Studies evaluating the outcome of these services support their effectiveness (Intagliata, 1986; Joyce, Singer, & Isralowitz, 1983; Upshur, 1983; Wikler, Hanusa, & Stoycheff, 1986). For example, families caring for developmentally disabled persons report improved level of functioning, including getting along better with each other, improved marital relationships, reduced social isolation, greater satisfaction with interactions with the disabled family member, and reduced likelihood of institutional placement (Joyce et al., 1983; Pagel & Whitling, 1978; Wikler et al., 1986).

Because the application of respite care services with geriatric populations is relatively recent (Crossman, London, & Barry, 1981; Lawton, Brody, & Saperstein, 1989), few large-scale empirical studies have been conducted to evaluate the impacts of formal respite care (Gonyea, Seltzer, Gerstein, & Young, 1988). However, one recent quasi-experimental study, comparing 25 families receiving formal respite service with 25 families waiting for service, offers beginning evidence that respite care can significantly reduce caregiver stress among families providing full-time, in-home care to a frail elderly relative (Marks, 1988). The present case study, which employs an experimental single-system design methodology ($A_1B_1A_2B_2$), attempts to garner additional empirical support for the effectiveness of respite care as an intervention to reduce caregiver burden. *Burden* for this caregiver included being homebound or trapped by caregiving responsibilities and feeling resentful and angry toward a frail, dependent, elderly mother.

Method and Procedures

Client

The client, Anne, a 69-year-old Caucasian woman, widowed for 7 years, was sole caregiver for her 99-year-old mother, Mrs. N. Anne had been caring for her mother for 12 years when the referral was received by a hospital-based elder care project for in-home evaluation and case management follow-up. The referral was initiated by Mrs. N's physician because of the "stress" created for Anne by her mother's progressively greater care needs. Anne complained of tension, heart palpitations, and fatigue.

A BA-level social worker, who functioned as case manager, made an initial visit to Anne's home, which was located in a rural-suburban community about 45 miles from a major northwest city. Assessment of Mrs. N's physical condition, ability to complete ADL, and mental status revealed her marked dementia and cognitive loss. The care situation was further complicated by the mother's recently fractured wrist secondary to a fall. A history of cardiac arrhythmias also was noted. Mrs. N was functionally dependent on her daughter for all her personal care, such as bathing, dressing, and toileting, and she needed standby assistance when ambulating. The mother revealed minimal awareness of her surrounding environment. She recognized her daughter and knew she was "at home," but she was unable to provide specific information regarding past or present events. Despite these impairments, Mrs. N was not prone to disoriented wandering or to verbally or physically abusive behavior. She was calm and composed during home visits and expressed positive feelings about her daughter. Although expressing unawareness of any problems or concerns, Mrs. N verbalized agreement to case management services.

An inventory or list of concerns was generated with Anne during subsequent discussions. She also completed the 13-item Caregiver Strain Index (CSI) (Robinson, 1983), which was used as an assessment tool to determine problem magnitude and to pinpoint and operationalize specific target concerns. The CSI assesses the level and source of caregiver stress among adult children who are primary caregivers for their aging parents. Data have been reported that suggest high reliability (.86) and construct validity. Responses to the CSI range from 0 to 12, with a mean and standard deviation both of 3.5, suggesting that a score of 7 or more indicates higher stress. Anne scored 8 on the CSI, denoting marked caregiver stress. Anne identified a number of specific strains, including her mother's bladder incontinence and need for 24-hour supervision, resulting in Anne's feeling "trapped," "a prisoner in my own home." Further assessment revealed that Anne typically experienced many conflicting and troubling thoughts both when preparing to leave the house (e.g., "I need to get away" and "I shouldn't leave Mom alone") and when she was out of the house, even for a short time (e.g., "I should be home" and "I'm not a good daughter"). She reported experiencing high levels of tension and anxiety and low levels of enjoyment or satisfaction during these ventures away from home. Often she would return home earlier than originally planned, feeling tired, weepy, and resentful of Mom (e.g., "I feel cheated" and "I feel trapped"). Thus, for Anne, caregiver burden included feelings of entrapment and lack of freedom to leave her home, as well as resultant negative feelings about herself and her mother.

The central target problem, jointly identified by Anne and the social worker, was lack of freedom to leave home because of the absence of substitute caregivers and her mother's need for constant supervision. Several service options, including nursing home placement for mother and stress reduction or relaxation training for Anne, were initially discussed but later dismissed. These alternatives were unacceptable to Anne, as they did not address the core issue as she perceived it. Anne wanted her mother to remain at home, and she desired some actual relief from her caregiving responsibility. She reasoned that having substitute home care would free her from the worries and guilt that now plagued her whenever she left her mother alone and that increased personal freedom and mobility would alter her growing negative attitude toward her mother. Her resentment and antagonism toward her mother was especially troubling to Anne, as she reported a history of a strong mother-daughter relationship. In consort with Anne's conceptualization of the problem, three specific outcome goals were selected and monitored. These included increasing the duration and enjoyment of time spent outside the home and improving Anne's attitude toward her mother.

Outcome Measures

Repeated collections of data on Anne's out-of-home behavior and feelings and on her attitude toward her mother constituted the outcome measures obtained over an 8-week period. Not only can multiple measures increase confidence in the validity of results from single-system design studies (Bloom & Fischer, 1982), but they can also facilitate interpretation of differential changes across behavioral, emotional, and cognitive response modalities (Levy & Richey, 1988).

Amount of Time away from Home
Increasing Anne's time away from home was viewed as an operational measure of greater personal freedom. Anne agreed to monitor in a daily log the amount of time she spent outside the home. Log entries were reviewed and discussed during semiweekly (Monday and Thursday) sessions, and weekly totals in hours were entered in the client's file and plotted on a graph.

Enjoyment of Time away from Home
Anne was also asked to enter in her daily log the level of enjoyment she experienced when away from home. Enjoyment was rated on a 5-point, self-anchored scale (1 = *not at all enjoyable,* and 5 = *very enjoyable*). Along with duration data, these ratings were also reviewed and summarized during sessions, with weekly aggregate scores entered in the case file and graphed. All raw, self-monitored data on daily logs were retained by the client. In an effort to enhance validity of client self-monitored data— in addition to apparent face validity—the social worker attempted to reduce the

possibility of socially desirable responding by telling Anne there were no correct responses and that honesty in completing the daily log was the most important dimension of record keeping.

Attitude toward Mother

Anne completed the Child's Attitude Toward Mother (CAM) scale during each Monday and Thursday session throughout the 2-month service period (Hudson, 1982). The CAM scale, like other standardized questionnaires in Hudson's Clinical Measurement Package, contains 25 positively and negatively worded items that are rated on a 5-point scale (1 = *rarely or none of the time*, 5 = *most or all of the time*). Items include, for example, "I feel very angry toward my mother" and "I really like my mother."

The Hudson scales were designed for single-system research (Bloom & Fischer, 1982). All scales include instructions to discourage socially desirable responding; are relatively easy to administer, score, and interpret; and have high internal consistency and test-retest reliabilities (.90 or better) and high face, concurrent, and construct validity (Bloom & Fischer, 1982).

The use of the CAM to gage the degree or magnitude of a relationship problem experienced by an adult child with her mother is a relatively innovative application of the scale that was tested for reliability and validity with much younger populations. However, examination of individual scale items indicated a high correlation between the issues it addresses and those thought to be major areas of concern in assessing the caregiver role for this client. Thus, although the scale has not been used extensively with adult children, its application in this study seemed appropriate and yielded interesting results.

Social Work Intervention

Intervention largely consisted of case management, with the hospital-based social worker taking central responsibility in assessing, planning, arranging, coordinating, evaluating, and advocating for services (Gambrill, 1983; Johnson & Rubin, 1983). In this case, concrete community resources, in the form of home-based respite care, were procured in order to alleviate caregiver burden and to prevent deterioration of familial bonds and quality of home care. Over the course of 8 weeks, the practitioner spent an estimated total of 27 hours performing tasks related to accessing, coordinating, and monitoring respite care services. These activities, when added to the 16 hours of face-to-face client contact, resulted in a total service output of 43 hours by the social worker.

After the initial assessment, both the practitioner and Anne identified respite care as the primary need for case management services. Steps were taken to (a) obtain COPES (Community Options Program Entry System) subsidization of a substitute caregiver and (b) locate a suitable care provider. Because Mrs. N received public assistance (SSI) benefits, she was eligible for a community-based care Medicaid waiver from the federal Department of Health and Human Services. These waivers were made possible through Section 21.76 of the 1981 Omnibus Reconciliation Act (PL 95-35). Basically, this is a welfare program, jointly funded by federal and state governments, designed to meet the needs of low-income persons for health care. During the 2 weeks required to determine COPES eligibility and to locate a suitable care provider, home visits continued, and baseline data were collected. With Anne's endorsement, provision was made for respite care in the home Monday through Friday, 6 hours daily, from 10 AM to 4 PM. Despite Anne's enthusiasm for the intervention plan, the social worker continued to encourage her utilization of these outside resources by reassuring her that relying on substitute care was not a sign of personal weakness or failure (Briar & Ryan, 1986; Gonyea et al., 1988; Lewis & Meredith, 1988).

Research Design

Originally, a basic *AB* single-system design was planned to reflect a 2-week baseline observation period (*A*) and a 6-week intervention period employing respite care (*B*). It should be noted that the *A* phase in this study was not entirely intervention free, as supportive home visits continued semiweekly throughout the course of service contact.

The *AB* design was altered after 5 weeks, when the COPES provider was unable to continue. The required change in the substitute caregiver resulted in a natural return to baseline (A_2) while an alternative provider was located. This unplanned shift during intervention created an experimental replication design (A_1, B_1, A_2, B_2) that provided stronger support for the causal efficacy of the intervention, respite care, than could the more simple *AB* design (Bloom & Fischer, 1982).

Results

All three outcome measures, amount and enjoyment of time out of the house and attitude toward mother, evidenced rather dramatic changes in predicted directions when respite care was introduced, withdrawn, and reintroduced.

Amount of Time away from Home

The caregiver's self-monitored daily log of time outside the home was used to calculate weekly totals. As illustrated in Figure B-1, baseline levels in the A_1 phase were very low, with weekly totals of less than one hour ($M = 0.7$, $SD = 0.14$). With the institution of respite care (B_1), weekly totals more than doubled to 2.2 hours after the first week of in-home care. The mean for B_1 phases was 1.7 hours, which indicated a 147 percent improvement over baseline. When respite care was not available during Week 6 (A_2), the client largely stayed at home ($M = 0.6$ hours). Out-of-home behavior again increased in B_2 when respite care was reinstituted ($M = 1.9$ hours). With the exception of Week 3 in the B_1 phase, which was the first week of respite care, introduction and withdrawal of intervention appeared to clearly coincide with changes in the amount of time the caregiver was away from home.

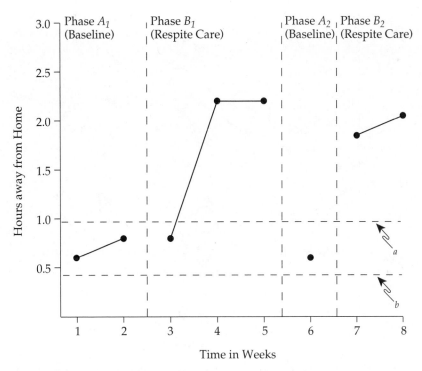

FIGURE B-1 Total Number of Hours Caregiver Reports Being away from Home Each Week

a. Upper two standard deviation band = .98
b. Lower two standard deviation band = .42

To determine whether changes in time away from home were statistically significant, two standard deviation bands (Shewart Charts) were calculated from baseline data (Bloom & Fischer, 1982). This procedure was judged appropriate because baseline data were not autocorrelated ($r = .5$), and there were limited observations. Based on this statistical procedure for time-series data, any two consecutive data points that fall beyond two standard deviations above or below the baseline mean indicate significant differences beyond the .05 level. As noted in Figure B-1, the increases in time away from home during Weeks 4 and 5 (B_1) and Weeks 7 and 8 (B_2) were statistically significant ($p < .05$), as they were well above the upper two standard deviation band.

Bloom and Fischer (1982) note that autocorrelation is a complex statistical problem with time-series data. Although computational steps are available for detecting autocorrelation, these may not be sensitive with small baselines. Hence results of the r formula with baseline data in this case must be cautiously interpreted (Bloom & Fischer, 1982). However, testing for autocorrelation may be unnecessary, if the statistical test is interpreted as only a rough indicator of association between intervention and subsequent data patterns (Blythe & Tripodi, 1989).

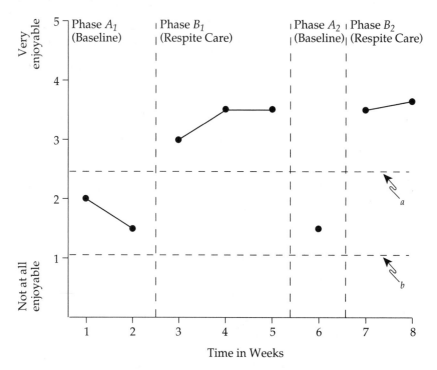

FIGURE B-2 **Weekly Averages of Caregiver Employment When away**
from Home

      a. Upper two standard deviation band = 2.45
      b. Lower two standard deviation band = 1.05

Enjoyment of Time away from Home

Figure B-2 summarizes weekly averages of the client's rating of her enjoyment level while away from home. Again data patterns reflect marked changes in predicted directions when respite care was and was not in place. Mean enjoyment level during the first 2 weeks of baseline (A_1) was low (M = 1.8, SD = 0.35), suggesting that the brief excursions made during that time offered very little satisfaction. Enjoyment plummeted to a very low level again (M = 1.5) during the 6th week, when the substitute caretaker was unavailable (A_2). The first introduction of respite care (B_1) appeared to occasion a marked and sustained increase in enjoyment of time away from home (M = 3.3). When respite care was reinstated during Weeks 7 and 8, enjoyment of time away again increased noticeably (M = 3.6).

    An initial test for autocorrelation revealed the absence of serial dependency in baseline data (r = –.5), so the two standard deviation band approach was again utilized. All enjoyment ratings during the respite care conditions (B_1 and B_2) were statistically significant above baseline levels (p < .05). These findings strongly support intervention effectiveness.

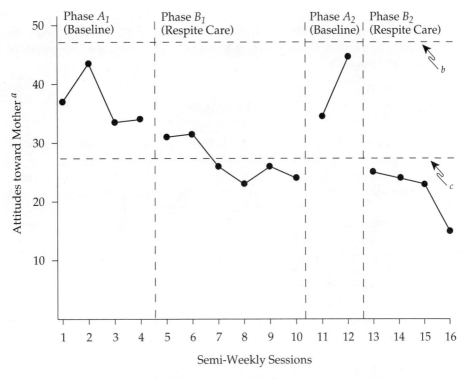

FIGURE B-3 Caregiver Attitude toward Mother on CAM Scale Assessed during Monday/Thursday Sessions over 2 Months

    a. Hudson's Child Attitude Mother (CAM) Scale. Higher scores = greater problem severity; clinical cutting score = 30
    b. Upper two standard deviation band = 45.5
    c. Lower two standard deviation band = 27.5

Attitude toward Mother

Figure B-3 summarizes scores on the CAM scale obtained during weekly Monday and Thursday sessions over the 2-month service period. The data reveal an average score of 36.5 (SD = 4.5) during the initial A_1 baseline phase. This score is above the clinical cutting point of 30 recommended for all Hudson scales, thus suggesting a clinically significant problem in Anne's attitude toward her mother before the introduction of respite care. Although attitude began to improve slightly during baseline, notable score decreases occurred during the initial 3 weeks of respite care (B_1), with an average CAM score of 26.8. This decrease is greater than the 5-point standard error of measurement for the Hudson scales, so it likely represents a "real" change in Anne's attitude. Consistent with data patterns from the other two measures, CAM scores spiked during the A_2 phase (M = 38), confirming apparent deterioration during the nonrespite week. More positive attitude scores emerged again during B_2, with all scores falling below the clinical cutoff (M = 22).

Analysis indicated that baseline data were not autocorrelated ($r = -.14$), and that attitude improvements in B_1 (Sessions 7–10) and B_2 (Sessions 13–16) were statistically significant above baseline levels ($p < .05$), using the two standard deviation band approach.

Discussion

The unintended $A_1B_1A_2B_2$ design in this case study supports the positive impact of respite care on caregiver burden. Despite the fact that the B_2 was not an exact replication of B_1 (each phase employed a different COPES provider), the core intervention, provision of an alternate caregiver, remained constant. Apparently, intervention effects were not limited to a particular respite care worker. Along with the experimental replication design, the statistically significant results also offer strong empirical evidence of intervention effectiveness.

The study was strengthened and practice knowledge increased by the use of multiple outcome measures, reflecting client behavior, feelings, and attitudes. The caregiver was highly motivated to improve her situation and remained an active participant by recording and discussing information throughout the study. The client's active involvement in collecting data might be challenged by some practitioners as disruptive to the development of a therapeutic relationship. On the contrary, participation of the caregiver in this study through self-monitoring and questionnaire completion represented an empowerment strategy, as well as a way to document change (Kopp, 1989). Self-assessment can provide a source of positive feedback and support to clients who may be unaware of small changes on a day-to-day basis. For instance, a series of single-case design studies with 66 home-based caregivers reported that caregivers enjoyed recording and graphing behavioral data and that the figural depictions of progress had great clinical value (Pinkston, Linsk, & Young, 1988).

A potential weakness of the study was the operationalization of a multifaceted problem such as burden. Although the definitions selected were supported by the caregiver, they nevertheless represented only a small part of the construct burden. Other variables of interest could have readily included depression and social isolation. Goal selection could represent another weakness. Although goals of increased time and enjoyment away from home and improved regard toward mother reflect pressing client concerns, these outcomes appear to emphasize relatively short-term changes that are primarily related to Anne's role as caretaker for another. To reduce possible gender bias and increase clinical relevance of goals selected, it might be important in casework with adult female caregivers to take time to focus on additional goals that are longer range (preparing Anne for a life without mother) and more personal (enhancing Anne's self-esteem and friendship networks; Gambrill & Richey, 1986).

The issue of clinical relevance must also be raised in this study with respect to levels of goal attainment, especially for duration of time away from home. Despite the statistical significance of increases in this measure, the clinical or practical significance of change must be addressed. Given the expanded opportunities to leave the house afforded by respite care (up to 6 hours daily, 30 hours weekly), a high of 2.2 hours a week away from home (or 7 percent of time available) seems a small respite indeed. Although these breaks from caretaking are important, they allow limited opportunity for extended interaction with friends or participation in community events. Perhaps Anne, like many caregivers whose opportunities to engage in reinforcing and pleasurable activities erode over time, was unable to think of things she would enjoy doing outside the home (Pinkston et al., 1988). On the other hand, it may be erroneous to conclude that Anne's time at home was unpleasant. Solitary activities, like reading, knitting, listening to music, or talking on the telephone may be more common "pleasant events" among caregivers than social activities requiring time away from their caregiver role (Lovett & Gallagher, 1988). Thus the presence of the respite care worker in the home not only allowed Anne the freedom to leave the house if she chose to, but it also relieved her of constant care responsibilities during most of the day, so she could pursue solitary activities at home without interruption. Future research could examine more specifically how relieved caregivers spend their respite time. For example, is time spent in activities that are active or sedentary, social or solitary?

A further limitation of the study involves the failure to systematically assess and document the quality of and satisfaction with caregiving provided by the respite care worker. Although the social worker routinely checked on Mrs. N during each home visit, no ongoing evaluation of the care itself was performed. Future research could contribute significantly to our understanding of respite care by studying the quality, appropriateness, and satisfaction of alternative care from the viewpoints of both the elder and the respite worker (Barer & Johnson, 1990).

As the number and proportion of older people increase, the importance of understanding and meeting the needs of caregivers also increases. Public policies supporting accessible and affordable community-based services for caregivers must become a high priority if we are to provide sound alternatives to institutionalization (Kane, 1985) and alter our narrow cost-containment mentality, which justifies cheap rather than humane long-term care options (Pilisuk & Parks, 1988). Because the family will continue to play an important support role with vulnerable individuals, it is imperative that the material, social, and emotional strains placed on relatives be recognized and addressed programmatically. This study offers one example of how empirical support for respite care and other support services can be collected by individual practitioners for purposes of both case and class advocacy (Hepworth & Larsen, 1990). Individual case data can be used to acquire, continue, or expand needed benefits and services for specific clients. To promote social policy change, ideographic data can be amassed and aggregated to form compelling evidence of intervention feasibility, efficiency, and efficacy for family caregivers as a group. Such evidence can boost efforts to develop social welfare policies and programs that support all family members in the pursuit of their caregiving roles.

References

American Association of Retired Persons. (1986). *A profile of older Americans.* Washington, DC: Author.

Archbold, P. G. (1983). Impact of parent-caring on women. *Family Relations, 32,* 39–45.

Arling, G., & McAuley, W. J. (1983). The feasibility of public payments for family caregiving. *Gerontologist, 23,* 300–306.

Bader, J. (1985). Respite care: Temporary relief for caregivers. *Women and Health, 10,* 39–51.

Barer, B. M., & Johnson, C. L. (1990). A critique of the caregiving literature. *Gerontologist, 30,* 26–28.

Biegel, D. E., Sales, E., & Schultz, R. (1991). *Family caregiving in chronic illness.* Newbury Park, CA: Sage.

Bloom, M., & Fischer, J. (1982). *Evaluating practice: Guidelines for the accountable professional.* Englewood Cliffs, NJ: Prentice-Hall.

Blythe, B. J., & Tripodi, T. (1989). *Measurement in direct practice.* Newbury Park, CA: Sage.

Briar, K. H., & Ryan, R. (1986). The anti-institution movement and women caregivers. *Affilia, 1*(1), 20–31.

Brody, E. M. (1985). Parent care as a normative family stress. *Gerontologist, 25,* 19–30.

Cantor, M. H. (1983). Strain among caregivers: A study of experience in the United States. *Gerontologist, 23,* 597–604.

Clark, N. M., & Rakowski, W. (1983). Family caregivers of older adults: Improving helping skills. *Gerontologist, 23,* 637–643.

Cohen, S. (1982). Supporting families through respite care. *Rehabilitation Literature, 43,* 7–11.

Crossman, L., London, C., & Barry, C. (1981). Older women caring for disabled spouses: A model for supportive services. *Gerontologist, 21,* 464–470.

Doll, W. (1976). Family coping with the mentally ill: An unanticipated problem of deinstitutionalization. *Hospital and Community Psychiatry, 27,* 183–185.

Foundation for Long Term Care. (1983). *Respite care for the frail elderly: A summary report on institutional respite research* (Monograph 1). Albany, NY: Author.

Gallagher, D. (1985). Intervention strategies to assist caregivers of frail elders: Current research status and future research directions. In M. P. Lawton & G. Maddox (Eds.), *Annual review of gerontology and geriatrics* (Vol. 5, pp. 249–282). New York: Springer.

Gambrill, E. D. (1983). *Casework: A competency-based approach.* Englewood Cliffs, NJ: Prentice-Hall.

Gambrill, E. D., & Richey, C. A. (1986). Criteria used to define and evaluate socially competent behavior among women. *Psychology of Women Quarterly, 10,* 183–196.

Gonyea, J. G., Seltzer, G. B., Gerstein, C., & Young, M. (1988). Acceptance of hospital-based respite care by families and elders. *Health and Social Work, 13,* 201–208.

Hepworth, D. H., & Larsen, J. A. (1990). *Direct social work practice.* Chicago: Dorsey.

Hickey, T., & Douglass, R. L. (1981). Mistreatment of the elderly in the domestic setting: An exploratory study. *American Journal of Public Health, 71,* 500–507.

Hooyman, N. R. (1987). Older women and social work curricula. In D. S. Burden & N. Gottlieb (Eds.), *The woman client: Providing human services in a changing world.* New York: Tavistock.

Hooyman, N. R., & Lustbader, W. (1986). *Taking care of your aging family members: A practical guide.* New York: Free Press.

Hudson, W. W. (1982). *The Clinical Measurement Package: A field manual.* Homewood, IL: Dorsey.

Intagliata, J. (1986). Assessing the impact of respite care services: A review of outcome evaluation studies. In C. L. Salisbury & J. Intagliata (Eds.), *Respite care: Support for persons with developmental disabilities and their families* (pp. 263–287). Baltimore, MD: Brookes.

Johnson, G. L. (1983). Dyadic family relations and social support. *Gerontologist, 23,* 377–384.

Johnson, P. J., & Rubin, A. (1983). Case management in mental health: A social work domain? *Social Work, 28,* 49–55.

Joyce, K., Singer, M., & Isralowitz, O. (1983). Impact of respite care on parent's perception of quality of life. *Mental Retardation, 2,* 153–156.

Kane, R. A. (1985). A family caregiving policy—should we have one? *Generations, 10,* 33–36.

Kopp, J. (1989). Self-observation: An empowerment strategy in assessment. *Social Casework, 70,* 276–284.

Lang, A. M., & Brody, E. M. (1983). Characteristics of middle-aged daughters and help to their elderly mothers. *Journal of Marriage and the Family, 45,* 193–201.

Lawton, M. P., Brody, E. M., & Saperstein, A. R. (1989). A controlled study of respite service for caregivers of Alzheimer's patients. *Gerontologist, 29,* 8–16.

Levy, R. L., & Richey, C. A. (1988). Measurement and design issues in behavioral medicine with women. In E. A. Blechman & K. Browell (Eds.), *Handbook of behavioral medicine for women* (pp. 421–438). New York: Pergamon.

Lewis, J., & Meredith, B. (1988). *Daughters who care: Daughters caring for mothers at home.* London: Routledge.

Lovett, S., & Gallagher, D. (1988). Psychoeducational interventions for family caregivers: Preliminary efficacy data. *Behavior Therapy, 19,* 321–330.

Marks, R. (1988, June). Families with frail elderly: An examination of family life, mechanisms of support and long-term care policy. In E. Rayne (Ed.), *Families in transition: Implications for social work and practice* (Tulane Studies in Social Welfare Vol. 17, pp. 149–167). New Orleans: Tulane University.

Montgomery, R., Gonyea, J., & Hooyman, N. (1985). Caregiving and the experience of subjective and objective burden. *Family Relations, 34*(1), 19–26.

Montgomery, R. J. V., & Prothero, J. (Eds.). (1986). *Developing respite services for the elderly.* Seattle: University of Washington Press.

Moroney, R. M. (1976). *The family and the state: Considerations for social policy.* New York: Longman.

Moroney, R. M. (1980). *Families, social services and social policy: The issue of shared responsibility.* Rockville, MD: National Institute of Mental Health.

Pagel, S. E., & Whitling, B. (1978). Readmissions to a state hospital for mentally retarded persons: Reasons for community placement and failure. *Mental Retardation, 16,* 164–166.

Pearlin, L. I., Mullan, J. T., Semple, S. J., & Skaff, M. M. (1990). Caregiving and the stress process: An overview of concepts and their measures. *Gerontologist, 30,* 583–591.

Pilisuk, M., & Parks, S. H. (1988). Caregiving: Where families need help. *Social Work, 33,* 436–440.

Pinkston, E. M., Linsk, N. L., & Young, R. N. (1988). Home-based behavioral family treatment of the impaired elderly. *Behavior Therapy, 19,* 331–344.

Poulshock, S. W., & Deimling, G. T. (1984). Families caring for elders in residence: Issues in the measurement of burden. *Journal of Gerontology, 39,* 230–239.

Pruchno, R. A., & Resch, N. L. (1989). Aberrant behaviors and Alzheimer's disease: Mental health effects of spouse caregivers. *Journal of Gerontology, 44,* 177–182.

Robinson, B. C. (1983). Validation of a caregiver strain index. *Journal of Gerontology, 38,* 344–348.

Salisbury, C. L., & Intagliata, J. (1986). *Respite care: Support for persons with developmental disabilities and their families.* Baltimore, MD: Brookes.

Sheehan, N. W., & Nuttall, P. (1988). Conflict, emotion, and personal strain among family caregivers. *Family Relations, 37*(1), 92–98.

Siegel, J. S., & Taeubex, C. M. (1982). The 1980 census and the elderly: New data available to planners and practitioners. *Gerontologist, 22,* 144–150.

Soldo, B. J., & Myllyluoma, J. (1983). Caregivers who live with dependent elderly. *Gerontologist, 23,* 605–611.

Stoller, E. P. (1983). Parental caregiving by adult children. *Journal of Marriage and the Family, 45,* 851–857.

Upshur, C. C. (1983). Developing respite care: A support for families with disabled members. *Family Relations, 32,* 13–20.

Wikler, L. M.,. Hanusa, D., & Stoycheff, J. (1986). Home-based respite care, the child with developmental disabilities, and family stress: Some theoretical and pragmatic aspects of process evaluation. In C. L. Salisbury & J. Intagliata (Eds.), *Respite care: Support for persons with developmental disabilities and their families* (pp. 243–261). Baltimore, MD: Brookes.

Zarit, S. H., Reever, K. E., & Bach-Peterson, J. (1980). Relatives of the impaired elderly: Correlates of feelings of burden. *Gerontologist, 20,* 649–655.

Zarit, S. H., Todd, P. A., & Zarit, J. M. (1986). Subjective burden of husbands and wives as caregivers: A longitudinal study. *Gerontologist, 26,* 260–266.

CASE STUDY C

The Effectiveness of Outreach Counseling and Support Groups for Battered Women: A Preliminary Evaluation

ALLEN RUBIN

Source: A. Rubin, *Research on Social Work Practice*, 1(4), pp. 332–357. Copyright © 1991 by Sage Publications, Inc. Reprinted by permission of Sage Publications, Inc.

PROGRAMS FOR BATTERED WOMEN have spread widely since their emergence in the 1970s and now exceed 900 in the United States (Davis, 1988). Although this growth has been accompanied by a proliferation in relevant literature, no well-controlled outcome studies testing the effectiveness of battered women's programs have been reported (Berk, Newton, & Berk, 1986; Davis, 1988; Wodarski, 1987). The dearth of such studies is understandable. Battered women are in crises that involve extreme stress and physical danger, often life-threatening danger. This danger may threaten their children as well (Jaffee, Wilson, & Wolfe, 1988). Outcome evaluations requiring the delay or withholding of services therefore are likely to be ruled out on ethical grounds (Berk et al., 1986).

The absence of rigorous outcome studies of programs for the victims of battering also can be attributed to practical and ideological constraints. Perhaps the most important practical constraint, one which also has ethical implications, is the difficulty that practitioners in battered women's programs encounter in engaging some battered women in their services. Denial, fear of stigma, fear of reprisal from the batterer, feelings of helplessness and hopelessness, psychological paralysis, depression, and fear of winding up alone and unable to support themselves or their children have been suggested as some of the prime factors (usually suggested as resulting from long-term abuse, not causing it) that make it difficult for many battered women to seek help (Aguirre, 1985; Bentzel & York, 1988; Bretton; 1988; McShane, 1979; Rounsaville, 1978; Rounsaville, Lifton, & Bieber, 1979; Wodarski, 1987). When battered women do seek services, social workers and other practitioners must respond to their needs in ways that will foster hope and motivate continued involvement. Delaying or withholding services in order to obtain experimental control, therefore, is unacceptable. Moreover, some might not see the need for rigorous outcome studies because they accept the value of battered women's programs as self-evident, especially when considering the protection offered by shelters for victimized women and their children. Also, service providers might see their services as part of a social movement or a commitment to women's issues (Bentzel & York, 1988; Davis, 1988) and thus might hold strong beliefs in the efficacy or value of their programs.

Despite these barriers, it is worth searching for ways to conduct scientifically useful evaluations of some services provided by battered women's programs. In the face of accountability concerns and shrinking fiscal support (Pfouts, Renz, & Renz, 1981), service providers in these programs are likely to encounter questions about their effectiveness, especially from sources of needed funding. Moreover, as these programs mature and as they become staffed by professionally trained social workers and other individuals who have learned the value of program evaluation and practice evaluation, some of their staff members may want scientific evidence as to the success of different service components or approaches in attaining program goals. Although these forces do not obviate the ethical and practical obstacles to conducting controlled group experiments, they may foster enthusiasm for outcome research using idiographic designs that control for threats to internal validity without delaying or withholding services. Edelson, Miller, Stone, and Chapman

(1985) demonstrated the applicability of single-case design methodology to evaluating programs to treat batterers. Might it also be useful in evaluating programs to treat the victims of battering?

External accountability pressures prompted the administrator of one of the oldest battered women's programs in the nation, the Austin Center for Battered Women, to express to her staff a wish for a way to evaluate the outcome of their program's outreach services that would have some scientific validity without requiring the delay or withholding of services. One of her staff members, a social worker, had recently completed a course on social work practice evaluation taught by the author of this article and suggested that the administrator contact him to explore using aggregated single-case designs in their agency. The author then designed a study for their agency using this methodology, engaging the administrator and staff members in the design process. He subsequently developed a field practicum for a second-year MSW student to implement the study under his supervision. This article reports that study.

Method

Agency Setting

The Austin Center for Battered Women (ACBW) began in 1977 as the first shelter for abused women and their children in Texas. It shelters approximately 600 women and 800 children per year. Although the shelter is the ACBW's core program, additional major services are provided. For example, an outreach program serves abused women who need support but do not feel they need shelter and those who want to enter the shelter but cannot because it is full. A telephone hotline program responds to crisis calls. A children's program is provided to deal with child abuse issues and provide children with emotional support. Other services provide legal support, substance abuse awareness groups, in-school peer support groups dealing with dating violence, and community education. The evaluation reported here focused on one major component of the outreach program, its counseling and support groups.

Clients

The counseling and support groups were selected as the most logical starting point to begin evaluating outcome in the agency because they provided an opportunity for obtaining adequate baselines without delaying the onset of intervention. The research required no delay to establish a baseline phase because of the variable time lapse that routinely occurred between the agency's intake interviews and when each client chose to begin attending group sessions. The agency procedure regarding this time lapse that was ongoing before the research was designed was not modified for the research (and thus conducting baselines required no ethical compromises regarding when clients could begin the intervention). In this procedure, on initial referral to the outreach program and prior to attending her first group session, one of the group leaders provides each client with an intake interview and information about the groups. Not all clients are referred to the groups; some are referred to other ACBW services. Those who are referred to the counseling and support groups are encouraged to begin attending groups as soon as possible. Some come to the very next meeting, but others might not begin attending until many weeks later. Some never return. For this study, whatever length of time that naturally elapsed between intake and attending the first group session comprised the baseline for each client. Those clients who were referred to the counseling and support groups during the study period were briefly informed about the groups during the initial interview and were asked if they would like to discuss participation in the outcome study with the MSW student placed at the agency for the study. If they agreed to meet with her, she then discussed their voluntary informed consent to participate.

During the course of the study, 17 women received initial agency interviews. Five of these women chose not to participate in the study. Of the remaining 12, sufficient data during both baseline and intervention phases were provided by six women. The other six provided sufficient baseline data but either had not yet begun attending group meetings by the end of the study period or had just attended their first meeting at the end of the study period and thus were able to provide only two data points during the intervention phase. (Nothing remarkable was observed in the data patterns of the latter six women. Their baselines were essentially flat or somewhat cyclical with no discernible slopes and with no clear shifts in the two data points during intervention.)

For the agency as a whole, the living situations of the clients participating in the groups are diverse. Some continue living with abusive partners in the hope that their partner will change and thus are not ready to enter a shelter or separate from the partner. They may know there is a problem but may deny or minimize the seriousness of the danger they face. Others may have left the batterer but continue to participate in the outreach counseling and support groups because they are still dealing with problems involving the batterer or issues regarding their relationship with the batterer. Some may be dating an abusive partner with whom they do not yet live. (The center offered another set of groups for women who, in addition to having left the batterer, are no longer dealing with problems regarding the batterer. This set of groups was omitted from the evaluation.)

Of the six clients who participated in this study, however, all but one (Client 6) were not living with the batterer at the start of the study. One of these five (Client 3) was divorced from the batterer before the study commenced, and three of them (Clients 1, 2, and 4) finalized a divorce from the batterer during the study. One of these three was in hiding and terminated participation when she left town in secrecy. Client 5 remained married to the batterer while living apart from him and then moved back in with the batterer in the midst of the intervention phase. This client reported only emotional abuse at intake; the others all reported physical and emotional abuse. The only client (Client 6) who was living with the batterer at the start of the study continued living with him throughout baseline but moved out one day before she began attending the group meetings. The six clients ranged in age from 24 to 38 years, with a median of 30.5 years. Five were employed, all in blue-collar or clerical jobs. Two had graduated from college, one had 2 years of college, and three were high school graduates.

Client 1 was a White mother of two in her late 30s. She was a high school graduate who had attended college for a while and now worked in a clerical job. She reported a long history of both physical and emotional abuse and was living apart from the batterer at the start of the study. She finalized a divorce from him during the study. Client 2 was an unemployed White mother in her mid-20s, whose education did not go beyond high school. She reported that in addition to the abuse she experienced, one of her young children was sexually abused by the batterer. She and her children lived in hiding at the start of the study and then secretly left town to escape the batterer. She had attended only two sessions of intervention at the time she left town. Client 3 was a White woman in her mid-20s who was divorced before entering the program. Her education did not go beyond high school, and she worked in a low-paying job. She had heard of the program through Alcoholics Anonymous. Client 4 was a White mother in her late 30s who had a college education and worked in a white-collar job. This woman, who at intake reported a history of depression, had been divorced in the past and was divorced from the batterer during the study. Client 5 was a White mother of three in her early 30s. Her education did not go beyond high school, and she worked in a low-paying blue-collar job. She reported no physical abuse—only emotional abuse—and remained married to the batterer. She lived apart from him at the start of the study, but after commencing intervention, she moved back in with him. Client 6 was the only study participant who was living with the batterer at the start of the study. This client was a White woman in her early 30s with a high school education and who worked in a clerical job. In addition to being physically abusive, her husband engaged in extremely dramatic behaviors in an effort to keep her from leaving and to entice her back. She moved away from the batterer two days before attending her first group session, moved back home about a week later, and then moved away again about two weeks after that. This woman reported at intake that it took her four years to decide to come to the battered women's program.

Outcome Measures

A telephone interview inventory was constructed for this study. It consisted of two outcome measures. The first measure listed thoughts, feelings, and behaviors and asked clients to approximate how often they felt or acted that way during the past 24 hours. Three response categories were used: *none of the time, a little of the time,* and *much of the time.* Responses to each item were scored from 0 to 2, with 2 representing *much of the time* for thoughts, feelings, or behaviors that are desirable from the standpoint of the objectives of the intervention and its underlying theory. Undesirable thoughts, feelings, and behaviors were scored 2 if *none of the time* was reported.

Two versions of this measure were developed: one for clients not living with the batterer and one for those living with the batterer. The two versions shared all but a few items and yielded a total score for 16 items with a possible range of 0 to 32. Items pertaining to feelings that appeared on both inventories asked how often clients felt happy, sad, helpless, good about themselves, isolated from friends or relatives, capable of living independently without a mate, able to find happiness without a mate, and that they must please a mate in order to be a worthwhile person. Additional items appearing on both versions asked how often they blamed themselves if their mate got upset, spent some time with friends or relatives, said no when asked to do something they did not want to do, enjoyed doing something special, and did what they wanted to do, even if others in the family wanted them to do something else.

Items only on the not-living-with-batterer version asked how often clients considered living with the batterer again or another partner who has abused them mentally or physically, spent some time speaking with the batterer, and spent some time seeing the batterer. Items only on the living-with-batterer version asked how often they felt angry about how their mate treats them (the response *much of the time* was deemed desirable and thus scored as a 2), considered taking actions to better protect themselves, and made a decision about what the family would do.

The second outcome measure attempted to operationally define the daily degree of abusive behaviors by the client's partners. It consisted of a checklist of five items that asked whether during the past 24 hours their current or previous partner belittled them; forced them to do something they did not want to do; became angry, scared them, screamed at them, or threw things at them; physically hurt them; and/or threatened them with a weapon, or acted like he would kill them. Scores on this section could range from 0 to 5, with a 1 assigned to each "yes" answer and a 0 to each "no." The purpose of this measure was not to see if the services succeeded in reforming the batterer, as the ACBW offers no services to treat batterers, believing instead that the clients need to concentrate on protecting themselves and to let go of their unrealistic hopes of changing the batterer. Rather, the purpose of this measure was to see if the services helped the clients find ways to avoid abuse. Another purpose of this measure was to see if the batterer's mere awareness that the client was attending the group would trigger retaliation. This concern was initiated by ACBW staff and was related to the findings of Berk et al. (1986) in connection to batterers' reactions to decisions of their partners to enter shelters.

Each measure was constructed in close collaboration with ACBW clinical and administrative staff. Each item attempted to operationally define an outcome goal identified by the staff (or, in the case of abusive acts committed by the batterer, to operationally define an unintended negative consequence of seeking help). Feedback as to the appropriateness of the indicators initially selected for the inventories was obtained from clients attending group meetings prior to initiation of the study. Pretesting was also done with these clients. Revisions were made based on the feedback and the pretesting.

Choosing the indicators for this study was not an easy process. The use of single-case design methodology required constructing inventory items that were limited to those goals of the counseling support groups which lent themselves to daily monitoring. The decision to develop a relatively large number of items on thoughts and feelings and to include very little in the way of behaviors representing dramatic acts of separation or self-protection was based on the intent to have an instrument that would be sensitive to subtle improvements that could be expected to occur soon after the clients began attending the group meetings, assuming the intervention is effective. More dramatic acts would occur very infrequently, could not be expected to coincide with the onset of treatment, and thus did not seem applicable to the logic of single-case methodology.

Direct service and administrative staff seemed pleased with the inventories, believed that they adequately operationalized some important intermediate objectives, and expressed optimism that the measurement would consistently detect changes coinciding with the onset of group intervention across cases. Nevertheless, the researcher was skeptical. Staff members initially had quite diverse views regarding what would be best to measure and how best to measure it. The researcher doubted whether changes in the indicators would occur soon enough after the onset of intervention to be detected in this brief study and to indicate visual significance. But given the absence of any better alternative approaches, he deferred to the judgment of the staff. He acknowledged that this study might turn out to be a first step in getting a better handle on measuring outcome but not a conclusive evaluation.

The decision to conduct the study was made despite awareness of some measurement limitations. The reliability and validity of the inventories was unknown. Triangulated measurement procedures were not feasible on a continual monitoring basis. The potential for social desirability bias in the interviews was troubling. Particularly worrisome was the prospect that once they started attending group meetings, clients might start reporting more desirable data simply because they thought they were expected to. Reactivity was another consideration. To what extent might any improvement be influenced by the daily monitoring, perhaps in interaction with the group intervention?

It was believed that these concerns could be addressed in subsequent research at the ACBW. In view of resource limitations and the agency's eagerness to obtain some outcome data, it seemed reasonable to table investigating those concerns until we learned whether the selected measures were capable of detecting change between baseline and treatment phases. If the outcome data supported the efficacy of the intervention, then concerns about social desirability and reactivity, for example, could be subsequently assessed as follows: After accumulating a larger sample of women, we could assess whether moving away from the batterer or back in with him was associated with increasing or decreasing scores on the inventory. If so, then concerns about social desirability bias would be offset. To deal with reactivity, we could administer the inventory to a subsequent sample of clients only once at the end of baseline (when they first appear for group) and one more time at a later point (a point to be determined based on the results of the first study, assuming that the results of the first study would indicate improved scores during intervention). To the extent that reactivity resulting from daily monitoring was influencing scores in the prior study (i.e., the current study), then the scores of the prior sample at the same two chronological points should be higher than the scores of the subsequent sample.

Thus the current study was conducted despite the aforementioned method-ological uncertainty. It was felt that the study would provide a valuable starting point either for sorting out the effects of a service that is hard to evaluate or for getting a better handle on whether and how to use single-case methodology to evaluate those effects. But readers are cautioned that the absence of data on the reliability and validity of the outcome measures is a serious limitation of this preliminary investigation. The outcome measures are available from the author on request, but future users are urged to use them cautiously and to consider ways to test their reliability and validity.

Intervention

At the time of this study, group meetings took place at four different meeting times per week. Each meeting lasted 90 minutes. Because of the emotional and practical obstacles to attending the meetings, clients were free to choose which times they attended from week to week or to skip attending at all. Sometimes, they did not show up for a while and then started attending again. Some came to more than one group meeting per week. Although there was some fluctuation in group composi-tion from week to week due to nonattendance, the clients tended to stay with the same group(s) when they did attend. These groups were composed of clients whose intervention began before this study was initiated as well as the six clients who were referred during the study period.

In designing this study, the author attempted to obtain information from ACBW staff that would enable him to explicate the intervention in specific terms. However, he was unable to get the level of specificity he desired. Certain agency constraints kept him from observing the intervention himself. Consequently, he asked his research assistant, a female MSW student doing fieldwork at the agency, to try to help him gain some operational specificity by taking notes about interven-tion specifics whenever she observed group sessions and discussed the intervention with agency practitioners. What follows is the most specific description of the intervention that the author was able to piece together under these circumstances. His inability to obtain a more replicable explication of the intervention may be due in large part to the apparent lack of structure in the intervention itself. It was the author's impression, based on all the feedback he was able to obtain, that agency practitioners providing the intervention engaged in a somewhat unsystematic pro-cess in which each session was planned, as it came up, in an idiosyncratic manner from session to session and across practitioners according to their clinical judg-ments, observations, and new ideas they had come across or intuited. In this process, the practitioners were guided by certain theoretical and ideological as-sumptions.

The group intervention combined elements of what Davis (1988) identified as the feminist and social services models of care for battered women. Techniques were drawn from various group treatment orientations, including cognitive-behavioral, humanistic, psychodynamic, mutual support, and feminist approaches. The specific techniques used were diverse and varied from session to session and across group leaders. Three full-time staff members led the groups. One was near completion of a part-time MSW program, and two had master's degrees in allied fields.

All three group leaders emphasized certain interventive commonalities and, as noted earlier, they shared key theoretical and ideological assumptions. Each emphasized that the safety of group members is the primary concern and that the aim of treatment is to maximize the sense of power that clients feel in their ability to protect themselves and their children from abuse. Each sought to empower clients to become emotionally and financially independent of their batterers. Each sought to overcome clients' denial and minimization of danger or their unrealistic hopes about the potential for the batterer to change. Each believed in accomplishing these objectives by drawing on the experience and support of group members. Underlying this common belief was the assumption that clients might become more fully aware of what has happened to them and the danger they are in once they see the reality of others' abuse. The leaders also encouraged group members to help their peers strategize plans for safely leaving a batterer and to provide encouragement and emotional support to members who initiated steps to begin protecting themselves. Newcomers to the group are asked to share their "story" with the group and describe themselves, and they then experience the group's empathy and support, borrowing a technique originated by Alcoholics Anonymous (1976).

The main interventive methods used in the group sessions fell into three categories: information provision, exploring feelings, and identifying discussion topics.

Information Provision

The empowerment objective was sought by providing information, social support, and efforts to enhance self-awareness. Group leaders provided information about forms of control other than physical violence, such as behaviors that serve to intimidate and isolate them. Walker's (1979) three-stage model of interactions that form a "cycle of violence" was emphasized in an effort to inform group members of the dynamics of abuse and to help them recognize warning signs and other stages in predictable patterns of abuse and how they get reinforced in their particular situations. (The three stages are tension-building, acute battering incident, and kindness and contrite loving behavior.)

Information was also provided about legal, financial, social service, and other resources that could be used to help members become less isolated, increase their safety, and attain independence. For example, the act of separating from an abusive partner may require resources and decisions concerning a peace bond or restraining order, filing assault charges, beginning divorce proceedings, making new childcare arrangements, obtaining employment or financial support, finding new living arrangements, and so on (Aguirre, 1985). Group leaders provided relevant information didactically as well as by encouraging group members to share their experiences in obtaining resources to deal with these issues.

Exploring Feelings

Trying to enhance self-awareness meant spending a great deal of time in group meetings exploring feelings. According to Walker's (1989) model, each time the cycle of violence is repeated, battered women become increasingly disoriented and lose self-awareness, self-esteem, and a sense of control. They blame themselves for their plight, become fearful and depressed, and retreat deeper into social isolation. The concept of learned helplessness has been used to describe the systematic destruction of a woman's perception of her ability to leave and not return to an abusive partner (Krish, 1974; Walker, 1979). Group leaders tried to make members more aware of their feelings so as to overcome denial, reduce their learned helplessness, and enhance their propensity to act in their own self-interest.

Discussion Topics

Group leaders often began sessions by identifying discussion topics for the group. In one session, they might suggest a discussion of coping and self-defense strategies. In another, they might suggest a discussion of self-blame and how batterers influence them to blame themselves for the abuse. Other common discussion foci of the groups included the dynamics and consequences of emotional numbness, role conflict resolution (some role playing was also done), healthy and unhealthy forms of anger, validating loss and grief through discussing the loss of idealized love or what each woman would miss if she left her partner, feelings of helplessness and the relationship of those feelings to abuse, and what is reasonable to try to accomplish about one's feelings.

Research Design

AB single-case designs were aggregated to assess the effectiveness of the outreach counseling and support groups. This approach was selected because it provides a scientifically credible way to assess outcome that does not conflict with agency concerns about withholding, withdrawing, or delaying service delivery. As noted earlier, the time lapse that routinely occurred between agency intake and when each client eventually chose to attend her first group meeting made it possible to collect baseline data without delaying the onset of intervention. Each client's baseline length depended on how long it took her, based on her own circumstances and reasons, to begin attending group sessions.

AB designs offer less internal validity than do more complex single subject designs, such as $A_1B_1A_2B_2$ designs and multiple baseline designs. The latter designs are stronger because replication is built into them within a single case or across cases. The principle is to look for unlikely successive coincidences (Jayaratne & Levy, 1979), but unlikely coincidences might also appear when we accumulate replications of AB designs. The design used in this study offered a natural opportunity to control somewhat for history because the women ended their baselines at different times.

Each woman who agreed to participate provided a telephone number and time of day where and when she could safely and conveniently provide outcome data via a brief (5- to 10-minute) daily interview in which the research assistant (the MSW student placed at the agency) administered the outcome measures over the telephone. All outcome data were collected in these telephone interviews, which were conducted only on weekdays. Thus five data points per week were established for each client. The data collection period lasted 11 weeks, coinciding with the duration of the block field placement (between mid-January and early April 1990).

Results

Graphs providing a visual basis for developing causal inferences about treatment effects are displayed in Figures C-1 through C-6. In interpreting graphs like these, we look for shifts in the level or slope of the data occurring after the onset of treatment in a consistent fashion across replications. To the extent that we find such unlikely successive coincidences, the data patterns can be deemed visually significant and thus supportive of causal inferences (Barlow & Hersen, 1984; Jayaratne & Levy, 1979). In these *AB* design graphs, the first phase (*A*) is the baseline, and the second phase (*B*) is the intervention period, which commences when the client first attends one of the counseling and support groups.

Two graphs are presented for each of the six clients who provided data across both the baseline and intervention phases. The top graphs in Figures C-1 through C-6 provide scores (on the vertical axis) for Clients 1 through 6 on the first outcome measure: thoughts, feelings, and behaviors. The bottom graphs provide scores (on the vertical axis) for the same clients regarding the degree of abusive behavior by their partners. Readers are reminded that each client's graph represents a different time period. The weekday numbers appearing at the bottom of the horizontal axis correspond to different dates for different clients. For example, all clients have their first data point appear as Weekday 1 on the horizontal axis, even though each of these clients supplied her first data point on a different date. Each data point on the horizontal axis corresponds to the 24 hours up to receiving the telephone interview. If the next day was a weekday, then the next data point represents the score for the 24 hours between the two calls. Thus the data points represent daily scores for weekday telephone interviews, omitting the 48 hours after Friday interviews.

In each of the top graphs in each figure, the higher the score, the more desirable the outcome regarding thoughts, feelings, and behaviors. Thus service efficacy would be indicated by data patterns in which scores during the intervention phase have a higher level or a more increased slope than scores during the baseline phase. In contrast, in each of the bottom graphs in each figure, lower scores are more desirable since they represent less abuse. For these graphs, service efficacy would be indicated by data patterns in which scores during the intervention phase have a lower level or a more sharply decreasing slope than scores during the baseline phase. Figures C-1 through C-6 provide very little evidence in support of service efficacy.

In the top graph (thoughts, feelings, and behaviors) for Client 1, the lowest data point during baseline might create an impression of some visual significance, but

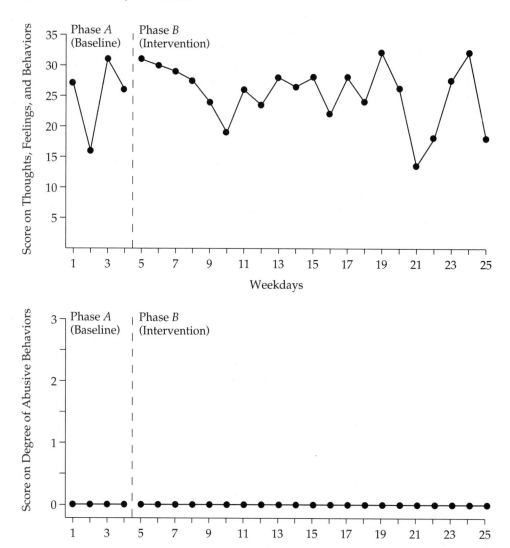

**FIGURE C-1 Summated Inventory Scores during Baseline and Intervention for
Client 1**

the intervention mean of 25.4 is not much higher than the baseline mean of 25.0.
With a baseline standard deviation of 6.4, the effect size is only .06. This client
attended four group sessions during the *B* phase (roughly once per week). Her
bottom graph (showing daily abuse scores) reflects no incidents of abuse during the
4 days of baseline or the 21 days of the intervention phase.

    In the top graph for Client 2, although there is one aberrantly high intervention
data point, the baseline and intervention means are identical (22.2), yielding an

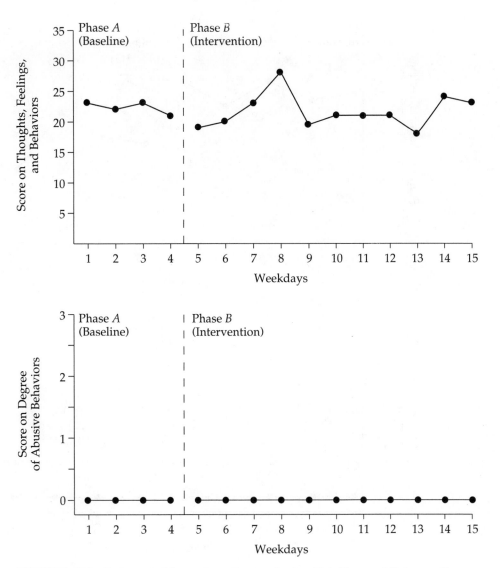

FIGURE C-2 Summated Inventory Scores during Baseline and Intervention for Client 2

effect size of zero. This client's intervention phase lasted 2 weeks, and she attended only one group session. Like Client 1, Client 2's bottom graph shows no incidents of abuse in either phase.

In the top graph for Client 3, the baseline mean of 24.2 drops to 16.8 during intervention. With a baseline standard deviation of 1.8, the effect size for these data is –4.1. The visual pattern for this graph is significant, and the difference between the means of the baseline and intervention phases is statistically significant ($p < .05$),

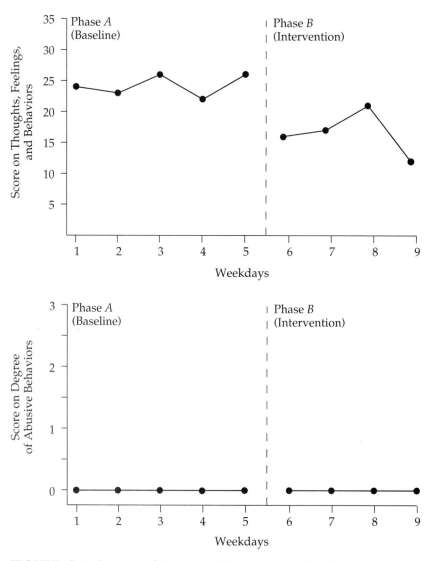

FIGURE C-3   Summated Inventory Scores during Baseline and
                      Intervention for Client 3

using the 2 standard deviation band approach. But the change is in an undesirable
direction. Although there is a clear drop in the level of inventory scores coinciding
with the onset of group attendance, the visual significance is offset by the small
number of data points. This client had attended only two group sessions at the
conclusion of this study. With only five points in baseline and four points in
intervention, our ability to rule out history, cyclicity, or other factors as plausible
alternative explanations for her data pattern is limited. The specific items on which

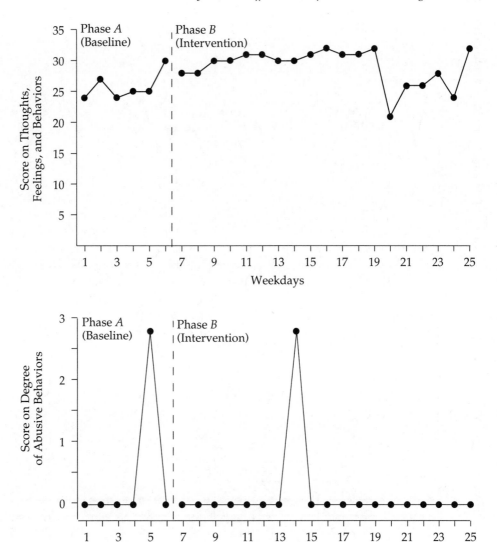

FIGURE C-4 **Summated Inventory Scores during Baseline and Intervention for Client 4**

this client's scores dropped the most dealt with feeling happy, sad, helpless, and good about herself. The day after her first attendance at group, she reported getting fired from her job. She said she was so upset after attending group that she could not go to work the next day. When we look at the bottom graph for Client 3 we again see, as with the previous two clients, no incidents of abuse in either phase.

The top graph for Client 4 comes closer to providing visual support for treatment efficacy than do the corresponding graphs for the previous 3 clients. In this

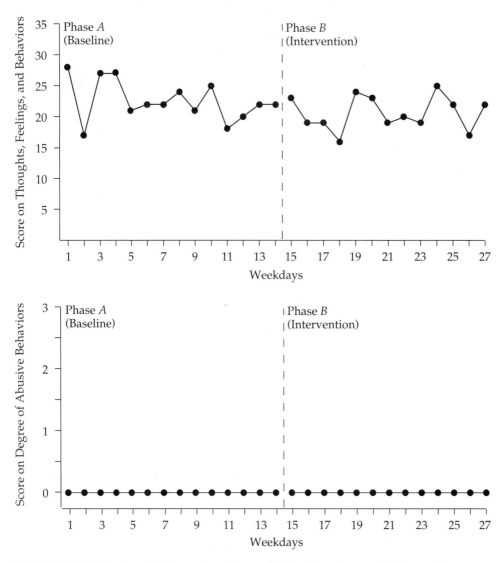

FIGURE C-5   Summated Inventory Scores during Baseline and Intervention for Client 5

graph, a stable and improved level of scores coincides with the onset of treatment. However, two factors weaken the visual significance of this graph. One is the fact that the first data point in the streak of improved scores occurred at the end of baseline, before the client attended her first group meeting. The other is the drop in scores for several data points near the end of the *B* phase. The mean score for this client improved from 25.8 in baseline to 28.8 in intervention, with an effect size of 1.3 (baseline standard deviation = 2.3). This change is not statistically significant. It is

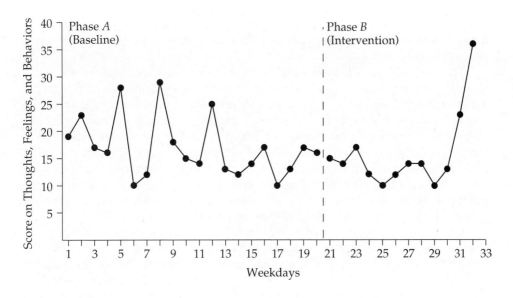

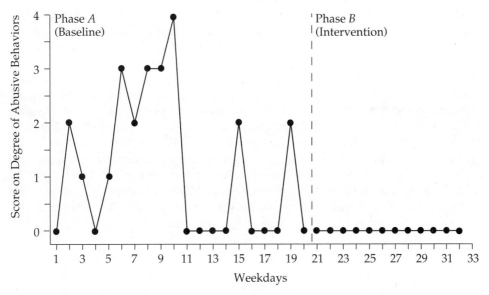

FIGURE C-6 Summated Inventory Scores during Baseline and Intervention for Client 6

conceivable that an extraneous event (or perhaps this client's problems with clinical depression) explains this client's dip in scores late during the intervention phase. At the same time that that dip occurred, her divorce was settled in court in a way that she perceived as favoring the batterer, and she reported that this upset her quite a bit. This client attended five group sessions, roughly on a weekly basis, during her intervention phase. Client 4 reported abusive mate behavior on only one day of baseline and one day of intervention, reflecting no differences between the two phases in her bottom graph.

The top graph for Client 5 shows that the intervention mean (20.5) was worse than the baseline mean (22.6). There is not much visual significance in this graph, and no statistical significance. With a baseline standard deviation of 3.3, the effect size is moderate at $-.636$ (which is relevant in light of the low statistical power of single-case studies with this number of data points). This woman attended group six times during the intervention phase, about once per week. She was not living with the batterer during baseline but moved back in with him about a week after intervention started, after attending her second session. This was at the fifth data point during the intervention phase. As with the first three clients, Client 5's bottom graph shows no incidents of abusive mate behavior in either phase.

Client 6 was the only one of the six participating in this study who was living with the batterer at the start of the study, and her two graphs are unlike those for the other five clients. Her top graph shows an ambiguous pattern. The baseline mean of 16.7 drops to 15.3 in intervention, and the effect size is $-.26$ (baseline standard deviation = 5.2). The final two data points of the intervention phase show a sharp upturn; however, these two data points occurred under special circumstances. The data for Client 6 should be interpreted in light of the fact that the client moved away from the batterer the weekend preceding the penultimate baseline data point and then moved back in with him temporarily after the fifth intervention data point. After the 10th data point in the intervention phase (the 30th data point overall), Client 6 again left the batterer to live with her mother. Two weeks then elapsed before the next data point was gathered, and another week elapsed before the final data point was gathered. Attributing either the positive or negative fluctuations in the top graph to the impact of group participation, therefore, is not warranted. The fluctuations could have been a reaction to the changing living arrangements. The same issues becloud the interpretation of Client 6's bottom graph. Client 6 reported abusive incidents on 10 of the 20 days of baseline but none during the 12 days of the intervention phase. Because she moved away from the batterer 1 day before starting intervention, there is reason to suppose that the cessation of battering simply is explained by leaving for a safer place before intervention even began rather than attributing the cessation to the intervention. And the continued absence of abuse during the five days of the intervention period when she moved back in with the batterer can be attributed to a "honeymoon" stage. One could perhaps argue that this client's anticipation of attending group helped her feel capable of moving away during baseline, but these data neither permit nor rule out such an explanation. This client attended group only two times during her *B* phase, which lasted five weeks.

Discussion and Applications to Social Work Practice

The foregoing data do not provide substantial grounds for optimism about the effectiveness of the counseling and support group intervention evaluated in this study. None of the six graphs on thoughts, feelings, and behaviors offer much visual or statistical support for concluding that the intervention groups are effective. Only the graphs for Client 4 and Client 6 show a potentially noteworthy period of improvement during the intervention phase, and in each of these it is unclear what caused the improvement and whether it would prove to be sustained or temporary.

Moreover, the results on thoughts, feelings, and behaviors for Client 3 are in an undesirable direction. This client, who had learned of the program from Alcoholics Anonymous, had a marked drop in scores on thoughts, feelings, and behaviors immediately after intervention commenced. She reported that the day after attending her first group session, she was so upset that she could not go to work and consequently got fired from her job. It is unclear what this means. One possible interpretation is that intervention may have been harmful for this client. However, one could argue that being upset after first attending group may be a positive sign, perhaps reflecting the discomfort of dealing with the denial of her situation. This client's entire intervention phase, which consisted of only four data points, may have reflected just a temporary deterioration associated with her reaction to dealing with denial. Getting fired for missing one day of work is unusual. Her attributing it to the impact of attending group may not be warranted and is perhaps being used as a way to avoid facing other factors that may have contributed. Getting fired may have been based on a longer history of problems, and the deterioration in scores during the intervention phase could have had more to do with her getting fired than with attending group. This client dropped out of the study after her fourth data point in the intervention phase and would not provide additional data that might facilitate a better interpretation.

It is conceivable that some clients exhibit a deterioration in the outcome indicators before they start exhibiting a sustained improvement. For example, Turner and Shapiro (1986) postulated that many battered women are engaged in denial and avoid acknowledging the painful impact on their already troubled lives of recent or anticipated losses of an idealized relationship, marital role, and emotional and other forms of security. It is not unreasonable to suppose that some women who might eventually benefit from the counseling and support groups will, during the first few weeks of attending the groups, find that confronting these issues initially increases the frequency of negative thoughts or feelings. Turner and Shapiro took issue with those who recommend concentrating on the needs of battered women for concrete services and who ignore or underemphasize emotional issues associated with the woman's need for security, closeness, and role fulfillment. The process of working through what Turner and Shapiro called "mourning the death of a relationship" may be lengthy, and practitioners who expect to see marked improvement in indicators like the ones used in this study may need to rethink their expectations. In fact, taking a psychosocial perspective as espoused by Turner and Shapiro, one could argue that an increase in reported frequencies of negative thoughts and feelings early in treatment might be a good sign—an indication that painful issues previously denied were being confronted.

Thus despite the fact that it is clear that in this brief study the intervention did not consistently yield beneficial effects, one could argue that conclusions about the efficacy of the intervention would be premature at this time. As noted earlier, the length of this study was limited by feasibility constraints. Although the clinical and administrative staff of the ACBW believed that improvements in inventory scores would be observed consistently across clients as soon as group attendance began, their optimism may have been unrealistic. Conceivably, the tested intervention really is effective, but a much longer intervention period is needed before the beneficial effects commence or become evident. This possibility can be tested with future single-subject evaluations that employ lengthier intervention phases. Perhaps consistent patterns will be detected in which beneficial treatment effects are observed much later in treatment, possibly following an initial period of deterioration. Of course, it is also possible that such studies will obtain results that provide no more support for treatment efficacy than do the results of this study. The point is to put the current results in proper perspective, not to discount them. Also, it does not seem premature to conclude at this time that if the tested intervention really is effective, its effects certainly do not consistently appear as soon as the staff expected them to—at least not on the indicators that were identified for this study.

As an alternative to much lengthier monitoring of clients, future studies might assess outcome indicators that conceivably have a better chance of reflecting desirable change early in treatment. For example, measures could be constructed to assess whether clients are beginning to overcome denial and to face some painful issues. Thus instead of asking about feeling happy or sad, good about herself, and so on, these measures might ask whether the client believes that she can excuse her partner's behavior in light of his problems, whether she believes her partner will stop abusing her if she just improves her behavior, and similar questions indicative of the extent to which the woman might be denying her painful situation, including anticipated or recent losses. Perhaps a Likert-type scale asking about such beliefs would be more appropriate than questions about the frequency of thoughts, feelings, and behaviors.

Future studies also might want to concentrate on women who are still living with the batterer when they begin receiving the intervention. Women who move out before attending groups may have already made too much progress to have visually significant results early in treatment, particularly on indicators like the ones selected in this study in collaboration with the ACBW staff. In the top graphs in Figures C-1 through C-6, the five women not living with the batterers at the start of the study (Clients 1 through 5) started out with higher scores on thoughts, feelings, and behaviors than did the woman still living with the batterer (Client 6), and the baseline scores of those five women were so near the maximum score of 32 that there was not much room for improvement to begin with.

Likewise, in the bottom graphs of Figures C-1 through C-6, it was only the woman still living with the batterer in baseline (Client 6) whose baseline data showed adequate room for improvement regarding scores indicating extent of abusive behaviors. It might be tempting to interpret that client's absence of abuse during the intervention phase as evidence of program effectiveness. But as noted in the findings, this woman moved away from the batterer before starting the intervention, and therefore the cessation of battering simply might be explained by leaving for a safer place before intervention rather than as an effect of intervention.

It could be argued that perhaps she was emboldened to leave by the knowledge that she was about to begin attending the counseling and support groups. Such an argument would presume the possibility of anticipatory treatment effects that could occur before treatment begins. This argument would conflict with traditional notions of logic that dictate that effects cannot be attributed to a treatment (i.e., the cause of the effects) unless they occur after the treatment (i.e., the cause) has commenced, but perhaps this argument is worth considering nonetheless.

In addition to their methodological relevance, the baseline data of the five women who were not living with the batterers during baseline (Clients 1 through 5) have implications for the staff of battered women's programs. Program planners and service providers may want to reexamine their assumptions about the needs of clients who are not living with the batterers when they enter the program and about what the treatment objectives for these women should be and how best to measure goal attainment with them. The baseline data in this study suggest that these clients may be faring better on this study's dependent variables before participating in the program than staff think they are. Practitioners may want to consider formulating objectives on an individualized basis, in collaboration with each client, rather than using the same outcome indicators with all the clients.

Practitioners also may want to provide more structure to the intervention and perhaps even develop an intervention manual. Better standardization of the intervention would provide several important benefits. First, it would help others replicate this intervention and assess it. Second, it would make it easier to interpret the results of future outcome studies. Third, perhaps new clients attempting to deal with the pain, trouble, and disarray that they are experiencing would find a more highly structured intervention more attractive and thus be more likely to begin intervention sooner and stay with it longer and more consistently. In this connection, it bears noting that there are two ways to look at the small number of group sessions attended by some of the clients. As noted earlier, one way is to cite that as a reason not to interpret the relatively negative data of this study too harshly; that is, to acknowledge that perhaps if the clients had attended more sessions the intervention would have appeared to be more effective. The other way, however, related to the *outreach* function of these counseling and support groups. The term outreach implies an effort to engage clients in treatment and to overcome barriers to their participation in treatment. To the extent that clients are participating in the intervention groups to a lesser degree than the staff anticipated, especially if that degree of participation is not yielding observable beneficial effects, then one can argue that the outreach aspect of the intervention is not as effective as desired.

Lewis (1983) described some problems that battered women encounter in mixed treatment groups like the ones evaluated in this study—problems that seem particularly relevant to the outreach function of the evaluated groups as well as to their relatively low degree of structure. Lewis argued that it is undesirable to lump into a mixed treatment group battered women who are at different stages of dealing with the battering and who therefore have diverse needs and concerns. Women who have been out of the relationship longer, and perhaps in treatment longer, may communicate impatience and annoyance with women at earlier stages of dealing with the problem. Some women may engage in a game of one-upmanship, in which each tries to convey the impression that she has suffered the most and which, in turn, may make other women feel that their cases are not so bad and that perhaps they do not belong in the group. Lewis suggests that these dynamics can evoke some women to withdraw from the group.

Although one can only hypothesize at this point as to the likelihood of getting better results with a more highly structured intervention, it is worth noting that the most recent reviews of social work practice effectiveness have found that studies with successful outcomes have usually evaluated more highly structured forms of practice and that evaluations of relatively unstructured forms of practice have generally not been found to be effective (Blythe & Briar, 1987; Reid & Hanrahan, 1982; Rubin, 1985). These reviews, as well as earlier reviews of the empirical literature on social work practice, have shown that despite the best of intentions, services that subjectively seem to be valuable sometimes turn out to be of no help to clients and in some cases are actually harmful (Fischer, 1973; Mullen & Dumpsen, 1972; Wood, 1978). This literature underscores the importance of evaluating services to battered women, a field of service delivery that has had virtually no rigorous empirical outcome evaluations to date.

This study has been an initial effort toward building the needed empirical base regarding the effectiveness of services for battered women. Because its results are inconclusive, much more research is needed to evaluate the effectiveness of outreach counseling and support groups for battered women and to sort out the alternative possible explanations for this study's findings. The author hopes that this report will have value in stimulating such research and in enhancing the methodologies of future studies using single-case designs to evaluate battered women's programs. We know how difficult it is to conduct well-controlled evaluations of battered women's programs using traditional group designs. Time will tell whether single-case designs offer a realistic alternative or whether the need for lengthy monitoring or for client improvements that commence soon after onset of treatment make these designs unworkable for this particular problem area. If they do prove to be workable, then time will also tell whether the current study's results signify the beginning of an empirical foundation for questioning the efficacy of interventions like the one described in this article and for searching for more effective approaches.

References

Aguirre, B. E. (1985). Why do they return? Abused wives in shelters. *Social Work, 30,* 350–354.

Alcoholics Anonymous. (1976). *Alcoholics anonymous* (3rd ed.). New York: Alcoholics Anonymous World Services, Inc.

Barlow, D., & Hersen, M. (1984). *Single case experimental designs.* New York: Pergamon.

Bentzel, S. B., & York, R. O. (1988). Influence of

feminism and professional status upon service options for the battered woman. *Community Mental Health Journal, 24,* 52–64.

Berk, R., Newton, P., & Berk, S. (1986). What a difference a day makes: An empirical study of the impact of shelters for battered women. *Journal of Marriage and the Family, 48,* 481–490.

Blythe, B. J., & Briar, S. (1987). Direct practice effectiveness. In A. Minahan (Ed.), *Encyclopedia of social work* (18th ed., pp. 399–409). Silver Spring, MD: National Association of Social Workers.

Bretton, T. (1988, April). Why battered women don't leave home. *New Woman*, pp. 104–108.

Davis, N. J. (1988). Shelters for battered women: Social policy response to interpersonal violence. *Social Science Journal, 25,* 401–419.

Edleson, J. L., Miller, D. M., Stone, G. W., & Chapman, D. G. (1985). Group treatment for men who batter. *Social Work Research and Abstracts, 21*(3), 18–21.

Fischer, J. (1973). Is casework effective? A review. *Social Work, 18,* 5–20.

Jaffee, P., Wilson, S. K., & Wolfe, D. (1988). Specific assessment and intervention strategies for children exposed to wife battering: Preliminary empirical investigations. *Canadian Journal of Community Mental Health, 7,* 157–163.

Jayaratne, S., & Levy, R. (1979). *Empirical clinical practice.* New York: Columbia University Press.

Kirsh, B. (1974). Consciousness-raising groups as therapy for women. In V. Franks & V. Burtle (Eds.), *Women in therapy* (pp. 326–354). New York: Brunner/Mazel.

Lewis, E. (1983). The group treatment of battered women. *Women & Therapy, 2,* 51–58.

McShane, C. (1979). Community services for bat-

tered women. *Social Work, 24,* 34–38.

Mullen, E. J., & Dumpsen, J. R. (Eds.). (1972). *Evaluation of social intervention.* San Francisco: Jossey-Bass.

Pfouts, J., Renz, H., & Renz, C. (1981). The future of wife abuse programs. *Social Work, 26,* 451–455.

Reid, W. J., & Hanrahan, P. (1982). Recent evaluations of social work: Grounds for optimism. *Social Work, 27,* 328–340.

Rounsaville, B. (1978). Battered wives: Barriers to identification and treatment. *American Journal of Orthopsychiatry, 48,* 487–494.

Rounsaville, B., Lifton, N., & Bieber, B. (1979). The natural history of a psychotherapy group for battered women. *Psychiatry, 42,* 63–78.

Rubin, A. (1985). Practice effectiveness: More grounds for optimism. *Social Work, 30,* 469–476.

Turner, S., & Shapiro, C. (1986). Battered women: Mourning the death of a relationship. *Social Work, 31,* 372–376.

Walker, L. E. (1989). *The battered woman.* New York: Harper & Row.

Wodarski, J. (1987). An examination of spouse abuse: Practice issues for the profession. *Clinical Social Work Journal, 15,* 173–187.

Wood, K. M. (1978). Casework effectiveness: A new look at the research evidence. *Social Work, 23,* 437–458.

GLOSSARY

YVONNE UNRAU

Accountability: A system of responsibility in which program administrators account for all program activities by answering to the demands of a program's stakeholders and by justifying the program's expenditures to the satisfaction of its stakeholders.

Accuracy: A standard of evaluation practice that requires technical adequacy of the evaluation process; includes matters of validity, reliability, measurement instruments, samples, and comparisons.

Activities: What practitioners do with their clients to achieve their practice and facilitative objectives.

Affective Program Objective: An objective that focuses on changing an individual's emotional reaction to him- or herself or to another person or thing.

Agency: A social service organization that exists to fulfill a broad social purpose. It functions as one entity, is governed by a single directing body, and has policies and procedures that are common to all of its parts.

Agency Goal: Broad unmeasurable outcomes the agency wishes to achieve. They are based on values and are guided by the agency's mission statement.

Agency Objective: A program established to help in the achievement of the agency's goal.

Area Probability Sampling: A form of cluster sampling that uses a three-stage process to provide the means to carry out a study when a comprehensive list of a population cannot be compiled.

Assessment: A professional activity that occurs prior to the intervention phase and investigates a client's present level of functioning in relevant areas so that an appropriate intervention plan can be established.

Baseline Measure: A numerical label assigned to a client's level of performance, knowledge, or affect *prior* to any intervention; the first measure to be made in any series of repeated measurements; designated as the *A* phase in formal case-level designs.

Behavioral Program Objective: An objective that aims to change the conduct or actions of clients.

Case Conferences: An informal, or nonempirical, method of case evaluation that requires professionals to meet and exchange descriptive client information for the purposes of making a case decision.

Classical Experimental Design: An explanatory research design with randomly selected and randomly assigned experimental and control groups in which the program's objective (the dependent variable) is measured before and

399

after the intervention (the independent variable) for both groups, but only the experimental group receives the intervention.

Client Log: A form whereby clients maintain annotated records of events related to their practice objectives; structured journals in which clients record events, feelings, and reactions relevant to their problem.

Clients: People who use human services—individuals, couples, families, groups, organizations, and communities.

Cluster Sampling: A multistage probability sampling procedure in which a population is divided into groups or clusters and the clusters, rather than the individuals, are selected for inclusion in the sample.

Comparison Group Posttest-Only Design: A descriptive research design with two groups, experimental and comparison, in which the program's objective (dependent variable) is measured once for both groups, and only the experimental group receives the intervention (the independent variable).

Comparison Group Pretest-Posttest Design: A descriptive research design with two groups, experimental and comparison in which the program's objective (the dependent variable) is measured before and after the intervention (the independent variable) for both groups, but only the experimental group receives the intervention.

Compensation: Attempts by evaluators or staff members to counterbalance the lack of treatment for control group clients by administering some or all of the intervention (the independent variable); a threat to internal validity.

Compensatory Rivalry: Motivation of control group clients to compete with experimental group clients; a threat to internal validity.

Computerized Data Systems: An automated method of organizing single units of data to generate summarized or aggregate forms of data.

Constants: A characteristic that has the same value for all clients in an evaluation.

Contextual Data: Empirical or subjective data that reflect the circumstances of the problem and help to explain the outcome or score.

Control Group: A group of randomly selected and randomly assigned clients in a study who do not receive the experimental intervention (the independent variable) and are used for comparison purposes.

Convenience Sampling: A nonprobability sampling procedure that relies on the closest and most available participants to constitute a sample.

Data: Isolated facts, presented in numerical or descriptive form, on which client or program decisions are based. Not to be confused with information.

Data Display: The manner in which collected data are set out on a page.

Decision Data Chart: A chart that lists, in chronological order, decisions to be made, the data needed to make each decision, and the data actually collected; used to ensure that adequate links exist between the data collected and the decisions made.

Demoralization: Feelings of deprivation among control group clients which may cause them to drop out of the evaluation study; a form of mortality which is a threat to internal validity.

Dependent Variable: A variable that is dependent on or caused by another variable; an outcome variable which is not manipulated directly but is measured to determine if the independent variable has had an effect. Program objectives are dependent variables.

Descriptive Design: A design that approximates a true experiment, but the worker does not have the same degree of control over manipulation of the intervention process; also known as quasi-experimental designs.

Differential Selection: The failure to achieve or maintain equivalency among the preformed groups; a threat to internal validity.

Diffusion of Treatment: Problems that may occur when experimental and control group clients talk to each other about a study; a threat to internal validity.

Duration Recording: A method of data collection that involves direct observation and documentation of the practice objective by recording the length of time of each occurrence within a specified observation period.

Efficiency Assessment: An evaluation to determine

the ratio of effectiveness or outcome to cost. Does not contain data that may explain why the program is or is not efficient.

Empirical Data: Isolated facts presented in numerical or descriptive form that have been derived from observation or testing, as opposed to data derived from inference or theory.

Empirical Evaluation: A method of appraisal based on the analysis of data collected by measuring instruments.

Evaluability Assessment: An appraisal of a program's components and operations intended to determine whether a program can, in fact, be evaluated for outcome, efficiency, or process. Mainly used to construct meaningful and measurable program objectives which are derived from the program's goal.

Evaluation: A form of appraisal using valid and reliable research methods. There are numerous types of evaluations geared to produce data which in turn produce information that helps in the decision-making process. Data from evaluations are used in the quality improvement process.

Evaluation Design: A process used to evaluate some aspect of a program; intended to elicit data that are required in making some decision.

Experimental Group: In an experimental research design, the group of clients exposed to the manipulation of the intervention (the independent variable); also referred to as the treatment group.

Explanatory Design: An attempt to demonstrate with certainty that specific activities caused specific reported changes in practice objectives. The professional manipulates certain factors in the intervention to gain a greater degree of control over the proceedings; also known as experimental designs.

Exploratory Design: A process in which a professional assesses the effects of an intervention process for the purpose of building a foundation of general ideas and tentative theories that can later be examined by more rigorous evaluative methods.

External Evaluation: An evaluation that is conducted by someone who does not have any connection with the program; usually an evaluation that is requested by the agency's funding sources. This type of evaluation complements an internal evaluation.

External Validity: The extent to which the findings of an evaluation study can be generalized outside the evaluative situation.

Extraneous Variables: Outside factors that occur at the same time as the intervention and thus may account for some of the measured change in practice objectives.

Facilitative Practice Objective: An objective that relates to the overall practice objective (it can be termed a practice subobjective); it also specifies an intended result and makes the achievement of the practice objective easier; constructed for the client's benefit.

Fairness: A standard of evaluation practice that requires evaluations to be conducted in a fair and ethical manner; includes the dissemination of evaluation results.

Feasibility: A standard of evaluation practice that requires evaluations to be conducted only under conditions that are practical and economically viable.

Field Error: A type of nonsampling error in which field staff show bias in their selection of a sample.

Flow Chart: A diagram of client service delivery in which symbols are used to depict client movement throughout the service delivery system.

Formal Case-Level Evaluation: An empirical method of appraisal in which a single client is monitored via repeated measurements over time in order to examine change in a practice objective.

Frequency Recording: A method of data collection involving direct observation and documentation in which each occurrence of the practice objective is recorded during a specified observation period.

Generalizability: Extending or applying the findings of an evaluation study to clients or situations which were not directly evaluated.

Graphic Rating Scale: A type of measuring instrument that describes an attribute on a continuum from one extreme to the other, with points of the continuum ordered in equal intervals and assigned numbers.

Hawthorne Effect: Effects on clients' behaviors or attitudes attributable to their knowledge that they are taking part in an evaluation project; a reactive effect that is a threat to internal validity.

History in Research Design: Any event that may affect the second or subsequent measurement of the program's objectives (the dependent variables) and which cannot be accounted for in the evaluation design; a threat to internal validity.

Hypothesis: A theory-based prediction of the expected results in an evaluation study; a tentative explanation of a relationship or supposition that a relationship may exist.

Independent Variable: A variable that is not dependent on another variable but is said to cause or determine changes in the dependent variable; an antecedent variable that is directly manipulated in order to assess its effect on the dependent variable. Interventions are independent variables.

Information: The interpretation given to data that have been collected, collated, and analyzed. Information is used to help in the decision-making process. Not to be confused with data.

Informed Consent: Procedures in which clients, or evaluation subjects, are told in advance about the major tasks and activities they will perform during an evaluation study; clients then participate in the evaluation study only if they are willing to engage in these activities.

Instrumental Practice Objective: An objective that bears no apparent relation to the practice objective, but when accomplished will remove practical impediments to the attainment of the practice objective; constructed for the client's benefit.

Instrumentation Error: Any flaws in the construction of a measuring instrument or any faults in the administration of a measuring instrument that affect the appraisal of program and practice objectives; a threat to internal validity.

Interaction Effect: Effects on the program's objective (the dependent variable) that are produced by the combination of two or more threats to internal validity.

Internal Evaluation: An evaluation that is conducted by someone who works within a program; usually an evaluation for the purpose of promoting better client services. This type of evaluation complements an external evaluation.

Internal Validity: The extent to which it can be demonstrated that the intervention (the independent variable) in an evaluation is the only cause of change in the program's objective (the dependent variable); soundness of the experimental procedures and measuring instruments.

Interrupted Time-Series Design: An explanatory evaluation design in which there is only one group and the program objective (the dependent variable) is measured repeatedly before and after the intervention (the independent variable).

Interval Recording: A method of data collection that involves continuous, direct observation and documentation of an individual's behavior during specified observation periods divided into equal time intervals.

Knowledge Program Objective: An objective that aims to change a client's level of information and understanding about a specific social area.

Longitudinal Case Study Design: An exploratory research design in which there is only one group and the program's objective (the dependent variable) is measured more than once; also referred to as a panel design, a cohort design, a developmental design, or a dynamic case study design.

Magnitude Recording: A method of data collection that involves direct observation and documentation of the amount, level, or degree of the practice objective during each occurrence.

Maintenance Program Objective: An objective formulated in an effort to keep a program financially viable; constructed for the program's benefit.

Manual Data Management: Noncomputerized

method of organizing single units of data to generate summarized or aggregate forms of the data.

Matched Pairs Method: A technique of assigning clients to groups so that the experimental and control groups are approximately equivalent in pretest scores or other characteristics, or so that all differences except the experimental condition are eliminated.

Maturation: Any unplanned change in clients due to mental, physical, or other processes which take place over the course of the evaluation project and which affect the program's objective; a threat to internal validity.

Measure: A label, usually numerical, assigned to an observation that has been subjected to measurement.

Measurement: The process of systematically assigning labels to observations; in statistics, measurement systems are classified according to level of measurement and usually produce data that can be represented in numerical form; the assignment of numerals to objects or events according to specific rules.

Measuring Instruments: Instruments such as questionnaires or rating scales used to obtain a measure for a particular client or client group.

Mission Statement: A unique written philosophical perspective of what an agency is all about; states a common vision for the organization by providing a point of reference for all major planning decisions.

Monitoring Approach to Quality Improvement: Evaluations that aim to provide ongoing feedback so that a program (or project) can be improved while it is still underway. It contributes to the continuous development and improvement of a human service program. This approach complements the project approach.

Mortality: The tendency for clients to drop out of an evaluation study before it is completed; a threat to internal validity.

Multigroup Posttest-Only Design: An exploratory research design in which there is more than one group and the program's objective (the dependent variable) is measured only once for each group.

Multiple-Treatment Interference: When a client is given two or more interventions in succession, the results of the first intervention may affect the results of the second or subsequent interventions; a threat to external validity.

Multistage Probability Sampling: Probability sampling procedures used when a comprehensive list of a population does not exist and it is not possible to construct one.

Needs Assessment: An evaluation that aims to assess the need for a human service by verifying that a social problem exists within a specific client population to an extent that warrants services.

Nonempirical Evaluation: An informal method of appraisal that is not based on empirical data; it depends on theories and descriptions that a professional considers to be relevant to the case.

Nonprobability Sampling: Sampling procedures in which all of the persons, events, or objects in the sampling frame have an unknown, and usually unequal, chance of being included in a sample.

Nonreactivity: An unobtrusive characteristic of a measuring instrument; nonreactive measuring instruments do not affect the behavior being measured.

Nonsampling Errors: Errors in study results that are not due to sampling procedures.

Norm: In measurement, an average or set group standard of achievement that can be used to interpret individual scores; normative data describing statistical properties of a measuring instrument, such as means and standard deviations.

One-Group Posttest-Only Design: An exploratory design in which the program's objective (the dependent variable) is measured only once; the simplest of all group evaluation designs.

One-Group Pretest-Posttest Design: A descriptive research design in which the program's objective (the dependent variable) is measured before and after the intervention (the independent variable).

One-Stage Probability Sampling: Probability sampling procedures in which the selection of a sample from a population is completed in one single process.

Outcome Assessment: An evaluation that determines how effectively a program is meeting its stated written program objectives.

Performance Appraisal: The process of evaluating the efficiency and effectiveness of a staff person's work; a possible misuse of evaluation practice.

Phase: Any relatively distinct part of the contact between a professional and a client; *A* represents a baseline phase and *B* an intervention phase.

Practice Objective: A statement of expected change identifying an intended therapeutic result tailored to the unique circumstances and needs of each client; logically linked to a program objective. Practice objectives, like program objectives, can be grouped into affects, knowledge, and behaviors.

Pretest-Treatment Interaction: Effects of the pretest on the responses of clients to the introduction of the intervention (the independent variable); a threat to external validity.

Principle of Parsimony: A principle stating that the simplest and most economical route to evaluating the achievement of the program's objective (the dependent variable) is the best.

Private Consultations: An informal method of case evaluation in which a professional exchanges descriptive information about client with another helping human service workers to obtain solid advice.

Probability Sampling: Sampling procedures in which every member of a designated population has a known chance of being selected for a sample.

Process Analysis: An evaluation in which the entire range and sequence of program activities, including decision making, are appraised.

Program: An organization that exists to fulfil some social purpose; must be logically linked to the agency's goal.

Program Goal: A statement defining the intent of a program which cannot be directly evaluated. It can, however, be evaluated indirectly by the program's objectives which are derived

from the goal. Not to be confused with program objectives.

Program Monitoring: A program activity comprised of the ongoing collection, analysis, reporting, and use of collected program data.

Program Objective: A statement that clearly and exactly specifies the expected change, or intended result, for individuals receiving program services. Qualities of well-chosen objectives are meaningfulness, specificity, measurability, and directionality. Program objectives, like practice objectives can be grouped into affects, knowledge, and behaviors. Not to be confused with program goal.

Project Approach to Quality Improvement: Evaluations whose purpose is to assess a completed or finished program (or project). This approach complements the monitoring approach.

Purposive Sampling: A nonprobability sampling procedure in which individuals with particular characteristics are purposely selected for inclusion in the sample; also known as judgmental or theoretical sampling.

Qualitative: A description of data that is given in words.

Quality Improvement Process: An ethical commitment to continually look for and seek ways to make services more responsive, efficient, and effective. It is a process that uses the data from all types of evaluations to improve the quality of human services.

Quantitative: A description of data which is given in numbers.

Quota Sampling: A nonprobability sampling procedure in which the relevant characteristics of a sample are identified, the proportion of these characteristics in the population is determined, and participants are selected from each category until the predetermined proportion (quota) has been achieved.

Random Assignment: The process of allocating clients to experimental and control groups so that the groups are equivalent; also referred to as randomization.

Random Sampling: An unbiased selection process conducted so that all members of a population have an equal chance of being selected to participate in the evaluation study.

Randomized Cross-Sectional Survey Design: A descriptive research design in which there is only one group, the program's objective (the dependent variable) is measured only once, the clients are randomly selected from the population and there is no intervention (the independent variable).

Randomized Longitudinal Survey Design: A descriptive research design in which there is only one group, the program's objective (the dependent variable) is measured more than once, and clients are randomly selected from the population before the intervention (the independent variable).

Randomized One-Group Posttest-Only Design: A descriptive research design in which there is only one group, the program's objective (the dependent variable) is measured only once and all members of a population have equal opportunity for participation in the evaluation.

Randomized Posttest-Only Control Group Design: An explanatory research design in which there are two or more randomly selected and randomly assigned groups; the control group does not receive the intervention (the independent variable), and the experimental groups receive different interventions.

Rating Scales: A type of measuring instrument in which responses are rated on a continuum or in an ordered set of categories, with numerical values assigned to each point or category.

Reactive Effects: An effect on outcome measures due to the clients' awareness that they are participating in an evaluation study; a threat to internal and external validity.

Reliability: (1) The degree of accuracy, precision, or consistency of results of a measuring instrument, including the ability to reproduce results when a variable is measured more than once or a test is repeatedly filled out by the same individual. (2) The degree to which individual differences on scores or in data are due either to true differences or to errors in measurement.

Repeated Measurements: The administration of one measuring instrument (or set of instruments) a number of times to the same client, under the same conditions, over a period of time.

Researcher Bias: The tendency of evaluators to find results that they expect to find; a threat to external validity.

Response Bias: The tendency for individuals to score items on a measuring instrument in such a manner that one score is reported for the majority of all items.

Response Error: A type of nonsampling error in which the participants of an evaluation present themselves differently than they actually are, perhaps in a manner that is socially desirable.

Rival Hypothesis: A theory-based prediction that is a plausible alternative to the research hypothesis and might explain results as well or better; a hypothesis involving extraneous variables other than the intervention (the independent variable); also referred to as the alternative hypothesis.

Sample: A subset of a population of individuals, objects, or events chosen to participate in or to be considered in a study; a group chosen by unbiased sample selection from which inferences about the entire population of people, objects, or events can be drawn.

Sampling Frame: A listing of units (people, objects, or events) in a population from which a sample is selected.

Sampling Theory: The logic of using methods to ensure that a sample and a population are similar in all relevant characteristics.

Selection-Treatment Interaction: The relationship between the manner of selecting clients to participate in an evaluation study and their responses to the intervention (the independent variable); a threat to external validity.

Self-Anchored Rating Scale: A type of measuring instrument in which respondents rate themselves on a continuum of values, according to their own referents for each point.

Simple Random Sampling: A one-stage probability sampling procedure in which members of a population are selected one at a time, without chance of being selected again, until the desired sample size is obtained.

Snowball Sampling: A nonprobability sampling procedure in which individuals selected for inclusion in a sample are asked to identify additional individuals who might be included from the population; can be used to locate people with divergent points of view.

Solomon Four-Group Design: An explanatory research design with four randomly assigned groups, two experimental and two control; the program's objective (the dependent variable) is measured before and after the intervention (the independent variable) for one experimental and one control group, but only after the intervention for the other two groups, and only the experimental groups receive the intervention.

Specificity of Variables: An evaluation project conducted with a specific group of clients at a specific time and in a specific setting may not always be generalizable to other clients at a different time and in a different setting; a threat to external validity.

Spot-Check Recording: A method of data collection that involves direct observation and documentation of the practice objective at specified intervals rather than continuously.

Stakeholder: A person or group of people having a direct or indirect interest in the results of an evaluation.

Standardized Measurement Instrument: A paper-and-pencil tool, usually constructed by researchers and used by human service professionals, to measure a particular area of knowledge, behavior, or feeling; provides for uniform administration and scoring and generates normative data against which later results can be evaluated.

Statistical Regression: The tendency for extreme high or low scores to regress, or shift, toward the average (mean) score on subsequent measurements; a threat to internal validity.

Stratified Random Sampling: A one-stage probability sampling procedure in which the population is divided into two or more strata to be sampled separately, using random or systematic random sampling techniques.

Subjective Data: Isolated facts, presented in descriptive terms, that are based on impressions, experience, values, and intuition.

Summated Scale: A multi-item measuring instrument in which respondents provide a rating for each item. The summation of items provides an overall score.

Systematic Random Sampling: A one-stage probability sampling procedure in which every person at a designated interval in the population list is selected to be included in the study sample.

Testing Effect: The effect that taking a pretest might have on posttest scores; a threat to internal validity.

Utility: (1) A characteristic of a measuring instrument that indicates its degree of usefulness (e.g., how practical is the measuring instrument in a particular situation?). (2) A standard of evaluation practice that requires evaluations to be carried out only if they are considered potentially useful to one or more stakeholders.

Validity: The degree to which a measuring instrument accurately measures the variable it claims to measure.

Valuation: Interpretation given to data produced by evaluations; the degree to which results are considered a success or failure.

Variable: A characteristic that can take on different values for different individuals; any attribute whose value, or level, can change; any characteristic (of a person, object, or situation) that can change value or kind from observation to observation.

REFERENCES AND FURTHER READINGS

Adams, G. R. & Schvaneveldt, J. D. (1985). *Understanding research methods*. White Plains, NY: Longman.

Afidi, R. J. (1971). Informed consent: A study of patient reaction. *Journal of the American Medical Association, 216*, 1325–1329.

Aiken, L. R. (1985). *Psychological testing and assessment*. Needham Heights, MA: Allyn and Bacon.

Allen, M. J. & Yen, W. M. (1979). *Introduction to measurement theory*. Monterey, CA: Brooks/Cole.

Alreck, P. L. & Settle, R. B. (1985). *The survey research handbook*. Homewood, IL: Irwin.

Alter, C. & Evens, W. (1990). *Evaluating your practice: A guide to self-assessment*. New York: Springer.

Altheide, D. (1987). Ethnographic content analysis. *Qualitative Sociology, 10*, 62–77.

American Association on Mental Deficiency. (1977). *Consent handbook* (No. 3). Washington, DC: Author.

American Psychological Association. (1973). *Ethical principles in the conduct of research with human participants*. Washington, DC: Author.

American Psychological Association. (1977). *Standards for providers of psychological services*. Washington, DC: Author.

American Psychological Association (1981). *Specialty guidelines for counseling psychologists*. Washington, DC: Author.

American Psychological Association (1984). *Publication manual* (3rd ed.). Washington, DC: Author.

Anastas, J. (1984). Studying practice using single-subject research. *Journal of Smith College School of Social Work, 42*, 19–23.

Anastasi, A. (1988). *Psychological testing* (6th ed.). New York: Macmillan.

Anderson, B. (1990). *First fieldwork: The misadventures of an anthropologist*. Prospect Heights, IL: Waveland Press.

Andrews, D. A. & Hoge, R. D. (1987). *The family service assessment and evaluation project*. Ottawa, Ontario, Canada: Family Service Canada.

askSam Systems (1987). *askSam: The information manager for the PC*. Perry, FL: Author.

Atherton, C. & Klemmack, D. (1982). *Research methods in social work*. Lexington, MA: Heath.

Austin, M. J. & Crowell, J. (1985). Survey research. In R. M. Grinnell, Jr. (Ed.), *Social work research and evaluation* (2nd ed., pp. 275–305). Itasca, IL: F.E. Peacock Publishers.

Babbie, E. (1992). *The practice of social research* (6th ed.). Belmont, CA: Wadsworth.

Bailey, K. D. (1992). *Methods of social research* (3rd ed.). New York: Free Press.

Barlow, D. H. & Hersen, M. (1984). *Single-case experimental designs: Strategies for studying behavior change* (2nd ed.). Elmsford, NY: Pergamon.

Barlow, D. H., Hayes, S. C., & Nelson, R. O. (1984). *The scientist-practitioner: Research and accountability in applied settings.* Elmsford, NY: Pergamon.

Baugher, D. (1981). *Measuring effectiveness.* San Francisco, CA: Jossey-Bass.

Beck, R. A. & Rossi, P. H. (1990). *Thinking about program evaluation.* Newbury Park, CA: Sage.

Beckman, D. (Ed.). (1987). *Using program theory in evaluation.* San Francisco, CA: Jossey-Bass.

Bell, A. (1983). *Assessing health and human service needs.* New York: Human Sciences Press.

Bernfeld, G. A., Blase, K. A., & Fixsen, D. L. (1990). Towards a unified perspective on human service delivery systems: Application of the teaching–family model. In R. J. McMahon and R. Peters (Eds.), *Behavior disorders of adolescence* (pp. 191–205). New York: Plenum Press.

Bisno, H. & Borowski, A. (1985). The social and psychological contexts of research. In R. M. Grinnell, Jr. (Ed.), *Social work research and evaluation* (2nd ed., pp. 83–100). Itasca, IL: F.E. Peacock Publishers.

Blase, K., Fixsen, D., & Phillips, E. (1984). Residential treatment for troubled children: Developing service delivery systems. In S. C. Paine, G. T. Bellamy, & B. Wilcox (Eds.), *Human services that work: From innovation to standard practice.* Baltimore: Paul H. Brooks.

Blazek, R. (Ed.). (1981). *Achieving accountability.* Chicago: American Library Association.

Blease, D. (1986). *Evaluating educational software.* London: Croom Helm.

Bloom, M., Fischer, J., & Orme, J. (1994). *Evaluating practice: Guidelines for the accountable professional* (2nd ed.). Englewood Cliffs, NJ: Prentice-Hall.

Blythe, B. J. & Tripodi, T. (1989). *Measurement in direct practice.* Newbury Park, CA: Sage.

Booth, A. & Higgins, D. (1984). *Human service planning and evaluation for hard times.* Springfield, IL: Charles C. Thomas.

Borowski, A. (1988). Social dimensions of research. In R. M. Grinnell, Jr. (Ed.), *Social work research and evaluation* (3rd ed., pp. 42–64). Itasca, IL: F.E. Peacock Publishers.

Boruch, R. F. (1985). *Randomization and field experimentation.* San Francisco, CA: Jossey-Bass.

Boruch, R. F. & Cecil, J. S. (Eds.). (1983). *Solutions to ethical and legal problems in applied social research.* New York: Academic Press.

Boruch, R. F. & Pearson, R. W. (1985). *The comparative evaluation of longitudinal surveys.* New York: Social Science Research Council.

Borus, M. E., Tash, W. R., & Buntz, C. G. (1982). *Evaluating the impact of health programs.* Cambridge, MA: MIT Press.

Bostwick, G. J. & Kyte, N. S. (1985a). Measurement. In R. M. Grinnell, Jr. (Ed.), *Social work research and evaluation* (2nd ed., pp. 149–160). Itasca, IL: F.E. Peacock Publishers.

Bostwick, G. J. & Kyte, N. S. (1985b). Validity and reliability. In R. M. Grinnell, Jr. (Ed.), *Social work research and evaluation* (2nd ed., pp. 161–184). Itasca, IL: F.E. Peacock Publishers.

Bostwick, G. J. & Kyte, N. S. (1988). Validity and reliability. In R. M. Grinnell, Jr. (Ed.), *Social work research and evaluation* (3rd ed., pp. 111–136). Itasca, IL: F.E. Peacock Publishers.

Bostwick, G. J., Jr. & Kyte, N. S. (1993). Measurement in research. In R. M. Grinnell, Jr. (Ed.), *Social work research and evaluation* (4th ed., pp. 174–197). Itasca, IL: F.E. Peacock Publishers.

Bouey, E. & Rogers, G. (1993). Retrieving information. In R. M. Grinnell, Jr. (Ed.), *Social work research and evaluation* (4th ed., pp. 402–426). Itasca, IL: F.E. Peacock Publishers.

Brownstein, I. & Lerner, N. B. (1982). *Guidelines for evaluating and selecting software packages.* New York: Elsevier.

Broxmeyer, N. (1979). Practitioner-research in treating a borderline child. *Social Work Research and Abstracts, 14,* 5–10.

Bryk, A. S. (1983). *Stakeholder-based evaluation.* San Francisco, CA: Jossey-Bass.

Buros, O. K. (Ed.). (1978). *The eighth mental measurements yearbook* (2 vols.). Highland Park, NJ: Gryphon Press.

Campbell, D. & Stanley, J. (1963). *Experimental and quasi-experimental designs for research.* Chicago, IL: Rand McNally.

Carley, M. (1981). *Social measurement and social indicators.* London: Allen & Unwin.

Carter, R. K. (1983). *The accountable agency.* Newbury Park, CA: Sage.

Catterall, J. R. (Ed.). (1985). *Economic evaluation of*

public programs. San Francisco, CA: Jossey-Bass.

Chambers, D. E., Wedel, K. R., & Rodwell, M. K. (1992). *Evaluating social programs*. Needham Heights, MA: Allyn and Bacon.

Ciarlo, J. A. (Ed.). (1981). *Utilizing evaluation: Concepts and management techniques*. Newbury Park, CA: Sage.

Cohen, B. P. (1980). *Developing sociological knowledge*. Englewood Cliffs, NJ: Prentice-Hall.

Collins, D. & Polster, R. (1993). Structured observation. In R. M. Grinnell, Jr. (Ed.), *Social work research and evaluation* (4th ed., pp. 244–261). Itasca, IL: F.E. Peacock Publishers.

Compton, B. R. & Galaway, B. (1989). *Social work processes* (4th ed.). Belmont, CA: Wadsworth.

Connor, R. F., Altmas, D. G., & Jackson, C. (Eds.). (1984). *Evaluation studies review annual*. Newbury Park, CA: Sage.

Connor, R. F., Clay, T., & Hill, P. (1980). *Directory of evaluation training*. Washington, DC: Pintail Press.

Corbeil, R. (1992). Evaluation assessment: A case study of planning an evaluation. In J. Hudson, J. Mayne, & R. Thomlison (Eds.), *Action-oriented evaluation in organizations* (pp. 107–134). Middletown, OH: Wall & Emerson.

Corcoran, K. J. (1985). Enhancing the response rate in survey research. *Social Work Research and Abstracts, 21*, 2.

Corcoran, K. J. (1988). Selecting a measuring instrument. In R. M. Grinnell, Jr. (Ed.), *Social work research and evaluation* (3rd ed., pp. 137–155). Itasca, IL: F.E. Peacock Publishers.

Corcoran, K. J. (Ed.). (1992). *Structuring client change*. Chicago IL: Lyceum Books.

Corcoran, K. J. & Fischer, J. (1994). *Measures for clinical practice* (2nd ed., 2 vols.). New York: Free Press.

Crane, J. A. (1982). *The evaluation of social policies*. Boston: Kluwer-Nijhoff.

Crnic, K., Greenberg, M., Ragozin, A., Robinson, N., & Basham, R. (1983). Effects of stress and social support on mothers and preterm and full-term infants. *Child Development, 54*, 209–217.

Daves, C. W. (Ed.). (1984). *The uses and misuses of tests*. San Francisco, CA: Jossey-Bass.

Davis, B. G. (Ed.). (1986). *Teaching of evaluation across the disciplines*. San Francisco, CA: Jossey-Bass.

Davis, B. G. & Humphreys, S. (1985). *Evaluating intervention programs*. New York: Teacher's College Press.

DeMillo, R. A. (1987). *Software testing and evaluation*. Menlo Park, CA: Benjamin/Cummings.

Deshler, D. (1984). *Evaluation for program improvement*. San Francisco, CA: Jossey-Bass.

Dillman, D. A. (1978). *Mail and telephone surveys: The total design method*. New York: Wiley.

Dolan, M. M. & Vourlekis, B. S. (1983). A field project: Single-subject design in a public social service agency. *Journal of Social Service Research, 6*, 29–43.

Dooley, D. (1984). *Social research methods*. Englewood Cliffs, NJ: Prentice-Hall.

Duehn, W. D. (1985). Practice and research. In R. M. Grinnell, Jr. (Ed.), *Social work research and evaluation* (2nd ed., pp. 19–48). Itasca, IL: F.E. Peacock Publishers.

Edelstein, B. A. & Berber, E. S. (1987). *Evaluation and accountability in clinical training*. New York: Plenum Press.

Epstein, I. (1985). Quantitative and qualitative methods. In R. M. Grinnell, Jr. (Ed.), *Social work research and evaluation* (2nd ed., pp. 263–274). Itasca, IL: F.E. Peacock Publishers.

Epstein, I. (1988). Quantitative and qualitative methods. In R. M. Grinnell, Jr. (Ed.), *Social work research and evaluation* (3rd ed., pp. 185–198). Itasca, IL: F.E. Peacock Publishers.

Evaluation Research Society. (1980). *Standards for program evaluation*. Potomac, MD: Evaluation Research Society.

Feldman, E. J. (1981). *A practical guide to the conduct of field research in the social sciences*. Boulder, CO: Westview Press.

Ferber, R. & Hirsch, W. Z. (1982). *Social experimentation and economic policy*. Cambridge, MA: Cambridge University Press.

Ferrari, D., Serazzi, G., & Zeigner, A. (1983). *Measurement and tuning of computer systems*. Englewood Cliffs, NJ: Prentice-Hall.

Fetterman, D. M. & Pitman, M. A. (1986). *Educational evaluation*. Newbury Park, CA: Sage.

Finsterbusch, K. (Ed.). (1983). *Social impact assessment methods*. Newbury Park, CA: Sage.

Fischer, J. (1985). Evaluating research reports. In

R. M. Grinnell, Jr. (Ed.), *Social work research and evaluation* (2nd ed., pp. 476–482). Itasca, IL: F.E. Peacock Publishers.

Fischer, J. (1993). Evaluating positivistic research reports. In R. M. Grinnell, Jr. (Ed.), *Social work research and evaluation* (4th ed., pp. 347–366). Itasca, IL: F.E. Peacock Publishers.

Fischer, J. & Greenberg, J. (1972). *An investigation of different training methods on indigenous non-professionals from diverse minority groups.* Paper presented at the National Association of Social Workers Conference on Social Justice, New Orleans.

Fitz-Gibbon, C. T. & Morris, L. L. (1987). *How to design a program evaluation.* Newbury Park, CA: Sage.

Forehand, G. A. (1982). *Applications of time series analysis to evaluation.* San Francisco, CA: Jossey-Bass.

Gabor, P. (1993). Sampling. In R. M. Grinnell, Jr. (Ed.), *Social work research and evaluation* (4th ed., pp. 154–170). Itasca, IL: F.E. Peacock Publishers.

Garbarino, J. (1976). Some ecological correlates of child abuse: the impact of socioeconomic stress on mothers. *Child Development, 47,* 178–185.

Garbarino, J. & Sherman, D. (1980). High-risk neighborhoods and high-risk families: The human ecology of child maltreatment. *Child Development, 51,* 188–198.

Garvin, C. D. (1981). Research-related roles for social workers. In R. M. Grinnell, Jr. (Ed.), *Social work research and evaluation* (pp. 547–552). Itasca, IL: F.E. Peacock Publishers.

Gilchrist, L. E. & Schinke, S. P. (1988). Research Ethics. In R. M. Grinnell, Jr. (Ed.), *Social work research and evaluation* (3rd ed., pp. 65–79). Itasca, IL: F.E. Peacock Publishers.

Gochros, H. L. (1985). Research interviewing. In R. M. Grinnell, Jr. (Ed.), *Social work research and evaluation* (2nd ed., pp. 306–342). Itasca, IL: F.E. Peacock Publishers.

Gochros, H. L. (1988). Research interviewing. In R. M. Grinnell, Jr. (Ed.), *Social work research and evaluation* (3rd ed., pp. 267–299). Itasca, IL: F.E. Peacock Publishers.

Green, G. R. & Wright, J. E. (1979). The retrospective approach to collecting baseline data. *Social Work Research and Abstracts, 15,* 25–30.

Greenwald, R. A., Ryan, M. K., & Mulvihill, J. E. (1982). *Human subjects research.* New York: Plenum Press.

Grinnell, R. M., Jr. (1985). Becoming a practitioner/researcher. In R. M. Grinnell, Jr. (Ed.), *Social work research and evaluation* (2nd ed., pp. 1–15). Itasca, IL: F.E. Peacock Publishers.

Grinnell, R. M., Jr., (1993a). Group research designs. In R. M. Grinnell, Jr. (Ed.), *Social work research and evaluation* (4th ed., pp. 118–153). Itasca, IL: F.E. Peacock Publishers.

Grinnell, R. M., Jr. (Ed.). (1993b). *Social work research and evaluation* (4th ed.). Itasca, IL: F.E. Peacock Publishers.

Grinnell, R. M., Jr., Rothery, M., & Thomlison, R. J. (1993). Research in social work. In R. M. Grinnell, Jr. (Ed.), *Social work research and evaluation* (4th ed., pp. 2–16). Itasca, IL: F.E. Peacock Publishers.

Grinnell, R. M., Jr. & Siegel, D. H. (1988). The place of research in social work. In R. M. Grinnell, Jr. (Ed.), *Social work research and evaluation* (3rd ed., pp. 9–24). Itasca, IL: F.E. Peacock Publishers.

Grinnell, R. M., Jr. & Stothers, M. (1988). Utilizing research designs. In R. M. Grinnell, Jr. (Ed.), *Social work research and evaluation* (3rd ed., pp. 199–239). Itasca, IL: F.E. Peacock Publishers.

Grinnell, R. M., Jr., Williams, M., & Tutty, L. (1995). *Research in social work: A primer.* (2nd ed.). Itasca, IL: F.E. Peacock Publishers.

Groves, R. M. (1989). *Telephone survey methodology.* New York: Wiley.

Guba, E. G. & Lincoln, Y. S. (1981). *Effective evaluation.* San Francisco, CA: Jossey-Bass.

Hornick, J. P. & Burrows, B. (1988). Program evaluation. In R. M. Grinnell, Jr. (Ed.), *Social work research and evaluation* (3rd ed., pp. 400–420). Itasca, IL: F.E. Peacock Publishers.

Hoshino, G. & Lynch, M. M. (1985). Secondary analyses. In R. M. Grinnell, Jr. (Ed.), *Social work research and evaluation* (2nd ed., pp. 370–380). Itasca, IL: F.E. Peacock Publishers.

House, E. R. (1981). *Evaluating with validity.* Newbury Park, CA: Sage.

House, E. R. (1986). *New directions in educational evaluation.* London: Falmer Press.

Hudson, J. & Grinnell, R. M., Jr. (1989). Program evaluation. In B. Compton & B. Galaway (Eds.), *Social work processes* (4th ed., pp. 691–711). Belmont, CA: Wadsworth.

Hudson, J., Mayne, J., & Thomlison R. (1992). (Eds.), *Action-oriented evaluation in organizations*. Middletown, OH: Wall & Emerson.

Hudson, W. W. (1981). Development and use of indexes and scales. In R. M. Grinnell, Jr. (Ed.), *Social work research and evaluation* (pp. 130–155). Itasca, IL: F.E. Peacock Publishers.

Hudson, W. W. (1982). *The clinical measurement package: A field manual*. Homewood, IL: Dorsey.

Hudson, W. W. (1985). Indexes and scales. In R. M. Grinnell, Jr. (Ed.), *Social work research and evaluation* (2nd ed., pp. 185–205). Itasca, IL: F.E. Peacock Publishers.

Hudson, W. W. (1990a). *Computer assisted social services*. Tempe, AZ: WALMYR Publishing.

Hudson, W. W. (1990b). *Index of self-esteem*. Tempe, AZ: WALMYR Publishing.

Hudson, W. W. (1990c). *The MPSI technical manual*. Tempe, AZ: WALMYR Publishing.

Hudson, W. W. (1990d). *WALMYR assessment scale scoring manual*. Tempe, AZ: WALMYR Publishing.

Hudson, W. W. (1991). *The WALMYR assessment scale scoring program*. Tempe, AZ: WALMYR Publishing.

Hudson, W. W. (1993). Standardized measures. In J. Krysik, I. Hoffart, & R. M. Grinnell, Jr. (1993). *Student study guide for the fourth edition of social work research and evaluation* (pp. 243–263). Itasca, IL: F.E. Peacock Publishers.

Hudson, W. W. & Thyer, B. A. (1987). Research measures and indices in direct practice. In A. Minahan (Ed.), *Encyclopedia of social work* (pp. 487–498). Washington, DC: National Association of Social Workers.

Ihilevich, D. & Gleser, G. C. (1982). *Evaluating mental health programs*. Lexington, MA: Lexington Books.

Isaac, S. & Michael, W. B. (1980). *Handbook in research and evaluation*. San Diego, CA: EDITS.

Jackson, G. B. (1980). Methods for integrative reviews. *Review of Educational Research, 50,* 438–460.

Joint Committee on Standards for Education

Evaluation. (1981). *Standards for evaluations of educational programs projects and materials*. Toronto, Ontario, Canada: McGraw-Hill.

Jordan, C., Franklin, C., & Corcoran, K. (1993). Standardized measuring instruments. In R. M. Grinnell, Jr. (Ed.), *Social work research and evaluation* (4th ed., pp. 198–220). Itasca, IL: F.E. Peacock Publishers.

Kerlinger, F. (1986). *Foundations of behavioral research* (3rd ed.). New York: Holt.

Kettner, P. M., Moroney, R. M., & Martin, L. L. (1990). Designing and managing programs: An effectiveness-based approach. Newbury Park, CA: Sage.

Keyser, D. J. & Sweetland, R. C. (1984). *Test critiques*. Kansas City, KS: Test Corporation of America.

Kidder, L. H. & Judd, C. M. (1986). *Research methods in social relations* (5th ed.). New York: Holt, Rinehart & Winston.

Krysik, J., Hoffart, I., & Grinnell, R. M., Jr. (1993). *Student study guide for the fourth edition of social work research and evaluation*. Itasca, IL: F.E. Peacock Publishers.

Lauffer, A. (1982). *Assessment tools*. Newbury Park, CA: Sage.

Lavrakas, P. J. (1987). *Telephone survey methods: Sampling, selection, and supervision*. Newbury Park, CA: Sage.

Lawler, E. E. & Nadler, D. (1980). *Organizational assessment*. Toronto, ON: Wiley.

LeCroy, C. W. (1985). Methodological issues in the evaluation of social work practice. *Social Service Review, 59,* 345–357.

LeCroy, C. W. & Solomon, G. (1993). Content analysis. In R. M. Grinnell, Jr. (Ed.), *Social work research and evaluation* (4th ed., pp. 304–316). Itasca, IL: F.E. Peacock Publishers.

Levin, H. M. (1983). *Cost-effectiveness: A primer*. Newbury Park, CA: Sage.

Lidz, C. S. (Ed.). (1987). *Dynamic assessment*. New York: Guilford Press.

Light, R. J. & Pillemer, D. B. (1984). *Summing up: The science of reviewing research*. Cambridge, MA: Harvard University Press.

Lincoln, Y. & Guba, E. (1985). *Naturalistic inquiry*. Newbury Park, CA: Sage.

Locke, L. F., Spirduso, W. W., & Silverman, S. (1987). *Proposals that work: A guide for plan-*

ning dissertations and grant proposals (2nd ed.). Newbury Park, CA: Sage.

Lockhart, D. C. (Ed.). (1984). *Making effective use of mailed questionnaires.* San Francisco, CA: Jossey-Bass.

Love, A. J. (1991). *Internal evaluation: Building organizations from within.* Newbury Park, CA: Sage.

Loveland, E. H. (1980). *Measuring the hard-to-measure.* San Francisco, CA: Jossey-Bass.

Madaus, G. F., Scriven, M., & Stufflebeam, D. (Eds.). (1983). *Evaluation models.* Boston, MA: Kluwer-Nijhoff.

Magura, S. & Moses, B. S. (1986). *Outcome measures for child welfare services.* Washington, DC: Child Welfare League of America.

Maloney, D. M. (1984). *Protection of human research subjects: A practical guide to federal laws and regulations.* New York: Plenum.

Mayne, J. (1992). Establishing internal evaluation in an organization. In J. Hudson, J. Mayne, & R. Thomlison (Eds.), *Action-oriented evaluation in organizations* (pp. 306–317). Middletown, OH: Wall & Emerson.

Mayne, J. & Hudson, J. (1992). Program evaluation: An overview. In J. Hudson, J. Mayne, & R. Thomlison (Eds.), *Action-oriented evaluation in organizations* (pp. 1–19). Middletown, OH: Wall & Emerson.

McMurtry, S. L. (1993). Survey research. In R. M. Grinnell, Jr. (Ed.), *Social work research and evaluation* (4th ed., pp. 262–289). Itasca, IL: F.E. Peacock Publishers.

Mendelsohn, H. N. (1987). *A guide to information sources for social work and the human services.* Phoenix, AZ: Oryx Press.

Miller, D. C. (1991). *Handbook of research design and social measurement* (4th ed). Newbury Park, CA: Sage.

Mindel, C. H. (1985). Instrument design. In R. M. Grinnell, Jr. (Ed.), *Social work research and evaluation* (2nd ed., pp. 206–230). Itasca, IL: F.E. Peacock Publishers.

Mindel, C. H. (1993). Instrument design. In R. M. Grinnell, Jr. (Ed.), *Social work research and evaluation* (4th ed., pp. 221–241). Itasca, IL: F.E. Peacock Publishers.

Mindel, C. H. & McDonald, L. (1988). Survey research. In R. M. Grinnell, Jr. (Ed.), *Social work*

research and evaluation (3rd ed., pp. 300–322). Itasca, IL: F.E. Peacock Publishers.

Morgan, D. (1988). *Focus groups as qualitative research.* Newbury Park, CA: Sage.

Morris, M. F. & Roth, P. F. (1982). *Computer performance evaluation.* New York: Van Nostrand Reinhold.

Moss, K. E. (1985). Research proposals. In R. M. Grinnell, Jr. (Ed.), *Social work research and evaluation* (2nd ed., pp. 445–458). Itasca, IL: F.E. Peacock Publishers.

Moss, K. E. (1988). Writing research proposals. In R. M. Grinnell, Jr. (Ed.), *Social work research and evaluation* (3rd ed., pp. 429–445). Itasca, IL: F.E. Peacock Publishers.

Mullen, E. J. (1988). Constructing personal practice models. In R. M. Grinnell, Jr. (Ed.), *Social work research and evaluation* (3rd ed., pp. 503–533). Itasca, IL: F.E. Peacock Publishers.

Murray, J. G. (1980). *Needs assessment in adult education.* Ottawa, Ontario, Canada: National Library of Canada.

Mutschler, E. (1979). Using single-case evaluation procedures in a family and children's service center: Integration of practice and research. *Journal of Social Service Research, 2,* 115–134.

Nelsen, J. C. (1988). Single-subject research. In R. M. Grinnell, Jr. (Ed.), *Social work research and evaluation* (3rd ed., pp. 362–399). Itasca, IL: F.E. Peacock Publishers.

Nowakowski, J. (Ed.). (1987). *The client perspective on evaluation.* San Francisco, CA: Jossey-Bass.

Nurius, P. S. (1986). Reappraisal of the self-concept and implications for counseling. *Journal of Consulting Psychology, 33,* 429–438.

Nurius, P. S. & Hudson, W. W. (1993). *Human services: Practice, evaluation, and computers.* Belmont, CA: Brooks/Cole.

Nurius, P. S. & Mutschler, E. (1984). Use of computer-assisted information processing in social work practice. *Journal of Education for Social Work, 20,* 83–94.

Owston, R. D. (1987). *Software evaluation.* Scarborough, Ontario, Canada: Prentice-Hall.

Paine, S. C., Bellamy, G. T., & Wilcox, B. (1984). *Human services that work: From innovation to standard practice.* Baltimore: Paul H. Brookes.

Palumbo, D. J. (1987). *The politics of program evalu-*

ation. Newbury Park, CA: Sage.

Patton, M. Q. (1982). *Practical evaluation*. Newbury Park, CA: Sage.

Patton, M. Q. (1986). *Utilization-focused evaluation* (2nd ed.). Beverly Hills: Sage.

Patton, M. Q. (1987). *Creative evaluation* (2nd ed.). Newbury Park, CA: Sage.

Patton, M. Q. (1990). *Qualitative evaluation and research methods* (2nd ed.). Newbury Park, CA: Sage.

Polansky, N., Chalmers, M., Buttenweiser, E., & Williams, E. (1978). Assessing child care: An urban scale. *Child Welfare, 57*, 439–448.

Polster, R. A. & Collins, D. (1993). Structured observation. In R. M. Grinnell, Jr. (Ed.), *Social work research and evaluation* (4th ed., pp. 244–261). Itasca, IL: F.E. Peacock Publishers.

Polster, R. A. & Collins, D. (1988). Measuring variables by direct observations. In R. M. Grinnell, Jr. (Ed.), *Social work research and evaluation* (3rd ed., pp. 156–176). Itasca, IL: F.E. Peacock Publishers.

Polster, R. A. & Lynch, M. A. (1985). Single-subject designs. In R. M. Grinnell, Jr. (Ed.), *Social work research and evaluation* (2nd ed., pp. 381–431). Itasca, IL: F.E. Peacock Publishers.

Posavac, E. J. & Carey, R. G. (1992). *Program evaluation: Methods and case studies* (4th ed.). Englewood Cliffs, NJ: Prentice-Hall.

Press, A. N., Lieberman, A. A., & McDonald, T. P. (1993a). Meta-analysis. In R. M. Grinnell, Jr. (Ed.), *Social work research and evaluation* (4th ed., pp. 367–385). Itasca, IL: F.E. Peacock Publishers.

Press, A. N., Lieberman, A. A., & McDonald, T. P. (1993b). Synthesizing the literature. In R. M. Grinnell, Jr. (Ed.), *Social work research and evaluation* (4th ed., pp. 427–438). Itasca, IL: F.E. Peacock Publishers.

Price, R. H. & Politser, P. E. (1980). *Evaluation and action in the social environment*. New York: Academic Press.

Puetz, B. E. (1985). *Evaluation in nursing staff development*. Rockville, MD: Aspen Systems.

Ramos, R. (1985). Participant observation. In R. M. Grinnell, Jr. (Ed.), *Social work research and evaluation* (2nd ed., pp. 343–356). Itasca, IL: F.E. Peacock Publishers.

Raymond, F. B. (1985). Program evaluation. In R. M. Grinnell, Jr. (Ed.), *Social work research and evaluation* (2nd ed., pp. 432–442). Itasca, IL: F.E. Peacock Publishers.

Reamer, F. G. (1979). Fundamental ethical issues in social work: An essay review. *Social Service Review, 53*, 229–243.

Reamer, F. G. (1982). *Ethical dilemmas in social service*. New York: Columbia University Press.

Reamer, F. G. (1983). Ethical dilemmas in social work practice. *Social Work, 28*, 31–35.

Reid, W. J. (1985). Writing research reports. In R. M. Grinnell, Jr. (Ed.), *Social work research and evaluation* (2nd ed., pp. 459–475). Itasca, IL: F.E. Peacock Publishers.

Reid, W. J. (1988). Writing research reports. In R. M. Grinnell, Jr. (Ed.), *Social work research and evaluation* (3rd ed., pp. 446–464). Itasca, IL: F.E. Peacock Publishers.

Reid, W. J. (1993). Writing research reports. In R. M. Grinnell, Jr. (Ed.), *Social work research and evaluation* (4th ed., pp. 332–346). Itasca, IL: F.E. Peacock Publishers.

Reid, W. J. & Smith, A. D. (1989). *Research in social work* (2nd ed.). New York: Columbia University Press.

Rich, R. F. (1981). *Social science information and public policy making: The interaction between bureaucratic politics and the use of survey data*. San Francisco, CA: Jossey-Bass.

Robinson, J. P. & Shaver, P. R. (1973). *Measures of social psychological attitudes* (rev. ed.). Ann Arbor, MI: Institute for Social Research.

Robyler, M. D. (1985). *Measuring the impact of computers in instruction*. Washington, DC: Association for Educational Data Systems.

Rogers, G. & Bouey, E. (1993). Reviewing the literature. In R. M. Grinnell, Jr. (Ed.), *Social work research and evaluation* (4th ed., pp. 388–401). Itasca, IL: F.E. Peacock Publishers.

Rossi, P. H. (1982). *Standards for evaluation practice*. San Francisco, CA: Jossey-Bass.

Rossi, P. H. & Freeman, H. E. (1989). *Evaluation: A systematic approach* (4th ed.). Newbury Park, CA: Sage.

Rothery, M. (1993a). The positivistic research approach. In R. M. Grinnell, Jr. (Ed.), *Social work research and evaluation* (4th ed., pp. 38–52). Itasca, IL: F.E. Peacock Publishers.

Rothery, M. (1993b). Problems, questions, and

hypotheses. In R. M. Grinnell, Jr. (Ed.), *Social work research and evaluation* (4th ed., pp. 17–37). Itasca, IL: F.E. Peacock Publishers.

Royse, D. (1991). *Research methods in social work.* Chicago, IL: Nelson-Hall.

Royse, D. (1992). *Program evaluation: An introduction.* Chicago, IL: Nelson-Hall.

Rubin, A. (1988). Secondary analyses. In R. M. Grinnell, Jr. (Ed.), *Social work research and evaluation* (3rd ed., pp. 323–341). Itasca, IL: F.E. Peacock Publishers.

Rubin, A. (1993). Secondary analysis. In R. M. Grinnell, Jr. (Ed.), *Social work research and evaluation* (4th ed., pp. 290–303). Itasca, IL: F.E. Peacock Publishers.

Rush, B. & Ogborne, A. (1991). Program logic models: Expanding their role and structure for program planning and evaluation. *The Canadian Journal of Program Evaluation, 6,* 95–106.

Rutman, L. (1980). *Planning useful evaluations.* Newbury Park, CA: Sage.

Saxe, L. & Fine, M. (1981). *Social experiments: Methods for design and evaluation.* Newbury Park, CA: Sage.

Schinke, S. P. (1985). Ethics. In R. M. Grinnell, Jr. (Ed.), *Social work research and evaluation* (2nd ed., pp. 101–114). Itasca, IL: F.E. Peacock Publishers.

Schinke, S. P. & Gilchrist, L. D. (1984). *Life skills counseling with adolescents.* Baltimore, MD: University Park Press.

Schinke, S. P. & Gilchrist, L. D. (1993). Ethics in research. In R. M. Grinnell, Jr. (Ed.), *Social work research and evaluation* (4th ed., pp. 79–90). Itasca, IL: F.E. Peacock Publishers.

Schuerman, J. R. (1983). *Research and evaluation in the human services.* New York: Free Press.

Scriven, M. (1991). *Evaluation thesaurus* (4th ed.). Newbury Park, CA: Sage.

Seaberg, J. R. (1985). Sampling. In R. M. Grinnell, Jr. (Ed.), *Social work research and evaluation* (2nd ed., pp. 133–148). Itasca, IL: F.E. Peacock Publishers.

Seaberg, J. R. (1988). Utilizing sampling procedures. In R. M. Grinnell, Jr. (Ed.), *Social work research and evaluation* (3rd ed., pp. 240–257). Itasca, IL: F.E. Peacock Publishers.

Selltiz, C., Wrightsman, L. S., & Cook, S. (1981). *Research methods in social relations* (4th ed.). New York: Holt, Rinehart, & Winston.

Shadish, W. R., Cook, T. D., & Leviton, L. C. (1992). *Foundations of program evaluation.* Newbury Park, CA: Sage.

Shapiro, S. H. & Louis, T. A. (Eds.). (1983). *Clinical trials: Issues and approaches.* New York: Marcel Dekker.

Siegel, D. H. (1988). Integrating data-gathering techniques and practice activities. In R. M. Grinnell, Jr. (Ed.), *Social work research and evaluation* (3rd ed., pp. 465–482). Itasca, IL: F.E. Peacock Publishers.

Siegel, D. H. & Reamer, F. G. (1988). Integrating research findings, concepts, and logic into practice. In R. M. Grinnell, Jr. (Ed.), *Social work research and evaluation* (3rd ed., pp. 483–502). Itasca, IL: F.E. Peacock Publishers.

Silkman, R. H. (Ed.). (1986). *Measuring efficiency.* San Francisco, CA: Jossey-Bass.

Smith, D. A. (1992). The evaluation of program efficiency. In J. Hudson, J. Mayne, & R. Thomlison (Eds.), *Action-oriented evaluation in organizations* (pp. 180–194). Middletown, OH: Wall & Emerson.

Smith, M. J. (1990). *Program evaluation in the human services.* New York: Springer.

Smith, N. J. (1985). Research goals and problems. In R. M. Grinnell, Jr. (Ed.), *Social work research and evaluation* (2nd ed., pp. 49–65). Itasca, IL: F.E. Peacock Publishers.

Smith, N. J. (1988). Formulating research goals and problems. In R. M. Grinnell, Jr. (Ed.), *Social work research and evaluation* (3rd ed., pp. 89–110). Itasca, IL: F.E. Peacock Publishers.

Stuart, P. (1988). Historical research. In R. M. Grinnell, Jr. (Ed.), *Social work research and evaluation* (3rd ed., pp. 342–361). Itasca, IL: F.E. Peacock Publishers.

Stuart, P. & Engeldinger, E. (1990). *Library instruction in social work education: New technologies for the 1990's.* Paper presented at the Annual Program Meeting of the Council on Social Work Education, Reno, NV.

Stufflebeam, D. & Shinkfield, A. (1984). *A systematic evaluation.* Boston: Kluwer Nijhoff.

Suchman, E. A. (1967). *Evaluative research.* New York: Russell Sage Foundation.

Suppe, F. (Ed.). (1977). *The structure of scientific*

theories. Urbana, IL: University of Illinois Press.

Susman, E., Trickett, P., Iannotti, R., Hollenbeck, B., & Zahn-Waxler, C. (1985). Child rearing patterns in depressed, abusive and normal mothers. *American Journal of Orthopsychiatry, 55*, 237–251.

Taylor, J. B. (1993). The naturalistic research approach. In R. M. Grinnell, Jr. (Ed.), *Social work research and evaluation* (4th ed., pp. 53–78). Itasca, IL: F.E. Peacock Publishers.

Taylor, S. & Bogdan, R. (1984). *Introduction to qualitative research methods: The search for meanings*. New York: Wiley.

Thomas, E. J. (1985). Developmental research. In R. M. Grinnell, Jr. (Ed.), *Social work research and evaluation* (2nd ed., pp. 483–499). Itasca, IL: F.E. Peacock Publishers.

Thompson, M. F. (1980). *Benefit-cost analysis for program evaluation*. Newbury Park, CA: Sage.

Thyer, B. A. (1993). Single-system research designs. In R. M. Grinnell, Jr. (Ed.), *Social work research and evaluation* (4th ed., pp. 94–117). Itasca, IL: F.E. Peacock Publishers.

Toseland, R. W. (1985). Research methods. In R. M. Grinnell, Jr. (Ed.), *Social work research and evaluation* (2nd ed., pp. 115–130). Itasca, IL: F.E. Peacock Publishers.

Toseland, R. W. (1993). Choosing a data collection method. In R. M. Grinnell, Jr. (Ed.), *Social work research and evaluation* (4th ed., pp. 317–328). Itasca, IL: F.E. Peacock Publishers.

Tripodi, T. (1974). *Uses and abuses of social research in social work*. New York: Columbia University Press.

Tripodi, T. (1983). *Evaluative research for social workers*. Englewood Cliffs, NJ: Prentice-Hall.

Tripodi, T. (1985). Research designs. In R. M. Grinnell, Jr. (Ed.), *Social work research and evaluation* (2nd ed., pp. 231–259). Itasca, IL: F.E. Peacock Publishers.

Tripodi, T., Fellin, P. A., & Meyer, H. J. (1983). *The assessment of social research: Guidelines for the use of research in social work and social service* (2nd ed.). Itasca, IL: F.E. Peacock Publishers.

Trochim, W. M. K. (1984). *Research design for program evaluation: The regression-discontinuity approach*. Newbury Park, CA: Sage.

Trochim, W. M. K. (Ed.). (1986). *Advances in quasi-experimental design and analysis*. San Francisco, CA: Jossey-Bass.

Udinsky, B., Osterlind, S., & Lynch, S. (1981). *Evaluation resource handbook: Gathering analyzing reporting data*. San Diego, CA: EDITS Publications.

Unrau, Y. (1993). A program logic model approach to conceptualizing social service programs. *The Canadian Journal of Program Evaluation, 8*.

Veney, J. E. & Kaluzny, A. D. (1984). *Evaluation and decision making for health services programs*. Englewood Cliffs, NJ: Prentice-Hall.

Washington, R. O. (1980). *Program evaluation in the human services*. Lanham, MD: University Press of America.

Watts, T. D. (1985). Ethnomethodology. In R. M. Grinnell, Jr. (Ed.), *Social work research and evaluation* (2nd ed., pp. 357–369). Itasca, IL: F.E. Peacock Publishers.

Webb, E., Campbell, D., Schwartz, R., & Sechrest, L. (1966). *Unobtrusive measures: Nonreactive research in the social sciences*. Chicago: Rand McNally.

Weinbach, R. W. (1985). The agency and professional contexts of research. In R. M. Grinnell, Jr. (Ed.), *Social work research and evaluation* (2nd ed., pp. 66–82). Itasca, IL: F.E. Peacock Publishers.

Weinbach, R. W. (1988). Agency and professional contexts of research. In R. M. Grinnell, Jr. (Ed.), *Social work research and evaluation* (3rd ed., pp. 25–41). Itasca, IL: F.E. Peacock Publishers.

Weinbach, R. W. & Grinnell, R. M., Jr. (1995). *Statistics for social workers* (3rd ed.). White Plains, NY: Longman.

Weingarten, H. R. (1988). Late life divorce and the life review. *Journal of Gerontological Social Work, 12*, 83–97.

Weiss, C. H. (1972). *Evaluation research: Methods of assessing program effectiveness*. Englewood Cliffs, NJ: Prentice-Hall.

Wholey, J. S. (Ed.) (1986). *Performance and credibility*. Lexington, MA: Lexington Books.

Williams, D. D. (1986). *Naturalistic evaluation*. San Francisco, CA: Jossey-Bass.

Williams, M. & Hudson, J. (1991). Evaluable

models of child sexual abuse treatment programs. *Journal of Child and Youth Care, 8*, 7–21.

Williamson, J. B., Karp, D. A., Dalphin, J. R., & Gray, P. S. (1982). *The research craft*. Boston, MA: Little Brown.

Wurman, R. (1989). *Information anxiety*. New York: Doubleday.

Yates, B. T. (1980). *Improving effectiveness and reducing costs in mental health*. Springfield, IL: Thomas.

Zeller, R. A. & Carmines, E. G. (1980). *Measurement in the social sciences: The link between theory and data*. New York: Cambridge University Press.

INDEX